Praise for *Advanced Android™ Application Development, Fourth Edition*

"This new edition of *Advanced Android™ Application Development* updates the definitive reference for Android developers, covering all major revisions of Android, including Android L. Whether you're just getting started, or need to brush up on the latest features of Android, this should be the first book you reach for."
—*Ray Rischpater, senior software engineer, Microsoft*

"This is the most comprehensive reference for programming Android. I still turn to it when I need to learn about a topic I am not familiar with."
—*Douglas Jones, senior software engineer, Fullpower Technologies*

"The problem with many Android development titles is that they either assume the developer is completely new to development or is already an expert. *Advanced Android™ Application Development, Fourth Edition,* cuts the fluff and gets to the need to know of modern Android development."
—*Phil Dutson, solution architect for mobile and UX, ICON Health & Fitness*

"*Advanced Android™ Application Development, Fourth Edition,* is an excellent guide for software developers, quality assurance personnel, and project managers who want to learn to plan, develop, and manage professional Android applications. The book explains several advanced Android topics through step-by-step running examples. The authors have done a great job explaining various Android APIs for threading, networking, location-based services, hardware sensors, animation, graphics, and more. This book is a classic investment."
—*B.M. Harwani, author,* The Android™ Tablet Developer's Cookbook

Advanced Android™ Application Development

Fourth Edition

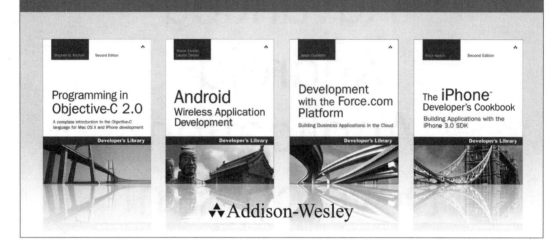

Developer's Library Series

Visit **developers-library.com** for a complete list of available products

---

The **Developer's Library Series** from Addison-Wesley provides practicing programmers with unique, high-quality references and tutorials on the latest programming languages and technologies they use in their daily work. All books in the Developer's Library are written by expert technology practitioners who are exceptionally skilled at organizing and presenting information in a way that's useful for other programmers.

Developer's Library books cover a wide range of topics, from open-source programming languages and databases, Linux programming, Microsoft, and Java, to Web development, social networking platforms, Mac/iPhone programming, and Android programming.

Advanced Android™ Application Development

Fourth Edition

Joseph Annuzzi, Jr.
Lauren Darcey
Shane Conder

♦♦Addison-Wesley

Upper Saddle River, NJ • Boston • Indianapolis • San Francisco
New York • Toronto • Montreal • London • Munich • Paris • Madrid
Capetown • Sydney • Tokyo • Singapore • Mexico City

Library of Congress Cataloging-in-Publication Data
  Revision of: Android wireless application development. Volume II, Advanced topics. ©2012.
  Includes bibliographical references and index.
  Summary: "This book—a renamed new edition of Android Wireless Application Development, Volume II—is the definitive guide to advanced commercial-grade Android development, updated for the latest Android SDK. The book serves as a reference for the Android API."— Provided by publisher.
  ISBN 978-0-13-389238-3 (pbk. : alk. paper)
  1. Application software—Development. 2. Android (Electronic resource) 3. Mobile computing. 4. Wireless communication systems.75 I. Darcey, Lauren, 1977- author. II. Conder, Shane, 1975- author. III. Title.
  QA76.76.A65A55 2015
  004.167—dc23
                                                                        2014033049

Editor-in-Chief
Mark L. Taub

Executive Editor
Laura Lewin

Development Editor
Songlin Qiu

Managing Editor
John Fuller

Full-Service Production Manager
Julie B. Nahil

Project Manager
Thistle Hill Publishing Services

Copy Editor
Barbara Wood

Indexer
Jack Lewis

Proofreader
Melissa Panagos

Technical Reviews
Douglas Jones
Raymond Rischpater
Valerie Shipbaugh

Editorial Assistant
Olivia Basegio

Cover Designer
Chuti Prasertsith

Compositor
Shepherd, Inc.

❖

This book is dedicated to Cleopatra (Cleo).
—Joseph Annuzzi, Jr.

This book is dedicated to ESC.
—Lauren Darcey and Shane Conder

❖

Contents at a Glance

Contents

Acknowledgments

This book is the result of collaboration among a great group, from the efforts of the team at Pearson Education (Addison-Wesley), from the suggestions made by the technical reviewers, and from the support of family, friends, coworkers, and acquaintances alike. We'd like to thank the Android developer community, Google, and the Open Handset Alliance for their vision and expertise. Special thanks go to Mark Taub for believing in the vision for this edition; Laura Lewin, who was the driving force behind the book—without her this book would not have become a reality; Olivia Basegio, who was instrumental in orchestrating the efforts of everyone involved; Songlin Qiu for performing countless iterations combing through the manuscript and making this book ready for production; and the technical reviewers: Doug Jones who suggested improvements of the fine details, Ray Rischpater, who made many beneficial recommendations, and Valerie Shipbaugh who spotted areas in need of clarification (as well as Mike Wallace, Mark Gjoel, Dan Galpin, Tony Hillerson, Ronan Schwarz, and Charles Stearns, who reviewed previous editions and incarnations of this book). Dan Galpin also graciously provided the clever Android graphics used for Tips, Notes, and Warnings. We also thank Hans Bodlaender for letting us use the nifty chess font he developed as a hobby project.

About the Authors

Joseph Annuzzi, Jr., is a freelance software architect, graphic artist, inventor, entrepreneur, and author. He usually can be found mastering the Android platform, implementing cutting-edge HTML5 capabilities, leveraging various cloud technologies, speaking in different programming languages, working with diverse frameworks, integrating with various social APIs, tinkering with peer-to-peer, cryptography, and biometric algorithms, or creating stunningly realistic 3D renders. He is always on the lookout for disruptive Internet and mobile technologies and has multiple patent applications in process. He graduated from the University of California, Davis, with a BS in managerial economics and a minor in computer science and lives where much of the action is: Silicon Valley.

When he is not working with technology, he has been known to lounge in the sun on the beaches of the Black Sea with international movie stars; he has trekked through the Bavarian forest in winter, has immersed himself in the culture of the Italian Mediterranean, and has narrowly escaped the wrath of an organized crime ring in Eastern Europe after his taxi dropped him off in front of the bank ATM they were liquidating. He also lives an active and healthy lifestyle, designs and performs custom fitness training routines to stay in shape, and adores his loyal beagle, Cleopatra.

Lauren Darcey is responsible for the technical leadership and direction of a small software company specializing in mobile technologies, including Android and iOS consulting services. With more than two decades of experience in professional software production, Lauren is a recognized authority in application architecture and the development of commercial-grade mobile applications. Lauren received a BS in computer science from the University of California, Santa Cruz.

She spends her copious free time traveling the world with her geeky mobile-minded husband and pint-sized geekling daughter. She is an avid nature photographer. Her work has been published in books and newspapers around the world. In South Africa, she dove with 4-meter-long great white sharks and got stuck between a herd of rampaging hippopotami and an irritated bull elephant. She's been attacked by monkeys in Japan, gotten stuck in a ravine with two hungry lions in Kenya, gotten thirsty in Egypt, narrowly avoided a coup d'état in Thailand, geocached her way through the Swiss Alps, drunk her way through the beer halls of Germany, slept in the crumbling castles of Europe, and gotten her tongue stuck to an iceberg in Iceland (while being watched by a herd of suspicious wild reindeer). Most recently, she can be found hiking along the Appalachian Trail with her daughter and documenting the journey with Google Glass.

Shane Conder has extensive application development experience and has focused his attention on mobile and embedded development for well over a decade. He has designed and developed many commercial applications for Android, iOS, BREW, BlackBerry, J2ME, Palm, and Windows Mobile—some of which have been installed on millions of phones worldwide. Shane has written extensively about the tech industry and is known for his keen insights regarding mobile development platform trends. Shane received a BS in computer science from the University of California, Santa Cruz.

A self-admitted gadget freak, Shane always has the latest smartphone, tablet, or wearable. He enjoys traveling the world with his geeky wife, even if she did make him dive with 4-meter-long great white sharks and almost get eaten by a lion in Kenya. He admits that he has to take at least three devices with him when backpacking ("just in case")—even where there is no coverage. Lately, his smart watch collection has exceeded his number of wrists. Luckily, his young daughter is happy to offer her own. Such are the burdens of a daughter of engineers.

Introduction

Android is a popular, free, and open-source mobile platform that has taken the wireless world by storm. This book and *Introduction to Android™ Application Development: Android Essentials, Fourth Edition*, provide comprehensive guidance for software development teams on designing, developing, testing, debugging, and distributing professional Android applications. If you're a veteran mobile developer, you can find tips and tricks to streamline the development process and take advantage of Android's unique features. If you're new to mobile development, these books provide everything you need to make a smooth transition from traditional software development to mobile development—specifically, its most promising platform: Android.

Who Should Read This Book?

This book includes tips for successful mobile development based upon our years in the mobile industry, and it covers everything you need to know to run a successful Android project from concept to completion. We cover how the mobile software process differs from traditional software development, including tricks to save valuable time and pitfalls to avoid. Regardless of the size of your project, this book is for you.

This book was written for various audiences:

- **Software developers who want to learn to develop professional Android applications.** The bulk of this book is targeted at software developers with Java experience who do not necessarily have mobile development experience. More seasoned developers of mobile applications can learn how to take advantage of Android and how it differs from the other technologies on the mobile development market today.

- **Other audiences.** This book is useful not only to software developers, but also to corporations looking at potential vertical market applications, entrepreneurs thinking about cool phone applications, and hobbyists looking for some fun with their new phones. Businesses seeking to evaluate Android for their specific needs (including feasibility analysis) can also find the information provided valuable. Anyone with an Android handset and a good idea for a mobile application can put the information in this book to use for fun and profit.

How This Book Is Structured

Advanced Android™ Application Development, Fourth Edition, focuses on advanced Android topics, including leveraging various Android application programming interfaces (APIs) for threading, networking, location-based services, hardware sensors, animation, graphics, and more. Coverage of advanced Android application components, such as services, application databases, content providers, and intents, is also included. Developers will learn to design advanced user interface (UI) components and integrate their applications deeply into the platform. Finally, developers will learn how to extend their applications beyond traditional boundaries using optional features of the Android platform, including the Android Native Development Kit (NDK), Google Cloud Messaging (GCM), Google Play In-app Billing APIs, Google Analytics APIs, Android Wear, Google Play game services, and more.

Advanced Android™ Application Development, Fourth Edition, is divided into nine parts. Here is an overview of the various parts:

- **Part I: Advanced Android Application Design Principles**

  Part I picks up where *Introduction to Android™ Application Development: Android Essentials, Fourth Edition,* leaves off in terms of application design techniques. We begin by talking about asynchronous processing. We then move on to some of the more complex Android application components, such as services, application databases (SQLite), content providers, intents, and notifications.

- **Part II: Advanced Android User Interface Design Principles**

  Part II dives deeper into some of the more advanced user interface tools and techniques available as part of the Android Software Development Kit (SDK), including working with action bars, gathering input through nonstandard methods such as gestures and voice recognition, and much more. You will also learn more about how to develop applications that are accessible to different types of users with impairments.

- **Part III: Leveraging Common Android APIs**

  Part III dives deeper into some of the more advanced and specialty APIs available as part of the Android SDK, including networking, web APIs, multimedia (including the camera), telephony, and hardware sensors.

- **Part IV: Leveraging Google APIs**

  Part IV is for those developers who need to integrate with the many available features provided by Google. We cover Google location services, Google Maps Android services, Google Cloud Messaging, Google In-app Billing, Google Analytics, and Google Play game services.

- **Part V: Drawing, Animations, and Graphics Programming with Android**

  Part V is for those developers incorporating graphics of any kind into their applications. We cover both 2D and 3D graphics (OpenGL ES), animation, and the Android NDK.

- **Part VI: Maximizing Android's Unique Features**

  Part VI discusses some of the many ways the Android platform is different from other mobile platforms and how your applications can leverage its unique features. Here you will learn how to extend your application features beyond the traditional borders of mobile applications, integrating them with the Android operating system. App Widgets, enabling searches, and backups are just some of the topics discussed.

- **Part VII: Advanced Topics in Application Publication and Distribution**

  Part VII covers more advanced topics in application publication and distribution, including how to internationalize your applications and taking measures to protect your intellectual property from software pirates.

- **Part VIII: Preparing for Future Android Releases**

  Part VIII introduces the newest version of the Android SDK, the L Developer Preview. We highlight many of the most anticipated features available in this release, including Android Runtime (ART), Project Volta, material design, and Android TV.

- **Part IX: Appendixes**

  Part IX includes a helpful quick-start guide for the Android Debug Bridge (ADB) tool, a refresher course on using SQLite, and a quick-start guide for the Android Studio IDE. There is also an appendix discussing Java for Android developers and one dedicated to providing answers to the quiz questions.

Key Questions Answered in This Book

This book answers the following questions:

1. How can developers write responsive applications?
2. How are Android applications structured? How are background operations handled with services? What are broadcast intents and how can applications use them effectively?
3. How do applications store data persistently using SQLite? How can applications act as content providers and why would they want to do so?
4. How do applications interact with the Android operating system? How do applications trigger system notifications, access underlying device hardware, and monitor device sensors?
5. How can developers design the best user interfaces for the devices of today and tomorrow? How can developers work with 2D and 3D graphics and leverage animation opportunities on Android?
6. How can developers write high-performance, computationally intensive applications using native code?
7. What are some of the most commonly used APIs for networking, location services, maps, multimedia, telephony, and Internet access?
8. What do managers, developers, and testers need to look for when planning, developing, and testing a mobile development application?
9. How do mobile teams design bulletproof Android applications for publication?

10. How can developers make their applications leverage everything Android has to offer in the form of App Widgets, live wallpapers, and other system perks?

11. How can applications take advantage of some of the optional third-party APIs available for use, such as Google Play's In-app Billing and License Verification Library, Google Analytics, Google Play game services, Google location services, Google Maps Android v2 services, and Google Cloud Messaging services?

12. How can developers make use of new Android preview features such as the new Android Studio or Android Wear?

An Overview of Changes in This Edition

When we began writing the first edition of this book, there were no Android devices on the market. Today there are hundreds of types of devices shipping all over the world—smartphones, tablets, e-book readers, smart watches, and specialty devices such as gaming consoles, Google TV, and Google Glass.

The Android platform has gone through extensive changes since the first edition of this book was published. The Android SDK has many new features, and the development tools have received much-needed upgrades. Android, as a technology, is now on solid footing in the mobile marketplace.

For this new edition, we took the opportunity to add content covering the latest and greatest features Android has to offer—but don't worry, it's still the book readers loved the first, second, and third time around; it's just bigger, better, and more comprehensive. In addition to adding new content, we've retested and upgraded all existing content (text and sample code) for use with the latest Android SDKs available while still remaining backward compatible. We created quiz questions to help readers ensure that they understand each chapter's content, and we added end-of-chapter exercises for readers to perform to dig deeper into all that Android has to offer. The Android development community is diverse, and we aim to support all developers, regardless of which devices they are developing for. This includes developers who need to target nearly all platforms, so coverage in some key areas of older SDKs continues to be included as it's often the most reasonable option for compatibility.

Here are some of the highlights of the additions and enhancements we've made in this edition:

- Coverage of the latest and greatest Android tools and utilities is included.

- The chapter on content providers has been rewritten with updated code samples in reference to a simpler application.

- The chapter on notifications has been rewritten to include a new application and code samples demonstrating how to create notifications with the new `NotificationCompat.Builder()` class, and we show how to create expandable and contractible notifications.

- There are totally new chapters that cover Google Cloud Messaging and Google Play game services, and a new appendix that shows you how to get up and running quickly with Android Studio.

- The chapter about location and map APIs has been rewritten to include the new Google location services APIs and the Google Maps Android v2 APIs, allowing you to build even more compelling location services into your applications.
- The chapter on Google Analytics has been rewritten and includes a new application with updated code demonstrating how to make use of the latest version of the Google Analytics SDK for Android.
- The telephony chapter includes information describing the latest changes that affect Short Message Service (SMS) applications, discussing the behavioral differences between the default SMS app and the nondefault SMS apps.
- We've added coverage of hot topics such as Android Wear, sensor event batching, state animations with scenes and transitions, OpenGL ES 3.0, Lock screen App Widgets, Daydream, and Google Play App Translation Service.
- All chapters and appendixes now include quiz questions and exercises for readers to test their knowledge of the subject matter presented.
- All existing chapters have been updated, often with entirely new sections.
- All sample code and accompanying applications have been updated to work with the latest SDK.

As you can see, we cover many of the hottest and most exciting features that Android has to offer. We didn't take this revision lightly; we touched every existing chapter, updated content, and added new chapters as well. Finally, we included many additions, clarifications, and, yes, even a few fixes based upon the feedback from our fantastic (and meticulous) readers. Thank you!

The Development Environment Used in This Book

The Android code in this book was written using the following development environments:

- Windows 7, Windows 8, and Mac OS X 10.9.x
- Android ADT Bundle (20140321 files were used)
- Android Studio (135.1078000 files were used)
- Android SDK Version 4.4, API Level 19 (KitKat)
- Android SDK Tools Revision 22.6.4
- Android SDK Platform Tools 19.0.2
- Android SDK Build Tools 19.1
- Android Support Library Revision 19.1 (where applicable)
- Google Analytics App Tracking SDK version 4 (where applicable)
- Google Play services Revision 17 (where applicable)
- Android NDK r9d (the `android-ndk-r9d-windows-x86.zip` file was used)

- Java SE Development Kit (JDK) 6 Update 45, and JDK 7 Update 55
- Android devices: Nexus 4 and 5 (phones), Nexus 7 (first- and second-generation 7-inch tablet), Nexus 10 (10-inch tablet), including various other devices and form factors

The Android platform continues to grow in market share against competing mobile platforms, such as Apple iOS and BlackBerry. New and exciting types of devices reach consumers' hands at a furious pace. Developers have embraced Android as a target platform to reach the device users of today and tomorrow.

Android's latest major platform update, Android 4.4, frequently called by its code name KitKat, has many new features that help differentiate Android from the competition. This book features the latest SDK and tools available, but it does not focus on them to the detriment of popular legacy versions of the platform. The book is meant to be an overall reference to help developers support all popular devices on the market today. As of the writing of this book, a sizable proportion of users (23.9 percent) have devices that run Android 4.3 or 4.4. Of course, some devices receive upgrades, and users purchase new devices as they become available, but for now, developers need to straddle this gap and support numerous versions of Android to reach the majority of users in the field. In addition, the next version of the Android operating system is likely to be released in the near future.

So what does this mean for this book? It means we provide legacy API support and discuss some of the newer APIs available only in later versions of the Android SDK. We discuss strategies for supporting all (or at least most) users in terms of compatibility. And we provide screenshots that highlight different versions of the Android SDK, because each major revision has brought with it a change in the look and feel of the overall platform. That said, we are assuming that you are downloading the latest Android tools, so we provide screenshots and steps that support the latest tools available at the time of writing, not legacy tools. Those are the boundaries we set when trying to determine what to include or leave out of this book.

Supplementary Materials Available

The source code is also available for download from our book's website: *http://advancedandroidbook.blogspot.com/2014/07/book-code-samples.html*.

Where to Find More Information

There is a vibrant, helpful Android developer community on the Web. Here are a number of useful websites for Android developers and followers of the wireless industry:

- **Android Developer website:** The Android SDK and developer reference site:
  http://developer.android.com/
- **Google Plus:** Android Developers Group:
  https://plus.google.com/+AndroidDevelopers/posts

- **YouTube:** Android Developers channels:

  http://youtube.com/user/androiddevelopers

- **Stack Overflow:** The Android website with great technical information (complete with tags) and an official support forum for developers:

  http://stackoverflow.com/questions/tagged/android

- **Open Handset Alliance:** Android manufacturers, operators, and developers:

  http://openhandsetalliance.com/

- **Google Play:** Buy and sell Android applications:

  https://play.google.com/store

- **Mobiletuts+:** Mobile development tutorials, including Android:

  http://code.tutsplus.com/categories/android-sdk

- **Android Tools Project Site:** The tools team discusses updates and changes:

  https://sites.google.com/a/android.com/tools/recent

- **FierceDeveloper:** A weekly newsletter for wireless developers:

  http://fiercedeveloper.com/

- **XDA-Developers Android forum:** From general development to ROMs:

  http://forum.xda-developers.com/android

- **Developer.com:** A developer-oriented site with mobile articles:

  http://developer.com/

Conventions Used in This Book

This book uses the following conventions:

- Code, directory paths, and programming terms are set in `monospace` font.
- Java import statements, exception handling, and error checking are often removed from printed code samples for clarity and to keep the book at a reasonable length.

This book also presents information in the following types of sidebars:

Tip
Tips provide useful information or hints related to the current text.

Note
Notes provide additional information that might be interesting or relevant.

Warning
Warnings provide hints or tips about pitfalls that may be encountered and how to avoid them.

Contacting the Authors

We welcome your comments, questions, and feedback. We invite you to visit our blog at:

- *http://advancedandroidbook.blogspot.com*

Or, email us at:

- *advancedandroidbook4e@gmail.com*

Circle us on Google+:

- Joseph Annuzzi, Jr.: *http://goo.gl/FBQeL*
- Lauren Darcey: *http://goo.gl/P3RGo*
- Shane Conder: *http://goo.gl/BpVJh*

Advanced Android Application Design Principles

1

Threading and Asynchronous Processing

Offloading intensive operations provides a smoother, more stable experience to the user. An application that is not responsive within 100 to 200 milliseconds creates the feeling of a slow application. Processing off the main UI thread may help speed up your applications. The Android SDK provides two easy ways to manage offload processing from the main UI thread: the `AsyncTask` class and the standard Java `Thread` class. An `Activity` or `Fragment` often needs to load data upon launch, which can be done asynchronously using a `Loader` class. In this chapter, you will learn how to make your applications more responsive by knowing when and how to move intensive operations off the main UI thread to be handled asynchronously.

The Importance of Processing Asynchronously

Users demand responsive applications, so time-intensive operations such as networking should not block the main UI thread. Some common blocking operations include:

- Any lengthy or complex calculation or operation
- Querying a data set of indeterminate size
- Parsing a data set
- Processing multimedia files, such as images, video, or audio
- Iterating over a data structure of indeterminate size
- Accessing network resources
- Accessing location-based services
- Accessing a content provider interface
- Accessing a local database
- Accessing a local file
- Accessing any service that uses any of the previous services

If your application is not responsive enough, it might be plagued with Application Not Responding (ANR) events. ANR events occur when the Android operating system decides that an application is not responding in a reasonable time and shuts that application down. Typically, these events happen when an application takes longer than 5 seconds to respond or complete a task or when an intent broadcast takes longer than 10 seconds to complete.

On API Level 11 and later, moving certain operations off the main UI thread is mandatory. For example, networking code must be completed asynchronously. Your code violates system-wide StrictMode policies otherwise. To ensure that your asynchronous code operates off the main UI thread properly, make sure to test your application on real devices.

Offloading intensive operations from the main UI thread helps avoid the dreaded ANR event and provides a smoother, more stable experience to the user. However, you must still perform all UI operations on the main thread, so some communication between these tasks may be desired. Even certain nonintensive operations are important to offload, such as reading or writing to the file system. While these are normally fast, occasionally a read or write might block for various reasons, including contention on the file or the file system itself. Mobile devices often use flash-based storage that uses wear-reduction algorithms that can significantly delay disk writes on occasion.

The Android SDK provides several ways to manage offload processing from the main UI thread:

- Use the AsyncTask helper class to easily complete tasks asynchronously and communicate back to the main UI thread.

- Use the standard Thread class to complete your processing, as you would in any Java application.

- Use the Loader class to facilitate the loading of data for use in an Activity or Fragment while still starting up quickly.

We discuss all three of these in this chapter.

Tip

Many of the code examples provided in this chapter are taken from the SimpleAsync application. The source code for this application is provided for download on the book's website.

Working with the AsyncTask Class

The AsyncTask class (android.os.AsyncTask) is a special class for Android development that encapsulates background processing and helps facilitate communication to the UI thread while managing the lifecycle of the background task within the context of the Activity lifecycle.

The AsyncTask class is an abstract helper class for managing background operations that eventually are posted back to the UI thread. It creates a simpler interface for asynchronous operations than manually creating a `Thread` class. Internally, `AsyncTask` improves with each new version of the Android SDK, and in later versions it can manage multiple tasks simultaneously using multiple physical cores and an internal thread pool.

Instead of creating threads for background processing and using messages and message handlers for updating the UI, you can create a subclass of `AsyncTask` and implement the appropriate callback methods. The important callbacks are:

- The `onPreExecute()` method runs on the UI thread before background processing begins.

- The `doInBackground()` method runs in the background on a separate thread and is where all the real work is done.

- The `publishProgress()` method, called from the `doInBackground()` method, periodically informs the UI thread about progress of the background process. This method sends information to the UI process. Use this opportunity to send updated information to a progress bar that the user can see.

- The `onProgressUpdate()` method runs on the UI thread whenever the `doInBackground()` method calls `publishProgress()`. This method receives information from the background process. Use this opportunity to update a `ProgressBar` control that the user can see or to update the UI in other ways.

- The `onPostExecute()` method runs on the UI thread once the background processing is completed.

When launched with the `execute()` method, the `AsyncTask` class handles processing in a background thread without blocking the UI thread.

Let's look at a simple example. Here we have an `Activity` class that simply displays a `TextView` control on the screen. In its `onCreate()` method, it launches an asynchronous task called `CounterTask`, which slowly counts to 100. Every time it makes some progress (defined here as 5 percent), it updates the `TextView` control in the UI. Here is the complete implementation:

```
public class SimpleAsyncActivity extends Activity {

    @Override
    public void onCreate(Bundle savedInstanceState) {
        super.onCreate(savedInstanceState);
        setContentView(R.layout.main);

        CountingTask tsk = new CountingTask();
        tsk.execute();
    }

    private class CountingTask extends AsyncTask<Void, Integer, Integer> {

        CountingTask() {}

        @Override
        protected Integer doInBackground(Void... unused) {
```

```
        int i = 0;
        while (i < 100) {
            SystemClock.sleep(250);
            i++;

            if (i % 5 == 0) {
                // update UI with progress every 5%
                publishProgress(i);
            }
        }
        return i;
    }

    protected void onProgressUpdate(Integer... progress) {
        TextView tv = (TextView) findViewById(R.id.counter);
        tv.setText(progress[0] + "% Complete!");
    }

    protected void onPostExecute(Integer result) {
        TextView tv = (TextView) findViewById(R.id.counter);
        tv.setText("Count Complete! Counted to " + result.toString());
    }
    }
}
```

There are two ways to start the task. The first, and default, is to simply instantiate the task and call the execute() method. Each task instantiation can be executed only once.

```
CountingTask tsk = new CountingTask();
tsk.execute();
```

On devices running at least API Level 11, tasks can be executed in parallel. On devices with multiple cores, this can allow execution to complete faster and, in the process, potentially increase your application's performance and smoothness. If you modify the previous code to take an identifier for TextView to update with the counter, you can execute several in parallel. Each task still has to be instantiated separately.

```
CountingTask tsk = new CountingTask();
tsk.executeOnExecutor(AsyncTask.THREAD_POOL_EXECUTOR, id1);
CountingTask tsk2 = new CountingTask();
tsk2.executeOnExecutor(AsyncTask.THREAD_POOL_EXECUTOR, id2);
```

Warning

On API Level 11, the execute() method behaves as if it were using a thread pool. If you do not want to parallel execute, call executeOnExecutor(AsyncTask .SERIAL_EXECUTOR). Although the documentation lists the plan to return execute to serial behavior after API Level 11, you can confirm that the behavior is serial only on API Level 14.

Working with the Thread Class

If you need to control a thread yourself, use the Thread class (java.lang.Thread).
Porting existing code might be simpler using the Thread class directly, instead of
AsyncTask. The Activity class that owns the thread is responsible for managing the
lifecycle of the thread. Generally speaking, the Activity includes a member variable of
type Handler. Then, when the Thread is instantiated and started, the post() method
of the Handler is used to communicate with the main UI thread. You can also communicate to the main UI thread using the runOnUiThread() method of the Activity
class and the post() and postDelayed() methods of the View class. For example, here
is a simple Activity class that performs an operation similar to the AsyncTask example
shown earlier in this chapter:

```
public class SimpleThreadActivity extends Activity {
    @Override
    public void onCreate(Bundle savedInstanceState) {
        super.onCreate(savedInstanceState);
        setContentView(R.layout.main);

        final TextView tv = (TextView) findViewById(R.id.counter);
        new Thread(new Runnable() {
            public void run() {

                int i = 0;

                while (i < 100) {
                    SystemClock.sleep(250);
                    i++;

                    final int curCount = i;
                    if (curCount % 5 == 0) {
                        // update UI with progress every 5%
                        tv.post(new Runnable() {
                            public void run() {
                                tv.setText(curCount + "% Complete!");
                            }
                        });
                    }
                }

                tv.post(new Runnable() {
                    public void run() {
                        tv.setText("Count Complete!");
                    }
                });
            }
        }).start();
    }
}
```

Here we create a new `Thread` object on the fly in the `onCreate()` method of the `Activity` class. Again, we count to 100 using the `post()` method to update the `Text View` with our progress in a thread-safe manner.

Tip

Today's Android devices contain multiple processor cores. To take advantage of running your application code across multiple processors to execute multiple operations in parallel, you could define a `ThreadPoolExecutor` to manage a pool of `Thread` objects to speed up your application's code even further. To determine the number of available processors on a device, use the following code:

```
Runtime.getRuntime().availableProcessors();
```

Working with Loaders

Android 3.0 (API Level 11) introduced the concept of a `Loader` class, which helps asynchronously load data for an `Activity` or `Fragment` from a data source such as a content provider or the network. When configured properly, a `Loader` also monitors the data source for changes, updating the `Activity` or `Fragment` as necessary, which helps avoid unnecessary queries. The most common reason to use a `Loader` involves pulling data from a content provider. To use a `Loader`, take the following steps:

1. Use your `Activity` or `Fragment` class's `LoaderManager` to initialize a `Loader`.
2. Provide an implementation of the `LoaderManager.LoaderCallbacks`.
3. The `onCreateLoader()` method is used to return a new `Loader` instance, typically a `CursorLoader` that queries a content provider from which the `Activity` or `Fragment` wants to display data.
4. The `onLoadFinished()` method signals that all data has been loaded and is ready for use. Typically, your screen contains some sort of control, such as a `ListView`, that leverages the `CursorAdapter` associated with the `CursorLoader`, so you want to swap the old and new `Cursor` objects in the adapter at this time.
5. The `onLoaderReset()` method is used to signify that the data is unavailable, and thus the `Cursor` used by the adapter is no longer valid. Typically, you need to swap out the `Cursor` again at this time.

Although the `Loader` class was added in API Level 11, it is part of the Android Support Package, so it can be used as far back as Android 1.6.

Tip

You can find an example of a `CursorLoader` in Chapter 4, "Building Android Content Providers." There are also numerous examples in the Android SDK samples.

Understanding `StrictMode`

`StrictMode` is a method developers can use to detect operations that should not be performed on the main thread. Beginning in API Level 9, developers can enable `StrictMode` in their own applications to detect when they are, for instance, performing network or disk operations on the main thread. In API Level 11, `StrictMode` was expanded with system-wide settings. These settings disallow some operations on the main thread and instead throw exceptions. To enable `StrictMode` in your own applications to behave like API Level 11 or later, use the following code:

```
StrictMode.ThreadPolicy policy = new StrictMode.ThreadPolicy.Builder()
    .detectAll().penaltyDeath().build();

StrictMode.setThreadPolicy(policy);
```

If you're not writing a production application and want to run some quick code without wiring up a full thread, you can disable the crashing and simply flash the screen instead (on API Level 11) or log the mistakes. You can also call `permitAll()` to skip `StrictMode` entirely. This is not recommended for production applications.

On Android 4.0 and later devices, a Developer options setting screen is available to turn the screen flashing on and off with `StrictMode`; however, it doesn't detect quite as many mistakes. It can be enlightening to turn it on, though.

Summary

Android applications perform many intensive operations on a regular basis, such as accessing resources on disk, services, content providers, databases, and the network. Other operations that can block the main thread include long processing and calculations, and even simple tasks that are performed on a large set of data. So that users don't perceive your applications as being slow, all of these tasks should be moved from the main UI thread of the application using some sort of asynchronous method, whether that be the `Thread` class, an `AsyncTask` implementation, a `Loader`, or a background service, which we talk about in the next chapter. Developers can use `StrictMode` to help identify areas of their applications that could be more responsive.

Quiz Questions

1. True or false: An ANR event means that the Android Notification Record has completed.
2. What `AsyncTask` method runs on the UI thread before background processing begins?

3. If you do not want parallel execution with your `AsyncTask`, what method, including parameters, should you use?

4. What class should you use when you want to load data asynchronously for an `Activity` or `Fragment`?

5. True or false: `StrictCode` is a method developers can use to detect operations that should not be performed on the main thread.

Exercises

1. Using the online documentation, create a list of the various things you should do to reinforce responsiveness in your applications.

2. Using the online documentation, explain the "important hierarchy" that Android uses for determining which processes are kept and which are destroyed.

3. Using the online documentation, determine at least one strategy you should use when your application needs to perform operations that take a long time to complete, and write a simple application demonstrating your knowledge of the strategy.

References and More Information

Android Training: "Keeping Your App Responsive":
  http://d.android.com/training/articles/perf-anr.html
Android API Guides: "Processes and Threads":
  http://d.android.com/guide/components/processes-and-threads.html
Android Reference documentation on the `Thread` class:
  http://d.android.com/reference/java/lang/Thread.html
Android Reference documentation on the `ThreadPoolExecutor` class:
  http://d.android.com/reference/java/util/concurrent/ThreadPoolExecutor.html
Android Reference documentation on the `AsyncTask` class:
  http://d.android.com/reference/android/os/AsyncTask.html
Android API Guides: "Loaders":
  http://d.android.com/guide/components/loaders.html
Android Reference documentation on the `StrictMode` class:
  http://d.android.com/reference/android/os/StrictMode.html

## 2

Working with Services

Services are important Android application components that can greatly enhance an application. An Android `Service` might be used to perform functions in the background that do not require user input or to supply information to other applications. In this chapter, you will learn how to create and interact with an Android `Service`. Then you will learn how to define a remote interface using the Android Interface Definition Language (AIDL). Finally, you will learn how to pass objects through this interface by creating a class that implements a `Parcelable` object.

Determining When to Use Services

A `Service` in the Android SDK can mean one of two things. First, a `Service` can mean a background process that performs some useful operation at regular intervals. Second, a `Service` can be an interface for a remote object, called from within an application. In both cases, the `Service` object extends the `Service` class from the Android SDK, and it can be a standalone component or part of an application with a complete user interface.

Certainly, not all applications require or use services. However, you might want to consider a `Service` if your application meets certain criteria, such as the following:

- The application performs lengthy or resource-intensive processing that does not require input from the user.
- The application must perform certain functions routinely, or at regular intervals, such as uploading or downloading fresh content or logging the current location.
- The application performs a lengthy operation that, if canceled because the application exits, would be wasteful to restart. An example of this is downloading large files.
- The application performs a lengthy operation while the user might be doing multiple activities. A `Service` can be used to span processing across the bounds of `Activity` lifecycles.
- The application needs to expose and provide data or information services (think web services) to other Android applications without the need of a user interface.

Understanding the `Service` Lifecycle

Before we get into the details of how to create a `Service`, let's look at how services interact with the Android operating system. First, it should be noted that a `Service` implementation must be registered in an application's manifest file using the `<service>` tag. The `Service` implementation might also define and enforce any permissions needed for starting, stopping, and binding to the `Service`, as well as make specific `Service` calls.

After it has been implemented, an Android `Service` can be started using the `Context.startService()` method. If the `Service` was already running when the `startService()` method was called, these subsequent calls don't start further instances of the `Service`. The `Service` continues to run until either the `Context.stop Service()` method is called or the `Service` completes its tasks and stops itself using the `stopSelf()` method.

To connect to a `Service`, interested applications use the `Context.bindService()` method to obtain a connection. If that `Service` is not running, the `Service` is created at that time. After the connection is established, the interested applications can begin making requests of that `Service` if the applications have the appropriate permissions. For example, a Magic Eight Ball application might have an underlying `Service` that can receive yes-or-no questions and provide Yoda-style answers. Any interested application can connect to the Magic Eight Ball `Service`, ask a question ("Will my app flourish in the Google Play store?"), and receive the result ("Signs point to Yes."). The application can disconnect from the `Service` when finished using the `Context.unbindService()` method.

Warning

Like applications, services can be killed by the Android operating system under low-memory conditions. Also like applications, services have a main thread that can be blocked, causing the system to become unresponsive. Always offload intensive processing to worker threads using whatever methodology you like, even when implementing a `Service`.

Creating a `Service`

Creating an Android `Service` involves extending the `Service` class and adding a `<service>` block to the `AndroidManifest.xml` permissions file. The `GPXService` class, discussed later in this section, overrides the `onCreate()`, `onStart()`, `onStartCommand()`, and `onDestroy()` methods to begin with. Defining the `Service` name enables other applications to start the `Service` that runs in the background and stop it. Both the `onStart()` and `onStartCommand()` methods are essentially the same, with the exception that `onStart()` is deprecated in API Level 5 and above. (The default implementation of the `onStartCommand()` on API Level 5 or greater is to call `onStart()`, which returns an appropriate value so that behavior is compatible with previous versions.) In the following example, both methods are implemented.

Tip

Many of the code examples provided in this chapter are taken from the SimpleService and UseService applications. The source code for these applications is provided for download on the book's website.

For this example, we implement a simple `Service` that listens for Global Positioning System (GPS) changes, displays notifications at regular intervals, and then provides access to the most recent location data via a remote interface. The following code gives a simple definition of the `Service` class called `GPXService`:

```
public class GPXService extends Service {
    public static final String GPX_SERVICE =
        "com.advancedandroidbook.GPXService.SERVICE";

    private LocationManager location = null;
    private NotificationManager notifier = null;

    @Override
    public void onCreate() {
        super.onCreate();
    }
    @Override
    public void onStart(Intent intent, int startId) {
        super.onStart(intent, startId);
    }

    @Override
    public void onStartCommand(Intent intent, int flags, int startId) {
        super.onStart(intent, startId);
    }

    @Override
    public void onDestroy() {
        super.onDestroy();
    }
}
```

You need to understand the lifecycle of a `Service` because it's different from that of an `Activity`. If a `Service` is started by the system with a call to the `Context.startService()` method, the `onCreate()` method is called just before the `onStart()` or `onStartCommand()` methods. However, if the `Service` is bound to with a call to the `Context.bindService()` method, the `onCreate()` method is called just before the `onBind()` method. The `onStart()` and `onStartCommand()` methods are not called in this case. We talk more about binding to a `Service` later in this chapter. Finally, when the `Service` is finished—that is, it is stopped and no other process is bound to it—the `onDestroy()` method is called. Everything for the `Service` must be cleaned up in this method.

With this in mind, here is the full implementation of the `onCreate()` method for the `GPXService` class previously introduced:

```
public void onCreate() {
    super.onCreate();
```

```
location = (LocationManager) getSystemService(Context.LOCATION_SERVICE);
notifier = (NotificationManager)
                getSystemService(Context.NOTIFICATION_SERVICE);
}
```

Because the object doesn't yet know if the next call is to either of the start methods or the `onBind()` method, we make a couple of quick initialization calls, but no background processing is started. Even this might be too much if neither of these objects is used by the interface provided by the binder.

Because we can't always predict what version of Android our code will run on, we can simply implement both the `onStart()` and `onStartCommand()` methods and have them call a third method that provides a common implementation. This enables us to customize behaviors on later Android versions while being compatible with earlier versions. To do this, the project needs to be built for an SDK of Level 5 or higher while having a `minSdkValue` of whatever earlier versions are supported. Of course, we highly recommend testing on multiple platform versions to verify that the behavior is as you expect. Here are sample implementations of the `onStartCommand()` and `onStart()` methods:

```
@Override
public int onStartCommand(Intent intent, int flags, int startId ) {
    Log.v(DEBUG_TAG, "onStartCommand() called, must be on L5 or later");

    if (flags != 0) {
        Log.w(DEBUG_TAG, "Redelivered or retrying service start: "+flags);
    }

    doServiceStart(intent, startId);
    return Service.START_REDELIVER_INTENT;
}

@Override
public void onStart(Intent intent, int startId) {
    super.onStart(intent, startId);
    Log.v(DEBUG_TAG, "onStart() called, must be on L3 or L4");
    doServiceStart(intent,startId);
}
```

Next, let's look at the implementation of the `doServiceStart()` method in greater detail:

```
@Override
public void doServiceStart(Intent intent, int startId) {
    updateRate = intent.getIntExtra(EXTRA_UPDATE_RATE, -1);
    if (updateRate == -1) {
        updateRate = 60000;
    }

    Criteria criteria = new Criteria();
    criteria.setAccuracy(Criteria.NO_REQUIREMENT);
    criteria.setPowerRequirement(Criteria.POWER_LOW);

    location = (LocationManager) getSystemService(Context.LOCATION_SERVICE);
```

```
String best = location.getBestProvider(criteria, true);

location.requestLocationUpdates(best, updateRate, 0, trackListener);

Intent toLaunch = new Intent(getApplicationContext(),
    ServiceControlActivity.class);
PendingIntent intentBack = PendingIntent.getActivity(
    getApplicationContext(), 0, toLaunch, 0);

NotificationCompat.Builder builder = new NotificationCompat.Builder(
    getApplicationContext());
builder.setTicker("Builder GPS Tracking");
builder.setSmallIcon(android.R.drawable.stat_notify_more);
builder.setWhen(System.currentTimeMillis());
builder.setContentTitle("Builder GPS Tracking");
builder.setContentText("Tracking start at " + updateRate
    + "ms intervals with [" + best + "] as the provider.");
builder.setContentIntent(intentBack);
builder.setAutoCancel(true);
Notification notify = builder.build();

notifier.notify(GPS_NOTIFY, notify);
}
```

The background processing starts in the two start methods. In this example, though, the background processing is actually just registering for an update from another `Service`. For more information about using location-based services and the `Location Manager`, see Chapter 17, "Using Location and Map APIs," and for more information on notification calls, see Chapter 6, "Working with Notifications."

Tip

The use of a callback to receive updates is recommended over doing background processing to poll for updates. Most mobile devices have limited battery life. Continual running in the background, or even just polling, can use a substantial amount of battery power. In addition, implementing callbacks for the users of your `Service` is more efficient for the same reasons.

In this case, we turn on the GPS for the duration of the process, which might affect battery life even though we request a lower-power method of location determination. Keep power management in mind when developing services so that your `Service` does not drain the user's battery.

The `Intent` extras object retrieves data passed in by the process requesting the `Service`. Here, we retrieve one value, `EXTRA_UPDATE_RATE`, for determining the length of time between updates. The string for this, `update-rate`, must be published externally, either in developer documentation or in a publicly available class file, so that users of the `Service` know about it.

The implementation details of the `LocationListener` object, `trackListener`, are not relevant to the discussion on services. However, processing should be kept to a minimum to avoid interrupting what the user is doing in the foreground. Some testing might be required to determine how much processing a particular phone can handle before the user notices performance issues.

There are two common methods of communicating data to the user. The first is to use notifications. This is the least intrusive method and can be used to drive users to the application for more information. It also means the users don't need to be actively using their phone at the time of the notification because it is queued. For instance, a weather application might use notifications to provide weather updates every hour.

The other method is to use Toast messages. From some services, this might work well, especially if the user expects frequent updates and those updates work well overlaid briefly on the screen, regardless of what the user is currently doing. For instance, a background music player could briefly overlay the current song title when the song changes.

The onDestroy() method is called when no clients are bound to the Service and a request for the Service to be stopped has been made via a call to the Context.stop Service() method, or a call has been made to the stopSelf() method from within the Service. At this point, everything should be gracefully cleaned up because the Service ceases to exist.

Here is an example of the onDestroy() method:

```
@Override
public void onDestroy() {
    if (location != null) {
        location.removeUpdates(trackListener);
        location = null;
    }

    Intent toLaunch = new Intent(getApplicationContext(),
        ServiceControlActivity.class);
    PendingIntent intentBack = PendingIntent.getActivity(
        getApplicationContext(), 0, toLaunch, 0);

    NotificationCompat.Builder builder = new NotificationCompat.Builder(
        getApplicationContext());
    builder.setTicker("Builder GPS Tracking");
    builder.setSmallIcon(android.R.drawable.stat_notify_more);
    builder.setWhen(System.currentTimeMillis());
    builder.setContentTitle("Builder GPS Tracking");
    builder.setContentText("Tracking stopped");
    builder.setContentIntent(intentBack);
    builder.setAutoCancel(true);

    Notification notify = builder.build();

    notifier.notify(GPS_NOTIFY, notify);
    super.onDestroy();
}
```

Here, we stop updates to the LocationListener object. This stops all our background processing. Then, we notify the user that the Service is terminating. Only a single call to the onDestroy() method happens, regardless of how many times the start methods are called.

The system does not know about a `Service` unless it is defined within the `Android Manifest.xml` permissions file using the `<service>` tag. Here is the `<service>` tag we must add to the Android manifest file:

```
<service
    android:enabled="true"
    android:name="GPXService">
    <intent-filter>
        <action android:name=
            "com.advancedandroidbook.GPXService.SERVICE" />
    </intent-filter>
</service>
```

This block of XML defines the `Service` name, `GPXService`, and that the `Service` is enabled. Then, using an intent filter, we use the same string that we defined within the class. This is the string that is used later when controlling the `Service`. With this block of XML inside the application section of the manifest, the system now knows that the `Service` exists and can be used by other applications.

Controlling a `Service`

At this point, the example code has a complete implementation of a `Service`. Now we write code to control the `Service` we previously defined:

```
Intent service = new Intent("com.advancedandroidbook.GPXService.SERVICE");
service.putExtra("update-rate", 5000);
startService(service);
```

Starting a `Service` is as straightforward as creating an `Intent` with the `Service` name and calling the `startService()` method. In this example, we also set the `Intent` extra parameter called `update-rate` to 5 seconds. That rate is quite frequent but works well for testing. For practical use, we probably want this set to 60 seconds or more. This code triggers a call to the `onCreate()` method, if the `Service` isn't bound to or running already. It also triggers a call to the `onStart()` or `onStartCommand()` methods, even if the `Service` is already running.

Later, when we finish with the `Service`, it needs to be stopped using the following code:

```
Intent service = new Intent("com.advancedandroidbook.GPXService.SERVICE");
stopService(service);
```

This code is essentially the same as the code for starting the `Service` but with a call to the `stopService()` method. This calls the `onDestroy()` method if there are no bindings to it. However, if there are bindings, `onDestroy()` is not called until those are also terminated. This means background processing might continue despite a call to the `stopService()` method. If there is a need to control the background processing separate from these system calls, a remote interface is required.

Implementing a Remote Interface

Sometimes it is useful to have more control over a Service than just system calls to start and stop its activities. However, before a client application can bind to a Service for making other method calls, you need to define the interface. The Android SDK includes a useful tool and file format for remote interfaces for this purpose.

To define a remote interface, you must declare the interface in an AIDL file, implement the interface, and then return an instance of the interface when the onBind() method is called.

Using the example GPXService service we already built in this chapter, we now create a remote interface for it. This remote interface has a method, which can be called especially for returning the last location logged. You can use only primitive types and objects that implement the Parcelable (android.os.Parcelable) protocol with remote Service calls. This is because these calls may cross process boundaries where memory can't be shared. The AIDL compiler handles the details of crossing these boundaries when the rules are followed. The Location object implements the Parcelable interface so it can be used.

Here is the AIDL file for this interface, IRemoteInterface:

```
package com.advancedandroidbook.services;

interface IRemoteInterface {
    Location getLastLocation();
}
```

When using the Android integrated development environment (IDE), you can add this AIDL file, IRemoteInterface.aidl, to the project under the appropriate package and the Android SDK does the rest. Now we must implement the code for the interface. Here is an example implementation:

```
private final IRemoteInterface.Stub
    mRemoteInterfaceBinder = new IRemoteInterface.Stub() {
        public Location getLastLocation() {
            Log.v("interface", "getLastLocation() called");
            return lastLocation;
        }
    };
```

The Service code has already stored the last location received as a member variable, so we can simply return that value. With the interface implemented, it needs to be returned from the onBind() method of the Service:

```
@Override
public IBinder onBind(Intent intent) {
    // we only have one, so no need to check the intent
    return mRemoteInterfaceBinder;
}
```

If multiple interfaces are implemented, the Intent passed in can be checked within the onBind() method to determine what action is to be taken and which interface should be returned. In this example, though, we have only one interface and don't expect any other information within the Intent, so we simply return the interface.

We also add the class name of the binder interface to the list of actions supported by the intent filter for the Service within the AndroidManifest.xml file. Doing this isn't required but is a useful convention to follow and allows the class name to be used. The following block is added to the <service> tag definition:

```
<action android:name ="com.advancedandroidbook.services.IRemoteInterface" />
```

The Service can now be used through this interface. This is done by implementing a ServiceConnection object and calling the bindService() method. When finished, the unbindService() method must be called so the system knows that the application has finished using the Service. The connection remains even if the reference to the interface is gone.

Here is an implementation of a ServiceConnection object's two main methods, onServiceConnected() and onServiceDisconnected():

```
public void onServiceConnected(ComponentName name,
    IBinder service) {

    mRemoteInterface = IRemoteInterface.Stub.asInterface(service);
    Log.v("ServiceControl", "Interface bound.");
}

public void onServiceDisconnected(ComponentName name) {
    mRemoteInterface = null;
    Log.v("ServiceControl", "Remote interface no longer bound");
}
```

When the onServiceConnected() method is called, an IRemoteInterface instance that can be used to make calls to the interface we previously defined is retrieved. A call to the remote interface looks like any call to an interface now:

```
Location loc = mRemoteInterface.getLastLocation();
```

Tip

Remember that remote interface calls operate across process boundaries and are completed synchronously. As such, you should place them within a separate thread, as any lengthy call would be.

To use this interface from another application, you should place the AIDL file in the project and appropriate package. The call to onBind() triggers a call to onService Connected() after the call to the Service's onCreate() method. Remember, the onStart() and onStartCommand() methods are not called in this case.

```
bindService(new Intent(IRemoteInterface.class.getName()),
    this, Context.BIND_AUTO_CREATE);
```

In this case, the Activity we call from also implements the ServiceConnection interface. This code also demonstrates why it is a useful convention to use the class name as an intent filter. Because we have both intent filters and we don't check the action on the call to the onBind() method, we can also use the other intent filter, but the code here is clearer.

When done with the interface, a call to unbindService() disconnects the interface. However, a callback to the onServiceDisconnected() method does not mean that the Service is no longer bound; the binding is still active at that point, just not the connection.

Implementing a `Parcelable` Class

In the example so far, we have been lucky in that the Location class implements the Parcelable interface. What if a new object needs to be passed through a remote interface?

Let's take the following class, GPXPoint, as an example:

```
public final class GPXPoint {
    public int latitude;
    public int longitude;
    public Date timestamp;
    public double elevation;

    public GPXPoint() {}
}
```

The GPXPoint class defines a location point that is similar to a GeoPoint but also includes the time the location was recorded and the elevation. This data is commonly found in the popular GPX file format. On its own, the GPX file format is not a basic format that the system recognizes for passing through to a remote interface. However, if the class implements the Parcelable interface and we then create an AIDL file from it, the object can be used in a remote interface.

To fully support the Parcelable type, we need to implement a few methods and a Parcelable.Creator<GPXPoint>. The following is the same class now modified to be a Parcelable class:

```
public final class GPXPoint implements Parcelable {
    public int latitude;
    public int longitude;
    public Date timestamp;
    public double elevation;

    public static final Parcelable.Creator<GPXPoint>
        CREATOR = new Parcelable.Creator<GPXPoint>() {

        public GPXPoint createFromParcel(Parcel src) {
            return new GPXPoint(src);
        }

        public GPXPoint[] newArray(int size) {
            return new GPXPoint[size];
        }
    };
```

```
public GPXPoint() {}

private GPXPoint(Parcel src) {
    readFromParcel(src);
}

public void writeToParcel(Parcel dest, int flags) {
    dest.writeInt(latitude);
    dest.writeInt(longitude);
    dest.writeDouble(elevation);
    dest.writeLong(timestamp.getTime());
}

public void readFromParcel(Parcel src) {
    latitude = src.readInt();
    longitude = src.readInt();
    elevation = src.readDouble();
    timestamp = new Date(src.readLong());
}

public int describeContents() {
    return 0;
}
}
```

The `writeToParcel()` method is required and flattens the object in a particular order using supported primitive types within a `Parcel`. When the class is created from a `Parcel`, the `Creator` is called, which in turn calls the private constructor. For readability, we also created a `readFromParcel()` method that reverses the flattening, reading the primitives in the same order that they were written and creating a new `Date` object.

Now you must create the AIDL file for this class. You should place it in the same directory as the Java file and name it `GPXPoint.aidl` to match. You should make the contents look like the following:

```
package com.advancedandroidbook.services;
parcelable GPXPoint;
```

Now the `GPXPoint` class can be used in remote interfaces. This is done in the same way as any other native type or `Parcelable` object. You can modify the `IRemote Interface.aidl` file to look like the following:

```
package com.advancedandroidbook.services;
import com.advancedandroidbook.services.GPXPoint;

interface IRemoteInterface {
    Location getLastLocation();
    GPXPoint getGPXPoint();
}
```

Additionally, we can provide an implementation for this method within the interface, as follows:

```
public GPXPoint getGPXPoint() {
    if (lastLocation == null) {
```

```
            return null;
        } else {
            Log.v("interface", "getGPXPoint() called");
            GPXPoint point = new GPXPoint();

            point.elevation = lastLocation.getAltitude();
            point.latitude = (int) (lastLocation.getLatitude() * 1E6);
            point.longitude = (int) (lastLocation.getLongitude() * 1E6);
            point.timestamp = new Date(lastLocation.getTime());

            return point;
        }
    }
```

As can be seen, nothing particularly special needs to happen. Just by making the object `Parcelable`, it can now be used for this purpose.

Using the `IntentService` Class

Offloading regularly performed tasks to a work queue is an easy and efficient way to process multiple requests without the cumbersome overhead of creating a full `Service`. The `IntentService` class (`android.app.IntentService`) is a simple type of `Service` that can be used to handle such tasks asynchronously by way of `Intent` requests. Each `Intent` is added to the work queue associated with that `IntentService` and is handled sequentially. You can send data back to the application by simply broadcasting the result as an `Intent` object and using a broadcast receiver to catch the result and use it within the application.

Certainly, not all applications require or use a `Service`, or more specifically an `IntentService`. However, you may want to consider one if your application meets certain criteria, such as:

- The application routinely performs the same or similar blocking or resource-intensive processing operations that do not require input from the user in which requests for such operations can "pile up," requiring a queue to handle the requests in an organized fashion. Image processing and data downloading are examples of such processing.

- The application performs certain blocking operations at regular intervals but does not need to perform these routine tasks so frequently as to require a permanent, "always on" `Service`. Examples of such operations are accessing local storage content providers, application databases, or a network, as well as heavy image processing or math to chug through.

- The application routinely dispatches "work" but doesn't need an immediate response. For example, an email application might use an `IntentService` work queue to queue up each message to be packaged up and sent out to a mail server. All networking code would then be separated from the main user interface of the application.

Now let's look at an example of how you might use `IntentService`.

Tip

The code examples in this section are taken from the `SimpleIntentService` sample application. The source code for this application is provided for download on the book's website.

Let's assume you have an application with a screen that performs some processing each time the user provides some input, and then displays the result. For example, you might have an `EditText` control for taking some textual input, a `Button` control to commit the text and start the processing, and a `TextView` control for displaying the result. The code in the `Button` click handler within the `Activity` class would look something like this:

```
EditText input = (EditText) findViewById(R.id.txt_input);
String strInputMsg = input.getText().toString();
SystemClock.sleep(5000);
TextView result = (TextView) findViewById(R.id.txt_result);
result.setText(strInputMsg + " "
    + DateFormat.format("MM/dd/yy h:mmaa", System.currentTimeMillis()));
```

All this click handler does is retrieve some text from an `EditText` control on the screen, hang around doing nothing for 5 seconds, and then generate some information to display in the `TextView` control as a result. In reality, your application would probably not just sit around sleeping but would do some real work. As written, the click processing runs on the main UI thread. This means that every time the user clicks on the `Button` control, the entire application becomes unresponsive for at least 5 seconds. The user must wait for the task to finish before continuing to use the application because the task is being completed on the main thread.

Wouldn't it be great if we could dispatch the processing request each time the user clicked the `Button`, but let the user interface remain responsive so the user can go about his or her business? Let's implement a simple `IntentService` that does just that. Here's our simple `IntentService` implementation:

```
public class SimpleIntentService extends IntentService {
    public static final String PARAM_IN_MSG = "imsg";
    public static final String PARAM_OUT_MSG = "omsg";

    public SimpleIntentService() {
        super("SimpleIntentService");
    }

    @Override
    protected void onHandleIntent(Intent intent) {
        String msg = intent.getStringExtra(PARAM_IN_MSG);
        SystemClock.sleep(5000);
        String resultTxt = msg + " " + DateFormat.format("MM/dd/yy h:mmaa",
                System.currentTimeMillis());
        Intent broadcastIntent = new Intent();
        broadcastIntent.setAction(ResponseReceiver.ACTION_RESP);
```

```
        broadcastIntent.addCategory(Intent.CATEGORY_DEFAULT);
        broadcastIntent.putExtra(PARAM_OUT_MSG, resultTxt);
        sendBroadcast(broadcastIntent);
    }
}
```

We use `Intent` extras to send some data associated with the specific task request, in a manner similar to passing data between `Activity` classes. In this case, we take the incoming `EditText` text value and package it into the `PARAM_IN_MSG` extra. Once the processing is complete, we use a broadcast `Intent` to tell anyone interested that the `Service` has finished the task. Your `IntentService` needs to do this only if the user interface needs to be updated. If the task simply updates the underlying application database or the shared preferences or what have you, your application would not need to be informed directly, as `Cursor` objects and such would be updated automatically when some underlying data changed.

Now, turn your attention back to the `Activity` class that hosts your application user interface with the `Button` control. Update the `Button` click handler to send a new task request to the `SimpleIntentService`. The request is packaged as an `Intent`, the incoming parameter is set (the data associated with the task), and the request is fired off using the `startService()` method.

```
EditText input = (EditText) findViewById(R.id.txt_input);
String strInputMsg = input.getText().toString();
Intent msgIntent = new Intent(this, SimpleIntentService.class);
msgIntent.putExtra(SimpleIntentService.PARAM_IN_MSG, strInputMsg);
startService(msgIntent);
```

Finally, define a `BroadcastReceiver` object for use by the application `Activity`, to listen for the results of each task completing and update the user interface accordingly:

```
public class ResponseReceiver extends BroadcastReceiver {
    public static final String ACTION_RESP =
        "com.mamlambo.intent.action.MESSAGE_PROCESSED";

    @Override
    public void onReceive(Context context, Intent intent) {
        TextView result = (TextView) findViewById(R.id.txt_result);
        String text = intent.getStringExtra(SimpleIntentService.PARAM_OUT_MSG);
        result.setText(text);
    }
}
```

The `BroadcastReceiver` class's `onReceive()` callback method does the work of reacting to a new broadcast from your `SimpleIntentService`. It updates the `TextView` control based upon the `Intent` extra data, which is the "result" from the task processing. Your application should register the broadcast receiver only when it needs to listen for results, and then unregister it when it's no longer needed. To manage this, first add a private member variable to your `Activity`, like this:

```
private ResponseReceiver receiver;
```

Activities typically register for broadcasts in their `onCreate()` or `onResume()` methods by creating an `IntentFilter`, like this:

```
IntentFilter filter = new IntentFilter(ResponseReceiver.ACTION_RESP);
filter.addCategory(Intent.CATEGORY_DEFAULT);
receiver = new ResponseReceiver();
registerReceiver(receiver, filter);
```

Similarly, it is typical to unregister the receiver when the `Activity` class no longer needs to react to results, such as in the `onPause()` or `onDestroy()` methods:

```
unregisterReceiver(receiver);
```

Finally, don't forget to register your `SimpleIntentService` in your Android manifest file, like this:

```
<service android:name="SimpleIntentService"/>
```

That's the complete implementation of our example `IntentService`. The `Activity` shoots off requests to the `SimpleIntentService` each time the `Button` control is clicked. The `Service` handles the queuing, processing, and broadcasting of the result of each task asynchronously. The `Service` shuts itself down when there's nothing left to do and starts back up if a new request comes in. Meanwhile, the application `Activity` remains responsive because it is no longer processing each request on the same thread that handles the UI. The user interface is responsive throughout all processing, allowing the user to continue to use the application. The user can hit the `Button` control five times in succession and trigger five tasks to be sent to the `IntentService` without having to wait 5 seconds between each click.

Summary

The Android SDK provides the `Service` mechanism that can be used to implement background tasks and to share functionality across multiple applications. By creating an interface through the use of AIDL, a `Service` can expose functionality to other applications without having to distribute libraries or packages. Creating objects with the `Parcelable` interface enables developers to extend the data that can also be passed across process boundaries.

Care should be taken when creating a background `Service`. Poorly designed background services might have a substantial negative impact on handset performance and battery life. In addition to standard testing, you should test a `Service` implementation with respect to these issues.

Prudent creation of a `Service`, though, can dramatically enhance the appeal of an application or service you might provide. `Service` creation is a powerful tool provided by the Android SDK for designing applications that are simply not possible on other mobile platforms. The `IntentService` class can be used to create a simple `service` that acts as a work queue.

Quiz Questions

1. True or false: Services should not be used for lengthy operations such as downloading large files.
2. What is the `Context` method used to connect to a `Service`?
3. What must be implemented to allow client applications to perform remote `Service` calls?
4. True or false: AIDL stands for Android Intent Data Layer.
5. What is the name of the `Service` class used for creating asynchronous work queue tasks?

Exercises

1. Use the online documentation to determine what method you should use to run a `Service` that is not allowed to be destroyed by the system when Android is low on memory.
2. In your own words, describe the difference between a bounded `Service` and an unbounded `Service`.
3. Use the online documentation to learn about the `Messenger` class. With this newfound knowledge, rewrite the `SimpleService` application using a `Messenger` rather than the AIDL used in the example code.

References and More Information

Android Reference: "`Service`":
   http://d.android.com/reference/android/app/Service.html
Android API Guides: "Services":
   http://d.android.com/guide/components/services.html
Android API Guides: "Bound Services":
   http://d.android.com/guide/components/bound-services.html
Android API Guides: "Android Interface Definition Language (AIDL)":
   http://d.android.com/guide/components/aidl.html
Android API Guides: "Processes and Threads":
   http://d.android.com/guide/components/processes-and-threads.html
Android API Guides: "Android Application Framework FAQ":
   http://d.android.com/guide/faq/framework.html

3

Leveraging SQLite Application Databases

Applications use a combination of application preferences, the file system, and database support to store information. In this chapter, we explore one of the most powerful ways you can store, manage, and share application data with Android: an application database powered by SQLite. Application databases provide structured data storage that is quick to access, search, and manipulate.

Note

For more information about designing SQLite databases and interacting with them via the `sqlite3` command-line tool, please see Appendix B, "Quick-Start Guide: SQLite." This appendix is divided into two parts. The first half is an overview of the most commonly used features of the `sqlite3` command-line interface and the limitations of SQLite compared to other flavors of SQL; the second half of the appendix includes a fully functional tutorial in which you build a SQLite database from the ground up and then use it. If you are new to SQLite or a bit rusty on your syntax, this appendix is for you.

Storing Structured Data Using SQLite Databases

When your application requires a more robust data storage mechanism, you'll be happy to hear that the Android file system includes support for application-specific relational databases using SQLite. SQLite databases are lightweight and file based, making them ideal for embedded devices.

Tip

Many of the code examples provided in this section are taken from the SimpleDatabase application. This source code for this application is provided for download on the book's website.

These databases and the data in them are private to the application. To share application data with other applications, you must expose the data you want to share by making your application a content provider.

The Android SDK includes a number of useful SQLite database management classes. Many of these classes are found in the `android.database.sqlite` package. Here you can find utility classes for managing database creation and versioning, database management, and query builder helper classes to help you format proper SQL statements and queries. The package also includes specialized `Cursor` objects for iterating query results. You can also find all the specialized exceptions associated with SQLite.

In this chapter, we focus on creating databases in our Android applications. For that, we use the built-in SQLite support to programmatically create and use a SQLite database to store application information. However, if your application works with a different sort of database, you can also find more generic database classes (in the `android.database` package) to help you work with data from other providers.

In addition to programmatically creating and using SQLite databases, developers can interact directly with their application's database using the `sqlite3` command-line tool that's accessible through the ADB shell interface. This can be a helpful debugging tool for developers and quality assurance personnel who might want to manage the database state (and content) for testing purposes.

Creating a SQLite Database

You can create a SQLite database for your Android application in several ways. To illustrate how to create and use a simple SQLite database, let's create an Android project called SimpleDatabase.

Creating a SQLite Database Instance Using the Application `Context`

The simplest way to create a new `SQLiteDatabase` instance for your application is to use the `openOrCreateDatabase()` method of your application `Context`, like this:

```
import android.database.sqlite.SQLiteDatabase;
...
SQLiteDatabase mDatabase;
mDatabase = openOrCreateDatabase("my_sqlite_database.db",
            SQLiteDatabase.CREATE_IF_NECESSARY,
            null);
```

Finding the Application Database File on the Device File System

Android applications store their databases (SQLite or otherwise) in a special application directory:

```
/data/data/<application package name>/databases/<databasename>
```

So, in this case, the path to the database would be:

```
/data/data/com.advancedandroidbook.SimpleDatabase/databases/my_sqlite_database.db
```

You can access your database using the `sqlite3` command-line interface using this path.

Configuring the SQLite Database Properties

Now that you have a valid `SQLiteDatabase` instance, it's time to configure it. Some important database configuration options include version and locale features:

```
import java.util.Locale;
...
mDatabase.setLocale(Locale.getDefault());
mDatabase.setVersion(1);
```

Creating Tables and Other SQLite Schema Objects

Creating tables and other SQLite schema objects is as simple as forming proper SQLite statements and executing them. The following is a valid `CREATE TABLE` SQL statement. This statement creates a table called `tbl_authors`. The table has three fields: a unique `id` number, which auto-increments with each record and acts as our primary key, and `firstname` and `lastname` text fields:

```
CREATE TABLE tbl_authors (
id INTEGER PRIMARY KEY AUTOINCREMENT,
firstname TEXT,
lastname TEXT);
```

You can encapsulate this `CREATE TABLE` SQL statement in a `static final String` variable (called `CREATE_AUTHOR_TABLE`) and then execute it on your database using the `execSQL()` method:

```
mDatabase.execSQL(CREATE_AUTHOR_TABLE);
```

The `execSQL()` method works for non-queries. You can use it to execute any valid SQLite SQL statement. For example, you can use it to create, update, and delete tables, views, triggers, and other common SQL objects. In our application, we add another table called `tbl_books`. The schema for `tbl_books` looks like this:

```
CREATE TABLE tbl_books (
id INTEGER PRIMARY KEY AUTOINCREMENT,
title TEXT,
dateadded DATE,
authorid INTEGER NOT NULL CONSTRAINT authorid REFERENCES tbl_authors(id) ON
DELETE CASCADE);
```

Unfortunately, SQLite does not enforce foreign key constraints. Instead, we must enforce them ourselves using custom SQL triggers, meaning that when a certain database event occurs, we run a particular SQL command. So we create triggers, such as this one that enforces that books have valid authors:

```
private static final String CREATE_TRIGGER_ADD =
"CREATE TRIGGER fk_insert_book BEFORE INSERT ON tbl_books
FOR EACH ROW
BEGIN
SELECT RAISE(ROLLBACK, 'insert on table \"tbl_books\" violates foreign key
```

```
constraint \"fk_authorid\"') WHERE (SELECT id FROM tbl_authors WHERE id =
NEW.authorid) IS NULL;
END;";
```

We can then create the trigger simply by executing the CREATE TRIGGER SQL statement:

```
mDatabase.execSQL(CREATE_TRIGGER_ADD);
```

We need to add several more triggers to help enforce our link between the author and book tables, one for updating tbl_books and one for deleting records from tbl_authors.

Creating, Updating, and Deleting Database Records

Now that we have a database set up, we need to create some data. The SQLiteDatabase class includes three convenience methods to do that. They are, as you might expect, insert(), update(), and delete().

Inserting Records

We use the insert() method to add new data to our tables. We use the Content Values object to pair the column names with the column values for the record we want to insert. For example, here we insert a record into tbl_authors for J. K. Rowling:

```
import android.content.ContentValues;
...
ContentValues values = new ContentValues();
values.put("firstname", "J.K.");
values.put("lastname", "Rowling");
long newAuthorID = mDatabase.insert("tbl_authors", null, values);
```

The insert() method returns the identifier of the newly created record. We use this author identifier to create book records for this author.

> **Tip**
>
> There is also another helpful method called insertOrThrow(), which does the same thing as the insert() method but throws a SQLException on failure, which can be helpful, especially if your inserts do not seem to be working and you'd like to know why. Generally, you'll want to check values before inserting and not rely on exceptions for common constraints.

You might want to create simple classes (that is, class Author and class Book) to encapsulate your application record data when it is used programmatically.

Updating Records

You can modify records in the database using the update() method. The update() method takes four arguments:

- The table in which to update records
- A ContentValues object with the modified fields to update

- An optional WHERE clause, in which ? identifies a WHERE clause argument
- An array of WHERE clause arguments, each of which is substituted in place of the ?s from the second parameter

Passing null to the WHERE clause modifies all records within the table, which can be useful for making sweeping changes to your database.

Most of the time, we want to modify individual records by their unique identifier. The following function takes two parameters: an updated book title and a bookId. We find the record in the table called tbl_books that corresponds to the id and update that book's title. Again, we use the ContentValues object to bind our column names to our data values:

```
public void updateBookTitle(Integer bookId, String newtitle) {
    ContentValues values = new ContentValues();
    values.put("title", newtitle);
    mDatabase.update("tbl_books",
        values, "id=?", new String[] { bookId.toString() });
}
```

Because we are not updating the other fields, we do not need to include them in the ContentValues object. We include only the title field because it is the only field we change.

Deleting Records

You can remove records from the database using the remove() method. The remove() method takes three arguments:

- The table from which to delete the record
- An optional WHERE clause, in which ? identifies a WHERE clause argument
- An array of WHERE clause arguments, each of which is substituted in place of the ?s from the second parameter

Passing null to the WHERE clause deletes all records in the table. For example, this function call deletes all records in the table called tbl_authors:

```
mDatabase.delete("tbl_authors", null, null);
```

Most of the time, though, we want to delete individual records by their unique identifiers. The following function takes a parameter bookId and deletes the record corresponding to that unique id (primary key) in the table called tbl_books:

```
public void deleteBook(Integer bookId) {
    mDatabase.delete("tbl_books", "id=?",
        new String[] { bookId.toString() });
}
```

You need not use the primary key (id) to delete records; the WHERE clause is entirely up to you. For instance, the following function deletes all book records in the table tbl_ books for a given author by the author's unique identifier:

```
public void deleteBooksByAuthor(Integer authorID) {
    int numBooksDeleted = mDatabase.delete("tbl_books", "authorid=?",
        new String[] { authorID.toString() });
}
```

Working with Transactions

Often there are multiple database operations that you want to happen all together or not at all. You can use SQL transactions to group operations together; if any of the operations fail, you can handle the error and either recover or roll back all operations. If all of the operations succeed, you can then commit them. Here we have the basic structure for a transaction:

```
mDatabase.beginTransaction();
try {
    // Insert some records, update others, delete a few.
    // Do whatever you need to do as a unit, then commit it.

    mDatabase.setTransactionSuccessful();
} catch (Exception e) {
    // Transaction failed. Failed! Do something here.
    // It's up to you.
} finally {
    mDatabase.endTransaction();
}
```

Now let's look at the transaction in a bit more detail. A transaction always begins with a call to the beginTransaction() method and a try/catch block. If your operations are successful, you can commit your changes with a call to the setTransaction Successful() method. If you do not call this method, all your operations are rolled back and not committed. Finally, you end your transaction by calling endTransaction() in the finally clause, guaranteeing that it will be called. It's as simple as that.

In some cases, you might recover from an exception and continue with the transaction. For example, if you have an exception for a read-only database, you can open the database and retry your operations.

Finally, note that transactions can be nested, with the outer transaction either committing or rolling back all inner transactions.

Querying SQLite Databases

Databases are great for storing data in any number of ways, but retrieving the data you want is what makes databases powerful. This is achieved partly by designing an appropriate database schema and partly by crafting SQL queries, most of which are SELECT statements.

Android provides many ways in which you can query your application database. You can run raw SQL query statements (strings), use a number of different SQL statement builder utility classes to generate proper query statements from the ground up, and bind specific user interface controls such as container views to your back-end database directly.

Working with Cursors

When results are returned from a SQL query, you often access them using a `Cursor` found in the `android.database.Cursor` class. `Cursor` objects are like file pointers; they allow random access to query results.

You can think of query results as a table in which each row corresponds to a returned record. The `Cursor` object includes helpful methods for determining how many results were returned by the query the `Cursor` represents and methods for determining the column names (fields) for each returned record. The columns in the query results are defined by the query, not necessarily by the database columns. These might include calculated columns, column aliases, and composite columns.

`Cursor` objects are generally kept around for a time. If you do something simple (such as get a count of records) or in cases when you know you retrieved only a single simple record, you can execute your query and quickly extract what you need. Don't forget to close the `Cursor` when you're done, as shown here:

```
// SIMPLE QUERY: select * from tbl_books
Cursor c = mDatabase.query("tbl_books", null, null, null, null, null, null);
// Do something quick with the Cursor here...
c.close();
```

Managing Cursors as Part of the Application Lifecycle

When a `Cursor` returns multiple records, or you do something more intensive, you need to consider running this operation on a thread separate from the UI thread. You also need to manage your `Cursor`.

`Cursor` objects must be managed as part of the application lifecycle. When the application pauses or shuts down, the `Cursor` must be deactivated with a call to the `deactivate()` method, and when the application restarts, the `Cursor` should refresh its data by requesting a new `Cursor`. When the `Cursor` is no longer needed, a call to `close()` must be made to release its resources.

As the developer, you can handle this by implementing `Cursor` management calls within the various lifecycle callbacks, such as `onPause()`, `onResume()`, and `onDestroy()`.

Iterating Rows of Query Results and Extracting Specific Data

You can use the `Cursor` to iterate those results, one row at a time, using various navigation methods such as `moveToFirst()`, `moveToNext()`, and `isAfterLast()`.

On a specific row, you can use the `Cursor` to extract the data for a given column in the query results. Because SQLite is not strongly typed, you can always pull fields out as strings using the `getString()` method, but you can also use the type-appropriate extraction utility function to enforce type safety in your application.

For example, the following method takes a valid `Cursor` object, prints the number of returned results, and then prints some column information (name and number of columns). Next, it iterates through the query results, printing each record.

```
public void logCursorInfo(Cursor c) {
    Log.i(DEBUG_TAG, "*** Cursor Begin *** " + " Results:" +
        c.getCount() + " Columns: " + c.getColumnCount());

    // Print column names
    String rowHeaders = "|| ";
    for (int i = 0; i < c.getColumnCount(); i++) {
        rowHeaders = rowHeaders.concat(c.getColumnName(i) + " || ");
    }

    Log.i(DEBUG_TAG, "COLUMNS " + rowHeaders);

    // Print records
    c.moveToFirst();
    while (c.isAfterLast() == false) {

        String rowResults = "|| ";
        for (int i = 0; i < c.getColumnCount(); i++) {
            rowResults = rowResults.concat(c.getString(i) + " || ");
        }

        Log.i(DEBUG_TAG, "Row " + c.getPosition() + ": " + rowResults);
        c.moveToNext();
    }
    Log.i(DEBUG_TAG, "*** Cursor End ***");
}
```

The output to the LogCat for this function might look something like Figure 3.1.

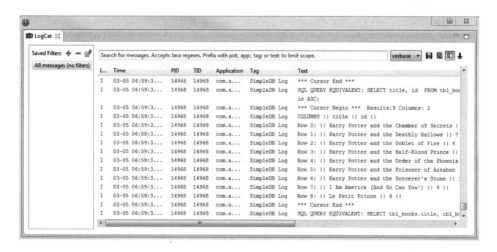

Figure 3.1 Sample log output for the `logCursorInfo()` method.

Executing Simple Queries

Your first stop for database queries should be the query() methods available in the SQLiteDatabase class. This method queries the database and returns any results in a Cursor object. The query() method we mainly use takes the following parameters:

- [String]: The name of the table against which to compile the query
- [String Array]: List of specific column names to return (use null for all)
- [String]: The WHERE clause: use null for all; might include selection args as ?s
- [String Array]: Any selection argument values to substitute for the ?s in the earlier parameter
- [String] GROUP BY clause: null for no grouping
- [String] HAVING clause: null unless the GROUP BY clause requires one
- [String] ORDER BY clause: if null, default ordering is used
- [String] LIMIT clause: if null, no limit

Previously, we called the query() method with only one parameter set to the table name, as shown in the following code:

```
Cursor c = mDatabase.query("tbl_books", null, null, null, null, null, null);
```

This is equivalent to the SQL query

```
SELECT * FROM tbl_books;
```

Tip

The individual parameters for the clauses (WHERE, GROUP BY, HAVING, ORDER BY, LIMIT) are all strings, but you do not need to include the keyword, such as WHERE. Instead, you include the part of the clause after the keyword.

Add a WHERE clause to your query, so you can retrieve one record at a time:

```
Cursor c = mDatabase.query("tbl_books", null, "id=?", new String[]{"9"},
                null, null, null);
```

This is equivalent to the SQL query

```
SELECT * tbl_books WHERE id=9;
```

Selecting all results might be fine for tiny databases, but it is not terribly efficient. You should always tailor your SQL queries to return only the results you require with no extraneous information included. Use the powerful language of SQL to do the heavy lifting for you whenever possible, instead of programmatically processing results yourself. For example, if you need only the titles of each book in the book table, you might use the following call to the query() method:

```
String asColumnsToReturn[] = { "title", "id" };
String strSortOrder = "title ASC";
```

```
Cursor c = mDatabase.query("tbl_books", asColumnsToReturn, null, null, null,
                null, strSortOrder);
```

This is equivalent to the SQL query

```
SELECT title, id FROM tbl_books ORDER BY title ASC;
```

Executing More Complex Queries Using SQLiteQueryBuilder

As your queries get more complex and involve multiple tables, you should leverage the SQLiteQueryBuilder convenience class, which can build complex queries (such as joins) programmatically.

When more than one table is involved, you need to make sure you refer to columns in a table by their fully qualified names. For example, the title column in the tbl_books table is tbl_books.title. Here we use a SQLiteQueryBuilder to build and execute a simple INNER JOIN between two tables to get a list of books with their authors:

```
import android.database.sqlite.SQLiteQueryBuilder;
...
SQLiteQueryBuilder queryBuilder = new SQLiteQueryBuilder();

queryBuilder.setTables("tbl_books, tbl_authors");
queryBuilder.appendWhere("tbl_books.authorid = tbl_authors.id");

String asColumnsToReturn[] = {
    "tbl_books.title",
    "tbl_books.id",
    "tbl_authors.firstname",
    "tbl_authors.lastname",
    "tbl_books.authorid" };
String strSortOrder = "title ASC";

Cursor c = queryBuilder.query(mDatabase, asColumnsToReturn, null, null, null,
                null,strSortOrder);
```

First, we instantiate a new SQLiteQueryBuilder object. Then we can set the tables involved as part of our JOIN and the WHERE clause that determines how the JOIN occurs. Then, we call the query() method of the SQLiteQueryBuilder that is similar to the query() method we have been using, except we supply the SQLiteDatabase instance instead of the table name. The earlier query built by the SQLiteQueryBuilder is equivalent to the SQL query

```
SELECT tbl_books.title,
tbl_books.id,
tbl_authors.firstname,
tbl_authors.lastname,
tbl_books.authorid
FROM tbl_books
INNER JOIN tbl_authors on tbl_books.authorid = tbl_authors.id
ORDER BY title ASC;
```

Executing Raw Queries without Builders and Column Mapping

All these helpful Android query utilities can sometimes make building and performing a nonstandard or complex query too verbose. In this case, you might want to consider the `rawQuery()` method. The `rawQuery()` method simply takes a SQL statement `String` (with optional selection arguments if you include ?s) and returns a `Cursor` of results. If you know your SQL and you don't want to bother learning the ins and outs of all the different SQL query-building utilities, this is the method for you.

For example, let's say we have a `UNION` query. These types of queries are feasible with the `QueryBuilder`, but their implementation is cumbersome when you start using column aliases and the like.

Let's say we want to execute the following SQL `UNION` query, which returns a list of all book titles and authors whose names contain the substring ow (such as Hallows, Rowling), as in the following:

```
SELECT title AS Name,
'tbl_books' AS OriginalTable
FROM tbl_books
WHERE Name LIKE '%ow%'
UNION
SELECT (firstname||' '|| lastname) AS Name,
'tbl_authors' AS OriginalTable
FROM tbl_authors
WHERE Name LIKE '%ow%'
ORDER BY Name ASC;
```

We can easily execute this by making a string that looks much like the original query and executing the `rawQuery()` method, as shown in the following code:

```
String sqlUnionExample = "SELECT title AS Name, 'tbl_books' AS
    OriginalTable from tbl_books WHERE Name LIKE ? UNION SELECT
    (firstname||' '|| lastname) AS Name, 'tbl_authors' AS OriginalTable
    from tbl_authors WHERE Name LIKE ? ORDER BY Name ASC;";

Cursor c = mDatabase.rawQuery(sqlUnionExample, new String[]{ "%ow%", "%ow%"});
```

We make the substrings (ow) into selection arguments, so we can use this same code to look for other substrings.

Closing and Deleting a SQLite Database

Although you should always close a database when you are not using it, you might on occasion also want to modify and delete tables and delete your database.

Deleting Tables and Other SQLite Objects

You delete tables and other SQLite objects in exactly the same way you create them. Format the appropriate SQLite statements and execute them. For example, to drop our tables and triggers, we can execute three SQL statements:

```
mDatabase.execSQL("DROP TABLE tbl_books;");
mDatabase.execSQL("DROP TABLE tbl_authors;");
mDatabase.execSQL("DROP TRIGGER IF EXISTS fk_insert_book;");
```

Closing a SQLite Database

You should close your database when you are not using it. You can close the database using the `close()` method of your `SQLiteDatabase` instance, like this:

```
mDatabase.close();
```

Deleting a SQLite Database Instance Using the Application Context

The simplest way to delete a `SQLiteDatabase` is to use the `deleteDatabase()` method of your application `Context`. You delete databases by name and the deletion is permanent. You lose all data and schema information.

```
deleteDatabase("my_sqlite_database.db");
```

Designing Persistent Databases

Generally speaking, an application creates a database and uses it for the rest of the application's lifetime—by which we mean until the application is uninstalled from the device. So far, we've talked about the basics of creating a database, using it, and then deleting it.

In reality, most mobile applications do not create a database on the fly, use it, and then delete it. Instead, they create a database the first time they need it and then use it. The Android SDK provides a helper class called `SQLiteOpenHelper` to help you manage your application's database.

To create a SQLite database for your Android application using the `SQLiteOpen Helper`, you need to extend that class and then instantiate an instance of it as a member variable for use in your application. To illustrate how to do this, let's create a new Android project called PetTracker.

Tip

Many of the code examples provided in this section are taken from the PetTracker application. The source code for this application is provided for download on the book's website.

Keeping Track of Database Field Names

You've probably realized by now that it is time to start organizing your database fields programmatically to avoid typos and such in your SQL queries. One easy way to do this is to create a class to encapsulate your database schema, such as `PetTrackerDatabase`, shown here:

```
import android.provider.BaseColumns;

public final class PetTrackerDatabase {

    private PetTrackerDatabase() {}

    public static final class Pets implements BaseColumns {
        private Pets() {}
        public static final String PETS_TABLE_NAME = "table_pets";
        public static final String PET_NAME = "pet_name";
        public static final String PET_TYPE_ID = "pet_type_id";
        public static final String DEFAULT_SORT_ORDER = "pet_name ASC";
    }

    public static final class PetType implements BaseColumns {
        private PetType() {}
        public static final String PETTYPE_TABLE_NAME = "table_pettypes";
        public static final String PET_TYPE_NAME = "pet_type";
        public static final String DEFAULT_SORT_ORDER = "pet_type ASC";
    }
}
```

By implementing the `BaseColumns` interface, we begin to set up the underpinnings for using database-friendly user interface controls in the future, which often require a specially named column called `_id` to function properly. We rely on this column as our primary key.

Extending the `SQLiteOpenHelper` Class

To extend the `SQLiteOpenHelper` class, we must implement several important methods, which help manage the database versioning. The methods to override are `onCreate()` and `onUpgrade()` and optionally `onDowngrade()` and `onOpen()`. We use our newly defined `PetTrackerDatabase` class to generate appropriate SQL statements, as shown here:

```
import android.content.Context;
import android.database.sqlite.SQLiteDatabase;
import android.database.sqlite.SQLiteOpenHelper;

import com.advancedandroidbook.PetTracker.PetTrackerDatabase.PetType;
import com.advancedandroidbook.PetTracker.PetTrackerDatabase.Pets;

class PetTrackerDatabaseHelper extends SQLiteOpenHelper {
```

```
    private static final String DATABASE_NAME = "pet_tracker.db";
    private static final int DATABASE_VERSION = 1;

    PetTrackerDatabaseHelper(Context context) {
        super(context, DATABASE_NAME, null, DATABASE_VERSION);
    }

    @Override
    public void onCreate(SQLiteDatabase db) {
        db.execSQL("CREATE TABLE " + PetType.PETTYPE_TABLE_NAME + " ("
            + PetType._ID + " INTEGER PRIMARY KEY AUTOINCREMENT ,"
            + PetType.PET_TYPE_NAME + " TEXT"
            + ");");
        db.execSQL("CREATE TABLE " + Pets.PETS_TABLE_NAME + " ("
            + Pets._ID + " INTEGER PRIMARY KEY AUTOINCREMENT ,"
            + Pets.PET_NAME + " TEXT,"
            + Pets.PET_TYPE_ID + " INTEGER" // FK to pet type table
            + ");");
    }

    @Override
    public void onUpgrade(SQLiteDatabase db, int oldVersion, int newVersion){
        // Housekeeping here.
        // Implement how to "move" your application data
        // during an upgrade of schema versions.
        // Move or delete data as required. Your call.
    }

    @Override
    public void onOpen(SQLiteDatabase db) {
        super.onOpen(db);
    }
}
```

Now we can create a member variable for our database like this:

```
PetTrackerDatabaseHelper mDatabase = new
    PetTrackerDatabaseHelper(this.getApplicationContext());
```

Now, whenever our application needs to interact with its database, we request a valid database object. We can request a read–only database or a database that we can also write to. We can also close the database. For example, here we get a database we can write data to:

```
SQLiteDatabase db = mDatabase.getWritableDatabase();
```

Binding Data to the Application User Interface

In many cases, you want to couple your user interface with the data in your application database. You might want to fill drop-down lists with values from a database table, or fill out form values, or display only certain results. There are various ways to bind database data to your user interface. You, as the developer, can decide whether to use built-in data-binding functionality provided with certain user interface controls, or build your own user interfaces from the ground up.

Working with Database Data Like Any Other Data

If you peruse the PetTracker application provided on the book's website, you notice that its functionality includes no magical data-binding features, yet the application clearly uses the database as part of the user interface.

Specifically, the database is leveraged

- When you fill out the Pet Species field; the AutoComplete feature is seeded with pet species already listed in the table_pettypes table (Figure 3.2, left).
- When you save new records using the Pet Entry form (Figure 3.2, middle).
- When you display the Pet List screen; you query for all pets and use a Cursor to programmatically build a TableLayout on the fly (Figure 3.2, right).

This might work for small amounts of data; however, there are various drawbacks to this method. For example, all the work is done on the main thread, so the more records you add, the slower your application response time becomes. Second, there's quite a bit of custom code involved to map the database results to the individual user interface components. If you decide you want to use a different control to display your data, you have quite a lot of rework to do.

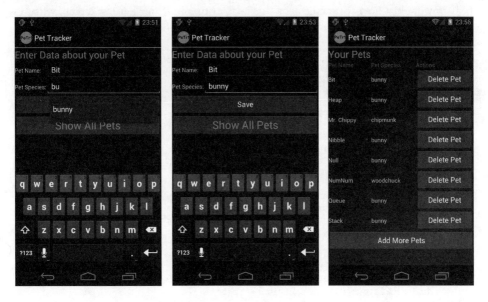

Figure 3.2   The PetTracker application: Entry screen (left, middle)
and Pet Listing screen (right).

Note

Yes, we really named our pet bunnies after data structures and computer terminology. We are that geeky. Null, for example, is a rambunctious little black bunny. Shane enjoys pointing at him and calling himself a Null pointer.

Binding Data to Controls Using Data Adapters

Ideally, you'd like to bind your data to user interface controls and let them take care of the data display. For example, we can use a fancy `ListView` to display the pets instead of building a `TableLayout` from scratch. We can spin through our `Cursor` and generate `ListView` child items manually, or even better, we can simply create a data adapter to map the `Cursor` results to each `TextView` child within the `ListView`.

The PetTracker2 application behaves much like the PetTracker sample application, except that it uses the `SimpleCursorAdapter` with `ListView` and an `ArrayAdapter` to handle `AutoCompleteTextView` features.

Tip

The source code for subsequent upgrades to the series of PetTracker applications is provided for download on the book's website.

Binding Data Using `SimpleCursorAdapter`

Let's now look at how we can create a data adapter to mimic our Pet List screen, with each pet's name and species listed. We also want to continue to have the ability to delete records from the list.

A `ListView` container can contain children such as `TextView` objects. In this case, we want to display each pet's name and type. We therefore create a layout file called `pet_item.xml` that becomes our `ListView` item template:

```xml
<?xml version="1.0" encoding="utf-8"?>
<RelativeLayout
    xmlns:android="http://schemas.android.com/apk/res/android"
    android:id="@+id/RelativeLayoutHeader"
    android:layout_height="wrap_content"
    android:layout_width="match_parent">
    <TextView
        android:id="@+id/TextView_PetName"
        android:layout_width="wrap_content"
        android:layout_height="?android:attr/listPreferredItemHeight"
        android:layout_alignParentLeft="true" />
    <TextView
        android:id="@+id/TextView_PetType"
        android:layout_width="wrap_content"
        android:layout_height="?android:attr/listPreferredItemHeight"
        android:layout_alignParentRight="true" />
</RelativeLayout>
```

Next, in our main layout file for the Pet List, we place our `ListView` in the appropriate place on the overall screen. The `ListView` portion of the layout file might look something like this:

```
<ListView
    android:id="@+id/petList"
    android:layout_width="wrap_content"
    android:layout_height="wrap_content"
    android:divider="#000"
    android:headerDividersEnabled="true"
    android:isScrollContainer="true"
    android:scrollbarAlwaysDrawVerticalTrack="true"
    android:scrollbars="vertical" />
```

Now to programmatically fill our `ListView`, we must take the following steps:

1. Perform the query and return a valid `Cursor` (a member variable).
2. Create a data adapter that maps the `Cursor` columns to the appropriate `TextView` controls within our `pet_item.xml` layout template.
3. Attach the adapter to the `ListView`.

In the following code, we perform these steps:

```
SQLiteQueryBuilder queryBuilder = new SQLiteQueryBuilder();
queryBuilder.setTables(Pets.PETS_TABLE_NAME
    + ", " + PetType.PETTYPE_TABLE_NAME);

queryBuilder.appendWhere(Pets.PETS_TABLE_NAME
    + "." + Pets.PET_TYPE_ID + "="
    + PetType.PETTYPE_TABLE_NAME + "." + PetType._ID);

String asColumnsToReturn[] = { Pets.PETS_TABLE_NAME + "." + Pets.PET_NAME,
    Pets.PETS_TABLE_NAME + "." + Pets._ID, PetType.PETTYPE_TABLE_NAME + "." +
    PetType.PET_TYPE_NAME };

mCursor = queryBuilder.query(mDB, asColumnsToReturn, null, null, null, null,
                Pets.DEFAULT_SORT_ORDER);

ListAdapter adapter = new SimpleCursorAdapter(this,
    R.layout.pet_item, mCursor,
    new String[]{Pets.PET_NAME, PetType.PET_TYPE_NAME},
    new int[]{R.id.TextView_PetName, R.id.TextView_PetType }, 1);

ListView av = (ListView) findViewById(R.id.petList);
av.setAdapter(adapter);
```

Notice that the `_id` column and the expected name and type columns appear in the query. This is required for the adapter and `ListView` to work properly.

Using a `ListView` (Figure 3.3, left) instead of a custom user interface enables us to take advantage of the `ListView` control's built-in features, such as scrolling when the list

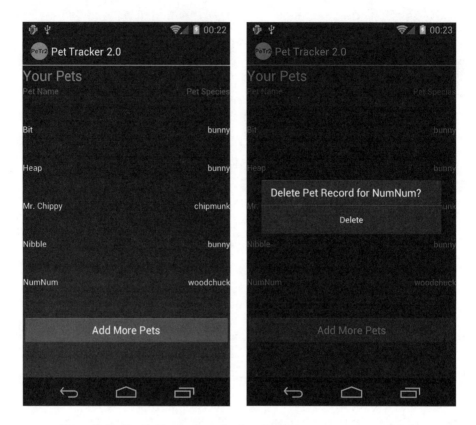

Figure 3.3   The PetTracker2 application: Pet List screen ListView (left)
with Delete feature (right).

becomes longer, and the ability to provide context menus as needed. The _id column is
used as the unique identifier for each ListView child node. If we choose a specific item
on the list, we can act on it using this identifier, for example, to delete the item.

Now we reimplement the Delete functionality by listening for onItemClick() events
and providing a Delete confirmation dialog (Figure 3.3, right):

```
av.setOnItemClickListener(new AdapterView.OnItemClickListener() {
    public void onItemClick(AdapterView<?> parent, View view, int position,
                    long id) {
        final long deletePetId = id;
        RelativeLayout item = (RelativeLayout) view;
        TextView nameView = (TextView) item.findViewById(R.id.TextView_PetName);
        String name = nameView.getText().toString();
        new AlertDialog.Builder(PetTrackerListActivity.this)
```

```
                       .setMessage("Delete Pet Record for " + name + "?")
                       .setPositiveButton("Delete",
                            new DialogInterface.OnClickListener() {
                                public void onClick(DialogInterface dialog, int which){
                                    deletePet(deletePetId);
                                    mCursor = queryBuilder.query(mDB,
                                        asColumnsToReturn,
                                        null, null, null, null,
                                        Pets.DEFAULT_SORT_ORDER, null);
                                    adapter = new SimpleCursorAdapter(
                                        getApplicationContext(),
                                        R.layout.pet_item, mCursor,
                                        new String[] { Pets.PET_NAME,
                                                    PetType.PET_TYPE_NAME },
                                        new int[] { R.id.TextView_PetName,
                                                R.id.TextView_PetType }, 1);
                                    av.setAdapter(adapter);
                                }
                }).show();
        }
});
```

Note that within the PetTracker2 sample application, we also use an `ArrayAdapter`
to bind the data in the `pet_types` table to the `AutoCompleteTextView` on the Pet
Entry screen. Although our next example shows how to do this in a preferred manner,
we left this code in the PetTracker sample to show you that you can always intercept
the data your `Cursor` provides and do what you want with it. In this case, we create
a `String` array for the `AutoText` options by hand. We use a built-in Android layout
resource called `android.R.layout.simple_dropdown_item_1line` to specify what
each individual item within the `AutoText` listing looks like. You can find the built-
in layout resources provided within your appropriate Android SDK version's resource
subdirectory.

Storing Nonprimitive Types (Such as Images) in the Database

Because SQLite is a single file, it makes little sense to try to store binary data in the database. Instead store the *location* of data, as a file path or a URI in the database, and access it
appropriately.

Summary

There are a variety of different ways to store and manage application data on the
Android platform. The method you use depends on what kind of data you need to store.
Application-specific SQLite databases are secure and efficient mechanisms for structured
data storage. You now know how to design persistent data access mechanisms in your
Android application, and you also learned how to bind data from various sources to user
interface controls, such as `ListView` objects.

Quiz Questions

1. True or false: SQLite enforces foreign key constraints.

2. What is the class used to pair column names to column values for inserting and updating records into a database?

3. What is the method call for committing transactions to a database?

4. True or false: The `SQLiteQueryBuilder` convenience class is used to build complex queries such as joins.

5. How should you store binary data in a database?

Exercises

1. Use the Android online documentation to compile a list of the `SQLiteDatabase` class constants and their respective constant values.

2. Use the Android online documentation to determine the `SQLiteQueryBuilder` method for marking a query as `DISTINCT`.

3. Create a simple CRUD social networking application and a schema that allows you to categorize your friends by their favorite programming language.

References and More Information

Android API Guides: "Storage Options":
   http://d.android.com/guide/topics/data/data-storage.html
Android SDK Reference for the `android.database.sqlite` package:
   http://d.android.com/reference/android/database/sqlite/package-summary.html
SQLite website:
   http://www.sqlite.org
SQLzoo.net: Interactive SQL Tutorial website:
   http://sqlzoo.net

4

Building Android
Content Providers

Applications can access data in other applications on the Android system through content provider interfaces, and they can expose internal application data to other applications by becoming content providers. Typically, a content provider is backed by a SQLite database where the underlying data is stored. In this chapter, you will build upon the knowledge of SQLite application databases from Chapter 3, "Leveraging SQLite Application Databases," by working through two content provider examples.

Acting as a Content Provider

Do you have data in your application? Can another application do something interesting with that data? To share the information in your application with other applications, you need to make the application a content provider by providing the standardized content provider interface for other applications; then you must register your application as a content provider in the Android manifest file. The most straightforward way to make an application a content provider is to store the information you want to share in a SQLite database.

Tip

The code examples provided in this section are taken from the SimpleSearchProvider application. The source code for this application is provided for download on the book's website.

Implementing a Content Provider Interface

Implementing a content provider interface is relatively straightforward. The following code shows the basic interface that an application needs to implement to become a content provider, requiring implementations of five important methods:

```
public class SimpleFieldnotesContentProvider extends ContentProvider {
    public int delete(Uri uri,
        String selection, String[] selectionArgs) {
        return 0;
    }
```

```
public String getType(Uri uri) {
    return null;
}

public Uri insert(Uri uri, ContentValues values) {
    return null;
}

public boolean onCreate() {
    return false;
}

public Cursor query(Uri uri, String[] projection,
    String selection, String[] selectionArgs, String sortOrder) {
    return null;
}

public int update(Uri uri, ContentValues values,
    String selection, String[] selectionArgs) {
    // no updates allowed
    return 0;
}
}
```

Tip

You can use the Android IDE to easily create a new class and include the basic overrides that you need. To do this, right-click on the package to which you want to add the new class, choose New, and then choose Class. Type the name of your content provider in the Name field, choose `android.content.ContentProvider` as your superclass, and check the box next to Inherited abstract methods.

Defining the Data URI

The provider application needs to define a base URI that other applications will use to access this content provider. This must be in the form of a `public static final Uri` named CONTENT_URI, and it must start with `content://`. The URI must be unique. The best practice for this naming is to use the fully qualified class name of the content provider. Here, we have created a URI name for our SimpleSearchProvider example:

```
public static final Uri CONTENT_URI =
    Uri.parse("content://com.advancedandroidbook.ssp." +
            "SimpleFieldnotesContentProvider/fieldnotes_provider");
```

Defining Data Columns

The user of the content provider needs to know what columns the content provider has available to it. In this case, the columns used are title and body. We also include a column for the record number, which is called _id.

```
public final static String _ID = "_id";
public final static String FIELDNOTES_TITLE = "fieldnotes_title";
public final static String FIELDNOTES_BODY = "fieldnotes_body";
```

Users of the content provider use these same strings. A content provider for data such as this often stores the data in a SQLite database. If this is the case, matching these columns' names to the database column names simplifies the code.

Implementing Important Content Provider Methods

This section shows example implementations of each of the methods that are used by the system to call this content provider when another application wants to use it. The system, in this case, is the ContentResolver interface that was used indirectly in the previous section when built-in content providers were used.

Some of these methods can make use of a helper class provided by the Android SDK, UriMatcher, which is used to match incoming URI values to patterns that help speed up development. The use of UriMatcher is described and then used in the implementation of these methods.

Implementing the `query()` Method

Let's start with a sample query implementation. Any query implementation needs to return a Cursor object. One convenient way to get a Cursor object is to return the Cursor from the underlying SQLite database that many content providers use. In fact, the interface to ContentProvider.query() is compatible with the SQLiteQuery Builder.query() call. This example uses it to quickly build the query and return a Cursor object:

```
public Cursor query(Uri uri, String[] projection,
    String selection, String[] selectionArgs,
    String sortOrder) {

    SQLiteQueryBuilder qBuilder = new SQLiteQueryBuilder();
    qBuilder.setTables(SimpleFieldnotesDatabase.FIELDNOTES_TABLE);

    int match = sURIMatcher.match(uri);
    switch (match) {
    case FIELDNOTES_SEARCH_SUGGEST:
        // selectionArgs has a single item; the query
        // adds wildcards around it
        selectionArgs = new String[] { "%" + selectionArgs[0] + "%" };
        queryBuilder
            .setProjectionMap(FIELDNOTES_SEARCH_SUGGEST_PROJECTION_MAP);
        break;

    case FIELDNOTES:
        break;

    case FIELDNOTE_ITEM:
        String id = uri.getLastPathSegment();
        queryBuilder.appendWhere(_ID + "=" + id);
        break;

    default:
        throw new IllegalArgumentException("Invalid URI: " + uri);
    }
```

```
SQLiteDatabase sql = database.getReadableDatabase();
Cursor cursor = queryBuilder.query(sql, projection, selection,
    selectionArgs, null, null, sortOrder);
cursor.setNotificationUri(getContext().getContentResolver(), uri);
return cursor;
}
```

First, the code gets an instance of a `SQLiteQueryBuilder` object, which builds a query with some method calls. Then, the `setTables()` method configures which table in the database is used. The `UriMatcher` class checks to see which specific rows are requested. `UriMatcher` is discussed in greater detail in the next section.

Next, the actual query is called. The content provider query has fewer specifications than the SQLite query, so the parameters are passed through and the rest is ignored. The instance of the SQLite database is read-only. Because this is only a query for data, it's acceptable.

Finally, the `Cursor` needs to know if the source data has changed. This is done by a call to the `setNotificationUri()` method telling it which URI to watch for data changes. The application's `query()` method might be called from multiple threads as it calls to `update()`, so it's possible the data can change after the `Cursor` is returned. Doing this keeps the data synchronized.

Exploring the `UriMatcher` Class

The `UriMatcher` class is a helper class for pattern matching on the URIs that are passed to this content provider. It is used frequently in the content provider functions that must be implemented. Here is the `UriMatcher` used in these sample implementations:

```
public static final String AUTHORITY =
    "com.advancedandroidbook.ssp.SimpleFieldnotesContentProvider"
public static final String BASE_DATA_NAME = "fieldnotes_provider";

private static final int FIELDNOTES = 0x1000;
private static final int FIELDNOTE_ITEM = 0x1001;
private static final int FIELDNOTES_SEARCH_SUGGEST = 0x1200;

private static final UriMatcher sURIMatcher =
    new UriMatcher(UriMatcher.NO_MATCH);
static {
    sURIMatcher.addURI(AUTHORITY, BASE_DATA_NAME, FIELDNOTES);
    sURIMatcher.addURI(AUTHORITY, BASE_DATA_NAME + "/#", FIELDNOTE_ITEM);
    sURIMatcher.addURI(AUTHORITY, BASE_DATA_NAME + "/"
        + SearchManager.SUGGEST_URI_PATH_QUERY,
        FIELDNOTES_SEARCH_SUGGEST);
    sURIMatcher.addURI(AUTHORITY, BASE_DATA_NAME + "/"
        + SearchManager.SUGGEST_URI_PATH_QUERY + "/*",
        FIELDNOTES_SEARCH_SUGGEST);
}
```

First, arbitrary numeric values are defined to identify each different pattern. Next, a static `UriMatcher` instance is created for use. The code parameter that the constructor wants is merely the value to return when there is no match. A value for this is provided for use within the `UriMatcher` class itself.

Next, the URI values are added to the matcher with their corresponding identifiers. The URIs are broken up into the authority portion, defined in AUTHORITY, and the path portion, which is passed in as a literal string. The path can contain patterns, such as the # symbol to indicate a number. The * symbol is used as a wildcard to match anything.

Implementing the `insert()` Method

The insert() method is used for adding data to the content provider. Here is a sample implementation of the insert() method:

```
public Uri insert(Uri uri, ContentValues values) {
    Uri newUri = null;
    int match = sURIMatcher.match(uri);
    if (match == FIELDNOTES) {
        SQLiteDatabase sql = database.getWritableDatabase();
        long newId = sql.insert(SimpleFieldnotesDatabase.FIELDNOTES_TABLE,
                            null, values);
        if (newId > 0) {
            newUri = ContentUris.withAppendedId(uri, newId);
            getContext().getContentResolver().notifyChange(uri, null);
        }
    }
    return newUri;
}
```

The Uri is first validated to make sure it's one where inserting makes sense. A Uri targeting a particular row would not, for instance. Next, a writable database object instance is retrieved. Using this, the database insert() method is called on the table defined by the incoming Uri and with the values passed in. At this point, no error checking is performed on the values.

If the insert was successful, a Uri is created for notifying the system of a change to the underlying data via a call to the notifyChange() method of the ContentResolver. Otherwise, an exception is thrown.

Implementing the `update()` Method

The update() method is used to modify an existing row of data. It has elements similar to the insert() and query() methods. The update is applied to a particular selection defined by the incoming Uri.

```
public int update(Uri uri, ContentValues values,
        String selection, String[] selectionArgs) {
    int match = sURIMatcher.match(uri);
    SQLiteDatabase sqlDB = mDB.getWritableDatabase();
    int rowsAffected;

    switch (match) {
        case FIELDNOTES:
            rowsAffected = sqlDB.update(
                SimpleFieldnotesDatabase.FIELDNOTES_TABLE,
                values, selection, selectionArgs);
            break;

        case FIELDNOTE_ITEM:
            String id = uri.getLastPathSegment();
```

```
        if (TextUtils.isEmpty(selection)) {
            rowsAffected = sqlDB.update(
                SimpleFieldnotesDatabase.FIELDNOTES_TABLE,
                values, _ID + "=" + id, null);
        } else {
            rowsAffected = sqlDB.update(
                SimpleFieldnotesDatabase.FIELDNOTES_TABLE,
                values, selection + " and " + _ID + "="
                + id, selectionArgs);
        }
        break;
    default:
        throw new IllegalArgumentException(
            "Unknown or Invalid URI " + uri);
    }

    getContext().getContentResolver().notifyChange(uri, null);
    return rowsAffected;
}
```

In this block of code, a writable SQLiteDatabase instance is retrieved and the Uri type the user passed in is determined with a call to the match() method of the UriMatcher. No checking of values or parameters is performed here. However, to block updates to a specific Uri, such as a Uri affecting multiple rows or a match on FIELDNOTE_ITEM, java.lang.UnsupportedOperationException can be thrown to indicate this. In this example, though, trust is placed in the user of this content provider.

After calling the appropriate update() method, the system is notified of the change to the Uri with a call to the notifyChange() method. This tells any observers of the Uri that data has possibly changed. Finally, the affected number of rows is returned, which is information conveniently returned from the call to the update() method.

Implementing the `delete()` Method

Now it's time to clean up the database. The following is a sample implementation of the delete() method. It doesn't check to see whether the user might be deleting more data than should be deleted. You also notice that this is similar to the update() method.

```
public int delete(Uri uri, String selection, String[] selectionArgs) {
    int match = sURIMatcher.match(uri);
    SQLiteDatabase sqlDB = mDB.getWritableDatabase();
    int rowsAffected = 0;

    switch (match) {

        case FIELDNOTES:
            rowsAffected = sqlDB.delete(
                SimpleFieldnotesDatabase.FIELDNOTES_TABLE,
                selection, selectionArgs);
            break;

        case FIELDNOTE_ITEM:
            String id = uri.getLastPathSegment();
            if (TextUtils.isEmpty(selection)) {
                rowsAffected =
```

```
                      sqlDB.delete(SimpleFieldnotesDatabase.FIELDNOTES_TABLE,
                      _ID + " = " + id, null);
              } else {
                 rowsAffected =
                      sqlDB.delete(SimpleFieldnotesDatabase.FIELDNOTES_TABLE,
                      selection + " and " + _ID + " = " + id, selectionArgs);
              }
              break;
        default:
              throw new IllegalArgumentException(
                 "Unknown or Invalid URI " + uri);
     }
     getContext().getContentResolver().notifyChange(uri, null);
     return rowsAffected;
}
```

Again, a writable database instance is retrieved and the Uri type is determined using
the match method of UriMatcher. If the result is a directory Uri, the delete is called
with the selection the user passed in. However, if the result is a specific row, the row
index is used to further limit the delete, with or without the selection. Allowing this
without a specific selection enables deletion of a specified identifier without having to
also know exactly where it came from.

As before, the system is then notified of this change with a call to the notify
Change() method of ContentResolver. Also as before, the number of affected rows is
returned, which we stored after the call to the delete() method.

Implementing the getType() Method

The last method to implement is the getType() method. The purpose of this method is
to return the MIME type for a particular Uri that is passed in. It does not need to return
MIME types for specific columns of data.

```
public static final String CONTENT_ITEM_TYPE =
    ContentResolver.CURSOR_ITEM_BASE_TYPE +
    "/vnd.advancedandroidbook.search.fieldnotes_provider";

public static final String CONTENT_TYPE =
    ContentResolver.CURSOR_DIR_BASE_TYPE +
    "/vnd.advancedandroidbook.search.fieldnotes_provider";

public String getType(Uri uri) {
    Uri newUri = null;
    int matchType = sURIMatcher.match(uri);
    switch (matchType) {

        case FIELDNOTES:
            return CONTENT_TYPE;

        case FIELDNOTE_ITEM:
            return CONTENT_ITEM_TYPE;

        default:
            return null;
    }
}
```

To start, a couple of MIME types are defined. The Android SDK provides some guideline values for single items and directories of items, which are used here. The corresponding strings for them are `vnd.android.cursor.item` and `vnd.android.cursor.dir`, respectively. Finally, the `match()` method is used to determine the type of the provided `Uri` so that the appropriate MIME type can be returned.

Updating the Manifest File

Finally, you need to update your application's `AndroidManifest.xml` file so that it reflects that a content provider interface is exposed to the rest of the system. Here, the class name and the authorities, or what might be considered the domain of the `content://` URI, need to be set. For instance, `content://com.advancedandroidbook.ssp.SimpleFieldnotesContentProvider` is the base URI used in this content provider example, which means the authority is `com.advancedandroidbook.ssp.SimpleFieldnotesContentProvider`. The following Extensible Markup Language (XML) shows an example of this:

```
<provider
    android:authorities=
        "com.advancedandroidbook.ssp.SimpleFieldnotesContentProvider"
    android:name=
        "com.advancedandroidbook.ssp.SimpleFieldnotesContentProvider"
    android:multiprocess="true"
    android:exported="true">
</provider>
```

The value of `multiprocess` is set to `true` because the data does not need to be synchronized among multiple running versions of this content provider. It's possible that two or more applications might access a content provider at the same time, so proper synchronization might be necessary. In addition, Android 4.2 (API Level 17) no longer exports content providers as the default setting, mainly for security reasons. If you would like other applications to make use of your application's data through your provider, you need to set the `android:exported` attribute to `true`.

Note

We frequently reference notifications that are sent to observers. In Chapter 6, "Working with Notifications," you learn about notifications that are sent to the device.

Enhancing Applications Using Content Providers

The concept of a content provider is complex and best understood by working through examples. The SimpleSearchProvider application is nice on its own, but allowing another application to access and display the provider data in its own user interface is what we would like to see.

Figure 4.1   The SimpleAccessProvider application screen.

Tip

The code examples provided in this section are taken from the SimpleAccessProvider application. The source code for this application is provided for download on the book's website.

In Figure 4.1, you can see the results of accessing the database information of the SimpleSearchProvider application through the application itself.

Locating Content on the Android System Using URIs

Most access to content providers comes in the form of queries: a list of contacts, a list of bookmarks, a list of calls, a list of pictures, and a list of audio files. Applications make these requests much as they would access a database, and they get the same type of structured results. The results of a query are often iterated through the use of a `Cursor`. However, instead of crafting queries, we use URIs.

You can think of a URI as an "address" to the location where content exists. URI addresses are hierarchical. Most content providers, such as the `Contacts` and the `MediaStore`, have URI addresses predefined. For example, to access thumbnails of the images on the external media device (sometimes a Secure Digital, or SD, card, not always user removable), we use the following URI:

```
Uri thumbnailUri = MediaStore.Images.Thumbnails.EXTERNAL_CONTENT_URI;
```

Setting Up Provider Access Permissions

The SimpleAccessProvider needs to request access from the SimpleSearchProvider application to be able to read the database. We need to add a `<uses-permission>` tag to our SimpleAccessProvider manifest file like so:

```
<uses-permission
    android:name=

        "com.advancedandroidbook.simplesearchprovider

        .SimpleFieldnotesContentProvider.READ_DATABASE" />
```

Retrieving Content Provider Data

We can query the SimpleSearchProvider content provider using a URI much as we would query a database. We `query()` a `ContentResolver` to return a `Cursor` containing all the field notes available from the SimpleSearchProvider:

```
private Uri mUri =
Uri.parse("content://com.advancedandroidbook.simplesearchprovider."
                        +
"SimpleFieldnotesContentProvider/fieldnotes_provider");
Cursor cursor = getContentResolver().query(mUri,
                    null, null, null,
                    "fieldnotes_title");
```

Then, we create a `ListView` and a `SimpleCursorAdapter`, and we load the `Cursor` object into the adapter, binding the `FIELDNOTES_TITLE` and the `FIELDNOTES_BODY` data to two text fields of the `SimpleCursorAdapter`. We complete the example by loading the adapter into the `ListView`:

```
ListView listView = (ListView) findViewById(R.id.provider);
SimpleCursorAdapter adapter = new SimpleCursorAdapter(this,
                        android.R.layout.two_line_list_item,
                        cursor,
                        new String[] { "FIELDNOTES_TITLE",
                                "FIELDNOTES_BODY" },
                        new int[] { android.R.id.text1,
                                android.R.id.text2 },
                        0);
listView.setAdapter(adapter);
```

We configured the example to retrieve the field note records of the SimpleSearchProvider content provider available within the application's database, for display within the SimpleAccessProvider application.

Summary

Your application can leverage the data available in other Android applications if they expose that data as content providers. Applications can also share data among themselves by becoming content providers. Becoming a content provider involves implementing a set of methods that manage how and what data you expose for use in other applications. Content providers are usually backed by data in the form of a private application database.

Quiz Questions

1. What methods are required to be defined when implementing a ContentProvider?

2. When defining a ContentProvider, what must the data URI start with?

3. True or false: Setting the multiprocess attribute of the <provider> tag in the manifest to true means that data needs to be synchronized among multiple running versions on that content provider.

4. True or false: As of Android 4.2 (API Level 17), all content providers are exported by default.

Exercises

1. Use the Android documentation to determine which ContentProvider data access methods must be thread-safe.

2. Use the Android documentation to determine what the manifest <provider> tag initOrder attribute is used for.

3. Create an application that is able to access the images located on the SD card of your device.

References and More Information

Android API Guides: "Content Providers":
http://developer.android.com/guide/topics/providers/content-providers.html
Android API Guides: "<provider>":
http://d.android.com/guide/topics/manifest/provider-element.html

Android SDK Reference documentation for the `android.provider` package:
http://d.android.com/reference/android/provider/package-summary.html

Android SDK Reference documentation for the `ContentProvider` class:
http://d.android.com/reference/android/content/ContentProvider.html

Android SDK Reference documentation for the `ContentResolver` class:
http://d.android.com/reference/android/content/ContentResolver.html

Android Tools: "Content Provider Testing":
http://d.android.com/tools/testing/contentprovider_testing.html

5

Broadcasting and Receiving Intents

The Android operating system enables applications to communicate with one another in a variety of ways. One way that information can be communicated across process or application boundaries is by using the broadcast event system built into the platform through the use of `Intent` objects. When an application has something it wants to communicate, it can broadcast that information to the system at large. Applications that are interested in that sort of event can listen for and react to that broadcast by becoming broadcast receivers. Although we develop numerous examples of broadcasts in the other chapters of this book, we felt it was worthwhile to cover some of the basics of broadcasting on the Android platform in their own chapter, free of other lessons.

Sending Broadcasts

The Android operating system uses broadcasts to communicate information to applications. The system generates numerous broadcasts about the state of the device, such as when the device is docked, an SD card is ejected, or a call is about to be placed. Applications can also generate and send broadcasts. Some system broadcasts can be initiated by applications (with the appropriate permissions), or applications can create their own events and broadcast them.

The Android framework supports two kinds of broadcasts. Normal broadcasts are delivered to all receivers and completed asynchronously in an undefined order. Ordered broadcasts are delivered to each receiver in priority order; the receiver can pass the event on to the next appropriate receiver in the queue or abort the broadcast before all receivers get it.

Broadcasts can also be sticky. This means that the `Intent` associated with the broadcast stays around after the broadcast has been completed, so that the broadcast receivers can retrieve valid `Intent` data from the `registerReceiver()` method return value. Both normal and ordered broadcasts can be sticky.

When dispatching a broadcast of any type, you have the option of specifying any permissions that the broadcast receiver must hold in order to receive your broadcast. These permissions are enforced by the Android operating system at runtime when matching occurs.

Tip

Many of the code examples provided in this chapter are taken from the SimpleBroadcasts application. The source code for this application is provided for download on the book's website.

Sending Basic Broadcasts

Sending basic broadcasts is as simple as configuring the appropriate `Intent` object and dispatching it to the system using the `sendBroadcast()` method of the `Context` class. For example, the following code creates a simple `Intent` with a custom action type:

```
Intent i = new Intent("ACTION_DO_A_LITTLE_DANCE");
sendBroadcast(i);
```

Intents may be much more specific, with data stored in the type, category, and extra data attributes. The Android operating system uses the action, data, and category information to match up the broadcast with the appropriate applications using intent filters. The `Intent` extra and flag information is not used as part of intent resolution but may be used by the broadcast receivers when handling a broadcast.

Tip

The `Intent` action namespace is globally shared. When you broadcast "custom" intents, make sure you define unique action types. (It's common to tack them onto your application package namespace.) If you want other developers to listen for and react to your broadcasts, be sure to clearly document the broadcasts your application generates and the `Intent` data stored in each type of broadcast.

To send a normal sticky broadcast, simply use the `sendStickyBroadcast()` method of the `Context` class instead of the `sendBroadcast()` method.

Sending Ordered Broadcasts

To send an ordered broadcast, simply create the appropriate `Intent` object as normal and then dispatch it to the system using the `sendOrderedBroadcast()` method of the `Context` class.

Tip

If multiple broadcast receivers that match a broadcast have the same priority, they will receive the broadcast in an arbitrary order.

To send an ordered sticky broadcast, simply use the `sendStickyOrderedBroadcast()` method of the `Context` class instead of the `sendOrderedBroadcast()` method.

Receiving Broadcasts

The Android operating system handles the transmission of broadcasts. Certain broadcasts can be initiated by any application, whereas others are protected or require certain permissions. The Android operating system matches up a broadcast with suitable application(s) using intent filters. Intent filters are criteria that the system uses as matching rules when determining what should handle an `Intent`. A simple intent filter might catch all intents of a given action type (like our sample application). A more specific intent filter might specify the `Intent` action, data (URI and data type), and category details.

In order to become a broadcast receiver, your application must

- Register to receive broadcasts, specifying a specific intent filter, which the Android operating system uses to match broadcasts to your receiver
- Implement a broadcast receiver class

After your application has received a broadcast, it is handled by your broadcast receiver class—specifically by its `onReceive()` callback. The lifecycle of a `BroadcastReceiver` is short; it is valid only for the duration of the `onReceive()` method. This means that you should not perform lengthy synchronous operations within this callback method. It also means that any asynchronous processing might be killed off before it finishes. To perform an operation that goes beyond these limitations, create and launch a `Service` instance instead. Android services are discussed in Chapter 2, "Working with Services." For more information on the lifecycle of a broadcast receiver, see the Android SDK documentation at: *http://d.android.com/reference/android/content/BroadcastReceiver .html#ReceiverLifecycle*

Let's look at a simple example of a broadcast receiver that can react to the dancing broadcast we sent earlier in this chapter. First, you must extend the `BroadcastReceiver` class and implement your own event handling in the `onReceive()` callback method. The following is an example implementation of a `BroadcastReceiver` called `MyDancingBroadcastReceiver`:

```
class MyDancingBroadcastReceiver extends BroadcastReceiver
{
    @Override
    public void onReceive(Context context, Intent intent) {
        Toast.makeText(context, "Get Down and Boogie!",
            Toast.LENGTH_LONG).show();
    }
}
```

If this is an inner class, say of your `Activity` class, it must be declared as `public static` so it can be instantiated on its own. This is particularly important if the registration is done in the manifest file; see "Registering to Receive Broadcasts Statically" in the next section.

Registering to Receive Broadcasts

To listen for and react to broadcast events, your application must register with the Android operating system as a broadcast receiver at runtime or in its Android manifest file. The type of events your application registers to listen for is dictated by what are called intent filters. You can filter on a variety of rules. For example, your application might want to listen only for broadcasts for specific `Intent` action types or some other `Intent` criteria.

Registering to Receive Broadcasts Dynamically

To register for specific broadcasts at runtime, use the `registerReceiver()` and `unregisterReceiver()` methods of the `Context` class. Registering dynamically enables your application to turn off receiving broadcasts of certain types when it can't handle them or doesn't need to. This can help improve performance compared to just ignoring broadcasts. It is fairly typical to register for broadcasts in the `onResume()` callback method of the `Activity` class, and unregister (stop listening for them) in the `onPause()` callback method. Here we have an example of how an `Activity` might manage its broadcast registration with a very simple intent filter that watches for a special `Intent` action type:

```
public class SimpleBroadcastsActivity extends Activity {
    public static String ACTION_DANCE =
        "com.advancedandroidbook.simplebroadcasts.ACTION_DANCE";

    MyDancingBroadcastReceiver mReceiver;

    @Override
    public void onCreate(Bundle savedInstanceState) {
        super.onCreate(savedInstanceState);
        setContentView(R.layout.main);
        mReceiver = new MyDancingBroadcastReceiver();
    }

    @Override
    protected void onPause() {
        super.onPause();
        unregisterReceiver(mReceiver);
    }

    @Override
    protected void onResume() {
        super.onResume();
        IntentFilter danceFilter =
            new IntentFilter(ACTION_DANCE);
        registerReceiver(mReceiver, danceFilter);
    }
}
```

Registering to Receive Broadcasts Statically

You can also register to receive broadcasts in your application's Android manifest file. Registering to receive broadcasts is useful when your application can always handle a particular broadcast. To re-create the same receiver configuration shown previously, where your broadcast receiver handles a specific `Intent` action type, you use the following XML in your application's Android manifest file inside the `<application>` tag:

```
<receiver android:name=

        "com.advancedandroidbook.simplebroadcasts

        .SimpleBroadcastsActivity$MyDancingBroadcastReceiver" >
    <intent-filter>
        <action
            android:name=
                "com.advancedandroidbook.simplebroadcasts.ACTION_DANCE" />
    </intent-filter>
</receiver>
```

You can also set numerous tag attributes, such as priority, on the intent filter.

Handling Incoming Broadcasts from the System

After you have registered your broadcast receiver and implemented its `onReceive()` callback method, you are ready to start processing broadcast events. In some cases, your application will send the broadcasts, but in many cases, you simply want to respond to broadcasts made by other applications or the Android operating system at large (the device). Some common broadcasts your application might want to listen for and react to are listed in Table 5.1.

Table 5.1 **Important System Broadcasts**

Broadcast Receiver `Intent` Action	Description
ACTION_AIRPLANE_MODE_CHANGED	A notification that the device has been switched into or out of airplane mode.
ACTION_BATTERY_CHANGED	The battery state has changed.
	Note: You must register for this broadcast dynamically.
ACTION_BATTERY_LOW	A warning issued by the device that the battery is low. Applications may want to adjust background services or cancel lengthy operations in response. The `ACTION_BATTERY_OKAY` event may occur later if the battery gets a charge.
ACTION_BOOT_COMPLETED	The device has finished booting up. You need the `RECEIVE_BOOT_COMPLETED` permission to receive this broadcast.

(continues)

Table 5.1 **Continued**

Broadcast Receiver **Intent** Action	Description
ACTION_CAMERA_BUTTON ACTION_MEDIA_BUTTON ACTION_DATE_CHANGED	The user pressed a specific button.
ACTION_TIMEZONE_CHANGED	A notification issued by the device that the system date or time zone has changed. Applications that rely upon dates and times, such as alarm clock apps, may wish to take note.
ACTION_DEVICE_STORAGE_LOW	A warning issued by the device when there is a low-memory condition. The ACTION_DEVICE_STORAGE_OKAY event may occur later if the storage gets freed up.
ACTION_DOCK_EVENT	A notification issued when the device has been attached to or detached from a dock.
ACTION_HEADSET_PLUG	A notification issued by the device that a headset has been plugged into the device or unplugged. Applications that leverage sound may wish to take note and adjust behavior.
ACTION_INPUT_METHOD_CHANGED	A notification that an input method has been changed.
ACTION_LOCALE_CHANGED	A notification issued by the device that the system locale has changed. Applications that have locale-sensitive code or use services that require locale information may take note.
ACTION_MEDIA_BAD_REMOVAL ACTION_MEDIA_CHECKING ACTION_MEDIA_EJECT ACTION_MEDIA_MOUNTED ACTION_MEDIA_NOFS ACTION_MEDIA_REMOVED ACTION_MEDIA_SHARED ACTION_MEDIA_UNMOUNTABLE ACTION_MEDIA_UNMOUNTED	Notifications related to external media availability and state. Applications that use external media, such as music, video, or camera applications, may want to pay special attention to these events. See the Android SDK documentation for details.
ACTION_MEDIA_SCANNER_STARTED ACTION_MEDIA_SCANNER_FINISHED ACTION_MEDIA_SCANNER_SCAN_FILE	Events related to the media scanner. You can request to scan a specific file and add it to the media database using the action ACTION_MEDIA_SCANNER_SCAN_FILE.
ACTION_MY_PACKAGE_REPLACED	This notification is sent to the new version of an application when the old version is replaced.
ACTION_NEW_OUTGOING_CALL	A notification that a call is about to be placed. The application needs the permission PROCESS_OUTGOING_CALLS to receive this broadcast.

Broadcast Receiver `Intent` Action	Description
ACTION_PACKAGE_ADDED ACTION_PACKAGE_CHANGED ACTION_PACKAGE_DATA_CLEARED ACTION_PACKAGE_FIRST_LAUNCH ACTION_PACKAGE_FULLY_REMOVED ACTION_PACKAGE_NEEDS_VERIFICATION ACTION_PACKAGE_REMOVED ACTION_PACKAGE_REPLACED ACTION_PACKAGE_RESTARTED	Events related to application package installation, usage, and removal. Normally the package in question is not notified, but other related applications may react to such events.
ACTION_POWER_CONNECTED ACTION_POWER_DISCONNECTED	Notifications regarding device power state in terms of being plugged in or not (separate from battery events).
ACTION_SCREEN_OFF ACTION_SCREEN_ON	Notifications regarding device screen state.
ACTION_SHUTDOWN	A notification that the device will be shut down. Most applications shut down gracefully as part of the application lifecycle, but if your application needs to know that this is a full shutdown (as opposed to a pause, and so on), this is the event to watch for.
ACTION_TIME_TICK	A notification that the system time has changed. This notification is sent every minute. You must register for this broadcast dynamically.
ACTION_UID_REMOVED ACTION_USER_PRESENT	Events related to users, including when user accounts are removed or when the user has woken up the device.
ACTION_WALLPAPER_CHANGED	A notification that the user has changed the device wallpaper.

Securing Application Broadcasts

Some broadcasts are meant to be "heard" by any application that is interested. Others are intended for specific recipients. For example, you might want to define a set of broadcasts that your suite of Android applications uses but that cannot be used by other applications. Here are some tips for securing the broadcasting and receiving ends of the broadcast system:

- Create unique `Intent` data for broadcast. If your application broadcasts only to specific target applications, create and enforce the permissions required for that broadcast when you send it.

- Send the most specific broadcasts you can and create the most specific intent filters possible. This helps avoid broadcasts accidentally making it to unintended receivers.

- As of API Level 14, you can specify the package limitations using the `setPackage()` method of the `Intent` class, and these limitations will be enforced. This is good for cross-application broadcasts that need to target just one application, for whatever reason.

- You can set the target `Class` of the broadcast through either the appropriate constructor or the `setClass()` method. Use this for sending a broadcast directly to a particular receiver in your app. This avoids needing to set up and configure intent filters if you know exactly which receiver must handle each broadcast and you have full control over them within your app.

- You can use the `android:exported` attribute of the `<intent-filter>` tag in your application's Android manifest file to prevent other applications from sending broadcasts to your receiver.

Tip

Want to broadcast within the boundaries of your application but are worried about privacy? Check out the Android Support Package class called `LocalBroadcastManager` (`android.support.v4.content.LocalBroadcastManager`). It is basically an application-scoped broadcast that is more efficient than a system broadcast, and it guarantees that your `Intent` data never leaves your app—great for sending private data.

Summary

Broadcasts are a simple yet powerful way to communicate data across process boundaries. Broadcasts are sometimes used to communicate between services and their application user interfaces and between applications at large. Many broadcasts are initiated by the operating system to notify applications of events such as changes in device state. When an application sends a broadcast out, the Android operating system matches it up with all applications that have intent filters that match that request. For security purposes, there are some ways to lock down a broadcast such that it is handled by a specific application, and no other.

Quiz Questions

1. What are the two types of broadcasts that Android supports?

2. True or false: The method `dispatchBroadcast()` is used for sending out broadcasts to the system.

3. What must your application do in order to become a broadcast receiver?

4. What broadcast receiver `Intent` action notifies the new version of an application when the old version is replaced?

5. True or false: The `android:exported` attribute is used to prevent other applications from sending broadcasts to your receiver.

Exercises

1. Use the Android documentation to determine why you would not want to unregister a receiver in `Activity.onSaveInstanceState()`.

2. Use the Android documentation to create a list of the broadcast receiver methods that work only when sent through `Context.sendOrderedBroadcast()`.

3. Create an application that is able to receive a `CALL_BUTTON` intent action and, upon doing so, broadcast a custom `Intent` that displays a success `Toast` message.

References and More Information

Android API Guides: "Application Fundamentals":
  http://d.android.com/guide/components/fundamentals.html
Android SDK Reference documentation regarding the `BroadcastReceiver` class:
  http://d.android.com/reference/android/content/BroadcastReceiver.html
Android API Guides: "Intent Resolution":
  http://d.android.com/guide/components/intents-filters.html#Resolution

6

Working with Notifications

Applications often need to communicate with users, even when the applications aren't actively running. Applications can alert users with text notifications, vibration, blinking lights, and even audio. In this chapter, you will learn how to build different kinds of notifications into your Android applications using modern APIs, while keeping them compatible with devices running Android versions all the way back to API Level 4.

Notifying the User

Applications can use notifications to greatly improve the user's experience. For example:

- An email application might notify a user when new messages arrive. A newsreader application might notify a user when there are new articles to read.
- A game might notify a user when a friend has signed in, or sent an invitation to play, or beaten a high score.
- A weather application might notify a user of special weather alerts.
- A stock market application might notify the user when certain stock price targets are met. (Sell now before it's too late!)

Users appreciate these notifications because they help drive application workflow, reminding the users when they need to launch the application. However, there is a fine line between just enough and too many notifications. Application designers need to consider carefully how they use notifications so as not to annoy users or interrupt them without good reason. Each notification should be appropriate for the specific application and the event the user is being notified of. For example, an application should not put out an emergency-style notification (think flashing lights, ringing noises, and generally making a "to-do") simply to notify the user that his or her picture has been uploaded to a website or that new content has been downloaded.

The Android platform provides a number of different ways of notifying the user. Notifications are often displayed on the status bar at the top of the screen. They may involve:

- Textual information
- Graphical indicators

- Action indicators
- Sound indicators
- Vibration of the device
- Control of the indicator light

Warning

Although the Android SDK provides APIs for creating a variety of notifications, not all notifications are supported by all devices. For example, the `BigTextStyle` and `BigPictureStyle` are not available on all Android devices. There is also a degree of variation in how different devices handle notifications. Always test any notification implementations on target devices.

Now let's look at how to use these different kinds of notifications in your applications. But first, let's talk a little about compatibility.

A Word on Compatibility

Notifications have been around since the beginning of the Android platform. They have undergone some changes, but the basics have pretty much stayed the same. However, over time, some areas have changed enough that they no longer work the way they originally did. While we're not attempting to cover every single type of notification or option allowed for notifications in this book, even this overview covers at least one area that behaves differently on different versions of Android. We point out these areas as we come across them.

Additionally, a new method of creating notifications was introduced in API Level 11. This method involves using the `Notification.Builder()` class, but in this book we describe how to maintain compatibility with devices that are running Android API versions older than API Level 11. To do so, we use the `NotificationCompat` library and the `NotificationCompat.Builder()` class, rather than the standard API Level 11 and `Notification.Builder()` class, so if you are developing only for devices at API Level 11 and higher, feel free to use the later class, as these two different approaches are easily interchangeable.

Notifying with the Status Bar

The standard location for displaying notifications and indicators on an Android device is the status bar that runs along the top of the screen. Typically, the status bar shows information such as the current date and time. It also displays notifications (such as incoming SMS messages) as they arrive—in short form along the bar and in full if the user pulls down the status bar to see the notification list. The user can clear certain notifications by pulling down the status bar and hitting the Clear button. Other notifications are intended to be ongoing, not dismissible by the user, and cleared only by the calling application or `Service`.

Developers can enhance their applications by using notifications from their applications to inform the user of important events. For example, an application might want to send a simple notification to the user whenever new content has been downloaded. A simple notification has a number of important components:

- An icon (appears on the status bar and the full notification)
- Ticker text (appears on the status bar)
- Notification title text (appears in the full notification)
- Notification body text (appears in the full notification)
- An Intent (launches if the user clicks on the full notification)

In this section, you will learn how to create this basic kind of notification.

Tip

Many of the code examples provided in this chapter are taken from the SimpleNotifications application. The source code for this application is provided for download on the book's website.

Using the `NotificationManager` Service

All notifications are created with the help of the `NotificationManager`. The `NotificationManager` (in the `android.app` package) is a system `Service` that must be requested. The following code demonstrates how to obtain a valid `Notification Manager` object using the `getSystemService()` method:

```
NotificationManager notifier = (NotificationManager)
    getSystemService(Context.NOTIFICATION_SERVICE);
```

The `NotificationManager` is not useful without having a valid `Notification` object to use with the `notify()` method. The `Notification` object defines what information displays to the user when the `Notification` is triggered. This includes text that displays on the status bar, a couple of lines of text that display on the expanded status bar, an icon displayed in both places, a count of the number of times this `Notification` has been triggered, and a time for when the last event that caused this `Notification` took place.

Creating a Simple Text Notification with an Icon

To remain backward compatible, first you must construct a `NotificationCompat.Builder` object, passing in the application `Context` as a parameter, like so:

```
NotificationCompat.Builder notifyBuilder = new
        NotificationCompat.Builder(getApplicationContext());
```

You can then set the icon, ticker text, and notification timestamp, each of which displays on the status bar, through the `notifyBuilder` variable, using the available methods of the object, as follows:

```
notifyBuilder.setSmallIcon(R.drawable.ic_launcher);
notifyBuilder.setTicker("Hello!");
notifyBuilder.setWhen(System.currentTimeMillis());
```

You need to set a couple more pieces of information before the call to the notify()
method takes place. First, you need to make a call to the setContentTitle() method
and the setContentText() method, which configure a View that displays in the
expanded status bar. Here is an example:

```
Intent toLaunch = new Intent(SimpleNotificationsActivity.this,
        SimpleNotificationsActivity.class);
notifyBuilder.setContentIntent(PendingIntent.getActivity(
        SimpleNotificationsActivity.this, 0, toLaunch, 0));
notifyBuilder.setContentTitle("Hi there!");
notifyBuilder.setContentText("This is even more text.");
```

Next, you must create the Notification object using the build() method, then call
the notify() method of the notification to supply the notification's title and body text as
well as the Intent triggered when the user clicks on the notification. In this case, we're
using our own Activity so that when the user clicks on the notification, our Activity
launches again.

Note

When the expanded status bar is pulled down, the current Activity lifecycle is still treated
as if it were the top (displayed) Activity. Triggering system notifications while running in
the foreground, though, isn't particularly useful. For an application that is in the foreground,
it is better to use a Dialog or Toast to notify the user, not a Notification.

Working with the Notification Queue

Now the application is ready to actually notify the user of the event. All that is needed is
a call to the notify() method of the NotificationManager with an identifier and the
Notification we configured using the Notification.Builder. This is demonstrated
with the following code:

```
private static final int NOTIFY_1 = 0x1001;
// ...
notifier.notify(NOTIFY_1, notify);
```

The identifier matches up a Notification with any previous Notification
instances of that type. When the identifiers match, the old Notification is updated
instead of a new one being created. You might have a Notification that some file is
being downloaded. You can update the Notification when the download is complete,
instead of filling the notification queue with a separate Notification, which quickly
becomes obsolete. This Notification identifier needs to be unique only in your
application.

The Notification displays as an icon and ticker text on the status bar. This is shown
at the top of Figure 6.1.

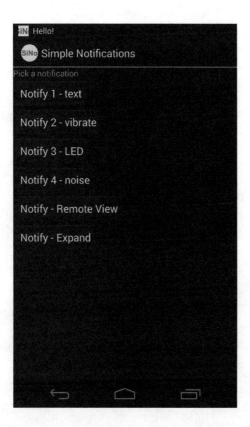

Figure 6.1   Status bar notification showing an icon and ticker text.

Shortly after the ticker text displays, the status bar returns to normal with each noti-fication icon shown. If the users expand the status bar, they see something like what is shown in Figure 6.2.

Updating Notifications

You don't want your application's notifications to pile up in the status bar. Therefore, you might want to reuse or update notifications to keep the notification list manage-able. For example, there is no reason to keep a notification informing the user that the application is downloading File X when you now want to send another notification say-ing File X has finished downloading. Instead, you can simply update the first notification with new information.

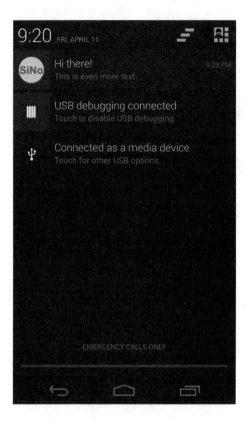

Figure 6.2   Expanded status bar showing the icon, both text fields,
and the time of the notification.

When the notification identifiers match, the old notification is updated. When a notification with a matching identifier is posted, the ticker text does not draw a second time. To show the user that something has changed, you can use a counter. The value of the number member variable of the `NotificationCompat.Builder()` object tracks and displays this. For instance, we can set it to the number 4, as shown here:

```
notifyBuilder.setNumber(4);
```

Figure 6.3 shows how this might look.

Clearing Notifications

When a user clicks on the notification, the `Intent` assigned is triggered. At some point after this, the application might want to clear the notification from the system

Figure 6.3   Status bar notification with the count of 4 showing
in the pull-down area.

notifications queue. This is done through a call to the `cancel()` method of the
`NotificationManager` object. For instance, the notification we created earlier
can be canceled with the following call:

```
notifier.cancel(NOTIFY_1);
```

This cancels the notification that has the same identifier. However, if the application
doesn't care what the user does after clicking on the notification, there is an easier way to
cancel notifications. Simply set a flag to do so, as shown here:

```
notifyBuilder.setAutoCancel(true);
```

Setting the `setAutoCancel()` method to `true` causes notifications to be canceled
when the user clicks on them. This is convenient and easy for the application when just
launching the `Intent` is good enough.

Vibrating the Phone

Vibration is a great way to enable notifications to catch the attention of a user in noisy environments or alert the user when visible and audible alerts are not appropriate (though a vibrating phone is often noisy on a hard surface). Android notifications give a fine level of control over how vibration is performed. However, before the application can use vibration with a notification, an explicit permission is needed. The following XML in your application's `AndroidManifest.xml` file is required to use vibration:

```
<uses-permission android:name="android.permission.VIBRATE" />
```

Warning

The vibrate feature must be tested on the device. The emulator does not indicate vibration in any way. Also, some Android devices do not support vibration.

Without this permission, the vibrate functionality does not work, nor are there any errors. With this permission enabled, the application is free to vibrate the phone however it wants. This is accomplished by describing the `vibrate` member variable using the `setVibrate()` method, which determines the vibration pattern. An array of `long` values describes the different vibration durations for turning the vibrator on and off. Thus, the following line of code enables a simple vibration pattern that occurs whenever the notification is triggered:

```
notifyBuilder.setVibrate(new long[] {0, 200, 200, 600, 600});
```

This pattern causes the device to vibrate for 200 milliseconds and then stop for 200 milliseconds. After that, it vibrates for 600 milliseconds and then stops for that long.

An application can use different patterns of vibrations to alert the user to different types of events or even present counts. For instance, think about a grandfather clock with which you can deduce the time based on the tones that are played.

Tip

Using short, unique patterns of vibration can be useful, and users become accustomed to them.

Blinking the Lights

Blinking lights are a great way to pass information silently to the user when other forms of alert are not appropriate. The Android SDK provides reasonable control over a multicolored indicator light, when such a light is available on the device. Users might recognize this light as a `Service` indicator or battery level warning. An application can also take advantage of this light by changing its blinking rate or color.

Warning

Indicator lights are not available on all Android devices. Also, the emulator does not display the light's state. Use of the indicator light mandates testing on actual hardware.

You must call methods on the `NotificationCompat.Builder()` object to use the indicator light. Then, the color of the light must be set as well as information about how it should blink. The following code configures the indicator light to shine green and blink at a rate of 1 second on and 1 second off:

```
notifyBuilder.setLights(Color.GREEN, 1000, 1000);
```

Although you can set arbitrary color values, a typical physical implementation of the indicator light has three small LEDs in red, green, and blue. Although the colors blend reasonably well, they won't be as accurate as the colors on the screen.

Warning

On some devices, certain notifications appear to take precedence when it comes to using the indicator light. For instance, the light on certain devices is always solid green when the device is plugged into a USB port, regardless of whether other applications are trying to use the indicator light. Additionally, on other devices, the color trackball is not lit unless the screen is off. You must unplug the phone from the USB port for the color to change.

An application can use different colors and different blinking rates to indicate different information to the user. For instance, the more times an event occurs, the more urgent the indicator light could be. The following block of code shows changing the light based on the number of notifications that have been triggered, and the blinking light continues until the notification is cleared by the user:

```
if (counterNotify3.getCount() < 2) {
    argb = Color.GREEN;
    onMs = 1000;
    offMs = 1000;
} else if (counterNotify3.getCount() < 3) {
    argb = Color.BLUE;
    onMs = 750;
    offMs = 750;
} else if (counterNotify3.getCount() < 4) {
    argb = Color.WHITE;
    onMs = 500;
    offMs = 500;
} else {
    argb = Color.RED;
    onMs = 50;
    offMs = 50;
}
counterNotify3.increment();
notifyBuilder.setLights(argb, onMs, offMs);
```

Color and blinking rates can also be used to indicate other information. For instance, temperature from a weather service can be indicated with red and blue plus a blink rate. Use of such colors for passive data indication can be useful even when other forms would work. It is far less intrusive than annoying, loud rings or harsh, vibrating phone noises. For instance, a simple glance at the device can tell the user some useful piece of information without the need to launch any applications or change what he or she is doing.

Making Noise

Sometimes, the device has to make noise to get the user's attention. Luckily, the Android SDK provides a means for doing this using the `NotificationCompat.Builder` object. Begin by calling the `setSound()` method and setting the URI of the sound, and also set the audio stream type to use when playing a sound. Generally, the most useful stream type is `STREAM_NOTIFICATION`. The following code demonstrates how to play a sound that is included as a project resource:

```
notifyBuilder.setSound(Uri.parse(
        "android.resource://com.advancedandroidbook.simplenotifications/"
        + R.raw.fallbackring),
        AudioManager.STREAM_NOTIFICATION);
```

By default, the audio file is played once. No specific permissions are needed for this form of notification.

> **Note**
>
> The sound file used in this example is included in the project as a raw resource. However, you can use any sound file on the device. Keep in mind that the sound files available on different Android devices may vary.

Customizing the Notification

Although the default notification behavior in the expanded status bar tray is sufficient for most purposes, developers can customize how notifications are displayed if they so choose. To do so, developers can use the `RemoteViews` object to customize the look and feel of a notification.

The following code demonstrates how to create a `RemoteViews` object and assign custom text to it:

```
RemoteViews remote = new RemoteViews(getPackageName(), R.layout.remote);

remote.setTextViewText(R.id.text1, "Big text here!");
remote.setTextViewText(R.id.text2, "Red text down here!");
notifyBuilder.setContent(remote);
```

To better understand this, here is the layout file `remote.xml` referenced by the preceding code:

```
<LinearLayout
    xmlns:android="http://schemas.android.com/apk/res/android"
    android:orientation="vertical"
    android:layout_width="match_parent"
    android:layout_height="match_parent">
    <TextView
        android:id="@+id/text1"
        android:layout_width="match_parent"
        android:layout_height="wrap_content"
        android:textSize="31sp"
        android:textColor="#ddd" />
    <TextView
```

```
        android:id="@+id/text2"
        android:layout_width="match_parent"
        android:layout_height="wrap_content"
        android:textSize="18sp"
        android:textColor="#f00" />
</LinearLayout>
```

This particular example is similar to the default notification but does not contain an icon. The `setContentTitle()` and `setContentText()` methods are normally used to assign the text to the default layout. In this example, we use our custom layout instead. The `Intent` still needs to be assigned, though, as follows:

```
Intent toLaunch = new Intent(SimpleNotificationsActivity.this,
        SimpleNotificationsActivity.class);
notifyBuilder.setContentIntent(PendingIntent.getActivity(
        SimpleNotificationsActivity.this, 0, toLaunch, 0));
Notification notify = notifyBuilder.build();
notifier.notify(NOTIFY_5, notify);
```

The end result looks something like Figure 6.4.

Figure 6.4   Custom notification showing just two lines of text.

Using a custom notification layout can provide better control over the information on the expanded status bar. Additionally, it can help differentiate your application's notifications from those of other applications by providing a themed or branded appearance.

Note
The size of the area that a layout can use on the expanded status bar is fixed for a given device. However, the exact details might change from device to device. Keep this in mind when designing a custom notification layout. Additionally, be sure to test the layout on all target devices in all modes of screen operation so that you can be sure the notification layout draws properly.

The default layout includes two fields of text: an icon and a time field for when the notification was triggered. Users are accustomed to this information. An application, where feasible and where it makes sense, should try to conform to at least this level of information when using custom notifications.

Expandable and Contractible Notifications

Android 4.1 (API Level 17) introduced the ability to create notifications that either expand or contract, depending on their order in the notification queue. Expanded notifications are the most recent notifications displayed in the status bar; are larger than contracted ones, as they provide more screen real estate for displaying notification content; and provide the option to include action buttons.

There are many different notification style types that allow you to include large image previews as an attachment using the `Notification.BigPictureStyle` class, larger amounts of text such as the contents of a long article using the `Notification.BigTextStyle` class, or multiple text snippets such as multiple unread messages from an email inbox using the `Notification.InboxStyle` class.

To create one of these `Notification` style types, use the `setStyle()` method of the `NotificationCompat.Builder` class. The `setStyle()` method requires passing in a `Style`, which is done as follows:

```
notifyBuilder.setStyle(new NotificationCompat.BigTextStyle()
        .bigText("This is a really long message that is used "
        + "for expanded notifications in the status bar"));
```

In this code sample, we call the `bigText()` method on our `BigTextStyle` class and include the text that we want displayed when the notification is expanded.

It is also possible to include action buttons in our `Notification`. To do so, we need to create a `PendingIntent` for each action that we include. The screen size of the device should determine how many action buttons you include, but we have found that more than two actions is usually too many. Figure 6.5 shows what our notification looks like when expanded, including two action buttons.

You should also include the `setContentTitle()` and `setContentText()` methods as we have demonstrated in past examples, to ensure that your notification displays properly when it is contracted; otherwise the notification content area will be empty if in the contracted state. Figure 6.6 shows what the same notification looks like when contracted.

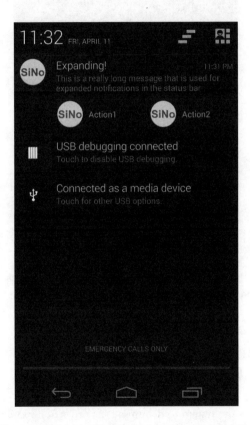

Figure 6.5   An expandable, big-view-style notification that is expanded, showing an icon, multiple lines of text, a timestamp, and two actions, each action accompanied by an icon.

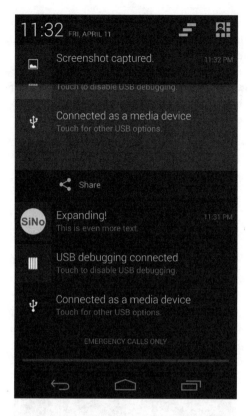

Figure 6.6   An expandable, big-view-style notification that is contracted
(second notification from the top), showing an icon, a title,
a line of text, and a timestamp.

Notification Priority

Starting with Android 4.1 (API Level 17), notifications include the ability to set a priority. The priority allows the system to determine the order of importance in which to display an application's activity to the device user. Here is a list of priorities you are able to set for your notifications:

- Min: Notifications do not show in the status bar when triggered, only when the user expands the notification tray.
- Low: Notifications show in the status bar with a low priority.
- Default: Notifications default to this when not specifically configured.

- High: Notifications for including messages such as, SMS, emails, etc.
- Max: Notifications for missed calls, voicemails, etc.

Introducing the Notification Listener

Android 4.3 (API Level 18) introduced the `NotificationListenerService`, and Android 4.4 (API Level 19) quickly released enhancements to this new `Service` class. The class is designed so that you can configure your application to listen for notifications as the system triggers responses to them. The Android 4.4 updates include special metadata with the notification messages sent by the system, allowing your application to learn more about the information included, such as the picture or title of a notification. This metadata is included as a `Bundle`, and Android 4.4 also includes a `Notification.Action` class that is useful for learning information about the actions posted by the notifications. You must include the `BIND_NOTIFICATION_LISTENER_SERVICE` permission on the `NotificationListenerService` class registered in your manifest, in addition to including an `<intent-filter>` action with a constant value of `android.service.notification.NotificationListenerService`.

Designing Useful Notifications

As you can see, the notification capabilities on the Android platform are quite robust—so robust that it is easy to overdo it and make your application tiresome for the user. Here are some tips for designing useful notifications:

- Use notifications only when your application is not in the foreground. When the application is in the foreground, use `Toast` or `Dialog` controls.
- Allow users to determine what types (text, lights, sound, and vibration) and frequency of notifications they receive, as well as what events to trigger notifications for.
- Whenever possible, update and reuse an existing notification instead of creating a new one.
- Clear notifications regularly so as not to overwhelm the user with dated information.
- When in doubt, generate "polite" notifications (read as quiet).
- Make sure your notifications contain useful information in the ticker, title, and body text fields and launch sensible intents.

The notification framework is lightweight yet powerful. However, some applications such as alarm clocks or stock market monitors might also need to implement their own alert windows above and beyond the notification framework provided. In this case, they may use a background `Service` and launch full `Activity` windows when certain events occur. In Android 2.0 and later, developers can use the `WindowManager.LayoutParams` class to enable `Activity` windows to display, even when the screen is locked with a keyguard.

Summary

Applications can interact with their users outside the normal activity boundaries by using notifications. Notifications can be visual, auditory, or sensory, using the vibrate feature of the device. Various methods can customize these notifications to provide rich information to the user. Special care must be taken to provide the right amount of appropriate information to the user without the application becoming a nuisance or the application being installed and forgotten about.

Quiz Questions

1. What method do you call to retrieve a `NotificationManager` object?
2. True or false: You should use the `setTicker()` method to set the ticker text of a `Notification`.
3. True or false: The `notify()` method is used to broadcast the `Notification`.
4. What method should you set on the `Notification.Builder` object to display a count of notifications?
5. What does the `setAutoCancel()` method cause?

Exercises

1. Add an `InboxStyle` `Notification` to the SimpleNotifications application included with this chapter.
2. Add a `Notification` that displays a progress indicator to the SimpleNotifications application included with this chapter.
3. Create a new Android application demonstrating how to use the `NotificationListenerService` class.

References and More Information

Android Design: "Notifications":
  http://d.android.com/design/patterns/notifications.html
Android Training: "Notifying the User":
  http://developer.android.com/training/notify-user/index.html
Android API Guides: "Notifications":
  http://d.android.com/guide/topics/ui/notifiers/notifications.html

Android Reference documentation for the `Notification` class:
http://d.android.com/reference/android/app/Notification.html

Android SDK Reference documentation for the `NotificationListenerService` class:
http://d.android.com/reference/android/service/notification/NotificationListenerService.html

Android SDK Reference documentation for the `StatusBarNotification` class:
http://d.android.com/reference/android/service/notification/StatusBarNotification.html

Android SDK Reference documentation for the `NotificationManager` class:
http://d.android.com/reference/android/app/NotificationManager.html

Android SDK Reference documentation for the `Notification.Builder` class:
http://d.android.com/reference/android/app/Notification.Builder.html

Android SDK Reference documentation for the `NotificationCompat` class:
http://d.android.com/reference/android/support/v4/app/NotificationCompat.html

YouTube Android Developers Channel: "Android Design in Action: Notifications and Design Process with Alex Faaborg":
http://www.youtube.com/watch?v=FaW8PwhU_BY

YouTube Android Developers Channel: "2012-10-18 Android Developer Lab+ - Notifications":
http://www.youtube.com/watch?v=s61Rbk3ynXQ

YouTube Android Developers Channel: "Android Design in Action: Local Video and Rich Notifications":
http://www.youtube.com/watch?v=2YeTxWtxgPQ

II

Advanced Android User Interface Design Principles

7

Designing Powerful User Interfaces

The Android platform has matured over time, especially when it comes to the user experience. We've already talked about many of the user interface controls you can leverage in your applications. Now we take a broader look at some of the UI features available in the Android SDK, including various kinds of action bars, styles, and themes. We also talk about the Android development team's initiative to document a set of guidelines and best practices for Android application design.

Following Android User Interface Guidelines

When we wrote the first edition of this book several years ago, design was not the focus, although today there is a growing interest in defining a set of application design principles. As the platform has matured, design patterns have arisen. Some have succeeded, and others have failed. It's hard to keep up, and developers have expressed no small amount of frustration over the number of UI overhauls that have occurred with each new revision of the Android platform. In early 2011, the Android development team launched a new Android developer education initiative called Android Design. Android Design is a website where you can learn all about the user interface principles recommended by the platform designers. These are recommendations, not requirements, but they are generally sound. That doesn't mean you can't break the mold and do something innovative, but the recommendations provide a nice baseline that will help developers with or without design talent raise the bar in terms of application user interface design. Check out Android Design at *http://d.android.com/design/index.html*.

Tip

We cover some of the most commonly used platform user interface features in this chapter, but there are many we do not have the space to include. For more information, see the resources listed at the end of this chapter.

> **Note**
>
> There's a famous quote by the late Steve Jobs that is appropriate here:
>
> > "People think it's this veneer—that the designers are handed this box and told,
> > 'Make it look good!' That's not what we think design is. It's not just what it looks like
> > and feels like. Design is how it works."
>
> From the November 30, 2003, *New York Times* article "The Guts of a New Machine" by Rob
> Walker, *http://www.nytimes.com/2003/11/30/magazine/30IPOD.html*

In this chapter, we show you how to add an action bar and how to customize and extend the action bar's capabilities. In addition, we also show you how to work with styles and themes so that you will be able to customize the look and feel of your application. Let's get started by working with action bars.

Enabling Action Bars

Action bars are a navigational user interface mechanism introduced in Android 3.0 (API Level 11). Action bars replace the older application title bar but provide a much richer set of features, allowing the user to traverse the screens and features of applications more quickly, with fewer clicks, and with less confusion. Action bars have also helped standardize application navigation as Android devices have been moving away from having physical hardware buttons to software buttons. Support for action bars has been added to the Android Support Library (revision 18), which allows you to add action bars to legacy applications running on devices with versions all the way back to Android 2.1 (API Level 7).

> **Tip**
>
> Many of the code examples provided in this section are taken from the SimpleActionBars
> application. The source code for this application is provided for download on the book's
> website.

The concept of the action bar is straightforward. If your application provides actions to a user, you may want to take advantage of the action bar features for including those actions in an easy-to-use way from within the title bar, as shown in Figure 7.1.

One tricky thing about action bars is that they look and behave differently depending on the Android platform version.

Building Basic Action Bars

Let's look at a simple example. Let's assume we have an application with four screens: a main `Activity` to launch into, and three other "cleaning" `Activity` classes for sweeping, scrubbing, and vacuuming. Now, we add an options menu to our main `Activity` that enables the user to jump to the three "cleaning" features easily, as shown in Figure 7.2.

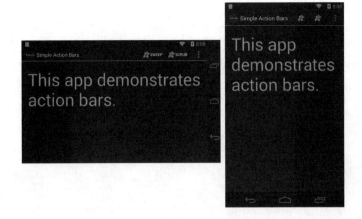

Figure 7.1   Action bar demonstration showing dynamic behavior.

Figure 7.2   A simple app with an options menu and four screens.

The two basic components of this application are the options menu resource file and the main `Activity` class. The other `Activity` classes simply display an `ImageView` and a `TextView` control. The options menu resource file defines the options menu items:

```xml
<?xml version="1.0" encoding="utf-8"?>
<menu
    xmlns:android="http://schemas.android.com/apk/res/android">
    <item
        android:id="@+id/sweep"
        android:icon="@drawable/ic_menu_sweep"
        android:title="@string/sweep"
        android:onClick="onOptionSweep" />
    <item
        android:id="@+id/scrub"
        android:icon="@drawable/ic_menu_scrub"
        android:title="@string/scrub"
        android:onClick="onOptionScrub" />
    <item
        android:id="@+id/vacuum"
        android:icon="@drawable/ic_menu_vac"
        android:title="@string/vacuum"
        android:onClick="onOptionVacuum" />
</menu>
```

The main `Activity` class loads this menu resource as an options menu and defines the `onClick()` handlers for each options menu item, as follows:

```java
public class SimpleActionBarsActivity extends Activity {
    @Override
    public void onCreate(Bundle savedInstanceState) {
        super.onCreate(savedInstanceState);
        setContentView(R.layout.main);
    }

    @Override
    public boolean onCreateOptionsMenu(Menu menu) {
        MenuInflater inflater = getMenuInflater();
        inflater.inflate(R.menu.cleaningoptions, menu);
        return true;
    }

    public void onOptionSweep(MenuItem i) {
        startActivity(new Intent(this, SweepActivity.class));
    }

    public void onOptionScrub(MenuItem i) {
        startActivity(new Intent(this, ScrubActivity.class));
    }

    public void onOptionVacuum(MenuItem i) {
        startActivity(new Intent(this, VacuumActivity.class));
    }
}
```

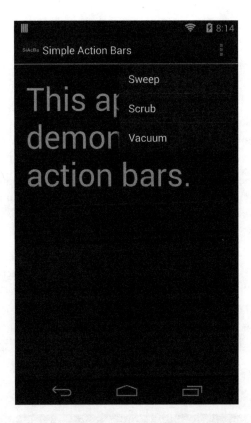

Figure 7.3   Action bar behavior on a device with API Level 7 and later.

We would like this application to work on devices as far back as we can, so we will set the minSdkVersion to API Level 7 in our manifest file, like so:

```
<uses-sdk android:minSdkVersion="7" />
```

By default, the title bar is thick. It shows the application icon, the application name, and what is called the overflow menu icon. Clicking this icon results in a textual menu that lists the options menu items, as shown in Figure 7.3.

Customizing Your Action Bar

When your application targets an API Level 7 platform or later, you can really take advantage of what the action bar widget has to offer by placing your options menu items right on the action bar, making them easily accessible to the user. The primary menu item attribute that controls this behavior is the `android:showAsAction` attribute. This attribute can have any of the following values:

- `always`: This value causes the menu item to always be shown on the action bar.
- `ifRoom`: This value causes the menu item to be shown on the action bar if there is sufficient room.
- `never`: This value causes the menu item to never be shown on the action bar.
- `withText`: This value causes the menu item to be displayed with its icon and its menu text.

You can modify the options menu resource file to use this attribute in different ways. First, look back at Figure 7.1; that is what the action bar looks like if you set each menu item to display if there's room, along with its name. In other words, each menu item has the following attribute:

```
android:showAsAction="ifRoom|withText"
```

Another reasonable setting is to display each menu item on the action bar, provided there is space, but without the clutter of the text. In other words, each menu item has the following attribute:

```
android:showAsAction="ifRoom"
```

Figure 7.4 shows what this change achieves on a typical device with API Level 7 or later.

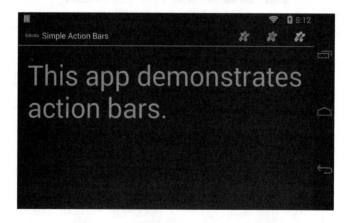

Figure 7.4   Showing menu items on the action bar
when room is available, not including text.

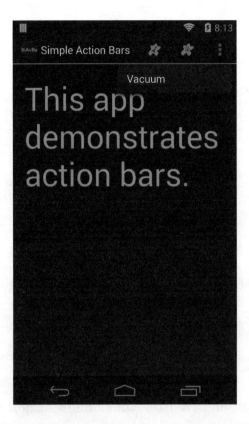

Figure 7.5   Showing some menu items on the action bar while others
never show (appearing instead in the overflow menu).

Finally, let's say that we never want to see the Vacuum menu item on the action bar:

`android:showAsAction="never"`

This results in two menu items on the action bar: Sweep and Scrub. Then, in the far right corner, you'll see the overflow menu again. Click it to see any menu items set to never (such as Vacuum) and any other menu items that might not have fit on the action bar, as shown in Figure 7.5.

Handling Application Icon Clicks on the Action Bar

Another feature of the action bar is that the user can click the application icon in the top left corner. Although clicking does nothing by default, adding a custom "home" functionality, perhaps to your launch screen, is easy. Let's say you want to update the default action bar in the SweepActivity class so that clicking the application icon causes the user to return to the main launch Activity (clearing the activity stack at the same time).

To do this, you would simply implement the onOptionsItemSelected() method for the SweepActivity class and handle the special menu item identifier called android.R.id.home, like this:

```
@Override
public boolean onOptionsItemSelected(MenuItem item) {
    switch (item.getItemId()) {
        case android.R.id.home:
            Intent intent = new Intent(this, SimpleActionBarsActivity.class);
            intent.addFlags(Intent.FLAG_ACTIVITY_CLEAR_TOP);
            startActivity(intent);
            return true;
        default:
            return super.onOptionsItemSelected(item);
    }
}
```

That's all there is to it (see the Sweep screen at the bottom right in Figure 7.2). You can also display a little arrow to the left of the application icon to identify that you are moving back up the screen hierarchy of your application; use the setDisplayHomeAs UpEnabled() method in your onCreate() method of the Activity in conjunction with implementing the special home menu item click handler:

```
ActionBar bar = getSupportActionBar();
bar.setDisplayHomeAsUpEnabled(true);
```

The resulting action bar, if we were to enable it on the Sweep screen, is shown in Figure 7.6.

Working with Screens That Do Not Require Action Bars

Once you've set your application target to API Level 7 or higher, all your screens will have action bars by default. However, you can remove the action bar from a screen in several ways. Perhaps the simplest way is to turn it off programmatically from within your Activity class. For example, we can turn off the action bar on the Vacuum screen with the following two lines of code added to the onCreate() method of the Activity class:

```
ActionBar bar = getSupportActionBar();
bar.hide();
```

This code removes the entire bar from the top of the screen (see the Vacuum screen at the left in Figure 7.2). The application name is not shown at all. You can also easily hide the action bar in layout files by creating a special custom theme. See the Android SDK documentation about action bars for details.

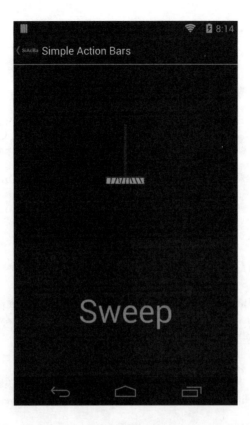

Figure 7.6 An action bar with a clickable Home button
and an Up indicator.

Contextual Action Mode

The design guidelines recommend that developers use contextual action bars instead of the older-style context menus. Contextual action mode can be enabled for a single View in response to an action, such as a long click. An ActionMode.Callback instance is assigned to handle creation and click handling on the contextual action mode action bar. As with other menus, creation of the menu is usually handled through a MenuInflater. Clicks are handled through the onActionItemClicked() method, and when the action is complete, the mode is returned to normal through a call to the finish() method of the ActionMode class.

With `ListView` and `GridView` controls, multiple items can be selected. Here you set the control to multiple-choice mode and then register a `MultiChoiceModeListener()` instance on the `View` control. This combines the selection handling and the contextual action mode listening into one callback class.

Tip

There's a lot more you can do with action bars. Action bars can be styled, including changing features such as the background graphic and other customizations. They also support several other more sophisticated `View` types and widgets, beyond those menu items found in the options menu, such as tabs and drop-downs. You can even add other types of `View` controls to create functional areas of the action bar. See the Android SDK documentation on action bars for details, found here—*http://d.android.com/training/ basics/actionbar/index.html*—and here—*http://d.android.com/guide/topics/ ui/actionbar.html.*

Working with Styles

Android user interface designers can group layout element attributes together in styles. A *style* is a group of common `View` attribute values that can be applied jointly to any user interface control. Styles can include such settings as the font to draw with or the color of text. The specific attributes depend on the `View` drawn. In essence, though, each style attribute can change the look and feel of the particular object drawn.

You can use a style to define your application's standard `TextView` attributes once and then refer to the style either in an XML layout file or programmatically from within Java. Styles are typically defined within the `/res/values/styles.xml` resource file using the `<style>` tag.

Building Simple Styles

Here's an example of a simple style resource file `/res/values/styles.xml` containing two styles, one for mandatory form fields and one for optional form fields, on `TextView` and `EditText` objects:

```
<?xml version="1.0" encoding="utf-8"?>
<resources>
    <style name="mandatory_text_field_style">
        <item name="android:textColor">#ffffff</item>
        <item name="android:textSize">14sp</item>
        <item name="android:textStyle">bold</item>
    </style>
    <style name="optional_text_field_style">
        <item name="android:textColor">#ffffff</item>
        <item name="android:textSize">12sp</item>
        <item name="android:textStyle">italic</item>
    </style>
</resources>
```

Many useful style attributes are colors and dimensions. It is more appropriate to use references to resources. Here's the `styles.xml` file again; this time, the color and text size fields are available in the other resource files `colors.xml` and `dimens.xml`:

```xml
<?xml version="1.0" encoding="utf-8"?>
<resources>
    <style name="mandatory_text_field_style">
        <item name="android:textColor">
            @color/mand_text_color
        </item>
        <item name="android:textSize">
            @dimen/important_text
        </item>
        <item name="android:textStyle">
            bold
        </item>
    </style>
    <style name="optional_text_field_style">
        <item name="android:textColor">
            @color/opt_text_color
        </item>
        <item name="android:textSize">
            @dimen/unimportant_text
        </item>
        <item name="android:textStyle">
            italic
        </item>
    </style>
</resources>
```

Now, if you can create a new layout with a couple of `TextView` and `EditText` text controls, you can set each control's style attribute by referencing it as such:

```
style="@style/name_of_style"
```

Here we have a form layout called `/res/layout/form.xml` that does that:

```xml
<?xml version="1.0" encoding="utf-8"?>
<LinearLayout
    xmlns:android="http://schemas.android.com/apk/res/android"
    android:orientation="vertical"
    android:layout_width="match_parent"
    android:layout_height="match_parent"
    android:layout_margin="20dp" >

    <TextView
        android:id="@+id/TextView01"
        style="@style/mandatory_text_field_style"
        android:layout_height="wrap_content"
        android:text="@string/mand_label"
        android:layout_width="match_parent" />

    <EditText
        android:id="@+id/EditText01"
```

```
        style="@style/mandatory_text_field_style"
        android:layout_height="wrap_content"
        android:text="@string/mand_default"
        android:layout_width="match_parent"
        android:background="#ffffff"
        android:textColor="#000000"
        android:singleLine="true" />

    <TextView
        android:id="@+id/TextView02"
        style="@style/optional_text_field_style"
        android:layout_width="match_parent"
        android:layout_height="wrap_content"
        android:text="@string/opt_label" />

    <EditText
        android:id="@+id/EditText02"
        style="@style/optional_text_field_style"
        android:layout_height="wrap_content"
        android:text="@string/opt_default"
        android:singleLine="true"
        android:background="#ffffff"
        android:textColor="#0f0f0f"
        android:layout_width="match_parent" />

    <TextView
        android:id="@+id/TextView03"
        style="@style/optional_text_field_style"
        android:layout_width="match_parent"
        android:layout_height="wrap_content"
        android:text="@string/opt_label" />

    <EditText
        android:id="@+id/EditText03"
        style="@style/optional_text_field_style"
        android:layout_height="wrap_content"
        android:text="@string/opt_default"
        android:singleLine="true"
        android:background="#ffffff"
        android:textColor="#0f0f0f"
        android:layout_width="match_parent" />
</LinearLayout>
```

The resulting layout has three fields, each made up of one `TextView` for the label and one `EditText` where the user can input text. The mandatory style is applied to the mandatory label and text entry. The other two fields use the optional style. The resulting layout looks something like Figure 7.7.

Styles are applied to specific layout controls such as `TextView` and `Button` objects. Usually, you want to supply the style resource `id` when you call the control's constructor. For example, the style named `myAppIsStyling` would be referred to as `R.style.myAppIsStyling`.

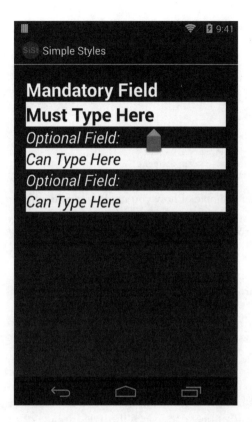

Figure 7.7   A layout using two styles, one for mandatory fields
and another for optional fields.

Leveraging Style Inheritance

Styles support inheritance; therefore, styles can also reference another style as a parent.
This way, they pick up the attributes of the parent style. Let's look at another example to
illustrate how style inheritance works. Here we have two different styles:

```xml
<?xml version="1.0" encoding="utf-8"?>
<resources>
    <style name="padded_small">
        <item name="android:padding">2dp</item>
        <item name="android:textSize">8sp</item>
    </style>
    <style name="padded_large">
        <item name="android:padding">4dp</item>
```

```
        <item name="android:textSize">16sp</item>
    </style>
</resources>
```

When applied, the `padded_small` style sets the padding to 2 dp and the `textSize` to 8 sp. The following is an example of how it is applied to a `TextView` from within a layout resource file:

```
<TextView
    style="@style/padded_small"
    android:layout_width="match_parent"
    android:layout_height="wrap_content"
    android:text="Small Padded" />
```

The following is an example of how you might use style inheritance:

```
<style name="red_padded">
    <item name="android:textColor">#F00</item>
    <item name="android:padding">3dp</item>
</style>

<style name="padded_normal" parent="red_padded">
    <item name="android:textSize">12sp</item>
</style>

<style name="padded_italics" parent="red_padded">
    <item name="android:textSize">14sp</item>
    <item name="android:textStyle">italic</item>
</style>
```

Here you find two common attributes in a single style and a reference to them from the other two styles that have different attributes. You can reference any style as a parent style; however, you can set only one style as the style attribute of a `View`. Applying the `padded_italics` style that is already defined makes the text 14 sp in size, italic, red, and padded. The following is an example of applying this style:

```
<TextView
    style="@style/padded_italics"
    android:layout_width="match_parent"
    android:layout_height="wrap_content"
    android:text="Italic w/parent color" />
```

As you can see from this example, applying a style with a parent is no different from applying a regular style. In fact, a regular style can be applied to `View` controls and used as a parent in a different style:

```
<style name="padded_xlarge">
    <item name="android:padding">10dp</item>
    <item name="android:textSize">100sp</item>
</style>
<style name="green_glow" parent="padded_xlarge">
    <item name="android:shadowColor">#0F0</item>
    <item name="android:shadowDx">0</item>
    <item name="android:shadowDy">0</item>
    <item name="android:shadowRadius">10</item>
</style>
```

Here the `padded_xlarge` style is set as the parent for the `green_glow` style. All six attributes are then applied to any `View` to which this style is applied.

Tip

When in the Graphical Layout editor or the XML editor for layouts, you can use the Android Development Tools (ADT) quick-fix capability to quickly make styles. When editing a `View`, simply add properties directly on it. Get them all correct. Then choose the quick-fix option for Extract as Style. This displays a dialog for you to name the style and choose which properties go in it. The tool then creates the style, sets it on the control on which you chose to do the action, and removes all of the properties that were included in the style.

Working with Themes

Themes are much like styles, but instead of being applied to one layout element at a time, they are applied to all elements of a given `Activity` or the application as a whole. Themes are defined in exactly the same way as styles. Themes use the `<style>` tag and should be stored in the `/res/values` directory. The only difference is that instead of applying that named style to a layout element, you define it as the `theme` attribute of an `<activity>` or `<application>` tag in the Android manifest file.

A *theme* is a collection of one or more styles (as defined in the resources), but instead of the style being applied to a specific control, it is applied to all `View` objects in a specified `Activity`. Applying a theme to a set of `View` objects all at once simplifies making the user interface look consistent and can be a great way to define color schemes and other common control attribute settings.

You can specify the theme programmatically by calling the `Activity` method `setTheme()` with the style resource identifier. Each attribute of the style is applied to each `View` within that `Activity`, as applicable. Styles and attributes defined in the layout files explicitly override those in the theme.

For instance, consider the following style:

```
<style name="right">
    <item name="android:gravity">right</item>
</style>
```

You can apply this as a theme to the whole screen, which causes any `View` displayed within that `Activity` to have its `gravity` attribute right-justified. Applying this theme is as simple as making the method call to the `setTheme()` method from within the `Activity`, as shown here:

```
setTheme(R.style.right);
```

You can also apply a theme to specific `Activity` instances by specifying it as an attribute within the `<activity>` element in the `AndroidManifest.xml` file, as follows:

```
<activity android:name=".MyActivityName"
    android:label="@string/app_name"
    android:theme="@style/myAppIsStyling">
```

Unlike applying a style in an XML layout file, multiple themes can be applied to a screen. This gives you flexibility in defining style attributes in advance while applying different configurations of the attributes based on what might be displayed on the screen. This is demonstrated in the following code:

```
setTheme(R.style.right);
setTheme(R.style.green_glow);
setContentView(R.layout.style_samples);
```

In this example, both the `right` style and the `green_glow` style are applied as a theme to the entire screen. You can see the results of green glow and right-aligned gravity, applied to a variety of `TextView` controls on a screen, in Figure 7.8. Finally, we set the layout to the `Activity`. You must do this after setting the themes. That is, you must apply all themes before calling the method `setContentView()` or the `inflate()` method so that the themes' attributes can take effect.

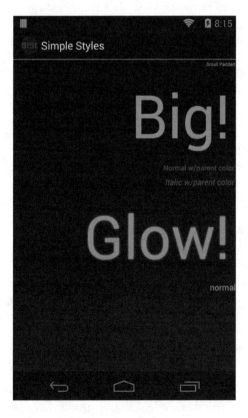

Figure 7.8 Packaging styles for glowing text, padding, and alignment into a theme.

A combination of well-designed and well-thought-out themes and styles can make the look of your application consistent and easy to maintain. Android comes with a number of built-in themes that can be a good starting point. These include such themes as `Theme_Black`, `Theme_Light`, and `Theme_NoTitleBar_Fullscreen`, as defined in the `android.R.style` class. They are all variations on the system theme, `Theme`, which built-in apps use.

Summary

The Android platform constantly changes as old user interface features are retired and new ones take their place. This chapter introduced you to action bars and how they behave under different circumstances. You also learned how to use styles and themes to provide a consistent user experience to your applications by "bottling up" groups of `View` attributes for reuse.

Quiz Questions

1. True or false: Action bars are available in the Android Support Library all the way back to API Level 4.
2. What are some of the values you are able to supply for defining the `showAsAction` attribute for action bar menu items?
3. What method should you use to implement an up navigation to the left of an `Activity`'s action bar application icon?
4. What method should you call on an action bar object to remove the action bar from the screen?
5. What method is used to programmatically apply a theme from within your application's code?

Exercises

1. Use the Android documentation to determine the constant value of the `Theme_Holo_NoActionBar` variable.
2. Use the Android documentation to determine how to declare the parent activity for enabling the Up button from an action bar.
3. Create an application that implements a split action bar.

References and More Information

Android Design website:

http://d.android.com/design/index.html

Android Design: "Action Bar":

http://d.android.com/design/patterns/actionbar.html

Android Training: "Adding the Action Bar":

http://developer.android.com/training/basics/actionbar/index.html

Android API Guides: "Action Bar":

http://d.android.com/guide/topics/ui/actionbar.html

Android SDK Reference documentation on the `ActionBar` class:

http://d.android.com/reference/android/app/ActionBar.html

Android Design: "Themes":

http://d.android.com/design/style/themes.html

Android API Guides: "Styles and Themes":

http://d.android.com/guide/topics/ui/themes.html

Android API Guides: "Style Resource":

http://d.android.com/guide/topics/resources/style-resource.html

8

Handling Advanced User Input

Users interact with Android devices in many ways, including using keyboards, touch-screen gestures, and even voice. Different devices support different input methods and have different hardware. For example, certain devices have hardware keyboards, and others rely only on software keyboards. In this chapter, you will learn about the different input methods available to developers and how you can use them to great effect within your applications.

Working with Textual Input Methods

The Android SDK includes input method framework classes that enable interested developers to use powerful input methods and create their own input methods, such as custom software keyboards and other Input Method Editors (IMEs). Users can download custom IMEs to use on their devices. For example, there's nothing stopping a developer from creating a custom keyboard with *Lord of the Rings*–style Elvish characters, smiley faces, or Greek symbols.

Tip

Most device settings related to input methods are available under the Settings, Language & input menu. Here, users can select the language, configure the custom user dictionary, and make changes to how their keyboards function.

The Android SDK also includes a number of other text input utilities that might benefit application users, such as text prediction, dictionaries, and the clipboard framework, which can be used to enable sophisticated cut-and-paste features in your application for text and much more.

Working with Software Keyboards

Because text input methods are locale-based (different countries use different alphabets and keyboards) and situational (numeric versus alphabetic versus special keys), the Android platform has trended toward software keyboards as opposed to relying on hardware manufacturers to deliver specialized hardware keyboards.

Choosing the Appropriate Software Keyboard

The Android platform has a number of software keyboards available for use. One of the easiest ways to enable your users to enter data efficiently is to specify the type of input expected in each text input field.

Tip

Many of the code examples provided in this section are taken from the SimpleTextInputTypes application. The source code for this application is provided for download on the book's website.

For example, to specify an `EditText` that should take only capitalized textual input, you can set the `inputType` attribute as follows:

```
<EditText
    android:layout_height="wrap_content"
    android:layout_width="match_parent"
    android:inputType="text|textCapCharacters">
</EditText>
```

Figure 8.1 shows a number of `EditText` controls with different `inputType` configurations.

The input type dictates which software keyboard is used by default, and it enforces appropriate rules, such as limiting input to certain characters. Figure 8.2 (left) illustrates what the software keyboard looks like for an `EditText` control with its `inputType` attribute set to all capitalized text input. Note that the software keyboard keys are all capitalized. If you were to set the `inputType` to `textCapWords` instead, the keyboard would switch to lowercase after the first letter of each word and then back to uppercase after a space. Figure 8.2 (middle) illustrates what the software keyboard looks like for an `EditText` control with its `inputType` attribute set to `number`. Figure 8.2 (right) illustrates what the software keyboard looks like for an `EditText` control with its `inputType` attribute set to textual input, where each sentence begins with a capital letter and the text can be multiple lines.

Depending on the user's keyboard settings (specifically, if the user has enabled the Show correction suggestions and Auto-correction options in the Android Keyboard settings of the device), the user might also see suggested words or spelling fixes while typing. For a complete list of `inputType` attribute values and their uses, see *http://developer.android.com/reference/android/R.attr.html#inputType*.

Tip

You can also have your `Activity` react to the display of software keyboards (to adjust where fields are displayed, for example) by requesting the `WindowManager` as a system `Service` and modifying the layout parameters associated with the `softInputMode` field.

For more fine-tuned control over input methods, see the `android.view.inputmethod.InputMethodManager` class.

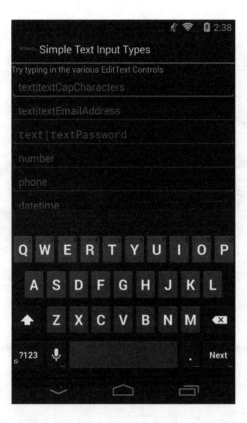

Figure 8.1   `EditText` controls with different input types.

Providing Custom Software Keyboards

If you are interested in developing your own software keyboards, we highly recommend the following references:

- IMEs are implemented as an Android `Service`. Begin by reviewing the Android packages called `android.inputmethodservice` and `android.view.inputmethod`, which can be used to implement custom input methods.

- The SoftKeyboard legacy sample application in the Android SDK provides an implementation of a software keyboard.

- The Android Developers Blog has articles on on-screen input methods (*http://android-developers.blogspot.com/2009/04/updating-applications-for-on-screen.html*) and creating an input method (*http://android-developers.blogspot.com/2009/04/ creating-input-method.html*). Don't forget to add voice typing to your input method (*http://android-developers.blogspot.com/2011/12/add-voice-typing-to-your-ime.html*).

Figure 8.2   The software keyboards associated with specific input types.

Working with Text Prediction and User Dictionaries

Text prediction is a powerful and flexible feature that is available on Android devices. We've already talked about many of these technologies in other parts of this book, but they merit mentioning in this context as well:

- In *Introduction to Android Application Development: Android Essentials, Fourth Edition*, you learned how to use AutoCompleteTextView and MultiAutoCompleteTextView controls to help users input common words and strings.

- In Chapter 3, "Leveraging SQLite Application Databases," you learned how to tie an AutoCompleteTextView control to an underlying SQLite database table.

- In *Introduction to Android Application Development: Android Essentials, Fourth Edition*, you learned about the UserDictionary content provider (android.provider .UserDictionary), which can be used to add words to the user's custom dictionary of commonly used words.

Using the Clipboard Framework

On Android devices running Android 3.0 and higher (API Level 11), developers can access the clipboard to perform copy and paste actions. Previous to this, the clipboard had no public API. To leverage the clipboard in your applications, you need to use the clipboard framework of the Android SDK. You can copy and paste different data structures—everything from text to references to files to application shortcuts—as Intent objects. The clipboard holds only a single set of clipped data at a time, and the clipboard is shared across all applications, so you can easily copy and paste content between applications.

Copying Data to the System Clipboard

To save data to the system clipboard, call getSystemService() and request the clipboard Service's ClipboardManager (android.content.ClipboardManager). Then, create a ClipData (android.content.ClipData) object and populate it with the data you want to save to the clipboard. Finally, commit the clip using the ClipboardManager class method setPrimaryClip().

Pasting Data from the System Clipboard

To retrieve data from the system clipboard, call getSystemService() and request the clipboard Service's ClipboardManager (android.content.ClipboardManager). You can determine whether the clipboard contains data by using the hasPrimaryClip() method. After you have determined whether there is valid data in the system clipboard, you can inspect its description and type and ultimately retrieve the ClipData object using the getPrimaryClip() method.

Handling User Events

You've seen how to do basic event handling in some of the previous control examples. For instance, you know how to handle when a user clicks on a button. There are a number of other events generated by various actions the user might take. This section briefly introduces you to some of these events. First, though, we need to talk about the input states in Android.

Listening for Touch Mode Changes

The Android screen can be in one of two states. The state determines how the focus on View controls is handled. When touch mode is on, typically only objects such as EditText get focus when selected. Other objects, because they can be selected directly by the user tapping on the screen, won't take focus but instead trigger their action, if any. When not in touch mode, however, the user can change focus among even more object types. These include buttons and other views that normally need only a click to trigger their action.

Knowing what mode the screen is in is useful if you want to handle certain events. If, for instance, your application relies on the focus or lack of focus on a particular control, your application might need to know whether the device is in touch mode because the focus behavior is likely different.

Your application can register to find out when the touch mode changes by using the addOnTouchModeChangeListener() method in the android.view.ViewTree Observer class. Your application needs to implement the ViewTreeObserver .OnTouchModeChangeListener class to listen for these events. Here is a sample implementation:

```
View all = findViewById(R.id.events_screen);
ViewTreeObserver vto = all.getViewTreeObserver();
vto.addOnTouchModeChangeListener(
    new ViewTreeObserver.OnTouchModeChangeListener() {
        public void onTouchModeChanged(
            boolean isInTouchMode) {
            events.setText("Touch mode: " + isInTouchMode);
        }
});
```

In this example, the top-level View in the layout is retrieved. A ViewTreeObserver listens to a View and all its child View objects. Using the top-level View of the layout means the ViewTreeObserver listens to events in the entire layout. An implementation of the onTouchModeChanged() method provides the ViewTreeObserver with a method to call when the touch mode changes. It merely passes in which mode the View is now in.

In this example, the mode is written to a TextView named events. We use this same TextView in further event handling examples to show on the screen which events our application has been told about. The ViewTreeObserver can enable applications to listen to a few other events on an entire screen.

By running this sample code, we can demonstrate the touch mode changing to true immediately when the user taps on the touchscreen. Conversely, when the user chooses to use any other input method, the application reports that touch mode is false immediately after the input event, such as a key being pressed.

Listening for Events on the Entire Screen

You saw in the last section how your application can watch for changes to the touch mode state of the screen using the ViewTreeObserver class. The ViewTreeObserver also provides other events that can be watched for on a full screen or an entire View and all of its children. Some of these are:

- Draw or PreDraw: Get notified before the View and its children are drawn.
- GlobalLayout: Get notified when the layout of the View and its children might change, including visibility changes.
- GlobalFocusChange: Get notified when the focus in the View and its children changes.

Your application might want to perform some actions before the screen is drawn. You can do this by calling the method addOnPreDrawListener() with an implementation of the ViewTreeObserver.OnPreDrawListener class interface or by calling the method `addOnDrawListener()` with an implementation of the `ViewTreeObserver.OnDraw Listener` class interface.

Similarly, your application can find out when the layout or visibility of a `View` has changed. This might be useful if your application dynamically changes the display contents of a `View` and you want to check to see whether a `View` still fits on the screen. Your application needs to provide an implementation of the `ViewTreeObserver.OnGlobal LayoutListener` class interface to the `addGlobalLayoutListener()` method of the `ViewTreeObserver` object.

Finally, your application can register to find out when the focus changes between a `View` control and any of its child `View` controls. Your application might want to do this to monitor how a user moves about on the screen. When in touch mode, though, there might be fewer focus changes than when touch mode is not set. In this case, your application needs to provide an implementation of the `ViewTreeObserver.OnGlobalFocus ChangeListener` class interface to the `addGlobalFocusChangeListener()` method. Here is a sample implementation of this:

```
vto.addOnGlobalFocusChangeListener(new
    ViewTreeObserver.OnGlobalFocusChangeListener() {
        public void onGlobalFocusChanged(
        View oldFocus, View newFocus) {
            if (oldFocus != null && newFocus != null) {
                events.setText("Focus \nfrom: " +
                    oldFocus.toString() + " \nto: " +
                    newFocus.toString());
            }
        }
    });
```

This example uses the same `ViewTreeObserver`, `vto`, and `TextView` events as the previous example. It shows that both the currently focused `View` object and the previously focused `View` object are passed to the listener as method parameters. From here, your application can perform needed actions.

If your application merely wants to check values after the user has modified a particular `View` object, though, you might need to register to listen for focus changes only of that particular `View` object. This is discussed later in this chapter.

Listening for Long Clicks

You can add a context menu or a contextual action bar to a `View` that is activated when the user performs a long click on that `View`. A long click is typically when a user presses on the touchscreen and holds a finger there until an action is performed. However, a long press event can also be triggered if the user navigates there with a non-touch method, such as via a keyboard or a button. This action is also often called a press-and-hold action.

Although the context menu is a great typical use case for the long-click event, you can listen for the long-click event and perform any action you want. However, this is the same event that triggers the context menu. If you've already added a context menu to a `View`, you might not want to listen for the long-click event as other actions or side effects might confuse the user or even prevent the context menu or contextual action bar from showing. As always with good user interface design, try to be consistent for usability's sake.

Tip

Usually a long click is an alternative action to a standard click. If a left-click on a computer is the standard click, a long click can be compared to a right-click.

Your application can listen to the long-click event on any `View`. The following example demonstrates how to listen for a long-click event on a `Button` control:

```
Button long_press = (Button) findViewById(R.id.long_press);
long_press.setOnLongClickListener(new View.OnLongClickListener() {
    public boolean onLongClick(View v) {
        events.setText("Long click: " + v.toString());
        return true;
    }
});
```

First, the `Button` object is requested by providing its identifier. Then the `setOnLong ClickListener()` method is called with our implementation of the `View.OnLong ClickListener` class interface. The `View` on which the user long-clicked is passed in to the `onLongClick()` event handler. Here again we use the same `TextView` as before to display text saying that a long click occurred.

Listening for Focus Changes

We have already discussed listening for focus changes on an entire screen. All `View` objects, though, can also trigger a call to listeners when their particular focus state changes. You do this by providing an implementation of the `View.OnFocusChange Listener` class to the `setOnFocusChangeListener()` method. The following is an example of how to listen for focus change events with an `EditText` control:

```
TextView focus = (TextView) findViewById(R.id.text_focus_change);
focus.setOnFocusChangeListener(new View.OnFocusChangeListener() {
    public void onFocusChange(View v, boolean hasFocus) {
        if (hasFocus) {
            if (mSaveText != null) {
                ((TextView)v).setText(mSaveText);
            }
        } else {
            mSaveText = ((TextView)v).getText().toString();
            ((TextView)v).setText("");
        }
    }
}
```

In this implementation, we also use a private member variable of type `String` for mSaveText. After retrieving the `EditText` control as a `TextView`, we do one of two things. If the user moves focus away from the control, we store the text in mSaveText and set the text to empty. If the user changes focus to the control, though, we restore this text. This has the amusing effect of hiding the text the user entered when the control is not active. This can be useful on a form on which a user needs to make multiple, lengthy text entries but you want to provide an easy way for the user to see which one to edit. It is also useful for demonstrating a purpose for the focus listeners on a text entry. Other uses might include validating text a user enters after the user navigates away or prefilling the text entry the first time the user navigates to it with something else entered.

Working with Gestures

Android devices often rely on touchscreens for user input. Users are now quite comfortable using common finger gestures to operate their devices. Android applications can detect and react to one-finger (single-touch) and two-finger (multitouch) gestures. Users can also use gestures with the drag-and-drop framework to enable the arrangement of `View` controls on a device screen.

Note

Even early Android devices supported simple single-touch gestures. Support for multitouch gestures was added in the Android 2.2 SDK and is available only on devices with capacitive touchscreen hardware. Some capacitive hardware is capable of tracking up to ten different points at once.

One of the reasons that gestures can be a bit tricky is that a gesture can be made of multiple touch events or motions. Different sequences of motion add up to different gestures. For example, a fling gesture involves the user pressing a finger down on the screen, swiping across the screen, and lifting the finger up off the screen while the swipe is still in motion (that is, without slowing down to stop before lifting the finger). Each of these steps can trigger motion events to which applications can react.

Detecting User Motions within a `View`

By now you've come to understand that Android application user interfaces are built using different types of `View` controls. Developers can handle gestures much as they do click events within a `View` control using the `setOnClickListener()` and `setOnLong ClickListener()` methods. Instead, the `onTouchEvent()` callback method is used to detect that some motion has occurred within the `View` region.

The `onTouchEvent()` callback method has a single parameter, a `MotionEvent` object. The `MotionEvent` object contains all sorts of details about what kind of motion occurs in the `View`, enabling the developer to determine what sort of gesture is happening by collecting and analyzing many consecutive `MotionEvent` objects. You can use all of the `MotionEvent` data to recognize and detect every kind of gesture you can possibly imagine. Alternatively, you can use built-in gesture detectors provided in the Android SDK to detect common user motions in a consistent fashion. Android currently has two different classes that can detect navigational gestures:

- The `GestureDetector` class can be used to detect common single-touch gestures.
- The `ScaleGestureDetector` can be used to detect multitouch scale gestures.

It is likely that more gesture detectors will be added in future versions of the Android SDK. You can also implement your own gesture detectors to detect any gestures not supported by the built-in ones. For example, you might want to create a two-fingered rotate gesture to, say, rotate an image, or a three-fingered swipe gesture that brings up an options menu.

In addition to common navigational gestures, you can use the android.gesture package with the GestureOverlayView to recognize commandlike gestures. For instance, you can create an S-shaped gesture that brings up a search or a zigzag gesture that clears the screen on a drawing app. Tools are available for recording and creating libraries of this style of gesture. As it uses an overlay for detection, it isn't well suited for all types of applications. This package was introduced in API Level 4.

Warning

The type and sensitivity of the touchscreen can vary by device. Different devices can detect different numbers of touch points simultaneously, which affects the complexity of gestures you can support.

Handling Common Single-Touch Gestures

Introduced in API Level 1, the GestureDetector class can be used to detect gestures made by a single finger. Some common single-finger gestures supported by the GestureDetector class include:

- onDown: Called when the user first presses the touchscreen.
- onShowPress: Called after the user first presses the touchscreen but before lifting the finger or moving it around on the screen; used to visually or audibly indicate that the press has been detected.
- onSingleTapUp: Called when the user lifts up (using the up MotionEvent) from the touchscreen as part of a single-tap event.
- onSingleTapConfirmed: Called when a single-tap event occurs.
- onDoubleTap: Called when a double-tap event occurs.
- onDoubleTapEvent: Called when an event within a double-tap gesture occurs, including any down, move, or up MotionEvent.
- onLongPress: Similar to onSingleTapUp, but called if the user holds down a finger long enough to not be a standard click but also without any movement.
- onScroll: Called after the user presses and then moves a finger in a steady motion before lifting the finger. This is commonly called *dragging*.
- onFling: Called after the user presses and then moves a finger in an accelerating motion before lifting it. This is commonly called a *flick gesture* and usually results in some motion continuing after the user lifts the finger.

You can use the interfaces available with the `GestureDetector` class to listen for specific gestures such as single and double taps (see `GestureDetector.OnDouble TapListener`), as well as scrolls and flings (see the documentation for `Gesture Detector.OnGestureListener`). The scrolling gesture involves touching the screen and moving a finger around on it. The fling gesture, on the other hand, causes (though not automatically) the object to continue to move even after the finger has been lifted from the screen. This gives the user the impression of throwing or flicking the object around on the screen.

Tip

You can use the `GestureDetector.SimpleOnGestureListener` class to listen to any and all of the gestures recognized by the `GestureDetector`.

Let's look at a simple example. Let's assume you have a game screen that enables the user to perform gestures to interact with a graphic on the screen. We can create a custom `View` class called `GameAreaView` that can dictate how a bitmap graphic moves around within the game area based upon each gesture. The `GameAreaView` class can use the `onTouchEvent()` method to pass along `MotionEvent` objects to a `GestureDetector`. In this way, the `GameAreaView` can react to simple gestures, interpret them, and make the appropriate changes to the bitmap, including moving it from one location to another on the screen.

Tip

How the gestures are interpreted and what actions they cause are completely up to the developer. You can, for example, interpret a fling gesture and make the bitmap graphic disappear . . . but does that make sense? Not really. It's important to always make the gesture jibe well with the resulting operation in the application so that users are not confused. Users are now accustomed to specific screen behavior based on certain gestures, so it's best to use the expected convention, too.

In this case, the `GameAreaView` class interprets gestures as follows:

- A double-tap gesture causes the bitmap graphic to return to its initial position.
- A scroll gesture causes the bitmap graphic to "follow" the motion of the finger.
- A fling gesture causes the bitmap graphic to "fly" in the direction of the fling.

Tip

Many of the code examples provided in this section are taken from the SimpleGestures application. The source code for this application is provided for download on the book's website.

To make these gestures work, the `GameAreaView` class needs to include the appropriate gesture detector, which triggers any operations upon the bitmap graphic. Based upon the specific gestures detected, the `GameAreaView` class must perform all translation animations and other graphical operations applied to the bitmap. To wire up the

`GameAreaView` class for gesture support, we need to implement several important methods:

- The class constructor must initialize any gesture detectors and bitmap graphics.
- The `onTouchEvent()` method must be overridden to pass the `MotionEvent` data to the gesture detector for processing.
- The `onDraw()` method must be overridden to draw the bitmap graphic in the appropriate position at any time.
- Various methods are needed to perform the graphics operations required to make a bitmap move around on the screen, fly across the screen, and reset its location based upon the data provided by the specific gesture.

All these tasks are handled by our `GameAreaView` class definition:

```
public class GameAreaView extends View {
    private static final String DEBUG_TAG =
        "SimpleGestures->GameAreaView";
    private GestureDetector gestures;
    private Matrix translate;
    private Bitmap droid;
    private Matrix animateStart;
    private Interpolator animateInterpolator;
    private long startTime;
    private long endTime;
    private float totalAnimDx;
    private float totalAnimDy;

    public GameAreaView(Context context, int iGraphicResourceId) {
        super(context);
        translate = new Matrix();
        GestureListener listener = new GestureListener(this);
        gestures = new GestureDetector(context, listener, null, true);
        droid = BitmapFactory.decodeResource(getResources(),
            iGraphicResourceId);
    }

    @Override
    public boolean onTouchEvent(MotionEvent event) {
        boolean retVal = false;
        retVal = gestures.onTouchEvent(event);
        return retVal;
    }

    @Override
    protected void onDraw(Canvas canvas) {
        Log.v(DEBUG_TAG, "onDraw");
        canvas.drawBitmap(droid, translate, null);
    }
```

```java
public void onResetLocation() {
    translate.reset();
    invalidate();
}

public void onMove(float dx, float dy) {
    translate.postTranslate(dx, dy);
    invalidate();
}

public void onAnimateMove(float dx, float dy, long duration) {
    animateStart = new Matrix(translate);
    animateInterpolator = new OvershootInterpolator();
    startTime = android.os.SystemClock.elapsedRealtime();
    endTime = startTime + duration;
    totalAnimDx = dx;
    totalAnimDy = dy;
    post(new Runnable() {
        @Override
        public void run() {
            onAnimateStep();
        }
    });
}

private void onAnimateStep() {
    long curTime = android.os.SystemClock.elapsedRealtime();
    float percentTime = (float) (curTime - startTime) /
        (float) (endTime - startTime);
    float percentDistance = animateInterpolator
        .getInterpolation(percentTime);
    float curDx = percentDistance * totalAnimDx;
    float curDy = percentDistance * totalAnimDy;
    translate.set(animateStart);
    onMove(curDx, curDy);

    if (percentTime < 1.0f) {
        post(new Runnable() {
            @Override
            public void run() {
                onAnimateStep();
            }
        });
    }
}
}
```

As you can see, the GameAreaView class keeps track of where the bitmap graphic should be drawn at any time. The onTouchEvent() method is used to capture motion events and pass them along to a gesture detector whose GestureListener we must implement as well (more on this in a moment). Typically, each method of the GameAreaView applies some operation to the bitmap graphic and then calls the invalidate() method, forcing the View to be redrawn.

Now we turn our attention to the methods required to implement specific gestures:

- For double-tap gestures, we implement a method called onResetLocation() to draw the bitmap graphic in its original location.

- For scroll gestures, we implement a method called onMove() to draw the bitmap graphic in a new location. Note that scrolling can occur in any direction—it simply refers to a finger swipe on the screen.

- For fling gestures, things get a little tricky. To animate motion on the screen smoothly, we used a chain of asynchronous calls and a built-in Android interpolator to calculate the location in which to draw the graphic based upon how long it has been since the animation started. See the onAnimateMove() and onAnimate Step() methods for the full implementation of fling animation.

Now we need to implement our GestureListener class to interpret the appropriate gestures and call the GameAreaView methods we just implemented. Here's an implementation of the GestureListener class that our GameAreaView class can use:

```
private class GestureListener extends
    GestureDetector.SimpleOnGestureListener {

    GameAreaView view;

    public GestureListener(GameAreaView view) {
        this.view = view;
    }

    @Override
    public boolean onDown(MotionEvent e) {
        return true;
    }

    @Override
    public boolean onFling(MotionEvent e1, MotionEvent e2,
        final float velocityX, final float velocityY) {
        final float distanceTimeFactor = 0.4f;
        final float totalDx = (distanceTimeFactor * velocityX / 2);
        final float totalDy = (distanceTimeFactor * velocityY / 2);

        view.onAnimateMove(totalDx, totalDy,
            (long) (1000 * distanceTimeFactor));
        return true;
    }

    @Override
    public boolean onDoubleTap(MotionEvent e) {
        view.onResetLocation();
        return true;
    }
```

```
    @Override
    public boolean onScroll(MotionEvent e1, MotionEvent e2,
        float distanceX, float distanceY) {
        view.onMove(-distanceX, -distanceY);
        return true;
    }
}
```

Note that you must return `true` for any gesture or motion event that you want to detect. Therefore, you must return `true` in the `onDown()` method as it happens at the beginning of a scroll-type gesture. Most of the implementation of the `GestureListener` class methods involves our interpretation of the data for each gesture. For example:

- We react to double taps by resetting the bitmap to its original location using the `onResetLocation()` method of our `GameAreaView` class.

- We use the distance data provided in the `onScroll()` method to determine the direction to use in the movement to pass in to the `onMove()` method of the `GameAreaView` class.

- We use the velocity data provided in the `onFling()` method to determine the direction and speed to use in the movement animation of the bitmap. The `timeDistanceFactor` variable with a value of 0.4 is subjective; it gives the resulting slide-to-a-stop animation enough time to be visible but is short enough to be controllable and responsive. You can think of it as a high-friction surface. This information is used by the animation sequence implemented in the `onAnimateMove()` method of the `GameAreaView` class.

Now that we have implemented the `GameAreaView` class in its entirety, you can display it on a screen. For example, you might create an `Activity` that has a user interface with a `FrameLayout` control and add an instance of a `GameAreaView` using the `addView()` method. Figure 8.3 shows a gesture example of dragging a droid around a screen.

Tip

To support the broadest range of devices, we recommend supporting simple, one-fingered gestures and providing alternative navigational items for devices that don't support multitouch gestures. However, users are beginning to expect support for multitouch gestures now, so use them where you can and where they make sense. Resistive touchscreens remain uncommon, typically appearing only on lower-end devices.

Handling Common Multitouch Gestures

Introduced in API Level 8 (Android 2.2), the `ScaleGestureDetector` class can be used to detect two-fingered scale gestures. The scale gesture enables the user to move two

Figure 8.3 Using gestures to drag the droid around the screen.

fingers toward and away from each other. Moving the fingers apart is considered scaling up; moving the fingers together is considered scaling down. This is the "pinch-to-zoom" style often employed by map and photo applications.

Tip

You can use the `ScaleGestureDetector.SimpleOnScaleGestureListener` class to detect scale gestures detected by the `ScaleGestureDetector`.

Let's look at another example. Again, we use the custom `View` class called `GameAreaView`, but this time we handle the multitouch scale event. In this way, the `GameAreaView` can react to scale gestures, interpret them, and make the appropriate changes to the bitmap, including growing or shrinking it on the screen.

Tip

Many of the code examples provided in this section are taken from the SimpleMulti TouchGesture application. The source code for this application is provided for download on the book's website.

To handle scale gestures, the GameAreaView class needs to include the appropriate gesture detector, a ScaleGestureDetector. The GameAreaView class needs to be wired up for scale gesture support similarly to the single-touch gestures implemented earlier, including initializing the gesture detector in the class constructor, overriding the onTouchEvent() method to pass the MotionEvent objects to the gesture detector, and overriding the onDraw() method to draw the View appropriately as necessary. We also need to update the GameAreaView class to keep track of the bitmap graphic size (using a Matrix) and provide a helper method for growing or shrinking the graphic. Here is the new implementation of the GameAreaView class with scale gesture support:

```
public class GameAreaView extends View {
    private ScaleGestureDetector multiGestures;
    private Matrix scale;
    private Bitmap droid;

    public GameAreaView(Context context, int iGraphicResourceId) {
        super(context);
        scale = new Matrix();
        GestureListener listener = new GestureListener(this);
        multiGestures = new ScaleGestureDetector(context, listener);
        droid = BitmapFactory.decodeResource(getResources(),
            iGraphicResourceId);
    }

    public void onScale(float factor) {
        scale.preScale(factor, factor);
        invalidate();
    }

    @Override
    protected void onDraw(Canvas canvas) {
        Matrix transform = new Matrix(scale);
        float width = droid.getWidth() / 2;
        float height = droid.getHeight() / 2;
        transform.postTranslate(-width, -height);
        transform.postConcat(scale);
        transform.postTranslate(width, height);
        canvas.drawBitmap(droid, transform, null);
    }

    @Override
    public boolean onTouchEvent(MotionEvent event) {
        boolean retVal = false;
        retVal = multiGestures.onTouchEvent(event);
        return retVal;
    }
}
```

As you can see, the GameAreaView class keeps track of what size the bitmap should be at any time using the Matrix variable called scale. The onTouchEvent() method is used to capture motion events and pass them along to a ScaleGestureDetector gesture detector. As before, the onScale() helper method of the GameAreaView applies some scaling to the bitmap graphic and then calls the invalidate() method, forcing the View to be redrawn.

Now let's take a look at the `GestureListener` class implementation necessary to interpret the scale gestures and call the `GameAreaView` methods we just implemented. Here's the implementation of the `GestureListener` class:

```
private class GestureListener implements
    ScaleGestureDetector.OnScaleGestureListener {

    GameAreaView view;

    public GestureListener(GameAreaView view) {
        this.view = view;
    }

    @Override
    public boolean onScale(ScaleGestureDetector detector) {
        float scale = detector.getScaleFactor();
        view.onScale(scale);
        return true;
    }

    @Override
    public boolean onScaleBegin(ScaleGestureDetector detector) {
        return true;
    }

    @Override
    public void onScaleEnd(ScaleGestureDetector detector) {
    }
}
```

Remember that you must return `true` for any gesture or motion event that you want to detect. Therefore, you must return `true` in the `onScaleBegin()` method as it happens at the beginning of a scale-type gesture. Most of the implementation of the `GestureListener` methods involves our interpretation of the data for the scale gesture. Specifically, we use the scale factor (provided by the `getScaleFactor()` method) to calculate whether we should shrink or grow the bitmap graphic, and by how much. We pass this information to the `onScale()` helper method we just implemented in the `Game AreaView` class.

Now, if you were to use the `GameAreaView` class in your application, scale gestures might look something like Figure 8.4.

Note

The Android emulator does not currently support multitouch input, although there is experimental support in the works. You will have to run and test multitouch input such as the scale gesture using a device running Android 2.2 or higher.

Figure 8.4   The result of scale-down (left) and scale-up (right) gestures.

Making Gestures Look Natural

Gestures can enhance your Android application user interfaces in new, interesting, and intuitive ways. Closely mapping the operations being performed on the screen to the user's finger motion makes a gesture feel natural and intuitive. Making application operations look natural requires some experimentation on the part of the developer. Keep in mind that devices vary in processing power, and this might be a factor in making things seem natural. Minimal processing, even on fast devices, will help keep gestures and the reaction to them smooth and responsive, and thus natural-feeling.

Using the Drag-and-Drop Framework

On Android devices running Android 3.0 and higher (API Level 11), developers can access the drag-and-drop framework to perform drag-and-drop actions. You can drag and drop View controls within the scope of a screen or Activity class.

The drag-and-drop process basically works like this:

- The user triggers a drag operation. How this is done depends on the application, but long clicks are a reasonable option for selecting a View for a drag under the appropriate conditions.

- The data for the selected View control is packaged in a ClipData object (also used by the clipboard framework), and the View.DragShadowBuilder class is used to generate a little visual representation of the item being dragged. For example, if you were dragging a filename into a directory bucket, you might include a little icon of a file.

- You call the startDrag() method on the View control to be dragged. This starts a drag event. The system signals a drag event with ACTION_DRAG_STARTED, which listeners can catch.

- There are a number of events that occur during a drag that your application can react to. The ACTION_DRAG_ENTERED event can be used to adjust the screen controls to highlight other View controls that the dragged View control might want to be dragged over to. The ACTION_DRAG_LOCATION event can be used to determine where the dragged View is on the screen. The ACTION_DRAG_EXITED event can be used to reset any screen controls that were adjusted in the ACTION_DRAG_ENTERED event.

- When the user ends the drag operation by releasing the shadow item over a specific target View on the screen, the system signals a drop event with ACTION_DROP, which listeners can catch. Any data can be retrieved using the getClipData() method.

For more information about the drag-and-drop framework, see the Android SDK documentation. There you can also find a great example of using the drag-and-drop framework called DragAndDropDemo.java.

Handling Screen Orientation Changes

Android devices have both landscape and portrait modes and can seamlessly transition between these orientations. The Android operating system automatically handles these changes for your application, if you so choose. You can also provide alternative resources, such as different layouts, for portrait and landscape modes. Also, you can directly access device sensors such as the accelerometer, which we talk about in Chapter 15, "Accessing Android's Hardware Sensors," to capture device orientation along three axes.

However, if you want to listen for simple screen orientation changes programmatically and have your application react to them, you can use the OrientationEventListener class to do this within your Activity.

Tip

Many of the code examples provided in this section are taken from the SimpleOrientation application. The source code for this application is provided for download on the book's website.

Warning

Orientation changes are best tested on real devices, not with the emulator.

Implementing orientation event handling in your Activity is simple. Simply instantiate an OrientationEventListener and provide its implementation. For example, the following Activity class called SimpleOrientationActivity logs orientation information to LogCat:

```
public class SimpleOrientationActivity extends Activity {
    OrientationEventListener mOrientationListener;

    @Override
    public void onCreate(Bundle savedInstanceState) {
        super.onCreate(savedInstanceState);
        setContentView(R.layout.main);

        mOrientationListener = new OrientationEventListener(this,
            SensorManager.SENSOR_DELAY_NORMAL) {

            @Override
            public void onOrientationChanged(int orientation) {
                Log.v(DEBUG_TAG,
                    "Orientation changed to " + orientation);
            }
        };

        if (mOrientationListener.canDetectOrientation() == true) {
            Log.v(DEBUG_TAG, "Can detect orientation");
            mOrientationListener.enable();
        } else {
            Log.v(DEBUG_TAG, "Cannot detect orientation");
            mOrientationListener.disable();
        }
    }

    @Override
    protected void onDestroy() {
        super.onDestroy();
        mOrientationListener.disable();
    }
}
```

You can set the rate to check for orientation changes to a variety of different values. There are other rate values appropriate for game use and other purposes. The default rate,

SENSOR_DELAY_NORMAL, is most appropriate for simple orientation changes. Other values, such as SENSOR_DELAY_UI and SENSOR_DELAY_GAME, might make sense for your application.

After you have a valid OrientationEventListener object, you can check if it can detect orientation changes using the canDetectOrientation() method, and enable and disable the listener using its enable() and disable() methods.

The OrientationEventListener has a single callback method, which enables you to listen for orientation transitions, the onOrientationChanged() method. This method has a single parameter, an integer. This integer normally represents the device tilt as a number between 0 and 359:

- A result of ORIENTATION_UNKNOWN (-1) means the device is flat (perhaps on a table) and the orientation is unknown.
- A result of 0 means the device is in its "normal" orientation, with the top of the device facing in the up direction. ("Normal" is defined by the device manufacturer. You need to test on each device to find out for sure what "normal" means.)
- A result of 90 means the device is tilted 90 degrees, with the left side of the device facing in the up direction.
- A result of 180 means the device is tilted 180 degrees, with the bottom side of the device facing in the up direction (upside down).
- A result of 270 means the device is tilted 270 degrees, with the right side of the device facing in the up direction.

Figure 8.5 shows an example of how the device orientation might read when the device is tilted to the right by 91 degrees.

Figure 8.5   Orientation of the device as reported by an
OrientationEventListener.

Summary

The Android platform enables great flexibility when it comes to ways that users can provide input to the device. Developers benefit from the fact that many powerful input methods are built into the View controls themselves, just waiting to be leveraged. Applications can take advantage of built-in input methods, such as software keyboards, or can customize them for special purposes. The Android framework also includes powerful features, such as a clipboard Service, gesture support, and a drag-and-drop framework, that your applications can use. It is important to support a variety of input methods in your applications, as users often have distinct preferences and not all methods are available on all devices.

Quiz Questions

1. True or false: IME stands for Input Method Editor.
2. Name the observer discussed in this chapter that listens to a View and all its child View objects.
3. What are two classes that are able to detect navigational gestures?
4. What method is called for a dragging single-finger gesture?
5. True or false: The MultiGestureDetector class can be used to detect two-fingered scale gestures.

Exercises

1. Use the online documentation to create a list of the core gestures supported by Android.
2. Modify the SimpleGestures application so that it makes use of the double-touch drag gesture design pattern.
3. Use the online documentation to create a list of the different inputType constants and their associated constant values.

References and More Information

Android API Guides: "Copy and Paste":
   http://d.android.com/guide/topics/text/copy-paste.html
Android SDK Reference regarding the ClipboardManager:
   http://d.android.com/reference/android/content/ClipboardManager.html

Android SDK Reference regarding the `ClipData` class:
http://d.android.com/reference/android/content/ClipData.html
Android API Guides: "Drag and Drop":
http://d.android.com/guide/topics/ui/drag-drop.html
Android SDK Reference regarding the `android.gesture` package:
http://d.android.com/reference/android/gesture/package-summary.html
Android Design: "Gestures":
http://d.android.com/design/patterns/gestures.html

9

Designing Accessible Applications

Android devices are as varied as their users. As the platform has matured and grown, its audience has become more diverse. The Android SDK includes numerous features and services for the benefit of users with physical impairments. Those users without impairments can also benefit from improved accessibility features such as speech recognition and text-to-speech services, especially when they are not paying complete attention to the device (such as when driving). In this chapter, we explore some of the accessibility features of Android devices and discuss how to make your applications accessible to as many different kinds of users as possible.

Exploring the Accessibility Framework

Accessibility is a commonly overlooked aspect of application development but one that is becoming increasingly important as time goes on. Many of the newest Android devices are well suited for new audiences, and the addition of the Android Accessory Development Kit (ADK) for building hardware accessories makes the issue that much more relevant.

Perhaps it would surprise you to know that the same sort of technology that drives Apple's Siri speech-recognizing assistant has been available on the Android platform for quite some time, if developers want to leverage it. Because speech recognition and text-to-speech applications are all the rage and their technologies are often used for navigation applications (especially because many states have passed laws that make it illegal to drive while using a mobile device without hands-free operation), we look at these two technologies in a little more detail.

Android applications can leverage speech input and output. Speech input can be achieved using speech recognition services, and speech output can be achieved using text-to-speech services. Not all devices support these services. However, certain types of applications—most notably hands-free applications such as directional navigation—often benefit from the use of these types of input.

Some of the accessibility features available in the Android SDK include the following:

- The speech recognition framework.
- The text-to-speech (TTS) framework.
- The ability to create and extend accessibility applications in conjunction with the Android accessibility framework. See the following packages to get started writing accessibility applications: `android.accessibilityservice` and `android.view` `.accessibility`. There are also a number of accessibility applications, such as TalkBack, that ship with the platform. For more information, see the device settings under Settings, Accessibility.

There are a number of subtle things you can do to greatly improve how users with disabilities can navigate your applications. For example:

- You can enable haptic feedback (the vibration you feel when you press a button, rather like a rumble pack game controller) on any `View` object (API Level 3 and higher). See the `setHapticFeedbackEnabled()` method of the `View` class.
- You can specify rich descriptions of visual controls, such as providing a text description for an `ImageView` control. This can be performed on any `View` control (API Level 4 and higher) and makes audio-driven screen navigation much more effective. This feature is often helpful for the visually impaired. See the `setContent` `Description()` method of the `View` class.
- You can review and enforce the focus order of screen controls. You can finely control screen navigation and control focus, overriding default behavior as necessary. See the focus-oriented methods of the `View` class for details on how to explicitly set the focus order of controls on the screen.
- If you implement custom `View` controls, it is your responsibility to send appropriate events to the accessibility `Service`. To do this, your custom `View` control must implement the `AccessibilityEventSource` interface (`android.view` `.accessibility.AccessibilityEventSource`) and fire off `Accessibility` `Event` events (`android.view.accessibility.AccessibilityEvent`) that let accessibility tools know what your control has done.
- Assume that users may configure their devices for larger font sizes and similar settings, and do not design screens that are overly cluttered or "break" under these conditions.
- Support alternative input methods, such as directional pads and trackballs, and do not assume your users will rely solely on touchscreen navigation.

Warning

Many of the most powerful accessibility features were added in later versions of the Android SDK, so check the API level for a specific class or method before using it in your application.

Tip

The Android `lint` tool is used to detect common coding and configuration mistakes. It has a section for accessibility. Enabling this in your Android Link Preferences will help catch known accessibility issues. Currently, this will only detect missing `contentDescription` fields on `ImageView`s and, as of API Level 17, `labelFor` fields on `EditText` objects, but it may eventually detect more accessibility issues.

Leveraging Speech Recognition Services

Speech services are available in the Android SDK in the `android.speech` package. The underlying services that make these technologies work might vary from device to device; some services might require a network connection to function properly.

Let's begin with speech recognition. You can enhance an application with speech recognition support by using the speech recognition framework provided in the Android SDK. Speech recognition involves speaking into the device microphone and enabling the software to detect and interpret that speech and translate it into a string.

There are several different methods of leveraging speech recognition in your application. First, the default Android keyboard (available in API Level 7+, shown in Figure 9.1) and many third-party input methods have a microphone that can be used whenever the user is presented with an input opportunity, such as on an `EditText` field. Second, applications can start a built-in speech recognition activity that will return text results (API Level 3+). Finally, applications can directly leverage the `SpeechRecognizer` class (API Level 8+) to more closely control the recognition and results.

We demonstrate using the built-in recognition activity. This has some advantages. First, your application needs no permissions, such as record audio and network access. (Although it does currently require network access, it does not require the permission because it's a different application handling the request.) Second, it's simple to use for developers and familiar to users. However, the disadvantage is that you can't easily enable long-form dictation with it. For that, the `SpeechRecognizer` class should be used. That said, the default input method for `EditText` fields may already allow for long-form, such as the continuous voice type available in Android 4.0.

Tip

Many of the code examples provided in this section are taken from the SimpleSpeech application. The source code for this application is provided for download on the book's website.

Warning

Speech services are best tested on a real Android device, not with the emulator.

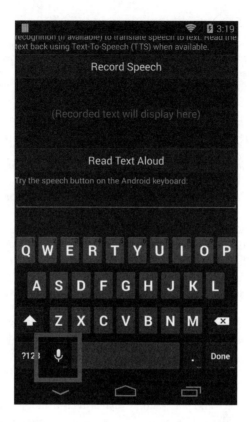

Figure 9.1   The Speech Recording option is available
on many software keyboards.

You can use the `android.speech.RecognizerIntent` intent to launch the built-in speech recorder. This launches the recorder (shown in Figure 9.2), allowing the user to record speech.

The speech is sent to an underlying recognition server for processing, so this feature is not practical for devices that don't have a reasonable network connection. You can then retrieve the results of the speech recognition processing and use them in your application. Note that you might receive multiple results for a given speech segment.

Note

Speech recognition technology is continually evolving and improving. Be sure to enunciate clearly when speaking to your device. Sometimes it might take several tries before the speech recognition engine interprets your speech correctly.

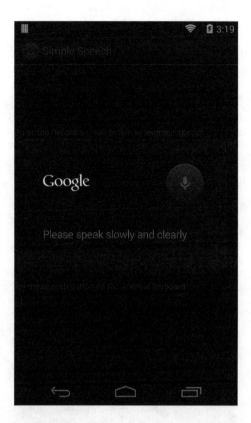

Figure 9.2   Recording speech with the `RecognizerIntent`.

The following code demonstrates how an application can be enabled to record speech using the `RecognizerIntent` intent:

```
public class SimpleSpeechActivity extends Activity
{
    private static final int VOICE_RECOGNITION_REQUEST = 1;

    @Override
    public void onCreate(Bundle savedInstanceState) {
        super.onCreate(savedInstanceState);
        setContentView(R.layout.main);
    }
    public void recordSpeech(View view) {
        Intent intent =
            new Intent(RecognizerIntent.ACTION_RECOGNIZE_SPEECH);
        intent.putExtra(RecognizerIntent.EXTRA_LANGUAGE_MODEL,
            RecognizerIntent.LANGUAGE_MODEL_FREE_FORM);
```

```
        intent.putExtra(RecognizerIntent.EXTRA_PROMPT,
            "Please speak slowly and clearly");
        startActivityForResult(intent, VOICE_RECOGNITION_REQUEST);
    }

    @Override
    protected void onActivityResult(int requestCode,
        int resultCode, Intent data) {
        if (requestCode == VOICE_RECOGNITION_REQUEST &&
            resultCode == RESULT_OK) {
            ArrayList<String> matches = data.getStringArrayListExtra(
                RecognizerIntent.EXTRA_RESULTS);
            TextView textSaid = (TextView) findViewById(R.id.TextSaid);
            textSaid.setText(matches.get(0));
        }
        super.onActivityResult(requestCode, resultCode, data);
    }
}
```

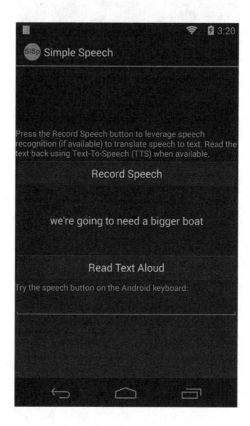

Figure 9.3   The text string resulting from the `RecognizerIntent`.

In this case, the `Intent` is initiated through the click of a `Button` control, which causes the `recordSpeech()` method to be called. The `RecognizerIntent` is configured as follows:

- The `Intent` action is set to `ACTION_RECOGNIZE_SPEECH` to prompt the user to speak and send the speech in for recognition.

- An `Intent` extra called `EXTRA_LANGUAGE_MODEL` is set to `LANGUAGE_MODEL_FREE_FORM` to simply perform standard speech recognition. There is also another language model especially for web searches called `LANGUAGE_MODEL_WEB_SEARCH`.

- An `Intent` extra called `EXTRA_PROMPT` is set to a string to display to the user during speech input.

After the `RecognizerIntent` object is configured, the `Intent` can be started using the `startActivityForResult()` method, and then the result is captured in the `onActivityResult()` method. The resulting text is then displayed in the `TextView` control called `TextSaid`. In this case, only the first result provided in the results is displayed to the user. So, for example, the user can press the button initiating the `record Speech()` method, say, "We're going to need a bigger boat," and that text is then displayed in the application's `TextView` control, as shown in Figure 9.3.

Leveraging Text-to-Speech Services

The Android platform includes a TTS engine (`android.speech.tts`) that enables devices to perform speech synthesis. You can use the TTS engine to have your applications "read" text to the user. You might have seen this feature used frequently with location-based service (LBS) applications that allow hands-free directions. Other applications use this feature for users who have reading or sight problems. The synthesized speech can be played immediately or saved to an audio file, which can be treated like any other audio file.

Note

To provide TTS services to users, an Android device must have both the TTS engine (available in Android SDK 1.6 and higher) and the appropriate language resource files. In some cases, the user must install the appropriate language resource files (assuming that there is space for them) from a remote location. The user can install the language resource files by going to Settings, Language & input, Text-to-Speech output, then choosing the Preferred Engine settings, then Install Voice Data. Unlike some other settings pages, this one doesn't have a specific `Intent` action defined under `android.provider.Settings`. You might also need to do this on your devices. Additionally, the application can verify that the data is installed correctly or trigger the installation if it's not.

For a simple example, let's have the device read back the text recognized in our ear-lier speech recognition example. First, we must modify the `Activity` to implement the `TextToSpeech.OnInitListener` interface, as follows:

```
public class SimpleSpeechActivity extends Activity
    implements TextToSpeech.OnInitListener {
    // class implementation
}
```

Next, you need to initialize TTS services in your `Activity`:

```
TextToSpeech mTts = new TextToSpeech(this, this);
```

Initializing the TTS engine happens asynchronously. The `TextToSpeech.OnInit Listener` interface has only one method, `onInit()`, that is called when the TTS engine has finished initializing successfully or unsuccessfully. Here is an implementation of the `onInit()` method:

```
@Override
public void onInit(int status) {
    Button readButton = (Button) findViewById(R.id.ButtonRead);
    if (status == TextToSpeech.SUCCESS) {
        int result = mTts.setLanguage(Locale.US);
        if (result == TextToSpeech.LANG_MISSING_DATA
            || result == TextToSpeech.LANG_NOT_SUPPORTED) {
            Log.e(DEBUG_TAG, "TTS Language not available.");
            readButton.setEnabled(false);
        } else {
            readButton.setEnabled(true);
        }
    } else {
        Log.e(DEBUG_TAG, "Could not initialize TTS Engine.");
        readButton.setEnabled(false);
    }
}
```

We use the `onInit()` method to check the status of the TTS engine. If it is initial-ized successfully, the `Button` control called `readButton` is enabled; otherwise, it is dis-abled. The `onInit()` method is also the appropriate place to configure the TTS engine. For example, you should set the language used by the engine using the `setLanguage()` method. In this case, the language is set to American English. The voice used by the TTS engine uses American pronunciation.

Note

The Android TTS engine supports a variety of languages, including English (in American or British accents), French, German, Italian, Korean, and Spanish. You can just as easily enable British English pronunciation using the following language setting in the `onInit()` method implementation instead:

```
int result = mTts.setLanguage(Locale.UK);
```

We amused ourselves trying to come up with phrases that illustrate how the American and British English TTS services differ. The best phrase we came up with was: *"We adjusted our schedule to search for a vase of herbs in our garage."* We often had "our garage" come out as "nerd haha."

Finally, you are ready to actually convert some text into speech. In this case, we grab the text string currently stored in the `TextView` control (where we set using speech recognition in the previous section) and pass it to TTS using the `speak()` method:

```
public void readText(View view) {
    TextView textSaid = (TextView) findViewById(R.id.TextSaid);
    mTts.speak((String) textSaid.getText(), TextToSpeech.QUEUE_FLUSH, null);
}
```

The `speak()` method takes three parameters: the string of text to say, the queuing strategy, and the speech parameters. The queuing strategy can either add some text to speak to the queue or flush the queue—in this case, we use the `QUEUE_FLUSH` strategy, so it is the only speech spoken. No special speech parameters are set, so we simply pass in `null` for the third parameter. Finally, when you are done with the `TextToSpeech` engine (such as in your `Activity` class's `onDestroy()` method), make sure to release its resources using the `shutdown()` method:

```
mTts.shutdown();
```

Now, if you wire up a `Button` control to call the `readText()` method when clicked, you have a complete implementation of TTS. When combined with the speech recognition example discussed earlier, you can develop an application that can record a user's speech, translate it into a string, display that string on the screen, and then read that string back to the user. In fact, that is exactly what the sample project called SimpleSpeech does.

Testing Application Accessibility

To prevent your application from suffering from unforeseen accessibility issues, it is important to understand what types of testing goals you should aim to achieve, what tests are required at a minimum, and what the recommended forms of testing are, among other factors.

There are two goals you should keep in mind when testing for accessibility. The first testing goal should be to allow your application to function without being assisted by sight. The second goal should be that directional controls provide an easy way to navigate through the application while responding appropriately to varying abilities of different users.

As with any other aspect of application development, accessibility needs to be taken into consideration and your application needs to be tested to ensure that it meets a minimum of accessibility needs. Make sure to incorporate accessibility testing into your application design and development workflow.

Summary

The Android platform includes extensive accessibility features, including speech recognition, text-to-speech support, and many subtle accessibility features peppered throughout the user interface classes of the Android SDK. All Android applications should be reviewed for basic accessibility features, such as providing text labels on graphical controls to accommodate eyes-free app navigation. Other applications might benefit from more comprehensive accessibility controls.

Give some thought to providing accessibility features, such as View metadata, in your applications. There's no excuse for not doing so. Your users will appreciate these small details, which make all the difference in terms of whether or not certain users can use your application at all. Also, make sure your quality assurance team verifies accessibility features as part of their testing process.

Quiz Questions

1. True or false: The Android SpeechRecognition class allows you to more closely control the recognition and results of speech services.

2. What Intent is used to launch the built-in speech recorder?

3. What is the Intent extra language model used for web searches?

4. True or false: The Read-Out-Loud speech synthesis engine allows your applications to "read" text to the user.

5. What method should you call on a TextToSpeech object to release its resources?

Exercises

1. Use the Android documentation to compile a checklist of design accessibility guidelines.

2. Use the Android documentation to compile a checklist of developer accessibility requirements, recommendations, and special cases and considerations.

3. Create an application that makes use of an accessibility service.

References and More Information

Android API Guides: "Accessibility":
   http://d.android.com/guide/topics/ui/accessibility/index.html
Android Design: "Accessibility":
   http://d.android.com/design/patterns/accessibility.html
Android Training: "Implementing Accessibility":
   http://d.android.com/training/accessibility/index.html
Android Tools: "Accessibility Testing Checklist":
   http://d.android.com/tools/testing/testing_accessibility.html
The Eyes-Free project:
   http://code.google.com/p/eyes-free/
YouTube Google Developers Channel: "Google I/O 2013—Enabling Blind and Low-Vision Accessibility on Android":
   http://www.youtube.com/watch?v=ld7kZRpMGb8

YouTube Google Developers Channel: "Google I/O 2011—Leveraging Android Accessibility APIs to Create an Accessible Experience":
http://www.youtube.com/watch?v=BPXqsPeCneA

Android SDK Reference documentation regarding the `android.speech.tts` package:
http://d.android.com/reference/android/speech/tts/package-summary.html

Android SDK Reference documentation regarding the `android.speech` package:
http://d.android.com/reference/android/speech/package-summary.html

10

Development Best Practices for Tablets, TVs, and Wearables

The Android platform may have started as a smartphone platform, but it has quickly moved into other device form factors. Android tablets have been especially popular. For TV, Google released Google TV. Most recently, the Android Wear SDK, released as a developer preview, will allow Android to work on smaller wearables.

Google has also released its design and development guidelines for these different types of devices, focused on maximizing where the devices are similar and handling the differences as necessary. In this chapter, we talk about some of the best practices to use when developing for different types of devices such as tablets, TVs, and wearables.

Understanding Device Diversity

Many application developers want to publish their applications to as many users (and therefore devices) as possible. This was relatively straightforward when Android was almost exclusively a smartphone platform. Developers could assume that the device screen size was within a certain reasonably small range. They could assume that the devices had telephony features, a camera, a numeric keypad, and the like.

These days, now that the Android platform has made its way onto tablets, TVs, toasters, e-book readers, net books, watches, and even car rearview mirrors (no joke: *http://www.autoblog.com/2012/01/19/android-integration-comes-to-your-cars-mirror-w-video/*), application developers cannot make these assumptions, which brings us to our first recommendation.

Don't Make Assumptions about Device Characteristics

Don't make assumptions about the device your application runs on, because tomorrow (or the day after) there will be yet another new type of Android device that breaks your assumptions. Instead, ensure that your application runs smoothly by configuring your application's Android manifest file appropriately to reflect what your application does and does not need to run correctly. Does it require a certain version of the Android SDK? If so, specify it. Does the application require a camera or telephony features? Declare those features using the `<uses-feature>` tag. Do you want your application to display correctly on a variety of device screens, whether they are large or small, portrait or landscape, high-definition, or otherwise? Start by using flexible user interface design that can attempt to smooth over and accommodate the differences among devices.

Designing Flexible User Interfaces

Regardless of what devices your application targets, there's no substitute for good application design. In many ways, all Android devices are created equal—they use the same operating system, the same SDKs, the same platform targets, the same tools for development. Designing for all device sizes, shapes, and form factors enables your application to look, behave, and run smoothly across the widest range of devices, regardless of type. Here are some things to consider with any Android project:

- Use flexible layout designs and controls such as `RelativeLayout`.
- Use dimension values such as `dp` instead of `px` to enable better scaling and support of multiple screen attributes with less work.
- Use scale values such as `sp` instead of `pt` to enable better scaling and support of text with less work.
- Make your graphics stretchable using graphic formats (nine-patch, XML-defined drawables) where possible.
- Provide alternative resources for various screen sizes and densities.
- Don't limit alternative resources to just images and layouts. Styles and values also make great alternative resources; they can sometimes be effective enough to reduce the need for some layouts.
- Adjust your user interface when hardware features aren't available. For instance, instead of requiring a camera, make it optional and present that option only when the camera is available. If it's not available, present an option to pick an image from the gallery instead. Perhaps the user has a device with a camera that is syncing to the gallery on the device without the camera.
- Use a `Fragment`-based application design from the start, as this new technology is supported in both smartphones and tablets and makes for flexible screen workflows and more code reuse.

These guidelines are just a start; there are so many different ways to approach the various combinations, they actually warrant explanations in their own book. Just know that following these guidelines as a baseline enables your application to display and function well on a variety of different devices. However, when working with devices that are often substantially larger (or smaller) than smartphones, scaling gracefully is not usually enough; you need to provide alternative resources for different resolutions and orientations.

Attracting New Types of Users

When you add new types of devices, different types of users buy them. This expands the user base—a good thing for developers who make a living from downloads. The audience for smartphones is different from that for tablets, TVs, and wearables. Understanding these new audiences can have an impact on your application design and development process.

Tablets can be used by individuals with special needs who are incapable of using smaller smartphones. This is especially true of the visually impaired, but certainly not limited to this crowd. Leverage the accessibility APIs available in the Android SDK to make your application as accessible as possible to these audiences, regardless of your device targets. The same design principles hold true for another audience—very young users—who generally require larger button controls, high-contrast colorations, and other such design features. Televisions are used by the whole family, not just the tech-savvy users or those who can afford (or are old enough to have) smartphones. Wearables seem to be targeted at users who are on the cutting edge of technology.

Tablets aren't phones and can sometimes be purchased outright without a wireless data plan for use on Wi-Fi networks. Wearables aren't phones either and often may require a dedicated device such as a phone or a tablet to connect to. Both of these enable new classes of Android users—those who live outside the current wireless coverage maps of the world, and those who demand more from their primary devices with wearables.

Leveraging Alternative Resources

You can achieve a lot by simply using alternative resources. The Android SDK enables you to supply project resources such as graphics and layout designs for different target device characteristics such as screen sizes, resolutions, orientations, and other device features. Used well, each class of device can have its own distinct look and feel while the underlying code remains unchanged. For more information on alternative resources, see the Android API Guides at *http://d.android.com/guide/topics/resources/providing-resources .html#AlternativeResources*.

Using Screen Space Effectively on Big Landscape Screens

Most tablets and televisions have screens that are 7 inches or larger. In terms of resources, tablets are usually defined as having large or extra-large screens. A large screen is defined as 5 inches to around 7 inches, and extra-large as 7 to 10 inches. There is some overlap in the definition, and the one a device uses is manufacturer dependent. When using the resource qualifier, you're looking at the `large` and `xlarge` values. Although `xlarge` was introduced at API Level 9, it is quietly ignored on earlier devices.

Tablets are most frequently held and used in landscape mode, and televisions are exclusively used in landscape mode. Although supporting both orientations is ideal, if you're going to focus on only one orientation for tablets and televisions, we recommend landscape mode. Keep in mind that you can use alternative resources to design a land-scape layout that differs substantially from the portrait layout. You'll want to consider different layouts using the `port` and `land` qualifiers.

Just scaling graphics up for these big screens is often not enough. Take, for example, a smartphone layout that has four buttons across, sized so that even big fingers will have no trouble tapping them. Enlarge that to a 10-inch tablet screen—which might be over 8 inches wide—and you now have buttons on the order of 2 inches wide. That might work for a toddler-friendly interface, but to most people those big buttons will look silly—and on television interfaces without touchscreens, they are a complete waste of space. Reduce the size of the buttons and find something else useful to put in the newly gained space. Be aware that even though you may be gaining inches on the screen in these circumstances, you may not necessarily be gaining pixels.

Note

One kind of application that may pose special challenges when it comes to design is games. Today's games use a lot of custom user interfaces, are fully 3D, and naturally scale by virtue of their rendering systems. These apps can transition easily to tablets and other larger devices, but they are not immune to problems—especially when a game has been designed as a "handheld" game.

Let's look at a simple example. You've got a great game that is normally played while held in landscape mode with side thumb controls. On a typical Android smartphone, this generally means that players can reach most of the screen with their thumbs. However, on a tablet, your thumbs go only so far. Entire areas of the screen are unreachable using thumb controls; if the user is required to tap in the middle of the screen, the tablet cannot be "held" or "cradled" as easily either.

Developing Applications for Tablets

Some say that 2011 was the year of the tablet (see Figure 10.1), the year tablets went mainstream (the way was paved by the success of the iPad—thanks, Apple!). Samsung, HTC, Motorola, ASUS, and many others shipped some fantastic tablet devices in various sizes and orientations. Amazon shipped the Kindle Fire to great fanfare. The tablet poses challenges for Android developers who are creating apps, so let's look at what it means to design, develop, test, and publish Android applications for tablet devices.

- From a developer perspective, a tablet can be considered just another device, pro-vided you haven't made any unfortunate development assumptions.
- Tablets run different versions of the Android platform, as far back as Android 1.0, although official tablet support by Google did not occur until Android 3.0.
- Tablets are not smartphones. This means that if your applications include telephony features, you will have to provide graceful alternative features for devices without these features, or effectively exclude these devices through Android manifest file configuration.

Figure 10.1   Tablets everywhere! (Google image search result).

- Unlike smartphones, most tablets default to landscape, not portrait, mode. Tablet users are more likely to change orientations than smartphone users.

- Tablets tend to have fewer hardware sensors than high-end smartphones.

- Fragments help separate user interface functionality from application logic. Using the Fragment class from the start greatly simplifies any shuffling of the user interface later on, speeds up development of tablet-centric user interfaces, and makes your app ready for the Android devices of the future.

- Google Play has no specific way to target or disable publication to specific types of devices such as tablets. You can, of course, use market filters to restrict your application to users with devices of certain screen sizes, libraries, and other device features, but there is no tablet "flag," per se.

Note
We do not recommend naming your app for its device target (for example, "The ACME App for Tablets").

Developing Applications for TV

Android and TVs are becoming a natural fit. There are two ways Android works with TVs. The first is Android directly integrated on the TV; the second involves Android installed on a set-top box that is connected to a TV.

Figure 10.2   Google TV devices are often set-top boxes (pictured here)
or are integrated directly into the TV.

Working with Google TV

Google announced a new platform initiative in early 2010—Google TV. The vision: a highly interactive and connected television experience that leverages the Android platform. Google wasn't going to do it alone but planned to partner with some of the top manufacturers in the television and set-top-box business, including Sony (Figure 10.2), VIZIO, LG, Samsung, and others.

Just as smartphones put apps in your pocket, Google TV brings them to your living room. The sky is the limit when it comes to the types of apps and content you might want to provide to Google TV users. Let's talk for a moment about what types of applications are suitable.

Google TV Variations

With Google TV, you have the option of purchasing a complete package (TV screen and all) or a set-top box that works with existing HDTV systems. There are two ways to bring your applications to Google TV devices: Chrome web apps and native Android apps. The Google TV website lists all supported Google TV devices you can purchase at *http://www.google.com/tv/get.html*.

Suitability may be less of an issue for web-based applications. However, many Android applications rely upon hardware assumptions that are not applicable to Google TV users, including the existence of cameras, location-based services, sensors, telephony, and such. In terms of user interface design, you don't have to worry so much about state changes like orientation changes or frequent network drops because your user is always connected. Therefore, only certain classes of existing Android applications are appropriate for the Google TV platform. Only you, the developer, can determine whether your app is suitable. There's nothing stopping you from developing interesting apps that fuse the power of existing smartphones and tablets (that have cameras, hardware sensors, and such) with the power of Google TV.

Optimizing Web Applications for Google TV

Your existing website and web applications, including those using HTML5 and Flash, can target Google TV. At this time, Google TVs run Chrome and support Adobe Flash. Optimizing your websites for display on a high-definition television screen involves many commonsense tweaks. You'll hear a lot of Google TV developers talk about "the 10-foot experience." This simply acknowledges the fact that Google TV users sit at some distance from the screen, and developers need to adjust their application's user experience to suit this typical use case.

Screen designs should be simple and elegant, using extra-large, readable fonts and graphics. There's quite a bit more wide-screen real estate with which to work, but scrolling is less appealing, and navigation, typically by D-pad, should be simple and straightforward. Some color schemes need to be adjusted for the high contrast and saturation levels typical of televisions. Finally, you'll want to come up with a high-resolution favicon so that your website looks slick in the Chrome bookmarks and other references.

Tip

When it comes to Flash, you'll want to check out Adobe's recommendations for optimizing Flash apps for televisions here: *http://www.adobe.com/devnet/devices/articles/video_content_tv.html*.

Developing Native Android Applications for Google TV

Native Google TV apps are written using the Android SDK and can be published through Google Play. At this time, some Google TVs are running the Honeycomb SDK (Android 3.1 or Android 3.2) and must be developed using the latest Android tools and the Google TV Add-on from the Android SDK Manager. Newer-generation Google TVs running on the ARM platform are running the Jelly Bean SDK (Android 4.2.2).

Developing native applications for Google TV is basically like developing for a large tablet without a touchscreen, camera, and so on. Here are some suggestions for porting an Android app to Google TV:

- Set the appropriate manifest file settings to allow for, market filter for, and not accidentally exclude Google TV devices.

- Use appropriate alternative resources for large, high-definition television displays (at 10 feet).

- Avoid certain methods and API calls that assume telephony device features.

- Adjust the user interface controls to be large and readable for television viewing.

- Adjust layout navigation to support D-pad as the primary input method.

- Add handling for the media keys for play, pause, and so on.

- Consider fast ways to get out of long lists; don't make a user traverse a long list just to get to a button at the bottom of the screen.

- Avoid using methods and APIs that assume telephony device features and other features unsupported by Google TV, such as the Android NDK. For more information, see the Google TV documentation for feature support at *https://developers .google.com/tv/android/docs/gtv_android_features*.

Tip

Once you have installed the Google TV Add-on, you can use it to create compatible Android Virtual Devices (AVDs) to run in the Google TV emulator. Find out more in the "Google TV Emulation" documentation at *https://developers.google.com/tv/android/docs/gtv_ emulator*.

Developing Applications for Wearables

A newly released developer preview SDK for Android, called Android Wear, is available for wearables. With the advent of smart watches, Google realized the need to create APIs that are optimized for delivering application notifications to a small, wearable form factor, such as a watch, notifications that originate from a primary device, such as a smartphone. This type of small wearable is meant to provide a richer Android experience and is used for displaying the most useful application information to users when they need it most and when it is most relevant to them.

The Android Wear SDK includes notification API capabilities that you can take advantage of to present rich application information to users:

- You can display actions for users to take to respond to notifications.

- Images can provide context so users have a visual understanding of what your application's notification is presenting.

- Your application icon can present application identity to users so they can easily determine which application is presenting the notification.

- Since wearable screens are so small, you may need to bundle your notification using two or more pages, swipe-able from left to right and back, for easy access to further notification content.

- When your application presents more than one notification at a time to which a user hasn't responded, stack them so users know how many notifications they have pending.

- Allow users to respond to notifications with voice replies, enabling them to speak "canned responses" you present for them to choose from for easy replies.

The Android Wear API is a brand-new feature that your application can take advantage of to keep your users engaged with your application's content in a simple and easy-to-use interface. Keep in mind that this API is new and, like many new APIs in Android, is subject to change.

Note

To learn more about how to begin testing the Android Wear developer preview SDK, sign up for access and start reading through the Android Wear documentation here: *http://d.android.com/wear/preview/start.html*. Some good sample applications are bundled with the preview release that demonstrate the capabilities of Android Wear. You also need to download the Android Wear system image for emulating a wearable, but as we have recommended before, always test on real hardware. Expect various manufacturers to make a few devices available for purchase in the near future.

Summary

Tablets, TVs, and wearables that run mobile operating systems are an exciting and popular category of Android device. As you have learned, designing and developing for these new niche devices is fairly simple when you keep your assumptions about device characteristics to a minimum and specify which device features and permissions your application requires in the Android manifest file. With planning, careful use of resources, and good development techniques, supporting these exciting new devices need not be a trial.

Quiz Questions

1. True or false: Don't make assumptions about device characteristics when planning your application.
2. What are some items you should take into consideration for designing flexible user interfaces?
3. True or false: Tablets tend to have more hardware sensors than high-end smartphones.
4. What are the two ways to bring your applications to Google TV devices?
5. What should you do when you need to present more than one notification at a time to a user on a wearable?

Exercises

1. Use the Android documentation to determine the guidelines you should follow for optimizing the user experience on both tablets and handsets.
2. Use the Android documentation to determine the three minimum system requirements for developing Google TV applications.
3. Use the Android documentation to determine the helper class for creating wearable notifications.

References and More Information

Android API Guides: "Supporting Tablets and Handsets":
http://d.android.com/guide/practices/tablets-and-handsets.html
Google TV Developers website:
https://developers.google.com/tv/
Google TV Developer Guide:
https://developers.google.com/tv/web/
Google TV "Build an Android App":
https://developers.google.com/tv/android/
Android Wear: "Building Apps for Wearables":
http://developer.android.com/training/building-wearables.html

III

Leveraging Common Android APIs

11

Using Android
Networking APIs

Applications written with networking components are far more dynamic and content rich than those that are not. Applications leverage the network for a variety of reasons: to deliver fresh and updated content, to enable social networking features of an otherwise standalone application, to offload heavy processing to high-powered servers, and to enable data storage beyond what the user can achieve on the device.

Those accustomed to Java networking will find the java.net package familiar. There are also some helpful Android utility classes for various types of network operations and protocols. This chapter focuses on Hypertext Transfer Protocol (HTTP), the most common protocol for networked mobile applications.

Understanding Mobile Networking Fundamentals

Networking on the Android platform is standardized, using a combination of powerful yet familiar technologies and libraries such as java.net. Network implementation is generally straightforward, but mobile application developers need to plan for less stable connectivity than one might expect in a home or office network setting—connectivity depends on the location of the users and their devices. Users demand stable, responsive applications. This means that you must take extra care when designing network-enabled applications. Luckily, the Android SDK provides a number of tools and classes for ensuring just that.

Warning

Recall that developers must agree to a number of network best practices as part of the Android SDK License Agreement. If you plan to use network support in your application, you might want to review these contractual points to ensure that your application complies with the agreement.

Understanding `StrictMode` with Networking

As discussed in Chapter 1, "Threading and Asynchronous Processing," `StrictMode` is a method that developers can use to detect operations performed on the main thread that should not be there. API Level 11 expanded upon `StrictMode` in ways that impact networking code. By default, if you perform network operations on the main thread, your application throws an exception, specifically `android.os.NetworkOnMainThread Exception`. The way to avoid this is to use proper coding techniques and put all networking operations on a thread other than the main thread. We show you how later in this chapter, or you can review Chapter 1 for the basics.

If you're not writing a production application and want to run some quick network code without wiring up a full thread, you can disable the crashing and simply flash the screen instead (on API Level 11) or log the mistakes. You can also call the `permitAll()` method to skip `StrictMode` entirely. This is not recommended for production applications.

Accessing the Internet (HTTP)

The most common way to transfer data to and from the network is to use HTTP. You can use HTTP to encapsulate almost any type of data and to secure the data with Secure Sockets Layer (SSL), which can be important when you transmit data that falls under privacy requirements. Also, most common ports used by HTTP are typically open from the device networks.

Tip

Many of the code examples provided in this chapter are taken from the SimpleNetworking application. The source code for this application is provided for download on the book's website.

Reading Data from the Web

Reading data from the Web can be simple. For example, if all you need to do is read some data from a website and you have the web address of that data, you can leverage the URL class (available as part of the `java.net` package) to read a fixed amount of text from a file on a web server, like this:

```
import java.io.InputStream;
import java.net.URL;

// ...

URL text = new URL("http://api.flickr.com/services/feeds/photos_public.gne" +
                   "?id=26648248@N04&lang=en-us&format=atom");

InputStream isText = text.openStream();
byte[] bText = new byte[250];
int readSize = isText.read(bText);
Log.i("Net", "readSize = " + readSize);
```

```
Log.i("Net", "bText = "+ new String(bText));
isText.close();
```

First, a new URL object is created with the URL to the data we want to read. A stream is then opened to the URL resource. From there, we read the data and close the InputStream. Reading data from a server can be that simple.

> **Note**
>
> As we state in the book's introduction, exception handling has been stripped from book code examples for readability. However, when it comes to networking code, you often need to add this handling for the code examples to compile. See the sample code provided on the book's website for examples of how to implement exception handling properly.

However, remember that because we work with a network resource, errors can be more common. Our device might not have network coverage; the server might be down for maintenance or disappear entirely; the URL might be invalid; and network users might experience long waits and time-outs.

This method might work in some instances—for example, when your application has lightweight, noncritical network features—but it's not particularly elegant. In many cases, you might want to know more about the data before reading from it from the URL. For instance, you might want to know how big it is.

Finally, for networking to work in any Android application, permission is required. Your application needs to have the following statement in its AndroidManifest.xml file:

```
<uses-permission android:name="android.permission.INTERNET"/>
```

Using HttpURLConnection

We can use the HttpURLConnection object to do a little reconnaissance on our URL before we transfer too much data. HttpURLConnection retrieves some information about the resource referenced by the URL object, including HTTP status and header information.

Some of the information you can retrieve from the HttpURLConnection includes the length of the content, content type, and date-time information so that you can check to see whether the data changed since the last time you accessed the URL.

Here is a short example of how to use HttpURLConnection to query the same URL previously used:

```
import java.io.InputStream;
import java.net.HttpURLConnection;
import java.net.URL;

// ...

URL text = new URL("http://api.flickr.com/services/feeds/photos_public.gne" +
                "?id=26648248@N04&lang=en-us&format=atom");

HttpURLConnection http = (HttpURLConnection) text.openConnection();
Log.i("Net", "length = " + http.getContentLength());
```

```
Log.i("Net", "respCode = " + http.getResponseCode());
Log.i("Net", "contentType = "+ http.getContentType());
Log.i("Net", "content = " + http.getContent());
```

The log lines demonstrate a few useful methods with the HttpURLConnection class. If the URL content is deemed appropriate, you can then call http.getInputStream() to get the same InputStream object as before. From there, reading from the network resource is the same, but more is known about the resource.

Parsing XML from the Network

A large portion of data transmitted among network resources is stored in a structured fashion in XML. In particular, Rich Site Summary (RSS) feeds are provided in a standardized XML format, and many web services provide data using these feeds. The Android SDK provides a variety of XML utilities. Parsing XML from the network is similar to parsing an XML resource file or a raw file on the file system. Android provides a fast and efficient XML Pull Parser, which is a parser of choice for networked applications.

The following code demonstrates how to use the XML Pull Parser to read an XML file from Flickr.com and extract specific data from within it. A TextView called status is assigned before this block of code is executed and displays the status of the parsing operation.

```
import java.net.URL;
import org.xmlpull.v1.XmlPullParser;
import org.xmlpull.v1.XmlPullParserFactory;

// ...

URL text = new URL("http://api.flickr.com/services/feeds/photos_public.gne" +
                "?id=26648248@N04&lang=en-us&format=atom");

XmlPullParserFactory parserCreator = XmlPullParserFactory.newInstance();
XmlPullParser parser = parserCreator.newPullParser();
parser.setInput(text.openStream(), null);
status.setText("Parsing...");
int parserEvent = parser.getEventType();

while (parserEvent != XmlPullParser.END_DOCUMENT) {
    switch(parserEvent) {
        case XmlPullParser.START_TAG:
            String tag = parser.getName();
            if (tag.compareTo("link") == 0) {
                String relType = parser.getAttributeValue(null, "rel");
                if (relType.compareTo("enclosure") == 0 ) {
                    String encType = parser.getAttributeValue(null, "type");
                    if (encType.startsWith("image/")) {
                        String imageSrc = parser.getAttributeValue(null,
                            "href");
                        Log.i("Net", "image source = " + imageSrc);
                    }
                }
```

```
            }
        }
        break;
    }
    parserEvent = parser.next();
}
status.setText("Done...");
```

After the URL is created, the next step is to retrieve an `XmlPullParser` instance from the `XmlPullParserFactory`. A Pull Parser has a main method that returns the next event. The events returned by a Pull Parser are similar to methods used in the implementation of a `SAXParser` handler class. Instead, though, the code is handled iteratively. This method is more efficient for mobile use.

In this example, the only event that we check for is the `START_TAG` event, signifying the beginning of an XML tag. Attribute values are queried and compared. This example looks specifically for image URLs in the XML from a Flickr feed query. When they are found, a log entry is made.

You can check for the following XML Pull Parser events:

- `START_TAG`: Returned when a new tag is found (that is, `<tag>`)
- `TEXT`: Returned when text is found (that is, `<tag>text</tag>` where text has been found)
- `END_TAG`: Returned when the end of a tag is found (that is, `</tag>`)
- `END_DOCUMENT`: Returned when the end of the XML file is reached

Additionally, the parser can be set to validate the input. Typically, parsing without validation is used when under constrained memory environments, such as a mobile environment. Compliant, nonvalidating parsing is the default for this XML Pull Parser.

Warning

The previous example executes on the main UI thread. Running network operations on the main UI thread is not a good idea because this is a blocking operation. In the following sections, we show you how to execute network operations without blocking the main UI thread.

Handling Network Operations Asynchronously

Networking operations can take an indefinite amount of time to complete and should not block the main UI thread. The style of networking presented so far causes the UI thread on which the operation runs to block until the operation finishes. You must move network operations off of the main UI thread.

Offloading networking operations is straightforward using the `AsyncTask` class and the standard Java `Thread` class. You can find out more about both methods in Chapter 1, "Threading and Asynchronous Processing."

Handling Network Operations with the `AsyncTask` Class

The simplest way to handle asynchronous processing is with the `AsyncTask` class. The following code demonstrates an example implementation of `AsyncTask` to perform the same functionality as the code earlier off the UI thread:

```
private class ImageLoader extends AsyncTask<URL, String, String> {
    @Override
    protected String doInBackground(URL... params) {
        // just one param
        try {
            URL text = params[0];
            // ... parsing code {
            publishProgress("imgCount = " + curImageCount);
            // ... end parsing code }
        }
        catch (Exception e ) {
            Log.e("Net", "Failed in parsing XML", e);
            return "Finished with failure.";
        }
        return "Done...";
    }

    protected void onCancelled() {
        Log.e("Net", "Async task Cancelled");
    }

    protected void onPostExecute(String result) {
        mStatus.setText(result);
    }

    protected void onPreExecute() {
        mStatus.setText("About to load URL");
    }

    protected void onProgressUpdate(String... values) {
        // just one value, please
        mStatus.setText(values[0]);
    }

}
```

When launched with the `AsyncTask.execute()` method, `doInBackground()` runs in a background thread while the other methods run on the UI thread. There is no need to manage a `Handler` or post a `Runnable` object to it. This simplifies coding and debugging.

Handling Network Operations with the `Thread` Class

If you're more comfortable working with traditional Java threads, you can use the `Thread` class instead. The following code demonstrates how to launch a new `Thread` that connects to a remote server, retrieves and parses some XML, and posts a response back to the UI thread to change a `TextView`:

```
import java.net.URL;
import org.xmlpull.v1.XmlPullParser;
import org.xmlpull.v1.XmlPullParserFactory;
```

```
// ...

new Thread() {
    public void run() {
        try {
            URL text = new URL("http://api.flickr.com/services/feeds/" +
                "photos_public.gne?id=26648248@N04&lang=en-us&format=atom");

            XmlPullParserFactory parserCreator =
                    XmlPullParserFactory.newInstance();
            XmlPullParser parser = parserCreator.newPullParser();

            parser.setInput(text.openStream(), null);

            mHandler.post(new Runnable() {
                public void run() {
                    status.setText("Parsing...");
                }
            });

            int parserEvent = parser.getEventType();
            while (parserEvent != XmlPullParser.END_DOCUMENT) {
                // Parsing code here ...
                parserEvent = parser.next();
            }

            mHandler.post(new Runnable() {
                public void run() {
                    status.setText("Done...");
                }
            });

        } catch (Exception e) {
            Log.e("Net", "Error in network call", e);
        }
    }
}.start();
```

For this example, an anonymous `Thread` object is reasonable. We create it and call its `start()` method immediately. However, now that the code runs on a separate thread, the user interface updates must be posted back to the main thread. This is done by using a `Handler` object on the main thread and creating `Runnable` objects that execute to call `setText()` on the `TextView` widget named `status`.

The rest of the code remains the same as in the previous examples. Executing both the parsing code and the networking code on a separate thread allows the user interface to continue to behave in a responsive fashion while the network and parsing operations are done behind the scenes, resulting in a smooth and friendly user experience. This also allows for handling of interim actions by the user, such as canceling the transfer. You can accomplish this by implementing the `Thread` to listen for certain events and check for certain flags.

Displaying Images from a Network Resource

Now that we have covered how you can use a separate thread to parse XML, let's take our example a bit deeper and talk about working with nonprimitive data types.

Continuing with the previous example of parsing for image locations from a Flickr feed, let's display some images from the feed. The following example reads the image data and displays it on the screen, demonstrating another way you can use network resources:

```
import java.io.InputStream;
import java.net.URL;
import org.xmlpull.v1.XmlPullParser;
import org.xmlpull.v1.XmlPullParserFactory;
import android.os.Handler;

// ...

final String imageSrc = parser.getAttributeValue(null, "href");
final String currentTitle = new String(title);

imageThread.queueEvent(new Runnable() {
    public void run() {
        InputStream bmis;
        try {
            bmis = new URL(imageSrc).openStream();
            final Drawable image = new BitmapDrawable(
                BitmapFactory.decodeStream(bmis));
            mHandler.post(new Runnable() {
                public void run() {
                    imageSwitcher.setImageDrawable(image);
                    info.setText(currentTitle);
                }
            });
        } catch (Exception e) {
            Log.e("Net", "Failed to grab image", e);
        }
    }
});
```

You can find this block of code in the parser thread, as previously described. After the image source and title of the image have been determined, a new `Runnable` object is queued for execution on a separate image-handling thread. The thread is merely a queue that receives the anonymous `Runnable` object created here and executes it at least 10 seconds after the last one, resulting in a slide show of the images from the feed.

Warning

Although the preceding code is sound for local resources and URLs, for sources over slow connections, it might not work properly. This is a known issue with the Android SDK and is caused by a buffering issue with loading large bitmaps over slow connections. There is a relatively straightforward workaround that you can find in the code provided for this chapter.

Figure 11.1   Screen showing a Flickr image
and decoding status of the feed.

As with the first networking example, a new URL object is created and an Input Stream retrieved from it. You need a Drawable object to assign to the Image Switcher. Then you use the BitmapFactory.decodeStream() method, which takes an InputStream.

Finally, from this Runnable object, which runs on a separate queuing thread, spacing out image drawing, another anonymous Runnable object posts back to the main thread to actually update the ImageSwitcher with the new image. Figure 11.1 shows what the screen might look like showing decoding status and displaying the current image.

Although all this continues to happen while the feed from Flickr is decoded, certain operations are slower than others. For instance, while the image is decoded or drawn on the screen, you may notice a distinct hesitation in the progress of the decoding. This is to be expected on current mobile devices because most have only a single thread of execution available for applications. You need to use careful design to provide a reasonably smooth and responsive experience to the user.

Retrieving Android Network Status

The Android SDK provides utilities for gathering information about the current state of the network. This is useful to determine whether a network connection is even available before trying to use a network resource. The ConnectivityManager class provides a

172   Chapter 11 Using Android Networking APIs

number of methods to do this. The following code determines whether the mobile
(cellular) network is available and connected to the device. In addition, it determines
the same for the Wi-Fi network:

```
import android.net.ConnectivityManager;
import android.net.NetworkInfo;

// ...

ConnectivityManager cm = (ConnectivityManager)
    getSystemService(Context.CONNECTIVITY_SERVICE);
NetworkInfo ni = cm.getNetworkInfo(ConnectivityManager.TYPE_WIFI);
boolean isWifiAvail = ni.isAvailable();
boolean isWifiConn = ni.isConnected();
ni = cm.getNetworkInfo(ConnectivityManager.TYPE_MOBILE);
boolean isMobileAvail = ni.isAvailable();
boolean isMobileConn = ni.isConnected();

status.setText("WiFi\nAvail = "+ isWifiAvail +
    "\nConn = " + isWifiConn +
    "\nMobile\nAvail = "+ isMobileAvail +
    "\nConn = " + isMobileConn);
```

First, an instance of the ConnectivityManager object is retrieved with a call to the
getSystemService() method, available as part of your application Context. Then this
instance retrieves NetworkInfo objects for both TYPE_WIFI and TYPE_MOBILE (for the
cellular network). These objects are queried for their availability but can also be queried

Figure 11.2   Network status with Wi-Fi turned off by the user.

at a more detailed status level to learn exactly what state of connection (or disconnection) the network is in. Figure 11.2 shows the typical output for the emulator in which the mobile network is simulated but Wi-Fi isn't available.

If the network is available, this does not necessarily mean the server that the network resource is on is available. However, a call to the `ConnectivityManager` method `requestRouteToHost()` can answer this question. This way, the application can give the user better feedback when there are network problems.

For your application to read the status of the network, it needs explicit permission. The following statement is required to be in its `AndroidManifest.xml` file:

```
<uses-permission android:name="android.permission.ACCESS_NETWORK_STATE"/>
```

Tip

Use the emulator networking settings to simulate various types of cellular networks, from GSM to HSDPA (and unlimited) data rates. Additionally, you can control the latency of the network to be similar to that of the cellular networks. Although this is useful for testing how your application behaves in good conditions for the chosen network type, it can't simulate the real behavior of the network out in the field when the user is in bad coverage, gets on an elevator, or is on a train rapidly losing and reacquiring network coverage. Only physical device testing can truly reveal these results.

Summary

Many applications use networking to enhance and improve the features they can provide to the user. However, a user's network connectivity is not a guaranteed, always-available service. Application developers need to design and implement networking features carefully to ensure a stable and responsive application. Integration of networking features into your mobile application needs to be considered at the design level. Deciding how much networking support your application should contain is part of the application design process.

Quiz Questions

1. True or false: The `android.permission.NETWORKING` is the permission required for networking in an Android application.

2. What is the name of the package for performing HTTP networking?

3. True or false: The XML Pull Parser event `START_TAG` occurs when a new `<tag>` is found.

4. What is the name of the class used to gather information about the current state of the network on the device?

5. What application permission is required in the `AndroidManifest.xml` file for reading the status of the network on the device?

Exercises

1. Use the Android documentation to determine the HttpURLConnection constant for the "404 not found" status code.

2. Use the Android documentation to determine the XmlPullParser method for setting the value of a property.

3. Write a simple application that communicates with a server for establishing a session with cookies.

References and More Information

Android SDK Reference documentation on the java.net package:

   http://d.android.com/reference/java/net/package-summary.html

Android SDK Reference documentation on the android.net package:

   http://d.android.com/reference/android/net/package-summary.html

Android SDK Reference documentation on the StrictMode class:

   http://d.android.com/reference/android/os/StrictMode.html

XML pull parsing:

   http://www.xmlpull.org/

Android SDK Reference documentation on Android XmlPullParser:

   http://d.android.com/reference/org/xmlpull/v1/XmlPullParser.html

## 12

Using Android Web APIs

Mobile developers often rely on web technologies to enrich their applications, provide fresh content, and integrate with popular web services such as social networks. Android applications can harness the power of the Internet in a variety of ways, including adding browser functionality to applications, using the special `WebView` control. Android 4.4 KitKat (API Level 19) introduces a brand-new `WebView` based on Chromium which supports many HTML5, CSS3, and JavaScript standards and technologies. Older versions of Android still use the original WebKit-based `WebView`. Android devices can also run Adobe AIR applications. In this chapter, we discuss the web technologies that are available on the Android platform.

Browsing the Web with `WebView`

Applications that retrieve and display content from the Web often end up displaying that data on the screen. Instead of customizing various screens with custom controls, Android applications can simply use the `WebView` control to display web content to the screen. You can think of the `WebView` control as a browser-like view.

The Android 4.4 `WebView` control uses the Chromium rendering engine to draw HTML content on the screen, and all devices running older versions of Android use the WebKit rendering engine. This content can be HTML pages on the Web or it can be locally sourced. Chromium and WebKit are open-source browser engines. You can read more about Chromium on its official website at *http://www.chromium.org/Home* and read more about WebKit on its official website at *http://www.webkit.org*.

> **Tip**
>
> Many of the code examples provided in this section are taken from the SimpleWeb application. The source code for this application is provided for download on the book's website.

Using the `WebView` control requires the `android.permission.INTERNET` permission. You can add this permission to your application's Android manifest file as follows:

```
<uses-permission android:name="android.permission.INTERNET" />
```

When deciding whether the `WebView` control is right for your application, consider that you can always launch a browser application using an `Intent` object. When you want the user to have full access to all browser features, such as bookmarking and browsing, you're better off launching into a browser application to a specific website, letting users do their browsing, and having them return to your application when they're done. You can do this as follows:

```
Uri uriUrl = Uri.parse("http://advancedandroidbook.blogspot.com/");
Intent launchBrowser = new Intent(Intent.ACTION_VIEW, uriUrl);
startActivity(launchBrowser);
```

Launching a browser via an `Intent` does not require any special permissions. This means that your application is not required to have the `android.permission.INTERNET` permission. In addition, because Android transitions from your application's current `Activity` to a specific browser application's `Activity`, and then returns when the user presses the Back key, the experience is nearly as seamless as implementing your own `Activity` class with an embedded `WebView` object.

Designing a Layout with a `WebView` Control

The `WebView` control can be added to a layout resource file like any other `View`. It can take up the entire screen or just a portion of it. A typical `WebView` definition in a layout resource might look like this:

```
<WebView
    android:id="@+id/web_holder"
    android:layout_height="match_parent"
    android:layout_width="match_parent" />
```

Generally speaking, you should give your `WebView` controls ample room to display text and graphics. Keep this in mind when designing layouts using the `WebView` control.

Warning

The Android IDE Layout Resource Editor does not display the `WebView` control properly. You need to run either the Android emulator or a device to make sure the layout displays properly.

Loading Content into a `WebView` Control

You can load content into a `WebView` control in a variety of ways. For example, a `WebView` control can load a specific website or render raw HTML content. Web pages can be stored on a remote web server or stored on the device.

Here is an example of how to use a `WebView` control to load content from a specific website:

```
final WebView wv = (WebView) findViewById(R.id.web_holder);
wv.loadUrl("http://www.perlgurl.org/");
```

You do not need to add any additional code to load the referenced web page on the screen. Similarly, you can load an HTML file called `webby.html` stored in the application's assets directory, like this:

```
wv.loadUrl("file:///android_asset/webby.html");
```

If, instead, you want to render raw HTML, you can use the `loadData()` method, which accepts a `data String`, a `mimeType String`, and an encoding `String`:

```
String strPageTitle = "The Last Words of Oscar Wilde";
String strPageContent = "<h1>" + strPageTitle +
    ": </h1>\"Either that wallpaper goes, or I do.\"";
String myHTML = "<html><title>" + strPageTitle
    +"</title><body>"+ strPageContent +"</body></html>";
wv.loadData(myHTML, "text/html", "utf-8");
```

The resulting `WebView` control is shown in Figure 12.1.

Figure 12.1   A `WebView` control used to display HTML.

Unfortunately, not all websites are designed for mobile devices. It can be handy to change the scale of the web content to fit comfortably in the `WebView` control. You can achieve this by setting the initial scale of the control, like this:

```
wv.setInitialScale(30);
```

The call to the `setInitialScale()` method scales the `View` to 30 percent of the original size. For pages that specify absolute sizes, scaling the `View` is necessary to see the entire page on the screen. Some text might become too small to read, though, so you might need to test and make page design changes (if the web content is under your control) for a good user experience.

Tip

If you want an entire screen to be a `WebView` control, you can simply create a `WebView` programmatically and pass it in to the `setContentView()` method in the `onCreate()` method of your `Activity`.

Adding Features to the `WebView` Control

You might have noticed that the `WebView` control does not have all the features of a full browser. For example, it does not display the title of a web page or provide buttons for reloading pages. In fact, if the user clicks on a link in the `WebView` control, that action does not load the new page in the `WebView`. Instead, it fires up the Browser application.

By default, all the `WebView` control does is display the web content provided by the developer using its internal rendering engine, Chromium or WebKit. You can enhance the `WebView` control in a variety of ways, though. You can use three classes, in particular, to help modify the behavior of the control: the `WebSettings` class, the `WebViewClient` class, and the `WebChromeClient` class.

Modifying `WebView` Settings with `WebSettings`

By default, a `WebView` control has various default settings: no zoom controls, JavaScript disabled, default font sizes, user-agent string, and so on. You can change the settings of a `WebView` control using the `getSettings()` method. The `getSettings()` method returns a `WebSettings` object that can be used to configure the desired `WebView` settings. Some useful settings include the following:

- Enabling and disabling zoom controls using the `setSupportZoom()` and `setBuiltInZoomControls()` methods
- Enabling and disabling JavaScript using the `setJavaScriptEnabled()` method
- Enabling and disabling mouse-overs using the `setLightTouchEnabled()` method
- Configuring font families, text sizes, and other display characteristics

You can also use the `WebSettings` class to configure `WebView` plug-ins and allow for multiple windows.

Handling `WebView` Events with `WebViewClient`

The `WebViewClient` class enables the application to listen for certain `WebView` events, such as when a page is loading, when a form is submitted, and when a new URL is about to be loaded. You can also use the `WebViewClient` class to determine and handle any errors that occur with page loading. You can tie a valid `WebViewClient` object to a `WebView` using the `setWebViewClient()` method.

The following is an example of how to use `WebViewClient` to handle the `onPageFinished()` method to draw the title of the page on the screen:

```
WebViewClient webClient = new WebViewClient() {
    public void onPageFinished(WebView view, String url) {
        super.onPageFinished(view, url);
        String title = wv.getTitle();
        pageTitle.setText(title);
    }};
wv.setWebViewClient(webClient);
```

When the page finishes loading, as indicated by the call to `onPageFinished()`, a call to the `getTitle()` method of the `WebView` object retrieves the title for use. The result of this call is shown in Figure 12.2.

Adding Browser Chrome with `WebChromeClient`

You can use the `WebChromeClient` class in a similar way to the `WebViewClient`. However, `WebChromeClient` is specialized for the sorts of items that are drawn outside the region in which the web content is drawn, typically known as *browser chrome*. The `WebChromeClient` class also includes callbacks for certain JavaScript calls, such as `onJsBeforeUnload()`, to confirm navigation away from a page. A valid `WebChromeClient` object can be tied to a `WebView` using the `setWebChromeClient()` method.

The following code demonstrates using `WebView` features to enable interactivity with the user. An `EditText` and a `Button` control are added below the `WebView` control, and a `Button` handler for loading a URL is implemented as follows:

```
Button go = (Button) findViewById(R.id.go_button);
go.setOnClickListener(new View.OnClickListener() {
    public void onClick(View v) {
        wv.loadUrl(et.getText().toString());
    }
});
```

Calling the `loadUrl()` method again, as shown, is all that is needed to cause the `WebView` control to download another HTML page for display, as shown in Figure 12.3. From here, you can build a generic web browser into any application, but you can apply restrictions so that the user is restricted to browsing relevant materials.

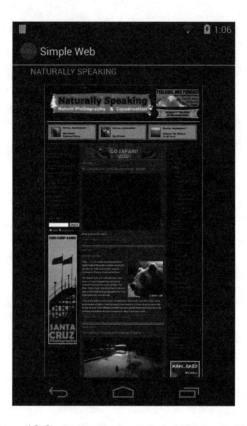

Figure 12.2   A `WebView` control showing a page title.

Using `WebChromeClient` can help add some typical chrome on the screen. For instance, you can use it to listen for changes to the title of the page, various JavaScript dialogs that might be requested, and even for developer-oriented pieces, such as console messages.

```
WebChromeClient webChrome = new WebChromeClient() {
    @Override
    public void onReceivedTitle(WebView view, String title) {
        Log.v(DEBUG_TAG, "Got new title");
        super.onReceivedTitle(view, title);
        pageTitle.setText(title);
    }
};
wv.setWebChromeClient(webChrome);
```

Here, the default `WebChromeClient` object is overridden to receive changes to the title of the page. The title of the web page is then set to a `TextView` visible on the screen.

Figure 12.3   `WebView` with `EditText` allowing entry of arbitrary URLs.

Whether you use `WebView` to display the main user interface of your application or use it sparingly to draw such things as help pages, there are circumstances where it might be the ideal control for the job to save coding time, especially when compared to a custom screen design. Leveraging the power of the open-source browser engine, `WebView` can provide a powerful, standards-based HTML viewer for applications.

Managing `WebView` State

On API Level 11 and higher, be sure to call the `onPause()` and `onResume()` methods of the `WebView` object. The `onPause()` call reduces or stops unnecessary processing activities, such as those from plug-ins and JavaScript. The `onResume()` method resumes after the `onPause()` method reduces or stops a `WebView`. Without making these calls, or in previous API versions, processing would continue in the background. These methods should be called from your `Activity onPause()` and `onResume()` methods, at minimum.

When the application is running on older versions of the platform, you can terminate the `WebView` instance entirely. If that's too much, you can make a call to `pause Timers()`, which stops some processing but also affects all `WebView` instances. Keep in mind that the rest of the device performance might be adversely affected if you don't do what you can to reduce processing. If your `WebView` doesn't allow plug-ins or JavaScript, only layout and parsing would continue.

You can have code such as the following in your `onPause()` method:

```
WebView wv = (WebView) findViewById(R.id.web_holder);
if (Build.VERSION.SDK_INT >= Build.VERSION_CODES.HONEYCOMB) {
    wv.onPause();
} else {
    wv.pauseTimers();
}
```

Building Web Extensions

All HTML rendering on the Android platform is done using either the Chromium or WebKit rendering engine. The `android.webkit` package provides a number of APIs for browsing the Internet using the powerful `WebView` control. You should be aware of the interfaces and classes available, as you are likely to need them to enhance the `WebView` user experience.

These are not classes and interfaces to the browser (although you can interact with the browser data using content providers). Instead, these are the classes and interfaces that you must use to control the browsing abilities of `WebView` controls you implement in your applications.

Browsing the WebKit APIs

These are some of the most helpful classes of the `android.webkit` package:

- The `CacheManager` class gives you some control over cache items of a `WebView`.
- The `ConsoleMessage` class can be used to retrieve JavaScript console output from a `WebView`.
- The `CookieManager` class is used to set and retrieve user cookies for a `WebView`.
- The `URLUtil` class is handy for validating web addresses of different types.
- The `WebBackForwardList` and `WebHistoryItem` classes can be used to inspect the web history of the `WebView`.

Now let's take a quick look at how you might use some of these classes to enhance a `WebView`.

Extending Web Application Functionality to Android

Let's take some of the `android.webkit` package features we have discussed so far in this chapter and work through an example. It is fairly common for mobile developers to design their applications as web applications to reach users across a variety of platforms. This minimizes the amount of platform-specific code to develop and maintain. However, on its own, a web application cannot call into native platform code and take advantage of the features that native apps (such as those written in Java for the Android platform) can, such as using a built-in camera or accessing some other underlying Android feature.

Developers can enhance web applications by designing a lightweight shell application in Java and using a `WebView` control as a portal to the web application content. Two-way communication between the web application and the native Java application is possible through scripting languages such as JavaScript.

Tip

Many of the code examples provided in this section are taken from the SimpleWebExtension application. The source code for this application is provided for download on the book's website.

Let's create a simple Android application that illustrates communication between web content and native Android code. This example requires that you understand JavaScript. To create this application, take the following steps:

1. Create a new Android application.

2. Create a layout with a `WebView` control called `html_viewer` and a `Button` control called `call_js`. Set the `onClick` attribute of the `Button` control to a method called `setHTMLText`.

3. In the `onCreate()` method of your application `Activity`, retrieve the `WebView` control using the `findViewById()` method.

4. Enable JavaScript in the `WebView` by retrieving its `WebSettings` and calling the `setJavaScriptEnabled()` method.

5. Create a `WebChromeClient` object and implement its `onConsoleMessage()` method to monitor the JavaScript console messages.

6. Add the `WebChromeClient` object to the `WebView` using the `setWebChromeClient()` method.

7. Allow the JavaScript interface to control your application by calling the `addJavascriptInterface()` method of the `WebView` control. You need to define the functionality that you want the JavaScript interface to control and in what namespace the calls will be available. In this case, we allow the JavaScript to initiate `Toast` messages.

8. Load your content into the `WebView` control using one of the standard methods, such as the `loadUrl()` method. In this case, we load an HTML asset we defined within the application package.

If you followed these steps, you should end up with your `Activity`'s `onCreate()` method looking something like this:

```
@Override
public void onCreate(Bundle savedInstanceState) {
    super.onCreate(savedInstanceState);
    setContentView(R.layout.main);
    final WebView wv = (WebView) findViewById(R.id.html_viewer);
    WebSettings settings = wv.getSettings();
    settings.setJavaScriptEnabled(true);
    WebChromeClient webChrome = new WebChromeClient() {
        @Override
        public boolean onConsoleMessage(ConsoleMessage consoleMessage) {
            Log.v(DEBUG_TAG, consoleMessage.lineNumber()
                + ": " + consoleMessage.message());
            return true;
        }
    };

    wv.setWebChromeClient(webChrome);
    wv.addJavascriptInterface(new JavaScriptExtensions(), "jse");
    wv.loadUrl("file:///android_asset/sample.html");
}
```

A custom `WebChromeClient` class is set so that any JavaScript `console.log` messages go out to LogCat output, using a custom debug tag as usual to enable easy tracking of log output specific to the application. Next, a new JavaScript interface is defined with the namespace called `jse`—the namespace is up to you. To call from JavaScript to this Java class, the JavaScript calls must all start with namespace `jse.`, followed by the appropriate exposed method—for instance, `jse.javaMethod()`.

You can define the `JavaScriptExtensions` class in the `Activity` as a subclass with a single method that can trigger Android `Toast` messages, as follows:

```
class JavaScriptExtensions {
    public static final int TOAST_LONG = Toast.LENGTH_LONG;
    public static final int TOAST_SHORT = Toast.LENGTH_SHORT;

    @JavascriptInterface
    public void toast(String message, int length) {
        Toast.makeText(SimpleWebExtension.this, message, length).show();
    }
}
```

The JavaScript code has access to everything in the `JavaScriptExtensions` class, including the member variables as well as the methods. Return values work as expected from the methods, too.

Warning

Forgetting to add the `@JavascriptInterface` annotation to methods exposed to JavaScript code will result in an error and prevent your application from compiling if your `targetSdkVersion` is 17 or newer.

Now switch your attention to defining the web page to load in the `WebView` control. For this example, simply create a file called `sample.html` in the `/assets` directory of the application. The contents of the `sample.html` file are shown here:

```html
<html>
    <head>
        <script type="text/javascript">
            function doToast() {
                jse.toast("'" + document.getElementById('form_text').value +
                "' -From Java!", jse.TOAST_LONG);
            }
            function doConsoleLog() {
                console.log("Console logging.");
            }
            function doAlert() {
                alert("This is an alert.");
            }
            function doSetFormText(update) {
                document.getElementById('form_text').value = update;
            }
        </script>
    </head>
    <body>
        <h2>This is a test.</h2>
        <input type="text" id="form_text" value="Enter something here..." />
        <input type="button" value="Toast" onclick="doToast();" /><br />
        <input type="button" value="Log" onclick="doConsoleLog();" /><br />
        <input type="button" value="Alert" onclick="doAlert();" />
    </body>
</html>
```

The `sample.html` file defines four JavaScript functions and displays the form shown in the `WebView`:

- The `doToast()` function calls into the Android application using the `jse` object defined earlier with the call to the `addJavascriptInterface()` method. The `addJavascriptInterface()` method, for all practical intents and purposes, can be treated literally as the `JavaScriptExtensions` class as if that class had been written in JavaScript. If the `doToast()` function had returned a value, we could assign it to a variable here.

- The `doConsoleLog()` function writes into the JavaScript console log, which is picked up by the `onConsoleMessage()` callback of the `WebChromeClient`.

- The `doAlert()` function illustrates how alerts work within the `WebView` control by launching a dialog. If you want to override what the alert looks like, you can override the `WebChromeClient.onJSAlert()` method.

The `doSetFormText()` function illustrates how native Java code can communicate back through the JavaScript interface and provide data to the web application. Finally, to demonstrate making a call from Java back to JavaScript, you need to define the click handler for the `Button` control within your `Activity` class. Here, the `onClick` handler, called `setHTMLText()`, executes some JavaScript on the currently loaded page by calling a JavaScript function called `doSetFormText()`, which we defined earlier in the web page. Here is an implementation of the `setHTMLText()` method:

```
public void setHTMLText(View view) {
    WebView wv = (WebView) findViewById(R.id.html_viewer);
    wv.loadUrl("javascript:doSetFormText('Java->JS call');");
}
```

This method of making a call to the JavaScript on the currently loaded page does not allow for return values. There are ways, however, to structure your design to allow checking of results, generally by treating the call as asynchronous and implementing another method for determining the response.

Figure 12.4   A simple Android application with a JavaScript interface.

Warning

Keep in mind that opening up the Android application to a JavaScript control using the `addJavascriptInterface()` method must be done securely. Make sure your `WebView` loads only the content under your control—not just any content on the Web. Also, the JavaScript interface does not run on the UI thread, so you need to employ normal cross-thread communication techniques, such as using a handler to post messages back to the other thread in order to communicate.

Figure 12.4 shows how this application might behave on an Android device.

This style of development has been popularized by the open-source PhoneGap project, which aims to provide a set of standard JavaScript interfaces to native code across a variety of platforms, including iOS, Android, BlackBerry, Symbian, and Palm. Learn more about PhoneGap at *http://phonegap.com*.

Debugging WebViews with Chrome DevTools

Android 4.4 KitKat (API Level 19) introduced an updated version of `WebView` based on the Chromium browser project. The new Chromium `WebView` supports many of the available features that can be found in Chrome for Android version 30, which includes many new features of HTML5, CSS3, and JavaScript. Since the new `WebView` is based on Chromium, the Chrome DevTools have been made available to developers for debugging WebViews.

To learn more about how to get started with debugging WebViews using the Chrome DevTools, you should read the tutorial titled "Debug WebViews" found here: *https://developer.chrome.com/devtools/docs/remote-debugging#debugging-webviews*.

Working with Adobe AIR and Flash

For those web developers who want to bring their Flash applications to mobile, browser-based Flash is no longer supported, but there are still ways developers can utilize Flash with Android, by using Adobe AIR. However, there are both benefits and drawbacks to including Flash technology on the platform. Let's look at some of the facts:

- Flash might not be the future (as opposed to HTML5, CSS3, and JavaScript), but it's the status quo in some web circles. There are millions of Flash applications and websites out there that are no longer accessible from Android devices.

- Flash on mobile browsers is most definitely not the future. Adobe has decided not to continue to create new mobile browser plug-ins. Instead, developers can use their tools to create HTML5 websites that work on mobile. Developers who use Adobe AIR to create packaged applications using Flash are not affected by this. See *http://blogs.adobe.com/conversations/2011/11/flash-focus.html* for more information.

- Native Android applications are always going to perform better, use fewer resources (read: drain the battery slower), provide tighter platform integration, have fewer platform prerequisites, and support more Android devices than Flash applications.

- Deciding to build Flash applications for the Android platform instead of native Java applications is a design decision that should not be made lightly. There are performance and security trade-offs as well as limited device support (and no backward compatibility) for Flash.

- You can't expect all Flash applications to just be loaded up and work. All the usual mobile constraints and UI paradigms apply. This includes designing around such constraints as a touch interface on a small screen, a relatively slow processor, and interruptions (such as phone calls) being the norm.

Adobe has created tools for developing cross-platform applications using its AIR tool suite in ActionScript 3, which is Adobe's web scripting language for web and Flash applications. Adobe AIR for Android enables developers to create AIR applications that can be compiled into native Android APK files that can then be published like any other Android application. Developers use Adobe's Flash Builder to create Flex Mobile projects to develop AIR applications that can be compiled into Android package files and distributed like native Android applications. A prerequisite (and limitation) of working with Adobe AIR is that users must also download and install Adobe AIR in order for your AIR application to work on their devices.

Summary

Android developers can add browser support to their applications using the versatile Web View control. Applications that require more control can enhance their applications with web features using powerful yet familiar technologies that come with browser engines such as Chromium and WebKit. In Android, Flash support is available on the Android platform only in the form of an Adobe AIR application that allows ActionScript to be compiled into Android APK files that can be distributed as native Android applications.

Quiz Questions

1. True or false: Android 4.4 KitKat (API Level 19) introduced a new version of WebView based on the Chromium browser engine.

2. What manifest permission is required in order to use a WebView control in your application?

3. What class is available to add browser chrome to your WebView?

4. What annotation is required for targetSdkVersion 17 and newer for exposing methods to JavaScript code?

5. True or false: The Chrome DevTools are used for debugging WebViews in Android 4.4 and newer.

Exercises

1. Use the Android documentation to determine what `android.webkit` class you should use for managing and manipulating cookies within a `WebView`.

2. Use the Android documentation to determine what `android.webkit` class is used to manage the `WebView` JavaScript storage APIs.

3. Go through the "Debug WebViews" tutorial link found in this chapter to learn how to use the Chrome DevTools for debugging WebViews.

References and More Information

Android API Guides: "Web Apps":
http://d.android.com/guide/webapps/index.html
Android API Guides: "Migrating to `WebView` in Android 4.4":
http://d.android.com/guide/webapps/migrating.html
Android Reference documentation on `WebView`:
http://d.android.com/reference/android/webkit/WebView.html
Android Reference documentation on `JavascriptInterface`:
http://d.android.com/reference/android/webkit/JavascriptInterface.html
Chrome: "Remote Debugging on Android with Chrome":
https://developer.chrome.com/devtools/docs/remote-debugging#debugging-webviews
The Chromium Blog: "Introducing Chromium-Powered Android `WebView`":
http://blog.chromium.org/2013/11/introducing-chromium-powered-android.html
The Chromium Projects: "Chromium":
http://www.chromium.org/Home
WebKit Open Source Project:
http://www.webkit.org
W3School's JavaScript tutorial:
http://www.w3schools.com/js/js_intro.asp
Adobe Developer Connection: "Hello World: Build a Mobile App in Five Minutes":
http://www.adobe.com/devnet/flash-builder/articles/hello-world.html
Adobe AIR 4:
http://www.adobe.com/products/air.html

## 13

Using Android Multimedia APIs

Multimedia—whether we're talking about images, videos, or audio—has become a key driver of mobile device sales. Many modern "smart devices" have built-in cameras to capture and display still images, video, and sophisticated music playback abilities. Your basic smartphone has at least one camera, sometimes two if you count the front-facing cameras used for video chat and self-portraits (selfies). In this chapter, you will learn how to capture still images using the camera, and you will learn how to record and play back audio and video files.

Working with Multimedia

The Android SDK provides a variety of methods for applications to incorporate audio and visual media, including support for many different media types and formats. Individual Android devices and developers can extend the list of supported media to other formats. Not every Android device has the same multimedia capabilities. Always verify the capabilities of target devices before publication.

The multimedia features of the Android platform generally fall into three categories:

- Still images (recorded with the camera)
- Audio (recorded with the microphone, played back with speakers or audio output)
- Video (recorded with the camera and microphone, played back with speakers or video output)

Tip
There have been several new classes, methods, and enhancements of the Multimedia APIs over the past few version releases of Android. This chapter focuses on the most widely used aspects of the Multimedia APIs, as there are far too many to document in a single chapter. To learn about all of the available features of the Multimedia APIs, refer to the Android documentation.

Multimedia hardware such as a built-in camera, speakers, and audio or video output ports is optional for Android devices.

In addition to requiring the appropriate permissions, you can specify which optional features your application requires within the Android manifest file. You can do this using the `<uses-feature>` tag of the Android manifest file to declare that your application uses the camera. Remember, though, that the `<uses-feature>` tag is not enforced by the Android platform. Instead, application stores such as Google Play use this data to filter which applications to sell for certain devices.

Any application that requests the `CAMERA` permission is assumed to use all camera features. If your application accesses the camera but can function properly without it, you can also set the `android:required` field of `<uses-feature>` to `false`. However, you can set the camera features your application requires specifically, for example, if your application requires a microphone and a camera with autofocus but not a flash to be present on the device:

```
<uses-feature android:name="android.hardware.microphone" />
<uses-feature android:name="android.hardware.camera" />
<uses-feature android:name="android.hardware.camera.autofocus" />
```

Tip

Many of the code examples provided in this chapter are taken from the SimpleMultimedia application. The source code for this application is provided for download on the book's website.

Working with the Camera

Many Android devices have at least one camera for capturing images and video. If the user's device has built-in camera hardware, the user can capture still images using the `Camera` object (`android.hardware.Camera`) of the Android SDK. You can use these images in a variety of ways, such as customizing the Home screen wallpaper using the `WallpaperManager` class.

Tip

Beginning in Android 4.1 (API Level 16), the `MediaActionSound` class allows you to produce sounds for a custom camera or media application when building your own UI.

Capturing Still Images Using the Camera

The `Camera` object controls the camera on devices that have camera support enabled. The preview feature of the camera relies on the assignment of a `SurfaceHolder` of an appropriate type. This enables applications to control the placement and size of the preview area that the camera can use.

Follow these steps to add camera capture capability to an application without having to draw preview frames (the `CameraSurfaceView` displays the camera `View`):

1. Create a new class extending `SurfaceView` and implement `SurfaceHolder` `.Callback`. For this example, we name this class `CameraSurfaceView`.

2. In the `surfaceCreated()` method, get an instance of the `Camera` object.

3. In the `surfaceChanged()` method, configure and apply the `Camera.Parameters;,` then call the `startPreview()` method.

4. Add a method in `CameraSurfaceView` for capturing images.

5. Add the `CameraSurfaceView` to an appropriate layout.

6. Include some way, such as a button, for the user to trigger the capturing of images.

7. Implement a `PictureCallback` class to handle storing of the captured image.

8. Add the `android.permission.CAMERA` permission to the `AndroidManifest.xml` file.

9. Release the `Camera` object in the `surfaceDestroyed()` method.

Let's start by looking at the `CameraSurfaceView` class:

```
import android.hardware.Camera;
import android.view.SurfaceHolder;
import android.view.SurfaceView;

private class CameraSurfaceView extends SurfaceView
    implements SurfaceHolder.Callback {

    private SurfaceHolder mHolder;
    private Camera camera = null;

    public CameraSurfaceView(Context context) {
        super(context);
        mHolder = getHolder();
        mHolder.addCallback(this);
    }

    public void surfaceChanged(SurfaceHolder holder,
        int format, int width, int height) {
    }

    public void surfaceCreated(SurfaceHolder holder) {
    }

    public void surfaceDestroyed(SurfaceHolder holder) {
    }

    public boolean capture(Camera.PictureCallback
        jpegHandler) {
    }
}
```

The constructor for the `CameraSurfaceView` configures the `SurfaceHolder`. The constructor is appropriate for calling from an `Activity`'s `onCreate()` method. When the display is ready, the `surfaceCreated()` method is called. Here we instantiate the `Camera` object:

```
public void surfaceCreated(SurfaceHolder holder) {
    camera = Camera.open();
    camera.setPreviewDisplay(mHolder);
}
```

The Camera object has a static method to retrieve a usable instance. Because the Surface is now available, the configured holder can be assigned to it. Information about the Surface might not yet be available, but at the next call to the surfaceChanged() method, the camera parameters will be assigned and the preview will start, as shown here:

```
public void surfaceChanged(SurfaceHolder holder,
        int format, int width, int height) {
    List<Camera.Size> sizes = params.getSupportedPreviewSizes();

    Camera.Size pickedSize = getBestFit(sizes, width, height);
    if (pickedSize != null) {
        params.setPreviewSize(pickedSize.width, pickedSize.height);
        camera.setParameters(params);
    }
    camera.startPreview();
}
```

The surfaceChanged() method provides the application with the proper width and height for use with the camera preview. After this is assigned to the Camera object, the preview starts. At this point, the user sees whatever is in front of the camera on the device. If, however, you debug this within the emulator, you see a black-and-white checkerboard with an animated square on it, as shown in Figure 13.1. This is the simulated camera preview, so camera testing can take place, to some extent, on the emulator.

Figure 13.1   Emulator screen showing a simulated camera View.

Note

The format parameter passed in to the `surfaceChanged()` method is not related to the format parameter of the `setPreviewFormat()` method of the `Camera` object.

When the `Surface` is no longer displayed, the `surfaceDestroyed()` method is called. Here is an implementation of the `surfaceDestroyed()` method suitable for this example:

```
public void surfaceDestroyed(SurfaceHolder holder) {
    camera.stopPreview();
    camera.release();
    camera = null;
}
```

In the `surfaceDestroyed()` method, the application stops the preview and releases the `Camera` object. If the `CameraSurfaceView` is used again, the `surfaceCreated()` method is called again, so this is the appropriate place to perform this operation.

The final step required to capture a still image is to add some way to call the `takePicture()` method of the `Camera` object. `CameraSurfaceView` can provide public access to the `Camera` object, but in this example, we provide a method to perform this within the `CameraSurfaceView` class:

```
public boolean capture(Camera.PictureCallback jpegHandler) {
    if (camera != null) {
        camera.takePicture(null, null, jpegHandler);
        return true;
    } else {
        return false;
    }
}
```

You can also use the `takePicture()` method to assign a callback suitable to play a shutter sound, or any other action, just before the image is collected from the sensor. In addition, you can assign a `PictureCallback` to get raw data from the camera.

Note

The format of the raw camera data can vary from device to device.

The `CameraSurfaceView` object is now ready for use in an `Activity`. For this example, an `Activity` with a layout that contains a `FrameLayout` widget for positioning the preview is used. Here is a sample implementation of assigning the `cameraView` to the layout:

```
final CameraSurfaceView cameraView = new
    CameraSurfaceView(getApplicationContext());
FrameLayout frame = (FrameLayout) findViewById(R.id.frame);
frame.addView(cameraView);
```

Next, a `Button` click handler calls the `capture()` method of the `CameraSurface View` object. A sample implementation is shown here:

```
public void onClick(View v) {
    cameraView.capture(new Camera.PictureCallback() {

        public void onPictureTaken(byte[] data,
            Camera camera) {
            FileOutputStream fos = null;

            try {
                String filename = "capture.jpg";
                fos = openFileOutput(filename,
                    MODE_PRIVATE);

                fos.write(data);
            } catch (Exception e) {
                Log.e("Still", "Error writing file", e);
            } finally {
                if (fos != null) {
                    try {
                        fos.close();
                    } catch (IOException e) {
                        Log.e("Still", "Error closing file", e);
                    }
                }
            }
        }
    });
}
```

The data that comes back from the callback can be written out directly to a JPG file in the application file directory. If written as shown, though, the captured image is usable only by the application. In some cases, this might be suitable. However, the application might want to share the image with the rest of the device, for example, by including it within the Gallery application, which uses the `MediaStore` content provider. You do this by using the `ContentResolver` object to place an entry for the image in the media library.

Warning

As with all lengthy operations, you should perform large file system writes from a separate thread to keep the application interface as responsive as possible.

Configuring Camera Mode Settings

You can use the `Camera` class to configure the specific capture settings for a picture. Many of the capture settings are stored in the `Camera.Parameters` class and set in the camera using the `setParameters()` method.

Working with Common Camera Parameters

Let's take a closer look at the `Camera.Parameters` class. Some of the most interesting camera parameters are:

- Flash modes (where flash hardware is available)
- Focus types (fixed point, depth of field, infinity, and so on)
- White balance settings (fluorescent, incandescent, and so on)
- Scene modes (snow, beach, fireworks, and so on)
- Effects (photo negative, sepia, and so on)
- Antibanding settings (noise reduction)

Different parameters are supported by different devices, so always check for support before trying to enable parameters. Use the `Camera.Parameters` class to determine what camera features are supported. For example, you can use the set of methods called `getSupportedFlashModes()`, `getSupportedFocusModes()`, and so on. Also, the `Camera.Parameters` class contains methods to access more technical camera settings, such as exposure compensation and EXIF information.

Tip

The `Camera` class received a major upgrade in Android 4.0. Application developers now have much finer camera control, including the ability to set focus or metering areas, enable continuous autofocusing, and more. See the `Camera` class documentation for details.

Zooming the Camera

The camera zoom setting is controlled using the `startSmoothZoom()` and `stopSmooth Zoom()` methods of the `Camera` class. As you might expect, you can set zoom parameters using the `Camera.Parameters` class. Useful zoom methods in the `Camera.Parameters` class include:

- Determining whether zooming is supported with `isZoomSupported()`
- Determining whether smooth zooming is supported with `isSmoothZoomSupported()`
- Determining the maximum zoom value with `getMaxZoom()`
- Retrieving the current zoom value with `getZoom()`
- Setting the current zoom value with `setZoom()`
- Calculating the zoom increments (for example, 1x, 2x, and 10x) with `getZoomRatios()`

Depending on the features available for a specific camera, zoom might be digital, optical, or some combination of the two.

Sharing Images

Storing an image in the local application directory, as demonstrated, might work for some applications; however, other applications might find it useful if the image goes in the shared image library on the device. The `ContentResolver` can be used in conjunction with the `MediaStore` object to push the image into the shared image library. The following example demonstrates storing the still image taken by the camera as an image file in the `MediaStore` content provider, using the same camera image callback:

```
public void onPictureTaken(byte[] data, Camera camera) {
    Log.v("Still", "Image data received from camera");
    try {
        Bitmap bm = BitmapFactory.decodeByteArray(
            data, 0, data.length);
        String fileUrl = MediaStore.Images.Media.
            insertImage(getContentResolver(), bm,
            "Camera Still Image",
            "Camera Pic Sample App Took");

        if (fileUrl == null) {
            Log.d("Still", "Image Insert failed");
            return;
        } else {
            Uri picUri = Uri.parse(fileUrl);
            sendBroadcast(new Intent(
                Intent.ACTION_MEDIA_SCANNER_SCAN_FILE,
                picUri));
        }
    } catch (Exception e) {
        Log.e("Still", "Error writing file", e);
    }
}
```

The image is turned into a `Bitmap` object, which is passed in to the `insertImage()` method. This method creates an entry in the shared image library. After the image is inserted, we use the returned `URL` to create a `Uri` object representing the new image's location, which we instruct the media scanner to pick up by broadcasting a specialized `Intent`. To determine whether the scan completed successfully, you can make a call to the static `MediaScannerConnection.scanFile()` method and provide a `MediaScannerConnection.OnScanCompletedListener` class implementation.

Now the image is available to all applications that use the `MediaStore` content provider, such as the Gallery application.

Warning

To use the `MediaStore` with the emulator, you must have a mounted SD card image.

Additionally, although it's technically not necessary to force the media scanner to scan for new images, we've found that the Gallery application on the emulator and device might crash if the `MediaStore` does not perform a scan before trying to access the image. It's a good idea to send the `Intent` or use the `MediaScannerConnection` class.

Assigning Images as Wallpapers

Wallpapers are a great way for users to personalize their phones with interesting and fun images. The `WallpaperManager` class is used for all wallpaper interaction. You will learn more about it in Chapter 26, "Extending Android Application Reach," when you create live wallpaper. For now, use it to set still image wallpapers.

The current wallpaper can be retrieved with a call to the `getDrawable()` or `peekDrawable()` methods. The methods `getDesiredMinimumHeight()` and `getDesiredMinimumWidth()` enable the application to programmatically determine the size that a wallpaper should be on the particular device. Finally, you can assign wallpaper through the `setResource()`, `setBitmap()`, and `setStream()` methods.

The following callback of the `Camera` object sets the wallpaper:

```
public void onPictureTaken(byte[] data, Camera camera) {
    Bitmap recordedImage =
        BitmapFactory.decodeByteArray(data, 0, data.length);
    try {
        WallpaperManager wpManager = WallpaperManager
            .getInstance(StillImageActivity.this);
        wpManager.setBitmap(recordedImage);
    } catch (Exception e) {
        Log.e("Still", "Setting wallpaper failed.", e);
    }
}
```

The image is copied locally for the wallpaper, so the original doesn't need to be kept, which is good in this case because it was never written to disk. You can remove the wallpaper completely with a call to the `clear()` method.

Finally, your application needs the `android.permission.SET_WALLPAPER` permission in the `AndroidManifest.xml` file.

Note

Prior to API Level 5 (Android 2.0), simple wallpaper commands were handled directly through the `Context` object. See the Android SDK documentation on the `Context` `.setWallpaper()` and `Context.getWallpaper()` methods for further information.

Choosing among Various Device Cameras

Many of the newer Android devices, especially the newer smartphones, have front-facing cameras in addition to the main camera. Since API Level 9, the Android SDK has provided a method for accessing multiple cameras on a device. Leveraging the front-facing camera lends itself to all kinds of interesting application features in the realm of selfie and video chat.

All device cameras are accessed using the `Camera` class. To determine which camera is the front-facing camera, you need to iterate through the available cameras on the device and look for those with the front-facing attribute, as follows:

```
private int findFirstFrontFacingCamera() {
    int foundId = -1;
```

```
int numCams = Camera.getNumberOfCameras();
for (int camId = 0; camId < numCams; camId++) {
    CameraInfo info = new CameraInfo();
    Camera.getCameraInfo(camId, info);
    if (info.facing == CameraInfo.CAMERA_FACING_FRONT) {
        foundId = camId;
        break;
    }
}
return foundId;
}
```

Here, we use the getNumberOfCameras() method of the Camera class to iterate over each camera instance and retrieve its CameraInfo. We then check the facing field to determine whether the camera is a CAMERA_FACING_FRONT (or CAMERA_FACING_BACK if we were looking for other cameras besides the default). If so, we have found a front-facing camera to use. After you've detected an appropriate camera, you can use it as you would the normal device camera, as discussed earlier in this chapter.

Working with Video

In recent years, video has become commonplace on devices. Most devices on the market now can record and play back video, and this is no different with Android, although the specific video features might vary from device to device.

Recording Video

Android applications can record video using the MediaRecorder class. Using Media Recorder is a matter of following a few simple steps:

1. Instantiate a new MediaRecorder object.
2. Set the video source.
3. Set the video output format.
4. Set the video size to record (optional).
5. Set the video frame rate (optional).
6. Set the video encoder.
7. Set the file to record to. (The extension must match the output format.)
8. Set the preview surface.
9. Prepare the object for recording.
10. Start the recording.
11. Stop and release the recording object when finished.

Using some standard button controls, you can create an `Activity` to record and play back video using the preceding steps. The `onClick()` method for a Record button might look like this:

```
public void onClick(View v) {
    if (videoRecorder == null) {
        videoRecorder = new MediaRecorder();
    }
    String pathForAppFiles =
        getFilesDir().getAbsolutePath();
    pathForAppFiles += RECORDED_FILE;

    videoRecorder.setVideoSource(
        MediaRecorder.VideoSource.CAMERA);

    videoRecorder.setOutputFormat(
        MediaRecorder.OutputFormat.MPEG4 );

    videoRecorder.setVideoSize(640, 480);
    videoRecorder.setVideoFrameRate(30);
    videoRecorder.setVideoEncoder(
        MediaRecorder.VideoEncoder.H264);

    videoRecorder.setOutputFile(pathForAppFiles);
    videoRecorder.setPreviewDisplay(surface);

    videoRecorder.prepare();
    videoRecorder.start();

    // button handling and other behavior here
}
```

The `videoRecorder` object is instantiated and given some video configuration values for the recording source. There are several values for each video configuration setting; however, supported values can vary by device.

A Stop button configured with an `onClick()` handler might look like this:

```
public void onClick(View v) {
    if (videoRecorder!= null) {
        videoRecorder.stop();
        videoRecorder.release();
        videoRecorder = null;
    }
    // button handling and other behavior here
}
```

Finally, applications wanting to record video require the explicit permission `android.permission.CAMERA` set in the `AndroidManifest.xml` file.

Tip

Beginning in Android 4.0 (API Level 14), you can take still photos during video sessions if the device supports this feature. To do this, first check that the device supports the feature using the `isVideoSnapshotSupported()` method, and then call the `takePicture()` method of the `Camera` class.

Playing Video

The simplest way to play back video with the Android SDK is to use the `VideoView` widget along with the `MediaController` widget to provide basic video controls. The following is an implementation of an `onCreate()` method in an `Activity` that demonstrates a workable video playback solution:

```
@Override
protected void onCreate(Bundle savedInstanceState) {
    super.onCreate(savedInstanceState);
    setContentView(R.layout.moving);

    VideoView vv = (VideoView) findViewById(R.id.video);
    MediaController mc = new MediaController(this);
    Uri video = Uri.parse(MOVIE_URL);

    vv.setMediaController(mc);
    vv.setVideoURI(video);
}
```

Note

The Android emulator doesn't play video files particularly well in all screen resolutions. Instead, it's best to test video code on the device.

A simple layout file with these controls might result in a display that looks like Figure 13.2. The `MediaController` presents a nice `ProgressBar` that shows download completion and the current location. The use of the `setAnchorView()` method of the `MediaController` is not needed when used with the `setMediaController()` method of `VideoView`—it's automatically set to the `VideoView`.

The call to the `setVideoURI()` method automatically starts playback. You can create a listener for when playback finishes using the `setOnCompletionListener()` method of the `VideoView`. The `VideoView` object has several other helpful methods, such as `getDuration()`, and direct control over playback through methods such as `pause()`. For finer control over the media, or for an alternative way to play back media, you can use the `MediaPlayer` object. Use of it is similar to using the camera—you need a `SurfaceHolder`.

Tip

If your application needs to protect the content of your media streams, you can use the `MediaDrm` class, introduced in Android 4.3 (API Level 18), which allows you to encrypt and decrypt your content. Refer to the Android documentation to learn more about the `MediaDrm` class for protecting your content: *http://d.android.com/reference/android/ media/MediaDrm.html*.

Warning

The `MediaController` can't be retrieved from a layout file XML definition by a call to `findViewById()`. It must be instantiated programmatically and uses the `Context` of the `Activity` class, not the application `Context`.

Figure 13.2   Screen showing video playback with
the default media controller displayed.

Note
When the URI to the video points to an Internet resource, your application will require the
`android.permission.INTERNET` permission in the manifest file.

Working with Face Detection

Beginning in Android 4.0 (API Level 14), the `Camera` class supports face detection.
To detect faces, you can register a `Camera.FaceDetectionListener`. Then start the
`Camera` and call the `startFaceDetection()` method to begin detecting faces. When
a face is detected, you'll get an `onFaceDetection()` callback event, which returns an
array of `Camera.Face` objects you can inspect. The `Camera.Face` class encapsulates a
plethora of information about the face, including a bounded rectangle representing the
facial area, a number of `Point` objects where the eyes and mouth of the face are thought
to be located, as well as a numeric score for how confident the face detection engine is

that you've detected a human face. When you're done, call `stopFaceDetection()`. For more information about face detection, see the most recent `Camera` class documentation.

Working with Audio

Much like video, the Android SDK provides methods for audio playback and recording. Audio files can be resources, local files, or `Uri` objects to shared or network resources. Audio recording takes place through the built-in microphone on the device, if one is present (typically a requirement for a phone because one speaks into it quite often).

Recording Audio

The `MediaRecorder` object of the Android SDK provides audio recording functionality. Using it is a matter of following a few simple steps you should now find familiar:

1. Instantiate a new `MediaRecorder` object.
2. Set the audio source.
3. Set the audio format to record with.
4. Set the file format to store the audio in.
5. Set the file to record to.
6. Prepare the object for recording.
7. Start the recording.
8. Stop and release the recording object when finished.

Using a couple of simple buttons, you can create a simple `Activity` to record and play back audio using the preceding steps. The `onClick()` method for a Record button might look like this:

```
public void onClick(View v) {
    if (audioRecorder == null) {
        audioRecorder = new MediaRecorder();
    }
    String pathForAppFiles =
        getFilesDir().getAbsolutePath();
    pathForAppFiles += RECORDED_FILE;

    audioRecorder.setAudioSource(
        MediaRecorder.AudioSource.MIC);
    audioRecorder.setOutputFormat(
        MediaRecorder.OutputFormat.DEFAULT);
    audioRecorder.setAudioEncoder(
        MediaRecorder.AudioEncoder.DEFAULT);

    audioRecorder.setOutputFile(pathForAppFiles);

    audioRecorder.prepare();
    audioRecorder.start();
```

```
    // button handling and other behavior here
}
```

The `audioRecorder` object is instantiated, if necessary. The default values for the recording source and output file work fine for our purposes. Of note are the values for `CAMCORDER`, which uses a microphone in the direction of the camera, and various voice values that can be used to record calls (beware of local laws) and choose the proper microphone for voice recognition.

Warning

If you find that recording does not start, check the file extension used. For instance, when using the MPEG4 container, the Android SDK requires that the file extension be `.mp4`; otherwise, the recording does not start.

A Stop button is configured with an `onClick()` handler that looks like this:

```
public void onClick(View v) {
    if (audioRecorder != null) {
        audioRecorder.stop();
        audioRecorder.release();
        audioRecorder = null;
    }
    // button handling and other behavior here
}
```

Finally, applications that want to record audio require the explicit permission `android.permission.RECORD_AUDIO` set within the `AndroidManifest.xml` file.

Now it is time to add the playback functionality, so we can listen to the audio we just recorded.

Playing Audio

The `MediaPlayer` object can be used to play audio. The following steps are required to prepare a file for playback:

1. Instantiate a new `MediaPlayer` object.
2. Set the path to the file using the `setDataSource()` method.
3. Call the `prepare()` method of the `MediaPlayer` object.
4. Call the `start()` method to begin playback.
5. Playback can then be stopped with a call to the `stop()` method.

The `onClick()` handler for a button to play the recorded audio from the previous example might look like the following:

```
public void onClick(View v) {
    if (player == null) {
        player = new MediaPlayer ();
    }
    try {
        String audioFilePath =
```

```
            getFilesDir().getAbsolutePath();
        audioFilePath += RECORDED_FILE;

        player.setDataSource(audioFilePath);

        player.prepare();
        player.start();
    } catch (Exception e) {
        Log.e("Audio", "Playback failed.", e);
    }
}
```

The audio data source can be a local file path, valid file object, or valid URI to an audio resource. You can programmatically stop the sound playback by a call to the stop() method. You can set a MediaPlayer.OnCompletionListener object to get a callback when the playback finishes. When done with the MediaPlayer object, you should use a call to the release() method to free up any resources it might be using, much like releasing the MediaRecorder object.

Tip

The AudioManager (android.media.AudioManager) is a system service. You can request the AudioManager by calling the getSystemService(Context.AUDIO_SERVICE) method. You can use the AudioManager to inspect, manage, and modify device-wide audio settings. A number of new APIs were added to the AudioManager in the Android 2.2 SDK for managing audio focus—that is, how multiple audio sources playing at the same time give one another "right of way" and so forth. This functionality can be crucial for audio-streaming applications like podcast and music players.

Sharing Audio

Audio can be shared with the rest of the system. The ContentResolver can send the file to the MediaStore content provider. The following code snippet shows how to configure an audio entry in the audio library on the device:

```
ContentValues values = new ContentValues(9);
values.put(MediaStore.MediaColumns.TITLE, "RecordedAudio");
values.put(MediaStore.Audio.Media.ALBUM,
    "Your Groundbreaking Album");
values.put(MediaStore.Audio.Media.ARTIST, "Your Name");
values.put(MediaStore.Audio.Media.DISPLAY_NAME,
    "The Audio File You Recorded In Media App");
values.put(MediaStore.Audio.Media.IS_RINGTONE, 1);
values.put(MediaStore.Audio.Media.IS_MUSIC, 1);
values.put(MediaStore.MediaColumns.DATE_ADDED,
    System.currentTimeMillis() / 1000);
values.put(MediaStore.MediaColumns.MIME_TYPE, "audio/mp4");
values.put(MediaStore.Audio.Media.DATA, pathForAppFiles);

Uri audioUri = getContentResolver().insert(
    MediaStore.Audio.Media.EXTERNAL_CONTENT_URI, values);
```

```
if (audioUri == null) {
    Log.d("Audio", "Content resolver failed");
    return;
}
```

Setting these values enables the recorded audio to be used by different audio-oriented applications on the device. For example, setting the `IS_MUSIC` flag enables the audio file to appear in the various sections of the music player and be sorted by its album information. Setting the `IS_RINGTONE` flag enables the audio file to appear in the list of ringtones for the device.

Periodically, the device scans for new media files. However, to speed up this process, a `BroadcastIntent` can be sent telling the system about new audio files. The following code demonstrates this for the audio added to the content library:

```
sendBroadcast(new Intent(
    Intent.ACTION_MEDIA_SCANNER_SCAN_FILE,audioUri));
```

After this `Intent` broadcast is handled, the audio file immediately appears in the designated applications.

Tip

Android 4.4 (API Level 19) introduced the `LoudnessEnhancer` class for increasing the volume of an application's audio. You could use this when your application has more than one audio track playing at one time and one needs to be louder than the others. To learn more about this class, see the Android documentation found here: *http://d.android.com/ reference/android/media/audiofx/LoudnessEnhancer.html*.

Searching for Multimedia

You can use the search `Intent` called `android.intent.action.MEDIA_SEARCH` to search for multimedia on a given device. You can also register an intent filter with your application to show up as a source for multimedia with this action. For example, you can perform a search for a specific artist and song like this:

```
Intent searchMusic = new Intent(
    android.provider.MediaStore.INTENT_ACTION_MEDIA_SEARCH);
searchMusic.putExtra(android.provider.MediaStore.EXTRA_MEDIA_ARTIST,
    "Cyndi Lauper");
searchMusic.putExtra(android.provider.MediaStore.EXTRA_MEDIA_TITLE,
    "I Drove All Night");
searchMusic.putExtra(android.provider.MediaStore.EXTRA_MEDIA_FOCUS,
    "audio/*");
startActivity(searchMusic);
```

If you load up a bunch of music on your device (such as Cyndi Lauper's "I Drove All Night") and launch this `Intent`, you are directed straight to the song you requested. Note that if you have many music apps installed, you might need to select an appropriate one (such as the Play Music application) the first time you send the `Intent`.

Figure 13.3   Screen showing a prompt to choose the application you
would like to use for searching for multimedia files on your device.

If you don't have any music on your device but have several music apps, you may be
prompted to pick the app that you want to perform this search. For example, Figure 13.3
shows what happens on one of our devices.

Working with Ringtones

Much like wallpapers, ringtones are a popular way to personalize a device. The Android
SDK provides a variety of ways to manage ringtones through the RingtoneManager
object. You can assign the recorded audio from the previous example as the current ringtone with the following static method call:

```
RingtoneManager.setActualDefaultRingtoneUri(
    getApplicationContext(),
    RingtoneManager.TYPE_RINGTONE, audioUri);
```

The type can also be TYPE_ALARM or TYPE_NOTIFICATION to configure sounds of
other system events that use audio tones. To successfully perform this operation, though,

the application must have the `android.permission.WRITE_SETTINGS` permission set in the `AndroidManifest.xml` file. You can also query the default ringtone with a call to the static `RingtoneManager.getActualDefaultRingtoneUri()` method. You can use the resulting URI to play the ringtone, which might be useful in applications that want to alert the user.

Introducing the Media Router

The Android Support Library (Revision 18) introduced the new v7 mediarouter library. This library allows an Android device to leverage the Google Cast SDK for routing Android content to another external device, such as a TV or speakers. For example, if you started to play a video on a small Android device such as a mobile phone, the media router APIs would allow you to reroute that media content to a larger screen.

Tip

The Google Cast SDK is composed of a sender and a receiver application. Senders are not limited to Android applications, as iOS and Chrome OS applications are also supported, although your Android applications would make use of the media router APIs found in the Android Support Library. To learn more about the media router APIs, see *http://d.android .com/guide/topics/media/mediarouter.html*.

A receiver application communicates with the sender application through the receiving device, and the media application is able to make use of the `MediaRouteProvider` APIs. To learn more about the `MediaRouteProvider` APIs, see *http://d.android.com/guide/ topics/media/mediarouteprovider.html*.

To learn more about the Google Cast SDK, see *https://developers.google.com/cast/*.

Summary

Use of multimedia in many applications can dramatically increase their appeal, usefulness, and even usability. The Android SDK provides a variety of APIs for recording audio, video, and images using the camera and microphone hardware; it also provides the capability to play audio and video and display still images. Other devices support more fine-tuned camera usage, including application-level access to front-facing cameras and face detection capabilities. Multimedia can be private to a specific application or shared among all applications using the `MediaStore` content provider.

Quiz Questions

1. True or false: Any application that requests the `CAMERA` permission is assumed to use all camera features.
2. What class should be extended and used for displaying the camera `View`?
3. What method should you use to determine the focus modes supported by the camera?

4. True or false: The setVideoURI() method automatically starts video playback of the provided video.

5. What permission do you need to declare in your application's manifest file to support recording of audio?

Exercises

1. Write an application that makes use of a device's existing Camera app for taking pictures.

2. Write an application that plays an audio file in the background using a Service to allow playback even while the application is no longer showing.

3. Use the Android documentation to determine the supported network protocols for playing audio and video.

References and More Information

Android API Guides: "Media and Camera":
   http://d.android.com/guide/topics/media/index.html
Android API Guides: "Supported Media Formats":
   http://d.android.com/guide/appendix/media-formats.html
Android SDK Reference documentation on the Camera class:
   http://d.android.com/reference/android/hardware/Camera.html
Android SDK Reference documentation on the android.media package:
   http://d.android.com/reference/android/media/package-summary.html
Android SDK Reference documentation on the MediaActionSound class:
   http://d.android.com/reference/android/media/MediaActionSound.html
Android SDK Reference documentation on the MediaDrm class:
   http://d.android.com/reference/android/media/MediaDrm.html
Android SDK Reference documentation on the LoudnessEnhancer class:
   http://d.android.com/reference/android/media/audiofx/LoudnessEnhancer.html
Android SDK reference documentation on the MediaPlayer class:
   http://d.android.com/reference/android/media/MediaPlayer.html

## 14

Using Android Telephony APIs

Although the Android platform has been designed to run on almost any type of device, many of the Android devices currently available on the market are smartphones. Applications can take advantage of this fact by integrating phone or telephony features into their feature set. This chapter introduces you to the telephony-related APIs available in the Android SDK.

Working with Telephony Utilities

The Android SDK provides a number of useful utilities to integrate phone features available on the device with applications. Although devices run applications, phone operations generally take precedence on smartphones. Your application should not interrupt a phone conversation, for example. To avoid this kind of behavior, your application should know something about what the user is doing, so that it can react differently. For instance, an application might query the state of the phone and determine that the user is talking on the phone, and then choose to vibrate instead of play an alarm.

Tip

There are many different types of Android devices now available to consumers. If your application uses telephony features, make sure you set the `<uses-feature>` tag with the `android.hardware.telephony` feature (or one of its sub-features) in your application's manifest file to ensure that your application is installed only on compatible devices. See the Android SDK documentation for more details.

In other cases, applications might need to place a call or send a text message. Phones typically support SMS, which is popular for texting (text messaging). Enabling the capability to leverage this feature from an application can enhance the appeal of the application and add features that can't be easily replicated on a desktop environment. Because many Android devices are phones, applications frequently deal with phone numbers and the contacts database; some might want to access the phone dialer to place calls or check phone status information. Adding telephony features to an application enables a more integrated user experience and enhances the overall value of the application to the users.

Tip

Many of the code examples provided in this chapter are taken from the SimpleTelephony application. The source code for this application is provided for download on the book's website.

Gaining Permission to Access Phone State Information

Let's begin by looking at how to determine the telephony state of the device, including the capability to request the hook state of the phone, information about the phone service, and utilities for handling and verifying phone numbers. The `TelephonyManager` object in the `android.telephony` package is a great place to start.

Many of the method calls in this section require explicit permission set with the Android application manifest file. The `READ_PHONE_STATE` permission is required to retrieve information such as the call state, handset phone number, and device identifiers or serial numbers. The `ACCESS_COARSE_LOCATION` permission is required for cellular location information.

The following block of XML is typically needed in an application's `Android Manifest.xml` file to access basic phone state information:

```
<uses-permission android:name="android.permission.READ_PHONE_STATE" />
```

Requesting Call State

You can use the `TelephonyManager` object to retrieve the state of the phone and some information about the phone service itself, such as the phone number of the handset.

You can request an instance of `TelephonyManager` using the `getSystemService()` method, like this:

```
TelephonyManager telManager = (TelephonyManager)
    getSystemService(Context.TELEPHONY_SERVICE);
```

With a valid `TelephonyManager` instance, an application can now make several queries. One important method is `getCallState()`. This method can determine the voice call status of the handset. The following block of code shows how to query for the call state and all the possible return values:

```
int callStatus = telManager.getCallState();
String callState = null;

switch (callStatus) {

    case TelephonyManager.CALL_STATE_IDLE:
        callState = "Phone is idle.";
        break;

    case TelephonyManager.CALL_STATE_OFFHOOK:
        callState = "Phone is in use.";
        break;
```

```
    case TelephonyManager.CALL_STATE_RINGING:
        callState = "Phone is ringing!";
        break;
}
Log.i("telephony", callState);
```

The three call states can be simulated with the emulator through the Dalvik Debug Monitor Service (DDMS) tool. Querying for the call state can be useful in certain circumstances. However, listening for changes in the call state can enable an application to react appropriately to something the user might be doing. For instance, a game might automatically pause and save state information when the phone rings so that the user can safely answer the call. An application can register to listen for changes in the call state by making a call to the listen() method of TelephonyManager:

```
telManager.listen(new PhoneStateListener() {
    public void onCallStateChanged(
        int state, String incomingNumber) {

        String newState = getCallStateString(state);
        if (state == TelephonyManager.CALL_STATE_RINGING) {
            Log.i("telephony", newState +
                " number = " + incomingNumber);
        } else {
            Log.i("telephony", newState);
        }
    }
}, PhoneStateListener.LISTEN_CALL_STATE);
```

The listener is called, in this case, whenever the phone starts ringing, the user makes a call, the user answers a call, or a call is disconnected. The listener is also called right after it is assigned so an application can get the initial state.

Another useful piece of information is determining the state of the telephony service. This information can tell an application if the phone has coverage at all, if it can make emergency calls only, or if the radio for phone calls is turned off as it might be when in airplane mode. To do this, an application can add the PhoneStateListener.LISTEN_SERVICE_STATE flag to the listener described earlier and implement the onService StateChanged method, which receives an instance of the ServiceState object. Alternatively, an application can check the state by constructing a ServiceState object and querying it directly, as shown here:

```
int serviceStatus = serviceState.getState();
String serviceStateString = null;

switch (serviceStatus) {
    case ServiceState.STATE_EMERGENCY_ONLY:
        serviceStateString = "Emergency calls only";
        break;

    case ServiceState.STATE_IN_SERVICE:
        serviceStateString = "Normal service";
        break;
```

```
    case ServiceState.STATE_OUT_OF_SERVICE:
        serviceStateString = "No service available";
        break;

    case ServiceState.STATE_POWER_OFF:
        serviceStateString = "Telephony radio is off";
        break;
}
Log.i("telephony", serviceStateString);
```

A status such as whether the handset is roaming can be determined by a call to the getRoaming() method. A friendly and frugal application can use this method to warn the user before performing any costly roaming operations such as data transfers within the application.

Requesting Service Information

In addition to call and service state information, your application can retrieve other information about the device. This information is less useful for the typical application but can diagnose problems or provide specialized services available only from certain provider networks. The following code retrieves several pieces of service information:

```
String opName = telManager.getNetworkOperatorName();
Log.i("telephony", "operator name = " + opName);

String phoneNumber = telManager.getLine1Number();
Log.i("telephony", "phone number = " + phoneNumber);

String providerName = telManager.getSimOperatorName();
Log.i("telephony", "provider name = " + providerName);
```

The network operator name is the descriptive name of the current provider that the handset connects to, typically the current tower operator. The SIM operator name is typically the name of the user's service provider. The phone number for this API is defined as the MSISDN, typically the directory number of a GSM handset (that is, the number someone would dial to reach that particular phone).

Monitoring Signal Strength and Data Connection Speed

Sometimes an application might want to alter its behavior based on the signal strength or service type of the device. For example, a high-bandwidth application might alter stream quality or buffer size based on whether the device has a low-speed connection (such as 1xRTT or EDGE) or a high-speed connection (such as EVDO or HSDPA). TelephonyManager can be used to determine such information.

If your application needs to react to changes in telephony state, you can use the listen() method of TelephonyManager and implement a PhoneStateListener to receive changes in service, data connectivity, call state, signal strength, and other phone state information.

Working with Phone Numbers

Applications that deal with telephony, or even just contacts, frequently have to deal with the input, verification, and usage of phone numbers. The Android SDK includes a set of helpful utility functions that simplify handling of phone number strings. Applications can have phone numbers formatted based on the current locale setting. For example, the following code uses the `formatNumber()` method:

```
String formattedNumber =
    PhoneNumberUtils.formatNumber("9995551212");
Log.i("telephony", formattedNumber);
```

The resulting output to the log would be the string 999-555-1212 in my locale. Phone numbers can also be compared using a call to the `PhoneNumberUtils.compare()` method. An application can also check to see whether a given phone number is an emergency phone number by calling `PhoneNumberUtils.isEmergencyNumber()`, which enables your application to warn users before they call an emergency number. This method is useful when the source of the phone number data might be questionable

Tip

There are a number of utilities for formatting phone numbers based upon locale. Keep in mind that different countries format their numbers in different ways. For example, there is a utility method called `formatJapaneseNumber()` for formatting numbers with special prefixes in the Japanese style. To learn more about these utilities, see the `PhoneNumberUtils` documentation: *http://d.android.com/reference/android/telephony/PhoneNumberUtils.html*.

The `formatNumber()` method can also take an `Editable` as a parameter to format a number in place. The useful feature here is that you can assign the `PhoneNumber FormattingTextWatcher` object to watch a `TextView` (or `EditText` for user input) and format phone numbers as they are entered. The following code demonstrates the ease of configuring an `EditText` to format phone numbers that are entered:

```
EditText numberEntry = (EditText) findViewById(R.id.number_entry);
numberEntry.addTextChangedListener(
    new PhoneNumberFormattingTextWatcher());
```

While the user is typing in a valid phone number, the number is formatted in a way suitable for the current locale. Just the numbers for 19995551212 were entered on the `EditText` shown in Figure 14.1.

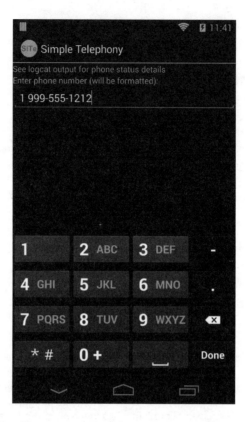

Figure 14.1   Screen showing formatting results after entering only digits.

Using SMS

Integrating messaging services into an application can provide familiar social functionality to the user. SMS functionality is provided to applications through the `android.telephony` package and the recently introduced `android.provider.Telephony` package added in Android 4.4 KitKat (API Level 19). The Android 4.4 editions provide public SMS APIs, allowing developers to avoid the temptation of using undocumented SMS features in their applications, which is a practice that is greatly discouraged as there is no way to guarantee API compatibility with particular devices.

Default Messaging Application

Android 4.4 introduced a new way for users to select your application as their device's default messaging application. This provides an opportunity for your application to remain front and center to your users whenever SMS and Multimedia Messaging Service (MMS) capabilities occur on their device. With that said, users are free to choose any messaging application as their default if other applications are also configured to become the default messaging application.

There are a few settings you need to declare in your application's manifest file to remain eligible to become the default messaging application. These settings include:

- An `Activity`: For other applications to send messages through the default SMS application, this `Activity` declaration requires including an `<intent-filter>` listing an `<action>` tag that names the `SENDTO` intent, and `<data>` tags for the sms, mms, smsto, and mmsto schema attributes.

- An SMS `BroadcastReceiver`: For the default messaging application to receive incoming SMS, include the `BROADCAST_SMS` permission and an `<intent-filter>` with the `SMS_DELIVER` `<action>` tag name attribute.

- An MMS `BroadcastReceiver`: For the default messaging application to receive incoming MMS, include the `BROADCAST_WAP_PUSH` permission, and an `<intent-filter>` with the `WAP_PUSH_DELIVER` `<action>` tag name attribute and a `<data>` tag with a mimeType of application/vnd.wap.mms-message.

- A `Service`: For the default messaging application to respond to incoming phone calls with a quick response text message, include the `SEND_RESPOND_VIA_MESSAGE` permission, and an `<intent-filter>` with the `RESPOND_VIA_MESSAGE` `<action>` tag name attribute, and `<data>` tags for the sms, mms, smsto, and mmsto schema attributes.

With these settings configured in the application's manifest, your application should show up in the device's Default SMS app system settings list. Locate this by navigating to the device's Settings application, and under Wireless & networks choose More . . ., then select Default SMS app to see your application listed in the settings. Figure 14.2 shows the Simple Telephony application listed in the Default SMS app list.

If a user chooses not to make your application the default SMS app, you must include code to ensure that your application accounts for this, in case the user still wants to use your application for reasons other than being the default SMS application.

SMS Provider

A new SMS Provider has been included along with the default SMS application capabilities. This provider is only writable by the default SMS application, but readable by all applications other than the default SMS application. This provider includes tables for received messages, draft messages, pending messages, and sent messages, but only the default SMS application is able to mark messages as read and to delete messages, and it is responsible for writing its own messages to the provider database.

SMS Applications Other than the Default

In case your users do not choose your application to be the default SMS application, you may still use the `android.telephony` features for sending SMS simply by including the appropriate permissions and writing the appropriate code.

Figure 14.2   Default SMS app settings list within the device settings.

Gaining Permission to Send and Receive SMS Messages

SMS functionality requires two different permissions, depending on whether the application sends or receives messages. The following XML, to be placed in AndroidManifest.xml, shows the permissions needed for both actions:

```
<uses-permission
    android:name="android.permission.SEND_SMS" />
<uses-permission
    android:name="android.permission.RECEIVE_SMS" />
```

Sending an SMS

To send an SMS, an application first needs to get an instance of the SmsManager. Unlike other system services, this is achieved by calling the static method getDefault() of SmsManager:

```
final SmsManager sms = SmsManager.getDefault();
```

Now that the application has an `SmsManager` instance, sending SMS is as simple as a single call:

```
sms.sendTextMessage("9995551212", null, "Hello!", null, null);
```

We can create a simple form for sending an SMS message very easily. The code for the button handling looks like the following:

```
Button sendSMS = (Button) findViewById(R.id.send_sms);
sendSMS.setOnClickListener(new View.OnClickListener() {
    public void onClick(View v) {
        String destination =
            numberEntry.getText().toString();

        String message =
            messageEntry.getText().toString();

        sms.sendTextMessage(destination, null, message,
            null, null);
    }
}
```

After this code is hooked in, the result should look something like Figure 14.3. In this application, we used the emulator "phone number" trick. This trick allows you to call

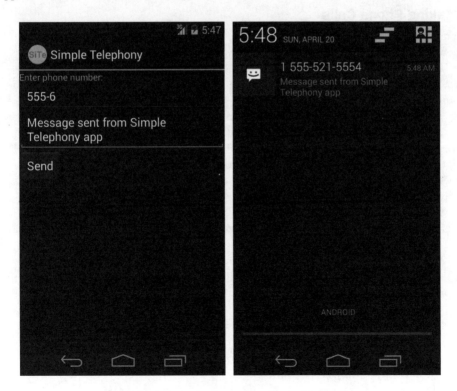

Figure 14.3   Two emulators, one sending an SMS from
an application (left) and one receiving an SMS (right).

another emulator instance by entering the port number of the emulator that you would like to call. This is a great way to test sending SMS messages without using hardware and without incurring charges by the handset operator.

A great way to extend this is to set the sent receiver to modify a graphic on the screen until the sent notification is received. Further, you could use another graphic to indicate when the recipient has received the message. Alternatively, you can use `ProgressBar` widgets to track the progress to the user.

Making and Receiving Phone Calls

It might come as a surprise to the younger generation (they usually just text), but phones are often still used for making and receiving phone calls. Any application can be made to initiate calls and answer incoming calls; however, these abilities should be used judiciously so as not to unnecessarily disrupt the calling functionality of the user's device.

Tip

You can also use two emulator instances to test calling to another handset. As with the SMS sending, the port number of the emulator is the phone number that can be called.

Making Phone Calls

You've seen how to find out if the handset is ringing. Now let's look at how to enable your application to make phone calls as well.

Building on the previous example, which sent and received SMS messages, we now walk through similar functionality that adds a Call button to the screen to call the phone number instead of messaging it.

The Android SDK enables phone numbers to be passed to the dialer in two different ways. The first way is to launch the dialer with a phone number already entered. The user then needs to press the Send button to actually initiate the call. This method does not require any specific permissions. The second way is to actually place the call. This method requires the `android.permission.CALL_PHONE` permission to be added to the application's `AndroidManifest.xml` file.

Let's look at an example of how to enable an application to take input in the form of a phone number and launch the phone dialer after the user presses a button, as shown in Figure 14.4.

We extract the phone number the user entered in the `EditText` field (or the most recently received SMS when continuing with the previous example). The following code demonstrates how to launch the dialer after the user presses the Call button:

```
Button call = (Button) findViewById(R.id.call_button);
call.setOnClickListener(new View.OnClickListener() {
    public void onClick(View v) {
        Uri number = Uri.parse("tel:" + numberEntry.getText().toString());
        Intent dial = new Intent(Intent.ACTION_DIAL, number);
        startActivity(dial);
    }
});
```

Figure 14.4   The user can enter a phone number in the `EditText` control and press the Call button to initiate a phone call from within the application.

First, the phone number is requested from the `EditText` and `tel:` is prepended to it, making it a valid URI for the `Intent`. Then, a new `Intent` is created with `Intent.ACTION_DIAL` to launch into the dialer with the number dialed in already. You can also use `Intent.ACTION_VIEW`, which functions in the same way. Replacing it with `Intent.ACTION_CALL`, however, immediately calls the number entered. This is generally not recommended; otherwise, calls might be made by mistake. Finally, the `startActivity()` method is called to launch the dialer, as shown in Figure 14.5.

Receiving Phone Calls

Much as applications can receive and process incoming SMS messages, an application can register to answer incoming phone calls. To enable this in an application, you must implement a broadcast receiver to process intents with the action `Intent.ACTION_ANSWER`.

Remember, too, that if you're not interested in the call itself but in information about the incoming call, you might want to consider using the `CallLog.Calls` content

Figure 14.5   One emulator calling (left) and the other receiving (right) after
the Call button initiates the phone call from the calling application.

provider (`android.provider.CallLog`) instead. You can use the `CallLog.Calls` class
to determine recent call information, such as:

- Who called
- When the person called
- Whether it was an incoming or outgoing call
- Whether or not anyone answered
- The duration of the call

Working with SIP

Session Initiation Protocol (SIP) is a protocol for controlling communication sessions. SIP
is at the same networking protocol level as HTTP or SMTP. The Android SDK addded
support for SIP in API Level 9. The SIP APIs can be found in the `android.net.sip`
package. Although the SIP APIs support generic sessions, the only type of session that is
handled automatically is a Voice-over-Internet Protocol (VoIP) session.

Using SIP requires that you have an SIP account with an SIP service provider. Using
SIP also requires the `android.permission.USE_SIP` permission to be set in your application's Android manifest file. Additionally, for market filtering, the `<uses-feature>`
tag should be set with `android.software.sip` and `android.software.sip.voip`
features.

For more information about creating an application that uses SIP, including a fully working sample application that comes with the Android SDK, please see the links provided in the reference section at the end of this chapter.

What can you use SIP for? After all, aren't most Android devices still phones? In-app voice communication can be useful. Perhaps your service provides a custom SIP server so that users can make voice connections with each other.

Summary

The Android SDK provides many helpful telephony utilities to handle making and receiving phone calls and SMS messages (with appropriate permissions) and tools to help with formatting phone numbers entered by the user or from other sources.

These telephony utilities enable applications to work seamlessly with the device's core phone features. Developers might also integrate voice calls and messaging features into their own applications, resulting in compelling new features. Messaging is more popular than ever, so integrating text messaging into an application can add a familiar and exciting social feature that users will likely enjoy.

Quiz Questions

1. What application permission is needed to access basic phone state information?
2. How would you retrieve an instance of `TelephonyManager` within your application?
3. True or false: The `getVoiceState()` method is used to determine the voice call status of a handset.
4. What are the four declarations you must make in your manifest file so your application is eligible for the default SMS app?
5. True or false: All SMS applications are capable of writing directly to the SMS Provider.

Exercises

1. Use the Android documentation to determine the class used for providing information about the signal strength of a phone.
2. Use the Android documentation to determine the `Telephony.SMS` class that provides information about outgoing messages.
3. Create an application that may operate as the default SMS application if a user selects it as the default SMS application and that may operate as an SMS application if a user selects another application as the default SMS application.

References and More Information

3GPP specifications (SMS):
  http://www.3gpp.org/specifications
Wikipedia's write-up on SMS:
  http://en.wikipedia.org/wiki/SMS
Android SDK Reference documentation on the `android.telephony` package:
  http://d.android.com/reference/android/telephony/package-summary.html
Android SDK Reference documentation on the `Telephony` class:
  http://d.android.com/reference/android/provider/Telephony.html
Android Developers Blog: "Getting Your SMS Apps Ready for KitKat":
  http://android-developers.blogspot.com/2013/10/getting-your-sms-apps-ready-for-kitkat.html
Android API Guides: "Session Initiation Protocol":
  http://d.android.com/guide/topics/connectivity/sip.html
Android SDK Reference documentation on the `android.net.sip` package:
  http://d.android.com/reference/android/net/sip/package-summary.html

15

Accessing Android's Hardware Sensors

The Android SDK provides a variety of APIs for accessing low-level hardware features on the device. In addition to the camera, Android devices might have a number of other sensors and hardware. Some popular device sensors include the magnetic and orientation sensors, light sensors, and temperature sensors. Applications can also access battery state information. In this chapter, you will explore the optional hardware APIs provided as part of the Android SDK.

Interacting with Device Hardware

The Android platform allows unprecedented access to the device's underlying hardware in a secure and robust manner. Because not all Android devices support or contain all hardware options, it is important to follow these guidelines when accessing underlying device hardware:

- Make no assumptions about the existence or availability of underlying hardware in code or otherwise.

- Always check and verify optional features before trying to access hardware programmatically.

- Pay special attention to exception handling and error and return value checking when working with hardware APIs.

- Understand that hardware features are device resources. Acquire them late, and release them as soon as you're done. In other words, play nice with the other apps. Don't hog the hardware or drain the device battery by misusing hardware resources.

 Warning

The Android emulator has limited to no support for simulating hardware sensors and the device battery. These are cases when testing on real devices is crucial. Much of the code and APIs discussed in this chapter work only on Android hardware and do little or nothing in the Android emulator.

The optional hardware features of different Android devices are key market differentiators to consumers. For example, some might want a device that can act as a Wi-Fi hotspot. Others might require Bluetooth, which we talk about in Chapter 16, "Using Android's Optional Hardware APIs." Still others might be interested in the data that can be collected from various sensors on the device. Finally, applications can access data about the battery and the power management state. We talk about other hardware-related features, such as the camera and location-based services, in Chapter 13, "Using Android Multimedia APIs," and Chapter 17, "Using Location and Map APIs."

> **Tip**
> Many of the code examples provided in this chapter are taken from the SimpleHardware application. The source code for this application is provided for download on the book's website.

Using the Device Sensors

The Android SDK provides access to raw data from sensors on the device. The sensors, and their precision and features, vary from device to device. Some of the sensors that applications can interact with include the magnetic sensor, which can be used as a compass, and the accelerometer sensor, which can detect motion.

You can access the device sensors through the `SensorManager` object (`android .hardware.SensorManager`). The `SensorManager` object listens for data from the sensors. It is a system `Service`, and you can retrieve an instance with the `getSystem Service()` method, as shown here:

```
SensorManager sensors =
    (SensorManager) getSystemService(Context.SENSOR_SERVICE);
```

Working with Different Sensors

The `Sensor` class (`android.hardware.Sensor`) defines a number of identifiers for the various sensors that you might find on a device. Not all sensors are available on each device. Some interesting sensors are listed here:

- `TYPE_ACCELEROMETER`: Measures acceleration in three directions (values are in SI units (m/s^2))
- `TYPE_AMBIENT_TEMPERATURE`: Measures temperature
- `TYPE_GYROSCOPE`: Measures angular orientation in three directions (values are angles in degrees)
- `TYPE_LIGHT`: Measures ambient light (values are in SI lux units)
- `TYPE_MAGNETIC_FIELD`: Measures magnetism in three directions; the compass (values are in micro-Teslas (µT))
- `TYPE_PRESSURE`: Measures barometric pressure

- `TYPE_PROXIMITY`: Measures the distance to an object (values are in centimeters, or "near" versus "far")

- `TYPE_RELATIVE_HUMIDITY`: Measures the relative humidity

- `TYPE_STEP_COUNTER`: Measures the total number of steps recorded since `Service` creation (API Level 19)

- `TYPE_STEP_DETECTOR`: Measures each step by recording a timestamp and a value of 1.0 (API Level 19)

The `SensorManager` class also has a number of constants that can be useful with certain sensors. For instance, you can use the `STANDARD_GRAVITY` constant with the accelerometer and the `LIGHT_SUNLIGHT` constant with the light sensor.

Tip

Not all sensors are available on all devices. For instance, the Galaxy Nexus Android device has a gravity sensor, linear acceleration sensor, magnetic sensor, pressure sensor, proximity sensor, and more, but no temperature sensor or humidity sensor.

Unfortunately, the emulator does not provide any sensor data. All sensor testing must be done on a physical device. Alternatively, OpenIntents.org also provides a handy Sensor Simulator (*http://code.google.com/p/openintents/wiki/SensorSimulator*). This tool simulates accelerometer, compass, and temperature sensors, and it transmits data to the emulator.

Configuring the Android Manifest File for Sensors

The `<uses-feature>` tag in the Android manifest file is used to indicate which sensors your application requires. For example, to declare that your application requires the barometer but can optionally use the gyroscope, you would add the following to your application's manifest file:

```
<uses-feature android:name="android.hardware.sensor.barometer" />
<uses-feature
    android:name="android.hardware.sensor.gyroscope"
    android:required="false" />
```

A full list of sensor declarations can be found in the Android SDK documentation at *http://d.android.com/guide/topics/manifest/uses-feature-element.html#hw-features*.

Acquiring a Reference to a Sensor

You can acquire a reference to a specific sensor using the `SensorManager` class method called `getDefaultSensor()`. This method takes a sensor type parameter. For example, you can acquire the default accelerometer sensor as follows:

```
Sensor accelSensor = sensors.getDefaultSensor(Sensor.TYPE_ACCELEROMETER);
```

Reading Sensor Data

After you have a valid `Sensor` object, you can read the sensor data periodically. Sensor values are sent back to an application using a `SensorEventListener` object that the application must implement and register using the `registerListener()` method:

```
boolean isAvailable = sensors.registerListener(SensorsActivity.this,
    accelSensor, SensorManager.SENSOR_DELAY_NORMAL);
```

In this case, the accelerometer sensor is watched. The `onSensorChanged()` method is called at particular intervals defined by the delay value in `registerListener()`, which is the default value in this case.

The `SensorEventListener` interface has two required methods that you must implement: `onAccuracyChanged()` and `onSensorChanged()`. The `onAccuracyChanged()` method is called whenever the accuracy of a given sensor changes. The `onSensorChanged()` method is called whenever the value of a sensor changes. The `onSensorChanged()` method is generally used to inspect sensor information.

Here is a sample implementation of `onSensorChanged()` that works for displaying various types of sensor data (not just the accelerometer):

```
@Override
public void onSensorChanged(SensorEvent event) {
    StringBuilder sensorMessage =
        new StringBuilder(event.sensor.getName()).append(" new values: ");

    for (float value : event.values) {
        sensorMessage.append("[").append(value).append("]");
    }

    sensorMessage.append(" with accuracy ").append(event.accuracy);
    sensorMessage.append(" at timestamp ").append(event.timestamp);

    sensorMessage.append(".");

    Log.i(DEBUG_TAG, sensorMessage);
}
```

The `onSensorChanged()` method has a single parameter, a `SensorEvent` object. The `SensorEvent` class contains all the data about the sensor, including which sensor caused the event, the accuracy of the sensor, the sensor's current readings, and a timestamp. For details about what data to expect for each type of sensor, see the `SensorEvent` class documentation provided with the Android SDK.

The accelerometer sensor provides three values corresponding to the acceleration currently felt by the device on the x, y, and z axes. The barometer provides the atmospheric pressure in millibars and fills only one of the value fields, as shown in Figure 15.1.

Warning

Depending on the sensor in use, the rate of sensor data might be high. Be aware that your application should do as little as possible in the `onSensorChanged()` method. Do not make blocking calls. If you must process the data, pass the data to a different thread, as

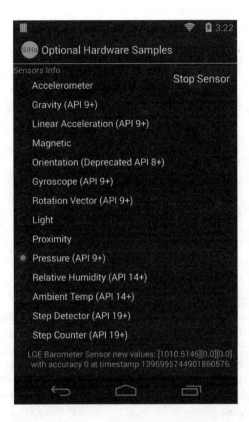

Figure 15.1   Sensor sample application showing barometric values.

described in Chapter 1, "Threading and Asynchronous Processing." Some devices modify the rate in other ways, such as slowing the rate down if the information is not changing quickly. Do not rely on the flow of sensor data for performing unrelated processing.

Calibrating Sensors

The sensor values won't be useful to the application until they are calibrated. One way to calibrate is to ask the user to click a button to calibrate the sensor. The application can then store the current values, and new values can be compared against the original values to see how they have changed (delta). Although the phone sensors have a specific orientation, this enables the user to use the app in either portrait or landscape mode, regardless of how the user holds the device.

When registering a sensor, the `registerListener()` method returns `true` if the sensor is available and can be activated. It returns `false` if the sensor isn't available or cannot be activated.

The sensor values are typically quite sensitive. For most uses, an application probably wants to provide some smoothing of the values to reduce the effects of any noise or shaking. How this is done depends on the purpose of the application. For instance, a simulated bubble level might need less smoothing than a game where too much sensitivity can be frustrating. The orientation values might be appropriate in cases where only the device's orientation is needed but not the rate at which it is changed (accelerometer) or the specific direction it's pointing (compass).

Determining Device Orientation

You can use the `SensorManager` class to determine the orientation of the device. Although the `Sensor.TYPE_ORIENTATION` sensor value is deprecated, it is still valid on most popular devices. However, the recommended way is to use the `getOrientation()` method of the `SensorManager` class instead.

The `getOrientation()` method takes two parameters: a rotation matrix and an array of three float values (azimuth [z], pitch [x], and roll [y]).

Finding True North

In addition to the `SensorManager`, there is a helpful class called `GeomagneticField` available in the `android.hardware` package. The `GeomagneticField` class uses the World Magnetic Model to estimate the magnetic field anywhere on the planet, which is typically used to determine magnetic variation between compass north and true north. This model, developed by the United States National Geospatial-Intelligence Agency (NGA), is updated for precision every five years. The current model expires in 2015, although results are accurate enough for most purposes for some time after that date, at which point the Android `GeomagneticField` class is likely to be updated to the latest model.

Sensor Event Batching

Android KitKat 4.4 (API Level 19) introduced ways to manage the battery usage of the device by batching sensor updates intended for an application's `SensorEventListener`. This means that `Sensor` updates are collected by the Android system and sent to your application as a batch at designated time intervals, only while the CPU is awake. API Level 19 introduced two new versions of the `registerListener()` method that reduce the number of Android system calls, allowing the device to operate in a low-power state.

If the CPU is not awake, you must take additional steps to ensure that your application's sensor memory does not reach capacity, as new sensor events will cause older ones to be removed if not executed as a batch before memory runs out.

Note

Not all Android devices are equipped with hardware sensors, but the new versions of `registerListener()` take this into account and degrade automatically to the older versions of `registerListener()` if only software sensors are supported.

Monitoring the Battery

Mobile devices operate with the use of the battery. Although many applications do not need to know the state of the battery, some types of applications might want to change their behavior based on the battery level, charging state, or power management settings. For instance, a monitoring application can reduce the monitoring frequency when the battery is low and can increase it if the device is powered by an external power source. The battery levels can also help indicate the efficiency of an application, allowing developers to find areas where behavior can be modified to improve battery life, which users will appreciate.

To monitor the battery, the application must have the BATTERY_STATS permission. The following XML added to the AndroidManifest.xml file is sufficient:

```
<uses-permission
    android:name="android.permission.BATTERY_STATS" />
```

Then the application needs to register for a particular BroadcastIntent. In this case, it must be Intent.ACTION_BATTERY_CHANGED. The following code demonstrates this:

```
registerReceiver(batteryRcv,
    new IntentFilter(Intent.ACTION_BATTERY_CHANGED));
```

Next, the application needs to provide an implementation of the Broadcast Receiver. The following is an example of a battery-monitoring BroadcastReceiver:

```
batteryRcv = new BroadcastReceiver() {

    public void onReceive(Context context, Intent intent) {
        int level =
            intent.getIntExtra(BatteryManager.EXTRA_LEVEL, -1);
        int maxValue =
            intent.getIntExtra(BatteryManager.EXTRA_SCALE, -1);
        int batteryStatus =
            intent.getIntExtra(BatteryManager.EXTRA_STATUS, -1);
        int batteryHealth =
            intent.getIntExtra(BatteryManager.EXTRA_HEALTH, -1);
        int batteryPlugged =
            intent.getIntExtra(BatteryManager.EXTRA_PLUGGED, -1);
        String batteryTech =
            intent.getStringExtra(BatteryManager.EXTRA_TECHNOLOGY);
        int batteryIcon =
            intent.getIntExtra(BatteryManager.EXTRA_ICON_SMALL, -1);
        float batteryVoltage =
            (float) intent.getIntExtra(BatteryManager.EXTRA_VOLTAGE,
                -1) / 1000;
        boolean battery =
            intent.getBooleanExtra(BatteryManager.EXTRA_PRESENT,
                false);
        float batteryTemp =
            (float) intent.getIntExtra(
                BatteryManager.EXTRA_TEMPERATURE, -1) / 10;
        int chargedPct = (level * 100)/maxValue ;

        String batteryInfo = "Battery Info:\nHealth=" +
            (String)healthValueMap.get(batteryHealth)+"\n" +
```

```
          "Status="+(String)statusValueMap.get(batteryStatus)+"\n" +
          "Charged % = "+chargedPct+"%\n"+
          "Plugged = " + pluggedValueMap.get(batteryPlugged) + "\n" +
          "Type = " + batteryTech + "\n"        +
          "Voltage = " + batteryVoltage + " volts\n" +
          "Temperature = " + batteryTemp + "°C\n"+
          "Battery present = " + battery + "\n";

      status.setText(batteryInfo);
      icon.setImageResource(batteryIcon);

      Toast.makeText(Battery.this, "Battery state changed",
          Toast.LENGTH_LONG).show();
    }

};
```

There are a couple of interesting items here. First, notice that the battery level isn't used directly. Instead, it's used with the scale, or maximum value, to find the percentage charged. The raw value wouldn't have much meaning to the user. The next property is the status. The values and what they mean are defined in the `android.os.BatteryManager` object. This is typically the charging state of the battery. Next, the health of the battery, also defined in the `android.os.BatteryManager` object, is an indication of how worn out the battery is. It can also indicate other issues, such as overheating. Additionally, the plugged value indicates whether the device is plugged in and, if it is, whether it uses AC or USB power. For more information about broadcast receivers, see Chapter 5, "Broadcasting and Receiving Intents."

Warning

On specific devices, not all this information is available or accurate. For instance, even though we see good data for most fields, we have noted in several instances that some devices return `false` for the `present` field or don't include it at all. Proper testing might be required before relying on battery data for a particular device.

Some other information is returned as well, including an icon identifier that can visually display the state of the battery and some technical details, such as the type of battery, current voltage, and temperature. All displayed, this information looks something like what is shown in Figure 15.2.

Summary

Unlike many other mobile platforms, Android allows complete access to the underlying hardware on the device, including the capability to read raw device sensor data and monitor battery usage. It is important to remember that different devices have different underlying hardware and sensors. Newer API features now allow you to batch sensor calls to conserve battery usage. Always verify the functionality available on each target phone platform during the planning stage of your Android project.

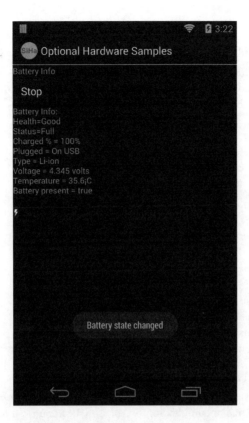

Figure 15.2 Screen capture showing values from the battery
monitor from a physical device.

Quiz Questions

1. True or false: The Android emulator supports simulating hardware sensors.

2. What method, including parameters, should you use to gain access to the device sensor service?

3. How would you acquire a reference to the TYPE_STEP_COUNTER sensor?

4. What method is called when the value of a sensor changes?

5. True or false: The TrueNorth class is used to determine the magnetic variation between compass north and true north.

Exercises

1. Use the Android documentation to determine the equation used to calculate the dew point temperature when using the humidity sensor.

2. Use the Android documentation to determine the Sensor constant that uses a magnetometer for calculating a rotation vector.

3. Create an application that is capable of batching sensor events.

References and More Information

Android API Guides: "Sensors Overview":
http://d.android.com/guide/topics/sensors/sensors_overview.html

Android API Guides: "Motion Sensors":
http://d.android.com/guide/topics/sensors/sensors_motion.html

Android API Guides: "Position Sensors":
http://d.android.com/guide/topics/sensors/sensors_position.html

Android API Guides: "Environment Sensors":
http://d.android.com/guide/topics/sensors/sensors_environment.html

Android SDK Reference documentation on the Sensor class:
http://d.android.com/reference/android/hardware/Sensor.html

Android SDK Reference documentation on the SensorEvent class:
http://d.android.com/reference/android/hardware/SensorEvent.html

Android SDK Reference documentation on the SensorEventListener class:
http://d.android.com/reference/android/hardware/SensorEventListener.html

Android SDK Reference documentation on the SensorManager class:
http://d.android.com/reference/android/hardware/SensorManager.html

Android SDK Reference documentation: SensorEvent values:
http://d.android.com/reference/android/hardware/SensorEvent.html#values

NOAA: "World Magnetic Model":
http://www.ngdc.noaa.gov/geomag/WMM/DoDWMM.shtml

16
Using Android's Optional Hardware APIs

The Android SDK provides a variety of APIs for accessing low-level hardware features on the device. In addition to the camera, Android devices have other hardware resources that developers can take advantage of in their applications, such as Wi-Fi, Near Field Communication (NFC), Bluetooth radios, and a variety of USB connectivity options. In this chapter, you will explore the optional hardware APIs provided as part of the Android SDK.

Working with Bluetooth

Bluetooth APIs have been available since API Level 5, though not all Android devices have Bluetooth hardware. However, this is a popular consumer feature that Android developers can use to their advantage. Android 4.3 (API Level 18) introduced support for Bluetooth Low Energy (BLE), which uses a lot less power than Classic Bluetooth and allows your application to connect to Bluetooth Low Energy peripheral devices. When Bluetooth hardware is present, Android applications can:

- Scan for and discover Bluetooth devices and interact with the Bluetooth adapter
- Establish RFCOMM connections and transfer data to and from devices via data streams
- Maintain point-to-point and multipoint connections with Bluetooth devices and manage multiple connections
- Connect to and communicate with Bluetooth Low Energy peripheral devices

Both Bluetooth APIs are part of the `android.bluetooth` package. As you might expect, the application must have permission to use the Bluetooth services. The `android.permission.BLUETOOTH` permission is required to connect to Bluetooth devices. Similarly, Android applications must have the `android.permission.BLUETOOTH_ADMIN` permission to administer Bluetooth hardware and related services, which includes managing tasks, enabling or disabling the hardware, and performing discovery scans.

Note

It is possible to communicate using either Classic Bluetooth or Bluetooth Low Energy, but not both at a given time.

For Classic Bluetooth, the APIs are divided into several useful classes, including the following:

- The `BluetoothAdapter` class represents the Bluetooth radio hardware on the local device.
- The `BluetoothDevice` class represents a remote Bluetooth device.
- The `BluetoothServerSocket` class is used to open a socket to listen for incoming connections and provides a `BluetoothSocket` object when a connection is made.
- The `BluetoothSocket` class is used by the client to establish a connection to a remote device. After the device is connected, the `BluetoothSocket` object is used by both sides to handle the connection and retrieve the input and output streams.

For Bluetooth LE, the APIs differ and are divided into their own classes:

- The `BluetoothManager` class is used to acquire the `BluetoothAdapter` using the `getSystemService()` method passing in the `Context.BLUETOOTH_SERVICE` value.
- The `BluetoothAdapter` class requires implementing the `LeScanCallback` interface to access the `BluetoothDevice` object using the `onLeScan()` method call.
- The `BluetoothDevice` class requires calling the `connectGatt()` method to connect to a peripheral Bluetooth LE device.

Note

For the rest of this chapter, when we refer to Bluetooth, we mean Classic Bluetooth. To learn more about how to use Bluetooth Low Energy, see the following "Bluetooth Low Energy" Android API Guides: *http://d.android.com/guide/topics/connectivity/bluetooth-le.html*.

Tip

Many of the code examples provided in this section are taken from the SimpleWireless application. The source code for this application is provided for download on the book's website.

Checking for the Existence of Bluetooth Hardware

The first thing to do when trying to enable Bluetooth functionality in your application is to establish whether or not the device has a Bluetooth radio. You can do this by calling and checking the return value of the `BluetoothAdapter` class's static method called `getDefaultAdapter()`:

```
BluetoothAdapter btAdapter = BluetoothAdapter.getDefaultAdapter();
if (btAdapter == null) {
    Log.d(DEBUG_TAG, "No bluetooth available.");
```

```
    // ...
} else {
    // bt available
}
```

Tip

Applications that use Bluetooth should declare as such in the Android manifest file to ensure installation only on compatible devices. You can use the `<uses-feature>` manifest tag to indicate this application requirement, like this: `<uses-feature android:name="android.hardware.bluetooth" />`.

Enabling Bluetooth

After you have determined that the device has a Bluetooth radio, you need to check to see whether it is enabled using the `BluetoothAdapter` class method called `isEnabled()`. If the Bluetooth adapter is enabled, you can proceed. Otherwise, you need to request that it be turned on. This can be done in several ways:

- Fire off the `BluetoothAdapter.ACTION_REQUEST_ENABLE` intent using the `startActivityForResult()` method. This launches an `Activity` that enables the user to choose to turn on the Bluetooth adapter. If the result is `RESULT_OK`, Bluetooth has been enabled; otherwise, the user canceled the Bluetooth-enabling process.

- Call the `BluetoothAdapter enable()` method. This method should be used only by applications that need to explicitly enable the Bluetooth radio. It requires the `BLUETOOTH_ADMIN` permission. In addition, it should be performed only as the result of a direct request from the user, such as through a button, menu item, or query dialog.

- The process of making an Android device discoverable also automatically enables Bluetooth. This can be achieved by firing off the `BluetoothAdapter.ACTION_REQUEST_DISCOVERABLE` intent using the `startActivityForResult()` method. This launches an `Activity` that presents the user with a choice to make the device discoverable for a set amount of time.

Querying for Paired Devices

You can use the `BluetoothAdapter` to query for available Bluetooth devices to connect to. The `getBondedDevices()` method returns a set of `BluetoothDevice` objects that represent the devices paired to the Bluetooth adapter:

```
Set<BluetoothDevice> pairedBtDevices = btAdapt.getBondedDevices();
```

Discovering Devices

New Bluetooth devices must be discovered and paired to the adapter before use. You can use the `BluetoothAdapter` to start and stop the discovery process for available Bluetooth devices to connect to. The startDiscovery() method starts the discovery process asynchronously. This method requires the android.permission.BLUETOOTH_ADMIN permission.

After you have initiated the discovery process, your application needs to register to receive broadcasts for the following Intent actions:

- ACTION_DISCOVERY_STARTED: Occurs when the discovery process initiates
- ACTION_FOUND: Occurs each time a remote Bluetooth device is found
- ACTION_DISCOVERY_FINISHED: Occurs when the discovery process completes

The discovery process is resource- and time-intensive. You can use the isDiscovering() method to test whether the discovery process is currently under way. The cancelDiscovery() method can be used to stop the discovery process. This method should also be used any time a connection is about to be established with a remote Bluetooth device.

Establishing Connections between Devices

The general idea behind connecting two devices via Bluetooth is for one device to find the other device by whatever means necessary, depending upon whether it is a previously paired device or is found through discovery. After it's found, the device calls the connect() method. Both devices then have a valid BluetoothSocket object that can be used to retrieve the InputStream and OutputStream objects for initiating data communications between the two devices.

Now, that's where the theory ends and reality sets in. If it's the same application running on both devices, both devices should find a remote device and both should be discoverable so they can also be found. Also, they should open a listening socket via the BluetoothServerSocket object so they can receive incoming connection requests and be able to connect to the other device. Add to that the fact that both the calls to the accept() method of the BluetoothServerSocket class and to the connect() method of the BluetoothSocket class are blocking synchronous calls, and you can quickly see that you need to use some threads here. Discovery also uses a fair amount of the Bluetooth hardware resources, so you need to cancel and then later restart this process as appropriate. Performing discovery during a connection or even while attempting a connection will likely lead to negative device performance.

Tip

The short code listings provided in the Bluetooth section are taken from the SimpleWireless application. The full source code for this application is provided for download on the book's website. The code required to establish and maintain connections between two devices is lengthy. Therefore, we have chosen to discuss it broadly here and not to include full Bluetooth code listings in this section. Instead, please consult the sample project for a complete implementation of Bluetooth, including the ability to cause one device to make a "ping" sound (sonar style) on the other device.

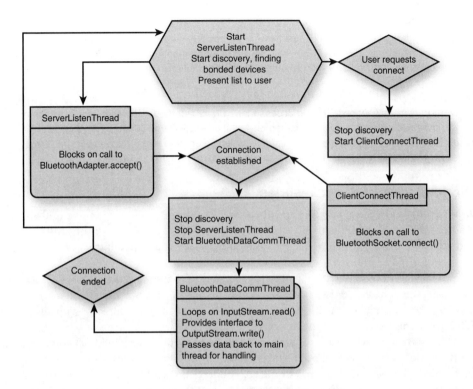

Figure 16.1   Diagram showing behavior flow
for a Bluetooth application on Android.

Figure 16.1 shows a reasonable layout for a Bluetooth implementation and the threads used in the SimpleWireless project.

Working with USB

The Android platform supports a variety of flexible USB-related features. Android devices can act as both USB peripherals (client devices) and USB hosts, depending on the circumstances. This expands the opportunities available for developers to extend the reach of their applications to a variety of situations. Android devices can act as remote controllers or be controlled by accessories. You can even use the Android Open Accessory Development Kit (ADK) to create new Android hardware accessories.

Tip

To debug on devices while they are connected to USB hardware, you can use adb over a network connection.

Warning

Not all Android devices support USB host and accessory modes, so make sure you declare the appropriate `<uses-feature>` tags in your Android manifest file to ensure your application is installed only on compatible Android devices.

Note

Want to develop your own Android accessories? Check out the Open Accessory Development Kit, available in Android 3.1. It is based on Arduino, and you can purchase development boards from a number of suppliers and get hacking. For more information about the ADK, see the Android Dev Guide at *http://d.android.com/tools/adk/index.html.*

Working with USB Accessories

In accessory mode, the approved accessory acts as a controller, providing power to the Android device. Data can be transferred in both directions. The USB accessory APIs can be found under the `android.hardware.usb` package; they were introduced in Android 3.1 (API Level 12).

Your application can interface with USB accessories by accessing the USB system service using the `Context.getSystemService()` method. You can use the `UsbManager` class (`android.hardware.usb.UsbManager`) to discover and communicate with any USB accessories connected to the device.

The `UsbManager` class has a `getAccessoryList()` method, which lists all connected USB accessories available to the application. You can also set up a broadcast receiver to be notified when specific USB accessories are connected. Each USB accessory is represented as a `UsbAccessory` (`android.hardware.usb.UsbAccessory`) object. In order to connect to a USB accessory, you need to request permission from the user. When your application has received permission to communicate with the accessory, it can open a connection to the accessory and communicate using streams; this communication should be handled off the main UI thread. When it is complete, you can terminate your application's connection to the accessory.

Applications that rely on USB accessories have numerous Android manifest file configuration details to consider. At minimum, applications should declare a `<uses-feature>` tag with the `android.hardware.usb.accessory` feature and set their minimum SDK to API Level 12 or higher. See the Android SDK class documentation for more details.

Tip

The USB accessory APIs were back-ported to Android 2.3.4 (API Level 10, though not Android 2.3.3, which is also API Level 10) as part of the Extras libraries, so many more devices now support this functionality. There are subtle differences when working with this version of the USB accessory APIs. This library is available for download in the Android SDK Manager and is named Google USB Driver.

Working as a USB Host

In host mode, the Android device acts as a controller, providing power to the connected USB device. Data can be transferred in both directions. The USB hosts APIs can be found under the `android.hardware.usb` package. It was introduced in Android 3.1 (API Level 12).

Your application can interface with USB devices by accessing the USB system service using the `Context.getSystemService()` method. You can use the `UsbManager` class (`android.hardware.usb.UsbManager`) to discover and communicate with any USB devices available. You can also set up a broadcast receiver to be notified when specific USB devices are connected.

The `UsbManager` class has a `getDeviceList()` method that lists all connected USB devices available to the application. Each USB device is represented as a `UsbDevice` (`android.hardware.usb.UsbDevice`) object. To connect to a USB device, you need to request permission from the user. After your application has received permission to communicate with the device, it can open a connection to the device; this communication should be handled off the main UI thread. The Android SDK includes a number of classes for facilitating communication, including the `UsbInterface`, `UsbEndpoint`, `Usb DeviceConnection`, and `UsbRequest` classes (see the `android.hardware.usb` package for class details). After it is complete, you can terminate your application's connection to the device.

Applications that act as USB hosts have numerous Android manifest file configuration details to consider. At minimum, applications should declare a `<uses-feature>` tag with the `android.hardware.usb.host` feature and set their minimum SDK to API Level 12 or higher. See the Android SDK class documentation for more details.

Working with Android Beam

NFC isn't a new technology, but lately it's been gaining traction with Google's introduction of NFC in Android handsets starting with API Level 9. Previously, you'd be lucky to find it in anything but Nokia devices. The NFC technology from Google is called Android Beam, which is an easy-to-market name for NDEF (NFC Data Exchange Format) Push over NFC and is available in API Level 14 and later.

Read on for a brief introduction to using Android Beam in your applications.

Tip

The code listings in this section are taken from the SimpleWireless application. The full source code for this application is provided for download on the book's website.

Enabling Android Beam Sending

In fact, sending is enabled by default and triggers automatically. When another NFC device is in range, the system shrinks the current screen of the foreground application

Figure 16.2   An app (Google Play Music) in "Touch to beam"
mode when near another NFC device.

and displays a message, "Touch to beam" (Figure 16.2). If your application has no data to
send, nothing happens.

What you want to know about is sending data with this tap. That's easy; just get
an instance of the `NfcAdapter` class and call the `setNdefPushMessageCallback()`
method with a valid `CreateNdefMessageCallback` instance. For example:

```
mNfcAdapter.setNdefPushMessageCallback(new CreateNdefMessageCallback() {
    @Override
    public NdefMessage createNdefMessage(NfcEvent event) {
        Time time = new Time();
        time.setToNow();
        String message = messageToBeam.getText().toString();
        String text = (message + " \n[Sent @ "
                + time.format("%H:%M:%S") + "]");
        byte[] mime = MIMETYPE.getBytes(Charset.forName("US-ASCII"));
        NdefRecord mimeMessage = new NdefRecord(
            NdefRecord.TNF_MIME_MEDIA, mime,
```

```
            new byte[0], text.getBytes());
        NdefMessage msg = new NdefMessage(
            new NdefRecord[] { mimeMessage,NdefRecord.
            createApplicationRecord("com.advancedandroidbook.simplewireless") });
        return msg;
    }
}, this);
```

The implementation of the `createNdefMessage()` method gets a `String` from an `EditText` control (`messageToBeam`), adds the time to it, and encapsulates it inside an `NdefRecord` object that is, itself, encapsulated in an `NdefMessage`. This message is returned and the system pushes it to the other device. You can register to be informed when the message has been successfully sent using the `setOnNdefPushComplete Callback()` method of the `NfcAdapter`.

Receiving Android Beam Messages

Receiving messages is even more straightforward. Your `Activity` needs a new intent filter. Conveniently, NDEF messages come in as normal `Intent` objects.

```
<intent-filter>
    <action android:name="android.nfc.action.NDEF_DISCOVERED" />
    <category android:name="android.intent.category.DEFAULT" />
    <data android:mimeType=
        "application/com.advancedandroidbook.simplewireless" />
</intent-filter>
```

Then you need to check the `Intent` content to see whether it has an NDEF message. If so, extract the data you're looking for (Figure 16.3). This is just reversing the `NdefMessage` and `NdefRecord` creation from previously.

```
@Override
public void onResume() {
    super.onResume();
    // Did we receive an NDEF message?

    Intent intent = getIntent();
    if (NfcAdapter.ACTION_NDEF_DISCOVERED.equals(intent.getAction())) {
        try {
            Parcelable[] rawMsgs = intent
                .getParcelableArrayExtra(NfcAdapter.EXTRA_NDEF_MESSAGES);

            // we created the message, so we know the format
            NdefMessage msg = (NdefMessage) rawMsgs[0];
            NdefRecord[] records = msg.getRecords();
            byte[] firstPayload = records[0].getPayload();
            String message = new String(firstPayload);
            mStatusText.setText(message);
        } catch (Exception e) {
            Log.e(DEBUG_TAG, "Error retrieving beam message.", e);
        }
    }
}
```

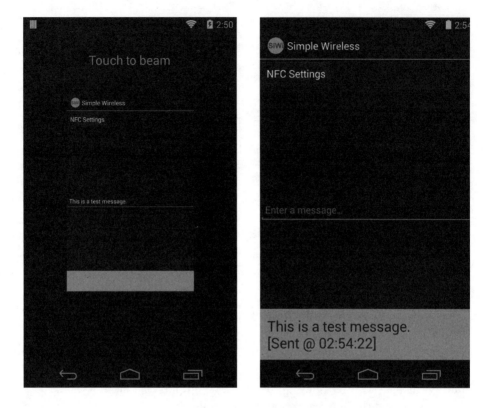

Figure 16.3   Sending the message (left) and receiving it (right).

Incorporating Android Beam into your applications can be that easy. Looking to do something more complex? Check out the resources provided at the end of this chapter for further reading on NFC topics.

Configuring the Manifest File for Android Beam

Android Beam requires API Level 14. Using NFC requires the `android.permission`
`.NFC` permission to be added to the application's Android manifest file. Additionally, `android.hardware.nfc` should be added as a `<uses-feature>` value to help app stores filter your application correctly to devices that have NFC hardware.

```
<uses-sdk
    android:minSdkVersion="14"
    android:targetSdkVersion="19" />
<uses-permission
    android:name="android.permission.NFC" />
```

```
<uses-feature
    android:name="android.hardware.nfc"
    android:required="true" />
```

Android Beam over Bluetooth

Android 4.1 (API Level 16) introduced a new feature for handing off NFC data transfers. NFC was not designed to transfer large amounts of data, nor does NFC transfer data quickly. One way to get around this limitation is to initiate the wireless connection using NFC with the device to which you want to transfer data, and then hand off the actual data transfer to a faster transfer method such as Bluetooth. To make use of this new feature, simply implement the `NfcAdapter.CreateBeamUrisCallback` interface or use the `setBeam PushUris()` method defining the `Uri` objects for transferring. The connection over Bluetooth is then handled automatically without your needing to implement any Bluetooth features yourself.

Introducing Host Card Emulation

Android 4.4 (API Level 19) brought new NFC functionality to the Android platform, known as host card emulation. Host card emulation allows an Android application to emulate an NFC card, rather than requiring the secure element of the device to act as the NFC card.

This feature opens up many possibilities for new NFC card applications that may not have been possible before, as data is transported securely from the NFC controller to your application and back.

Warning

If your application accesses data elsewhere on the system to send to the NFC controller, this may create potential security vulnerabilities, as the data your application sends may not be what it is supposed to be. To learn more about how you can secure your host card emulation applications, read the following "Security Tips" documentation: *http://d.android .com/training/articles/security-tips.html*.

Working with Wi-Fi

Developers can also integrate Wi-Fi features into their applications in two main ways. They can work with the Wi-Fi system service to find and connect to various Wi-Fi networks. Newer versions of the Android SDK also support Wi-Fi Direct, which helps facilitate connections.

Introducing Wi-Fi Direct

Wi-Fi Direct is a relatively new standard that attempts to solve the problems and difficulties with ad hoc Wi-Fi—namely, configuration and connection management—and it first appeared in the Android SDK in Android 4.0 (API Level 14). In doing so, a host Wi-Fi Direct device basically becomes an access point, and a variation of the Protected Setup protocol is used to connect the two devices. With its longer range, faster data communications, and simpler networking than Bluetooth, some think Wi-Fi Direct will ultimately replace Bluetooth for certain kinds of connections.

Using Wi-Fi Direct on Android is fairly straightforward; start by checking out the peer-to-peer Wi-Fi package `android.net.wifi.p2p`. Using the `WifiP2pManager` class (`android.net.wifi.p2p.WifiP2pManager`), you configure several callback classes that are used to asynchronously get the status of requests you make. You can also configure a broadcast receiver to handle various notifications as the state of Wi-Fi Direct changes, both in response to your requests and in changing availability of devices.

In terms of permissions, there is no distinction between regular Wi-Fi and Internet access and Wi-Fi Direct and peer-to-peer networking access. Thus, you need permissions for `INTERNET`, `ACCESS_WIFI_STATE`, `ACCESS_NETWORK_STATE`, `CHANGE_WIFI_STATE`, and `CHANGE_NETWORK_STATE`. Wi-Fi Direct requires API Level 14.

The fastest way to get started with exploring Wi-Fi Direct in code is using the WifiDirectDemo sample application that ships with the Android SDK. To create this project in the Android IDE, simply choose New, then select Project and open the Android folder, then select Android Sample Project, choose Android API 19, and then choose WiFiDirectDemo from the list of legacy samples.

Monitoring Wi-Fi State

The Wi-Fi sensor can read network status and determine nearby wireless access points. The Android SDK provides a set of APIs for retrieving information about the Wi-Fi networks available to the device and Wi-Fi network connection details. This information can be used for tracking signal strength, finding access points of interest, or performing actions when connected to specific access points. This section describes how to get Wi-Fi information. However, if you are looking for information on networking, it is more thoroughly discussed as part of Chapter 11, "Using Android Networking APIs."

The following samples require two explicit permissions in the `AndroidManifest.xml` file. The `CHANGE_WIFI_STATE` permission is needed when an application is accessing information about Wi-Fi networks that can turn on the Wi-Fi radio, thus changing its state. The `ACCESS_WIFI_STATE` permission is also needed to request any information from the Wi-Fi device. You can add these to the `AndroidManifest.xml` file as follows:

```
<uses-permission
    android:name="android.permission.CHANGE_WIFI_STATE" />
<uses-permission
    android:name="android.permission.ACCESS_WIFI_STATE" />
```

The next thing the application needs is an instance of the `WifiManager` object. It is a system service, so the `getSystemService()` method works:

```
WifiManager wifi =
    (WifiManager) getSystemService(Context.WIFI_SERVICE);
```

Now that the `WifiManager` object is available, the application can do something interesting or useful with it. First, the application performs a Wi-Fi scan to see what access points are available in the local area. You need to complete a few steps to perform a scan:

1. Start the scan with the `startScan()` method of the `WifiManager` object.

2. Register a `BroadcastReceiver` for the SCAN_RESULTS_AVAILABLE intent.

3. Call `getScanResults()` to get a list of `ScanResult` objects.

4. Iterate over the results and do something with them.

You can perform the first two steps with the following code:

```
wifi.startScan();
registerReceiver(rcvWifiScan,
    new IntentFilter(WifiManager.SCAN_RESULTS_AVAILABLE_ACTION));
```

The sample `BroadcastReceiver` object, shown here, performs the last two steps. It is called regularly until the `stopScan()` method is called on the `WifiManager` object.

```
rcvWifiScan = new BroadcastReceiver() {
    public void onReceive(Context context, Intent intent) {
        List<ScanResult> resultList = wifi.getScanResults();
        int foundCount = resultList.size();

        Toast.makeText(WiFi.this,
            "Scan done, " + foundCount + " found",
            Toast.LENGTH_SHORT).show();
        ListIterator<ScanResult> results = resultList.listIterator();
        String fullInfo = "Scan Results : \n";
        while (results.hasNext()) {
            ScanResult info = results.next();
            String wifiInfo = "Name: " + info.SSID +
                "; capabilities = " + info.capabilities +
                "; sig str = " + info.level + "dBm";

            Log.v("WiFi", wifiInfo);

            fullInfo += wifiInfo + "\n";
        }
        status.setText(fullInfo);
    }
};
```

The `ScanResult` object contains a few more fields than are demonstrated here. However, the Service Set Identifier (SSID), or name, property is probably the most recognizable to users. The capabilities property lists such things as what security model can be used (such as WEP). The signal strength (level), as given, isn't all that descriptive for most users.

However, the `WifiManager` object provides a couple of helper methods for dealing with signal levels. The first is `calculateSignalLevel()`, which effectively turns the number into a particular number of "bars" of strength. You can use the second, `compare SignalLevel()`, to compare the relative signal strengths of two results.

Note

The emulator does not provide Wi-Fi emulation, but the `WifiManager` APIs do work. However, there are not any results when you use them. Perform testing of Wi-Fi APIs on actual hardware that has a functional Wi-Fi radio.

You can use the `WifiManager` object to list known access points. These are typically access points that the user has configured or connected to in the past. The following code demonstrates the use of the `getConfiguredNetworks()` method:

```
ListIterator<WifiConfiguration> configs =
    wifi.getConfiguredNetworks().listIterator();

String allConfigs = "Configs: \n";
while (configs.hasNext()) {
    WifiConfiguration config = configs.next();
    String configInfo = "Name: " + config.SSID +
        "; priority = " + config.priority;

    Log.v("WiFi", configInfo);

    allConfigs += configInfo + "\n";
}

status.setText(allConfigs);
```

The returned `WifiConfiguration` object does not include all the fields that it could. For instance, it does not fill any network key fields. It does, however, fill in similar fields to those found in the `ScanResults` object. This can be used, for instance, to notify the users when they are in range of known Wi-Fi networks if their devices are set to not automatically connect.

You can use the `WifiManager` object to configure Wi-Fi networks, get the state of the Wi-Fi radio, and more. See the `android.net.wifi` package for more information.

Summary

Unlike many other mobile platforms, Android allows substantial access to the underlying hardware as well as devices attached via USB. Application developers can create new and exciting applications that leverage the Bluetooth, NFC, Wi-Fi, and Wi-Fi Direct technologies. They can also create applications that enable the device to act as a USB host or accessory. Developers can even use the ADK to develop their own Android USB accessories. It is important to remember that different devices have different underlying hardware. Always verify the functionality available on each target platform during the planning stage of your Android project.

Quiz Questions

1. True or false: The Bluetooth Low Energy APIs have been added to the `android` `.bluetooth_le` package.

2. What permissions do you need to declare to connect to Bluetooth devices and to administer Bluetooth hardware?

3. What class is used to discover and communicate with the available USB devices?

4. What does NDEF stand for?

5. What `WifiManager` method should you call to scan for Wi-Fi access points available in the local area?

Exercises

1. Use the Android documentation to determine what method to use to terminate accessory communication when the device is detached.

2. Use the Android documentation to determine what Bluetooth profiles are supported by the Android Bluetooth API.

3. Use the Android documentation to determine what NFC tag technologies are supported by the Android platform.

References and More Information

Android API Guides: "Bluetooth":
   http://d.android.com/guide/topics/connectivity/bluetooth.html
Android API Guides: "Bluetooth Low Energy":
   http://d.android.com/guide/topics/connectivity/bluetooth-le.html
Android SDK Reference documentation on the `android.net.wifi.p2p` package:
   http://d.android.com/reference/android/net/wifi/p2p/package-summary.html
Android API Guides: "Wi-Fi Peer-to-Peer":
   http://d.android.com/guide/topics/connectivity/wifip2p.html
Wikipedia entry on Wi-Fi Direct:
   http://en.wikipedia.org/wiki/Wi-Fi_Direct
Android Training: "Sharing Files with NFC":
   http://d.android.com/training/beam-files/index.html
Android API Guides: "Near Field Communication":
   http://d.android.com/guide/topics/connectivity/nfc/index.html
Android SDK Reference documentation on the `android.nfc` package:
   http://d.android.com/reference/android/nfc/package-summary.html
Android API Guides: "USB Host and Accessory":
   http://d.android.com/guide/topics/connectivity/usb/index.html
Android Tools: "Android Open Accessory Development Kit":
   http://d.android.com/tools/adk/index.html

IV

Leveraging
Google APIs

17

Using Location and Map APIs

Whether for safety or for convenience, incorporating location information, navigation, and mapping features into your project can make your application much more robust. In this chapter, you will learn how to leverage two different location services available for Android: the Android location services APIs and the Google location services APIs. You will learn how to determine the location of the device using both APIs. You will also learn how to translate raw location coordinates into descriptive location names—and how to do the reverse. Finally, we explore a couple of different methods for mapping and utilities that work with maps.

Tip

Many of the code examples provided in this chapter are taken from the SimpleLocation application. The source code for this application is provided for download on the book's website.

Incorporating Android Location APIs

The Android location APIs are built directly into the Android SDK. Until Google Play services introduced the new Google location services APIs, the `android.location` package provided the sole means for working with the location features of a device. Even though the new Google location APIs are much more robust, here are some reasons why you should care about the Android location APIs:

- Not all devices are capable of having Google Play services installed; therefore, it is impossible to access the Google location APIs on these devices.

- There are many classes available in the Android location APIs that are not available in the Google location APIs. This means that you are able to make use of the best of both APIs (provided they are both available), rather than relying on one over the other.

Let's now take a look at some of the features available in the Android location APIs.

Using the Global Positioning System (GPS)

The Android location APIs provide the means for accessing location via built-in GPS hardware, when it's available. Generally speaking, just about every Android phone has some location capabilities. For example, in the United States, emergency services use mobile phone location information. That said, not all Android devices are phones, nor do all phones enable consumer usage of location services. If GPS features are disabled, or an Android device does not have location hardware, the Android SDK provides additional APIs for determining alternative location providers. These other providers might have advantages and disadvantages in terms of power use, speed, and accuracy of reporting.

Using GPS Features in Your Applications

Location services and hardware such as built-in precision GPS are optional features for Android devices. In addition to requiring the appropriate permissions, you can specify which optional features your application requires in the Android manifest file. You can declare that your application uses or requires specific location services using the `<uses-feature>` tag of the Android manifest file. Although this tag is not enforced by the Android operating system, it enables popular publication mechanisms such as the Google Play store to filter your app and provide it only to users with appropriate devices. If your application functions well only on devices with some sort of method for determining the current location, you can use the following `<uses-feature>` tag in your application's manifest file:

```
<uses-feature android:name="android.hardware.location" />
```

If your application requires a precise location fix (that is, the device has functional GPS hardware, not just cell tower triangulation or other such mechanisms), use the following `<uses-feature>` tag instead:

```
<uses-feature android:name="android.hardware.location.gps" />
```

Determining the Location of the Device

To determine device location with the Android location APIs, you need to perform a few steps and make some choices. The following list summarizes this process:

1. Retrieve an instance of the `LocationManager` using a call to the `getSystemService()` method using the `LOCATION_SERVICE`.

2. Add an appropriate permission to the `AndroidManifest.xml` file, depending on what type of location information the application needs.

3. Choose a provider using either the `getAllProviders()` method or the `getBestProvider()` method.

4. Implement a `LocationListener` class.

5. Call the `requestLocationUpdates()` method with the chosen provider and the `LocationListener` object to start receiving location information.

Specific permissions are not needed to retrieve an instance of the `LocationManager` object. Instead, the permissions determine the available providers. The following code retrieves an instance of the `LocationManager` object:

```
import android.location.*;
...
LocationManager locationManager =
    (LocationManager)getSystemService(Context.LOCATION_SERVICE);
```

The following block of XML provides the application with both coarse and fine location permissions when added within the `AndroidManifest.xml` permissions file:

```
<uses-permission
    android:name="android.permission.ACCESS_FINE_LOCATION" />
<uses-permission
    android:name="android.permission.ACCESS_COARSE_LOCATION" />
```

Requesting fine permission implies coarse support as well, but it's helpful to be explicit.

Now that the application has permissions to use location information and the `LocationManager` object is valid, we must determine what provider to use for location information. The following code configures a `Criteria` object and requests the provider based on this information:

```
Criteria criteria = new Criteria();
criteria.setAccuracy(Criteria.NO_REQUIREMENT);
criteria.setPowerRequirement(Criteria.NO_REQUIREMENT);

String bestProvider = locationManager.getBestProvider(criteria, true);
```

The `setAccuracy()` method can take values for `ACCURACY_COARSE` and `ACCURACY_FINE` that can be used (along with the appropriate permissions) to request a provider that the application has permissions to use. You can use the `setPowerRequirement()` method to find a provider that fits certain power use requirements, such as `POWER_HIGH` or `POWER_LOW`. The `Criteria` object also enables you to specify whether the provider can incur a monetary cost to the user, whether altitude is needed, and some other details. If the application has specific requirements, this is where you set them. However, setting these criteria doesn't imply that the provider is available to the user. Some flexibility might be required to allow use on a broad range of devices. A `boolean` parameter of the `getBestProvider()` method enables the application to ask for only enabled providers.

Using the provider returned by the `getBestProvider()` method, the application can request the location. Before doing so, however, the application needs to provide an implementation of `LocationListener`. The `LocationListener` implementation consists of several methods: to tell the application whether the provider has been disabled or enabled, to give the status about the provider (such as the number of satellites the GPS receiver can see), and to tell the application location information. The following is a sample implementation for the last method, the `onLocationChanged()` method:

```
public void onLocationChanged(Location location) {
    String locInfo = String.
```

```
            format("Current loc = (%f, %f) @ (%f meters up)",
            location.getLatitude(), location.getLongitude(),
            location.getAltitude() );
    if (lastLocation != null) {
        float distance = location.distanceTo(lastLocation);
        locInfo += String.
            format("\n Distance from last = %f meters", distance);
    }
    lastLocation = location;
    status.setText(locInfo);
}
```

The onLocationChanged() method receives a Location object with the most recent
location information from the chosen provider. In this example, the application merely
prints out the location, including the altitude, which might be returned by the provider.
Then, it uses a utility method of the Location object, distanceTo(), to calculate how
far the device has moved since the last time onLocationChanged() was called.

It is up to the application to determine how to use this location information. The
application might want to turn the location information into an address, display the location on an embedded map, or launch the built-in Maps application (if the Google applications are installed) centered at the location.

Tip

To use many Android location services APIs, you should use AVD configurations that target
the Android SDK with the Google APIs. Using the Google APIs target puts applications like
Maps on the emulator. Other times, location services design and testing are best done on a
real Android device.

Locating Your Emulator

The Android emulator can simulate location services, but as you would expect, it does
not have any "underlying hardware" to get a real satellite fix. The Android SDK provides
a means to simulate location data with the use of a single location point, GPX file, or
KML file. This works only with the emulator, not the physical device, but it can be useful for testing your location-based application.

Geocoding Locations

Determining latitude and longitude is useful for precise location, tracking, and measure-
ments; however, this data is not usually descriptive to users. The Android SDK provides
some helper methods to turn raw location data into addresses and descriptive place names.
These methods can also work in reverse, turning place names or addresses into raw location coordinates, which is referred to as reverse geocoding.

Warning

According to the Android documentation, AVDs that target the Google APIs enable
developers to test on emulator instances with Google Play services. The Google APIs provide
the capability to use Google Maps as well as a back-end geocoder service. Although it is not

documented, not all AVD API levels support these geocoder services. For example, AVDs for API Level 6 with the Google APIs provide geocoder services, whereas AVDs with API Levels 7 and 8 with the Google APIs do not (as of this writing). When you use an AVD without back-end geocoder services, you simply get an exception stating there is no back-end service. The code in this chapter is best run in an emulator running an AVD with API Level 6 plus the Google APIs, or on a real device with true geocoder back-end services.

The `Geocoder` object can be used without any special permission. The following block of code demonstrates using the `Geocoder` object to get the location names of a `Location` object passed in to the `onLocationChanged()` method of a `LocationListener`:

```
if (Geocoder.isPresent()) {
    Geocoder coder = new Geocoder(this);
    try {
        List<Address> addresses = coder.getFromLocation(
                location.getLatitude(), location.getLongitude(), 3);
        if (addresses != null) {
            for (Address namedLoc : addresses) {
                String placeName = namedLoc.getLocality();
                String featureName = namedLoc.getFeatureName();
                String country = namedLoc.getCountryName();
                String road = namedLoc.getThoroughfare();
                locInfo.append(String.format("[%s][%s][%s][%s]\n",
                        placeName, featureName, road, country));
                int addIdx = namedLoc.getMaxAddressLineIndex();
                for (int idx = 0; idx <= addIdx; idx++) {
                    String addLine = namedLoc.getAddressLine(idx);
                    locInfo.append(String.format("Line %d: %s\n", idx,
                            addLine));
                }
            }
        }
    } catch (IOException e) {
        Log.e("GPS", "Failed to get address", e);
    }
} else {
    Toast.makeText(GPSActivity.this, "No geocoding available",
            Toast.LENGTH_LONG).show();
}
```

You can extract information from the results of the call to the `getFromLocation()` method in two ways, both of which are demonstrated. Note that a particular location might have multiple `Address` results in the form of a `List<Address>` object. Typically, the first `Address` is the most detailed, and the subsequent `Address` objects have less detail and describe a broader region.

The first method is to query for specific information, such as by using the `getFeature Name()` method or the `getLocality()` method. These methods are not guaranteed to return useful information for all locations. They are useful, though, when you know you need only a specific piece of general information, such as the country.

The second method for querying information is by address lines. This is generally used for displaying the address of a location to the user. It might also be useful to use the location in directions and in other cases where a street address is desired. That said, the addresses returned might not be complete. Simply use the `getMaxAddressLineIndex()` and `getAddressLine()` methods to iterate through the addresses. Figure 17.1 shows a sample location with three resulting addresses.

The `Geocoder` object also supports using named locations or address lines to generate latitude and longitude information. The input is forgiving and returns reasonable results in most cases. For instance, all of the following return valid and correct results: "Eiffel Tower," "London, UK," "Iceland," "BOS," "Yellowstone," and "1600 Pennsylvania Ave, DC."

The following code demonstrates a button `onClick()` handler that computes location data based on user input:

```
public void onClick(View v) {
    if (Geocoder.isPresent()) {
        String placeName = name.getText().toString();

        try {
            // coder initialized elsewhere
            List<Address> geocodeResults = coder
                    .getFromLocationName(placeName, 3);
```

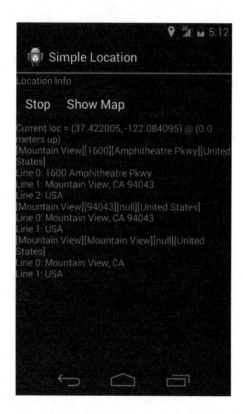

Figure 17.1   Image showing a location geocoded to three "addresses."

```
        StringBuilder locInfo = new StringBuilder("Results:\n");
        double lat = 0f;
        double lon = 0f;

        for (Address loc : geocodeResults) {
            lat = loc.getLatitude();
            lon = loc.getLongitude();
            locInfo.append("Location: ").append(lat)
                    .append(", ").append(lon).append("\n");
        }

        results.setText(locInfo);
    } catch (IOException e) {
        Log.e("GeoAddress", "Failed to get location info", e);
    }
} else {
    Toast.makeText(GeoAddressActivity.this,
            "No geocoding available", Toast.LENGTH_LONG).show();
}
}
```

The result of the call to the `getFromLocationName()` method is a `List` of `Address` objects, much like the previous example. Figure 17.2 shows the results for entering *Eiffel Tower.*

Figure 17.2   The results for geocoding the term *Eiffel Tower.*

Always assume that you will get more than one result. It is good form to provide a picker so that the user can select the most appropriate location from the results. Another good way to confirm that the user entered the correct location is to map it. We will discuss later a couple of different methods for mapping locations using Google Maps.

Warning

Geocoding operations typically require a network connection and therefore should not be run on the main UI thread. Instead, perform geocoding tasks in a separate thread so as not to cause your application's responsiveness to degrade.

Doing More with Android Location-Based Services

You have been introduced to a number of different location tools provided by the Android location APIs; however, you should be aware of several more.

The `LocationManager` supports proximity alerts, which are alerts that trigger a `PendingIntent` when the device comes within some distance of a location. This can be useful for warning the user of an upcoming turn in directions, for scavenger hunts, or for help in geocaching.

The `GpsStatus`, `GpsStatus.Listener`, and `GpsSatellite` classes provide more detailed information about the GPS satellites used by the GPS engine. The `GpsStatus` class and its `Listener` subclass monitor the GPS engine and get a list of the satellites used. The `GpsSatellite` class represents the current state of an individual satellite used by the GPS engine with state information such as satellite elevation and whether the particular satellite was used in the most recent GPS fix.

Tip

Location services applications are a popular category of Android applications. Location services are like networking services: sometimes unreliable or unresponsive. Make sure to consider application responsiveness when designing location services applications. This means completing location-related tasks asynchronously using threads or `AsyncTask` as well as considering Android services.

Incorporating Google Location Services APIs

The Google location services APIs were added into the Google Play services SDK and are compatible with devices that have Google Play installed and running Android version 2.2 (API Level 8) or newer. If you are looking for an easier way to add location features to your application with increased accuracy and low power consumption, use the Google location services APIs.

Locating with the Fused Location Provider

Now that the location features have been integrated into Google Play services, rather than each application having to implement its own code for managing location features,

Google Play services handles all of this tedious work for you and makes this information available to you via the fused location provider, in a convenient set of APIs. Developers no longer need to be concerned with managing power consumption on their own and are able to locate with fine-grained accuracy with very little coding effort.

To make use of the fused location provider, there are a few simple steps you need to follow:

1. Add the appropriate permissions to the Android manifest file, declaring the accuracy that your application requires, such as ACCESS_COARSE_LOCATION or ACCESS_FINE_LOCATION.

2. Make sure to check that Google Play services have been installed on the device; otherwise, your application will crash. Failure to implement the appropriate checks and handling cases where Google Play services are not installed could result in a bad user experience and bad user reviews if your application crashes unexpectedly.

3. Implement the appropriate callback methods for the OnConnectionFailed Listener and ConnectionCallbacks. For the OnConnectionFailedListener, implement the onConnectionFailed() method, and for the Connection Callbacks class, implement the onConnected() and onDisconnected() methods.

4. Create a location client using the LocationClient class in the onCreate() method of your application, and handle the appropriate lifecycle events to connect() and disconnect() the location client where appropriate.

5. Use the getLastLocation() method of the location client to retrieve the location of the device. The permissions you have requested and the location features users have enabled on their device will determine the type of location information available to your application.

Doing More with Google Location Services

The fused location provider is just the first improvement of the Google location services API. In addition, there are two other APIs that you should be aware of, the activity recognition APIs and the geofencing APIs.

Understanding Activity Recognition APIs

The activity recognition APIs are used for detecting the user's current physical activity. Here is a list of the activities, by their constant value and description, that your application is able to detect:

- IN_VEHICLE: Determine if a user is driving a vehicle.
- ON_BICYCLE: Determine if a user is riding on a bike.
- ON_FOOT: Determine if a user is walking or running.
- STILL: Determine if a user is not moving at all.

- TILTING: Determine if a user is tilting the device.

- UNKNOWN: If the user's current activity does not fit into one of these classifications, the activity is unknown.

Tip

To learn more about how to implement activity recognition API features, download the sample application found on the Android documentation website: *http://d.android.com/ shareables/training/ActivityRecognition.zip.*

Understanding Geofencing APIs

A `Geofence` is an area that you define for detecting whether a user has entered or exited a particular latitude, longitude, and specified radius. To set up a `Geofence` for your application, there are a few things you need to do:

1. Add the appropriate location permissions to the Android manifest file.

2. Verify that your app is able to access Google Play services, as geofencing APIs are available only if the Google Play application is installed.

3. Define a `Geofence` storage mechanism using `SharedPreferences`.

4. Create a `Geofence` using a latitude, longitude, and radius.

5. Monitor for when a user enters or exits a `Geofence` and handle the intents appropriately.

6. Stop monitoring and remove the geofences.

Tip

To learn more about how to implement geofencing API features, download the sample application found on the Android documentation website: *http://d.android.com/shareables/ training/GeofenceDetection.zip.*

Incorporating Google Maps Android API v2

Determining the location of a device or specific geographic coordinates does not necessarily provide meaningful information to users; therefore, it is best to display that information on a map with which users are familiar. Luckily, Google provides a set of Map APIs for Android. The current version is 2, and this version provides a number of features and enhancements that were not available in the first version.

Note

The first version of Google Maps for Android is no longer available for new developer signups. This means that you will no longer be able to request an API key to access the first version, but the service is still supported for users who already have an existing API key.

Mapping Locations

The Android SDK provides two different methods to show a location with Google Maps. The first method is to use a location URI to launch the built-in Google Maps application with the specified location. The second method is to use a `MapFragment` embedded within your application to display the map location.

Mapping Intents

Earlier in this chapter, we demonstrated how to determine the latitude and longitude for a place name. Now we map the location using the built-in Maps application. The following block of code demonstrates how to perform this:

```
String geoURI = String.format("geo:%f,%f", lat, lon);
Uri geo = Uri.parse(geoURI);
Intent geoMap = new Intent(Intent.ACTION_VIEW, geo);
startActivity(geoMap);
```

The first task is to create a `String` that conforms to the URI handled by the mapping application. In this case, it's `geo:` followed by the latitude and longitude. This URI is then used to create a new `Uri` object for creating a new `ACTION_VIEW` intent. Finally, we call the `startActivity()` method. If the latitude and longitude are valid, such as the location for the Hoover Dam, the screen would look like Figure 17.3.

Using this method of mapping launches the user into a built-in mapping application—in this case, Google Maps. If you do not want to bother with the details of a full mapping application or do not need to provide any further control over the map, this is a fast and easy method to use. Users are typically accustomed to the controls of the mapping application on their device, too.

Getting Your Map API Key

Before you are able to work with Maps in your application, you first need to obtain a Google Maps for Android API key from Google. The key is generated from a SHA-1 fingerprint of a certificate that you use to sign your applications.

For testing purposes, you can use the debug certificate that is created by the Android SDK, as mentioned in step 1 below. For production distribution, substitute the debug certificate with your release distribution signing certificate.

You need to do the following to generate the appropriate API key:

1. Generate a SHA-1 fingerprint for your debug certificate.
2. Sign in to the Google Developer Console, and choose the project for which you would like to generate an API key.
3. Under the Services link, make sure that Google Maps Android API v2 is turned on.
4. Navigate to the API Access link, and under Simple API Access, click Create new Android key.
5. Paste in the fingerprint from step 1 and follow the additional instructions for configuring an Android key for your project, then press Create.

Figure 17.3   The resulting map for geocoding the term
Hoover Dam and launching a geo URI.

The first step is performed on your development machine. Locate the debug certificate
used by the Android SDK. On all platforms, the filename is debug.keystore by default.
If you use the Android IDE, the location of the file is listed under the Android Build
preferences. Using this file, you then need to execute the following command (make sure
the Java tools are in your path):

```
keytool -list -keystore /path/to/debug.keystore -storepass android
```

The result is the fingerprint that you must paste into the form in step 5.

Tip

The default debug keystore on the Android SDK lasts for only one year and is unique to
a developer's computer. We highly recommend making a debug key that lasts longer and
can be shared among team members. This enables your Google Maps Android API key to

last much longer. In addition, you won't have to uninstall apps from a shared device before you can install one with someone else's debug key. Luckily, it's easy to do this using the `keytool` command-line tool with the following command:

```
keytool -genkey -keypass android -keystore debug.keystore
   alias androiddebugkey -storepass android
   -validity 10000
   -dname "CN=Android Debug,O=Android,C=US"
```

This command generates a valid debug keystore that can be shared among team members and lasts for 10,000 days. After creating it, make sure you reference it from the Android IDE if it's not in the default location.

When you have successfully completed the steps to get your key, you can reference your map key in the Android manifest file of your application by including the following `<meta-data>` tag:

```
<meta-data
   android:value="API_KEY"
   android:name="com.google.android.maps.v2.API_KEY" />
```

Tip

If you work on multiple development machines or work as part of a team, you need to have an API key for everyone's debug certificate. Alternatively, you can copy the debug certificate from one machine to other machines so that the signing and check against the Android Maps API key is successful. This can save you time because you don't have to modify the code or layout files for each developer on the team.

Map Fragments

A `MapFragment` is a user interface component that allows you to add a map to your application in the form of a `Fragment`. Simply create a layout that includes a `Map Fragment` (or a `SupportMapFragment` when working with the Support Library), like so:

```
<fragment
   android:id="@+id/map"
   android:layout_width="match_parent"
   android:layout_height="match_parent"
   class="com.google.android.gms.maps.SupportMapFragment" />
```

Then extend a `FragmentActivity`, and within your `Activity`, access the map in your code using the `getFragmentManager()` or `getSupportFragmentManager()` method using the `getMap()` method of the `Fragment` like so:

```
map = ((SupportMapFragment) getSupportFragmentManager()
          .findFragmentById(R.id.map))
          .getMap();
```

Once you have the map, you are ready to manipulate the presentation to provide meaningful information to your users. When you execute the SimpleLocation code, you should be presented with a screen that looks like Figure 17.4.

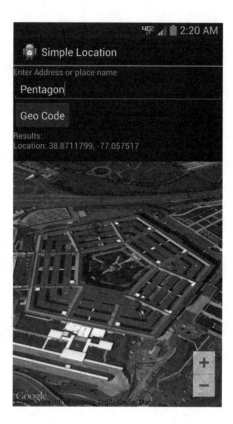

Figure 17.4 `MapFragment` results for geocoding the term *Pentagon*.

Marking the Spot

There are times when you want to mark a particular geographic location on the screen to clearly distinguish a point of reference on the map. Google Maps provides a convenience method for adding a marker to a map at a specific position:

```
map.addMarker(new MarkerOptions()
          .position(new LatLng(0, 0))
          .title("Marker"));
```

First you call the `addMarker()` method on the map and pass in a new `Marker Options()` object with a new coordinate position and a title for the marker. When the user clicks the marker, the marker displays the information you passed to the `title()` method of the `MarkerOptions()` class as shown in Figure 17.5.

Positioning and Animating the Map Camera

There are times when you may like to navigate to a different location on the map as the user interacts with your application. The map is viewable through what is known as the

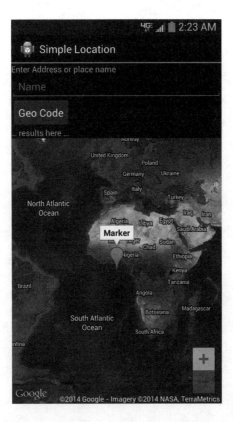

Figure 17.5   Displaying a marker with title information.

camera, whose position can be zoomed, rotated, tilted, or moved. The following code
will move and animate the map to a different location, zoom, rotation, and tilt:

```
destBuilder = new CameraPosition.Builder();
CameraPosition dest = destBuilder.target(new LatLng(lat, lon))
                            .zoom(15.5f)
                            .bearing(300)
                            .tilt(50)
                            .build();
map.animateCamera(CameraUpdateFactory.newCameraPosition(dest));
```

First you create a new `CameraPosition.Builder()` object. Then you define the
target where you would like the camera to move; provide any zoom, orientation, and
tilt options; and then call `build()` to create a new `CameraPosition` object. Then you
call the `animateCamera()` method of the map object and pass in a `CameraUpdate`
`Factory` object with the new camera position to navigate to. Figure 17.6 shows what
the SimpleLocation application looks like after having animated the camera to a new
location on the map.

Figure 17.6   A map after animating the camera to the Giza pyramids.

Summary

Google Maps for Android v2 support is available to developers who register for a key, and it can be used to enhance Android applications with location-rich information. Some applications want to build in seamless map support, whereas others might just launch the built-in map application for the user to leverage. There are tremendous opportunities for using the built-in Android location services APIs, the Google location services APIs, and the Google Maps Android v2 services APIs to improve your Android applications.

Quiz Questions

1. True or false: The Android manifest `<uses-feature>` attribute for adding a precise hardware GPS location fix is `android.hardware.location`.

2. What permission should you add to your Android manifest file to access fine location?

3. When working with a `LocationClient` object, what method should you call to retrieve the location of the device?

4. True or false: A `MapView` is used to display a map with the Google Maps Android v2 services APIs.

5. What method should you call on a `Fragment` to access the `MapFragment`?

Exercises

1. Write an application that makes use of the geofencing APIs.

2. Write an application that makes use of the activity recognition APIs.

3. Use the Google Developer Console to create an API key for Google Maps Android API v2 and install and run the SimpleLocation application provided with this chapter.

References and More Information

Android Google Services: "Location APIs":
   http://d.android.com/google/play-services/location.html
Android Training: "Making Your App Location-Aware":
   http://d.android.com/training/location/index.html
Android API Guides: "Location and Maps":
   http://d.android.com/guide/topics/location/index.html
Android API Guides: "Location Strategies":
   http://d.android.com/guide/topics/location/strategies.html
Android Reference documentation on the `android.location` package:
   http://d.android.com/reference/android/location/package-summary.html
Android Google Services Reference documentation on the `com.google.android.gms`
   `.location` package:
   http://d.android.com/reference/com/google/android/gms/location/package-summary.html
Android Google Services: "Google Maps Android API v2":
   http://d.android.com/google/play-services/maps.html
Google Developers: "Google Maps Android API v2":
   https://developers.google.com/maps/documentation/android/
Android Google Services Reference documentation on the `com.google.android.gms`
   `.maps` package:
   http://d.android.com/reference/com/google/android/gms/maps/package-summary.html
Android Google Services Reference documentation on the `com.google.android.gms`
   `.maps.model` package:
   http://d.android.com/reference/com/google/android/gms/maps/model/package-summary.html

18

Working with Google Cloud Messaging

Does your application need to connect to a server and download data to keep its content fresh? Does the data come in at random times, as opposed to on a schedule (such as a once-a-day news article download)? Are you considering implementing a polling mechanism so that your Android application can routinely check your application server for new content? If this is the case, you might want to look into the Google Cloud Messaging for Android (usually referred to as GCM) service instead, because it can save you a lot of work and results in more efficient use of the user's device resources. In this chapter, we talk about this Google-provided third-party service, which is available to Android developers.

An Overview of GCM

GCM is a messaging service offered by Google that supports push-style messaging from servers and receiving messages from users. It basically allows third-party developers like you to use a single messaging service on the device instead of creating one. The GCM service is free to use and has no quota limitations.

Note

GCM is the successor of a Google Labs–style project named Cloud to Device Messaging (C2DM). C2DM has been deprecated, and Google is no longer accepting new users or increasing quota limits for existing users. If you are still using C2DM in your application, you are encouraged to transition to GCM. There is a great write-up on how to migrate your application over to GCM from C2DM that is easy to follow here: *http://d.android.com/ google/gcm/c2dm.html*.

The GCM service was introduced in Android 4.1 (API Level 16). It gives your servers the ability to push data to applications efficiently. Instead of your application constantly checking for new data on its application server, a notification can be initiated from the server side. This has substantial positive ramifications in terms of device power usage and application responsiveness. In addition, your application on a user's device is able to send messages of its own to your servers.

Note

Using the GCM service basically means you're using the shared messaging channel that Google developed for its own Android applications, such as Gmail. This cuts down on the number of individual applications that must constantly stay "awake" in order to poll their application servers and check for new stuff.

Understanding GCM Message Flow

Here are the basics of how the GCM messaging process works. To push data to an application, the developer's application server sends a simple notification to Google's GCM servers via HTTP or Google Cloud Connection Server (CCS) using a token that a specific application installation received when it was registered. Google's servers handle the message delivery details, pushing the data to the user's device when it becomes available on the network. The shared messaging channel on the user's Android device receives the message and sends out a broadcast. Your application implements a broadcast receiver, so it can wake up, receive the message, and inspect its contents. Your application can then take whatever action is necessary, such as contacting its application server for more information or to download additional content.

Understanding the Limitations of the GCM Service

Because this is a free service and all applications on the device use the same service to communicate with the Google messaging servers, there are a number of limitations to using GCM. Some of these limitations include the following:

- The GCM service requires Android 2.2 (API Level 8) or higher.
- The GCM service is available only on Android devices that have the Google Play store application installed. This means that devices (such as the Amazon Kindle Fire line) cannot take advantage of such services and so developers must use other alternatives.
- Mobile devices that are running Android versions earlier than 3.0 must have their Google account set up on the device. Devices running Android version 4.0.4 or higher do not require this.
- The messages pushed to the device have a size limit for message data payload. At the time of this writing, that limit is 4096 bytes, and messages are stored by the GCM service for a maximum of four weeks.
- Google has imposed a throttling mechanism that is intended to prevent abuse of the service by oversending messages to a user's device. Google does this by providing tokens for sending messages, and once all the tokens have been used, GCM will not be able to send out messages until more tokens become available. The GCM service is not intended for time-critical situations. Messages are delivered in a timely manner, but there is no time limit. Therefore, it's not appropriate for alarm apps and the like.

- Of course, the GCM service requires the user to have a network-enabled device. The good news is that Google has created a robust push mechanism that stores messages to be sent to the device and is fault-tolerant enough to handle the sporadic network connectivity frequently experienced with mobile devices. Still, your users may incur data charges for network activity, as normal.

These limitations are pretty reasonable for most small- and medium-size applications that are published on Google Play. Given how straightforward the implementation is, we see no reason not to use the GCM service.

If your application cannot work within these limitations, you need to use an alternative method of messaging within your application. See the alternatives discussed at the end of this chapter for some options.

Signing Up for GCM

To use Google's GCM service, you must have a Google Developer Console account so that you can create a Google API project. You create a project number when creating a Google API project, which you will need to use as the sender ID for your application. You can create an account or log in to the Google Developer Console at *https://cloud .google.com/console*. Within the Google Developer Console, you need to enable the Google Cloud Messaging for Android service, and then you must create a Public API key that you will use on your application servers.

Note
When you incorporate GCM services into your Android applications, you are subject to additional terms of service, so make sure you read the fine print carefully to ensure that your application complies with the rules.

Incorporating GCM into Your Applications

After you have turned on GCM for Android, you are ready to begin using the service. Make sure you take the time to familiarize yourself with the documentation and sample code available at *http://d.android.com/google/gcm/index.html*.

Integrating GCM Services on the Android Client Side
The basic process for integrating GCM into your Android application is as follows:

1. Your application requires setting up the Google Play services SDK.
2. Your application requires several GCM-specific permissions.
3. If GCM messaging is required by your application, you will want to set the minimum SDK supported by your application to API Level 8.
4. Your application must register to receive GCM messages from a specific sender identifier.

5. The registration on the client side results in a registration identifier that must be delivered to the server and stored for future use.

6. Your application must implement a broadcast receiver for receiving GCM messages.

7. Your application is responsible for retrieving any data payload that is spawned by a GCM message arriving.

Integrating GCM Services on the Android Application Server Side

The process of sending notifications to Google's GCM servers is as follows:

1. Your application server must support HTTP or CCS, which uses Extensible Messaging and Presence Protocol (XMPP) as the message transport layer. In order to make use of the CCS service, you must first sign up for it, which you can do by filling out this form: *https://services.google.com/fb/forms/gcm/*. Your application server should also be able to queue message requests and, ideally, perform exponential backoffs.

2. Your application server needs to maintain an authentication token and refresh it occasionally.

3. To send a message to the GCM servers, your application server must create an HTTP POST message or an XMPP <message>. This message must include information about the registration identifier, authentication token, message data, and message delivery behavior details.

4. The application server should be able to handle numerous response codes (successful and erroneous) from the GCM servers.

For more information on how to configure your application server for GCM messaging, see the GCM documentation at *http://d.android.com/google/gcm/server.html*.

Exploring the GCM Sample Applications

Google provides a few sample applications that help illustrate how to use GCM. There are two different client applications available, along with two different server applications, and one application showing how to use Google App Engine as your back-end server with GCM. To learn more about these applications and to download the code, check out the Google Cloud Messaging for Android project hosted by Google here: *https://code .google.com/p/gcm/*.

What Alternatives to GCM Exist?

In some cases, the GCM service may not be right for your application. Perhaps you are targeting devices that do not have the Google Play store installed, or your application requires a different type of message traffic from what the GCM service currently allows.

In such cases, you are perfectly welcome to implement your own messaging solutions. Some options include:

- Implement a simple server polling solution in a background `Service`. This works well for infrequent messages or messages that aren't time-sensitive.
- Leverage XMPP to implement your own messaging capabilities.
- Find a third-party service provider that offers mobile push messaging capabilities.
- Check the app markets through which your application is published. Some third-party app markets now publish their own push services for use by their subscribers. For example, Amazon provides notification services as part of the Amazon Web Services SDK for Android. These services can incur fees to the developer and the user.

Summary

There are numerous third-party APIs and services that can be used to create robust and interesting applications on the Android platform. One service that can greatly improve the experience your users have with their Android devices is the Google Cloud Messaging for Android service available from Google. This service allows applications to share a messaging channel, making for longer battery life and more responsive applications.

Quiz Questions

1. True or false: The GCM service was introduced in Android 2.2 (API Level 8).
2. What is the size limit for messages with the GCM service?
3. True or false: The Google Play services SDK is not required for implementing the GCM service in your application.
4. What must your client application implement in order to receive messages from the GCM service?
5. True or false: The Google Cloud Connection Server uses XMPP as the message transport layer.

Exercises

1. Review the `GoogleCloudMessaging` client reference documentation found here: *http://d.android.com/reference/com/google/android/gms/gcm/GoogleCloudMessaging.html*.
2. Read through the "GCM Advanced Topics" documentation found here: *http://d.android.com/google/gcm/adv.html*.
3. Obtain an API key for the Google Cloud Messaging for Android service, download the sample applications from Google Code, and configure them to work with your API key. Then study the code to make sure you understand how the GCM service works.

References and More Information

Google Code Project: "Google Cloud Messaging for Android":
  https://code.google.com/p/gcm/
Android Google Services: "Google Cloud Messaging":
  http://d.android.com/google/gcm/index.html
Android Google Services: "Getting Started":
  http://d.android.com/google/gcm/gs.html
Android Google Services: "Implementing GCM Client":
  http://d.android.com/google/gcm/client.html
Android Google Services: "Implementing GCM Server":
  http://d.android.com/google/gcm/server.html
Android Google Services for migrating from C2DM to GCM: "Migration":
  http://d.android.com/google/gcm/c2dm.html
Android Google Services reference documentation for the `GoogleCloudMessaging` class:
  http://d.android.com/reference/com/google/android/gms/gcm/GoogleCloudMessaging.html
Android Google Services reference documentation for the `com.google.android.gcm`
  `.server` package:
  http://d.android.com/reference/com/google/android/gcm/server/package-summary.html
Amazon: "AWS SDK for Android":
  http://aws.amazon.com/sdkforandroid/

19

An Overview of In-App Billing APIs for Android

Developers can monetize their Android applications in a variety of ways. In addition to selling applications outright, developers can integrate billing APIs into their applications in order to sell specific content. In this chapter, we discuss some of the in-app billing APIs available to Android developers, how they might be used, and what some of their limitations are.

What Is In-App Billing?

The freemium business model—where apps are published free of charge but contain content for purchase—is perhaps the most popular way to monetize Android applications these days. Users are more likely to sample a free application, and if the content is sufficiently interesting, they are more likely to pay for it.

Developers can implement freemium applications in a variety of ways. For example:

- A role-playing game might provide a shop where users can purchase items. These items might be available for free in the game if users are willing to play longer, or users can purchase items if they don't have the time or inclination.

- That same game might provide content that is solely available for purchase. For example, perhaps users can customize a character's appearance only if they pay for the privilege.

- A platform game might entice users with a couple of free levels or a time limit (three-day trial), and then provide more levels or game play time for purchase thereafter.

- A wallpaper, ringtone, music, or video download application might allow users to browse and preview content and then purchase only the content they want.

- A cloud-based music storage application might limit the number of songs that can be stored, unless the user upgrades to a purchased storage plan (unlimited or a tiered setup).

- A photo filter app might enable only certain features, such as the ability to share photos with friends, when the user pays up. That same photo filter app might sell new filters right in the app, as they become available.

- A messaging application might enable little extras, such as emoticons or video sending, for users who pay for them.

- A developer might provide tiered or priority service to those willing to pay for it. This might mean "faster" service (usage of a higher-performance server, for example), among other things. Maybe a user can buy VoIP support calls that are handled right from the app.

- Developers might accept donations from users who like their app. Users could even "vote" with their dollars to get more features in the next update to the application.

These are just a few of the many ways that in-app purchases can make the monetization of Android applications that much more achievable. Think creatively.

Using In-App Billing

Android developers have numerous options when it comes to designing freemium applications. Most choose to use one of the several well-respected services that offer libraries for handling secure in-app purchases. Many in-app billing services work only for applications published by specific providers.

Developers are responsible for managing the content they wish to sell to users through the billing APIs. In-app billing is nontrivial to implement. There are third-party APIs to use, limitations to consider, security and export concerns, and usually substantial code to write—code that needs to be unique and private to your application to help avoid reverse engineering, piracy, and exploitation of your valuable content.

We discuss several specific in-app billing opportunities for developers in this chapter:

- Google Play's In-app Billing APIs
- The Amazon Appstore for Android in-app purchasing API
- The PayPal Android SDK APIs

All billing APIs have several things in common:

- All in-app billing APIs use a secure Internet connection to complete a financial transaction. This means all billing APIs require the INTERNET permission and a working network connection to function properly.

- All implementations of billing APIs are only as secure as your code is. Protect your digital signatures and any billing API keys provided to you, the developer. Your implementation of billing features should be unique and obfuscated to help avoid piracy and exploitation of your application.

- All in-app billing services that we know of charge a commission or fees for use.

- All in-app billing APIs impose additional terms of service and limitations on your applications. We strongly recommend reading the fine print and consulting your financial and law experts if you have questions.

- In-app billing may be tied to a particular device feature, such as having Google Play or Amazon Appstore for Android installed.

- All applications that leverage billing APIs must comply with international law in terms of taxes and export and with local laws regarding financial transactions.

Note

For these reasons, we do not provide sample applications for the in-app billing mechanisms discussed in this chapter, but we have reviewed the sample applications provided with each technology and are confident that they are adequate for most developers. If you were hoping for working samples in this book, we would have to tell you to change them completely; otherwise, they wouldn't be very secure.

Leveraging Google Play In-App Billing APIs

Google Play has an in-app billing system that enables you to sell content from within applications. You need a Google Play developer account and Google Wallet merchant account to use these APIs, and they have a number of requirements and limitations, such as the following:

- You can use the APIs only for applications that are published through Google Play. These can be free or paid applications.

- You can sell only digital content using these APIs. You cannot use them to sell physical goods or services. (This is not an auction payment service, for example.)

- The 30 percent commission applies to in-app purchases, just as it does for applications sold on Google Play.

- You can test your applications before you publish them using test accounts you create with your Google Play publisher account.

- The In-app Billing APIs have a number of system requirements you need to comply with. In-app Billing API version 2 is available for devices running Android 1.6 (API Level 4) and higher, and In-app Billing API version 3 is available for devices running Android 2.2 (API Level 8) and higher. Other system requirements also exist.

For more information about Google Play In-app Billing APIs, see the Android "Selling In-app Products" Training link in the references section at the end of this chapter.

Tip

There is an excellent sample application that illustrates how to use Google Play In-app Billing services that is worth looking over. You can find out more about the sample application by downloading the library from the Android SDK Manager under Extras, Google Play Billing Library, and then using the Android IDE wizard to import the TrivialDrive billing sample application.

Leveraging Amazon Appstore for Android In-App Purchasing APIs

With the success of Android-powered e-book readers such as the Amazon Kindle Fire, developers are looking to monetize applications published through venues other than Google Play. Amazon runs its own Android application marketplace in the form of the Amazon Appstore for Android. The in-app purchasing APIs are appropriate for developers publishing on the Amazon Appstore only. If you are interested in joining this program, we recommend signing up here: *https://developer.amazon.com/appsandservices/apis/earn/in-app-purchasing.*

Leveraging PayPal Billing APIs

PayPal is a popular e-commerce service that facilitates financial transactions between somewhat trusted parties. PayPal publishes the PayPal Android SDK which can be used to integrate PayPal functionality into your Android applications. You can find the libraries through PayPal's GitHub account for download (see the direct link in the references section at the end of this chapter). We recommend reading over the PayPal Android SDK README.md file and reviewing the javadocs.

Note

To publish applications that leverage the PayPal Android SDK, you need to create a PayPal developer account and submit your applications for review. You can submit and manage your applications from the PayPal.com website. After your application has been approved, you will receive a key for use with the APIs.

Leveraging Other Billing APIs

There are other billing APIs available for use on the Android platform. If you happen to prefer a specific financial service, see whether it has (or is developing) a mobile API. As always, read the fine print. Third-party libraries, especially those that deal with finances, often have additional terms of use. Also, be aware that you, as the developer, are often responsible for handling taxes and tariffs and other financial law compliance, especially when exporting your application to other countries.

Summary

The in-app billing APIs provide the tools you need for monetizing your applications, without the need for you to roll your own billing solution. This chapter introduced you to some of the many ways developers are monetizing their applications and highlighted the freemium business model. In addition, different services have been presented for integrating in-app billing into your applications, such as Google Play services, Amazon, and

PayPal. You should now be equipped with enough information to determine what type of monetization strategy and billing solution to choose for your applications.

Quiz Questions

1. What is a freemium business model?
2. What are three ways developers can implement freemium applications?
3. True or false: You may use the Google Play In-app Billing APIs to sell physical goods or services.
4. True or false: Google Play In-app Billing APIs are available only for devices running Android 4.0 (API Level 14).

Exercises

1. Import the TrivialDrive Android sample application into the Android IDE and review the code so that you understand how Google Play In-app Billing integration functions.
2. Read the Google Services "Google Play In-app Billing" documentation, the link to which is found in the following section, to become familiar with the latest information on in-app billing.

References and More Information

Wikipedia discussion on the freemium business model:
   http://en.wikipedia.org/wiki/Freemium
Android Training: "Selling In-App Products":
   http://d.android.com/training/in-app-billing/index.html
Google Services: "Google Play In-App Billing":
   http://d.android.com/google/play/billing/index.html
Amazon Appstore for Android In-App Purchasing API:
   https://developer.amazon.com/appsandservices/apis/earn/in-app-purchasing
PayPal Android SDK:
   https://github.com/paypal/PayPal-Android-SDK
PayPal Android SDK javadocs:
   http://paypal.github.io/PayPal-Android-SDK/

## 20

Enabling Application Statistics with Google Analytics

Most Android developers want to know what their users are up to. How long do users spend in the application? How often do they use it? What features of the application are they using and not using? Is the user interface designed so that users can find what they need? What sorts of devices are users using? In this chapter, we discuss how application developers can use the Google Analytics SDK for Android to collect and track information about their application users in a consistent, robust fashion.

Tip

Many of the code examples provided in this chapter are taken from the SimpleStats application. The source code for this application is provided for download on the book's website.

Creating a Google Account for Analytics

To send data to the Google Analytics service and later access the statistics your application gathers on the Google Analytics Dashboard, you need to create a developer account at *http://www.google.com/analytics*. Much like your Google Play account, your Google Analytics account must be tied to an underlying Google account. The accounts are free to start. Figure 20.1 shows the Google Analytics signup page for a registered Google account.

Note

The account setup is primarily targeted at website statistics tracking, but mobile developers use the same workflow, so don't get confused and think you're in the wrong place.

As part of the account creation, you'll be asked to log in with your Google account credentials. Then you'll be prompted to enter some information to set up your account. When you are prompted to enter a website or mobile app for tracking purposes, choose the mobile app option and enter an Account Name (ideally including the name of your app and company domain, such as *http://simplestats.advancedandroidbook.com*) and an App Name such as SimpleStats. You also need to set the Industry Category and the Reporting

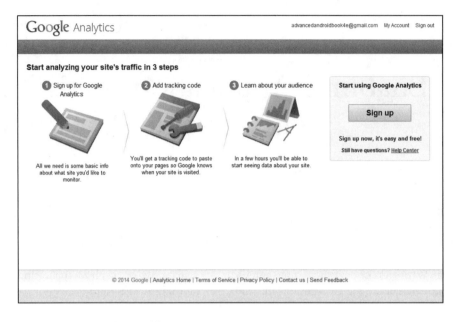

Figure 20.1   The Google Analytics signup page.

Time Zone to which you want to normalize statistics. Next, you enter sharing options for the account. Finally, you need to press Get Tracking ID and accept the Google Analytics Terms of Service.

Tip

For the same reason as for Google Play, it's recommended that you create your Google Analytics account with a generic Google account, such as one for a company entity, as opposed to an individual's account, so you're not trying to track down a specific person's login information on a weekend or some other inconvenient time. It's just more professional that way. You can add other people to the account with the Analytics account settings, too.

The resulting account creation generates a Tracking ID for your application to use with your SDK. The Tracking ID is displayed within the Google Analytics Admin console preceded by the letters "UA-" followed by some numbers (as shown in Figure 20.2). Save this information—you will need to use this number in your application to send statistics to the proper Google Analytics account. You can create different accounts with different tracking identifiers from your Google Analytics account, or use the same one for all your apps. It depends on what you want out of the reports.

When you navigate to the Reporting section, you may be greeted with an empty Dashboard when you first log in to your account, as shown in Figure 20.3.

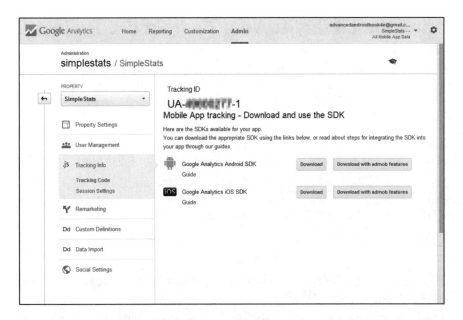

Figure 20.2   The Google Analytics Admin section.

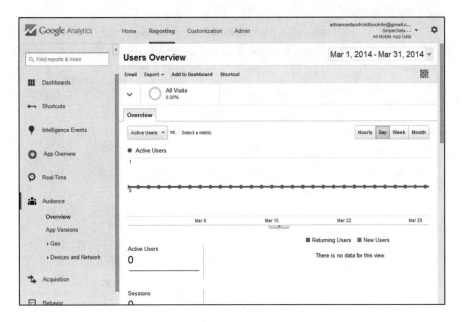

Figure 20.3   The Google Analytics Reporting section.

Adding the Library to Your Android IDE Project

Now you're ready to work with the Google Analytics SDK for Android. This library is available via the Android SDK Manager by installing the Google Play services library. When installed, the Google Play services library is located in the SDK directory under `<path_to_sdk>/extras/google/google_play_services/libproject/google-play-services_lib`.

> **Note**
> At the time of this writing, we used the Google Analytics SDK for Android version 4.

To use the Google Analytics SDK for Android, you must first import the `google-play-services_lib` project into your Android IDE as a library project. To integrate the SDK into your Android IDE project, follow these steps:

1. Add the `google-play-services_lib` to your project.
2. Add two permissions to your Android manifest file.
3. Add the Google Play services library as a dependency to the `<application>` element in the Android manifest file.

Adding the `google-play-services_lib` to your project in the Android IDE is easy:

1. Right-click the application to which you would like to add Analytics support and choose Properties.
2. Under the Android settings, select the Add . . . button under the Library heading.
3. Choose the `google-play-services_lib` project and select OK, then select OK again.

Because you are sending information over the network, you need to add two permissions to your application. To do this, follow these steps:

1. Click the Permissions tab of the Android manifest file for your application.
2. Add the permission called `android.permission.INTERNET`.
3. Add the permission called `android.permission.ACCESS_NETWORK_STATE`.
4. Save your Android manifest file.

You also must add the Google Play services library as a dependency to your Android manifest file. To do this, follow these steps:

1. Add the following line of code as a child element within the `<application>` element of the manifest file:

```
<meta-data android:name="com.google.android.gms.version"
        android:value="@integer/google_play_services_version" />
```

2. Save your Android manifest file.

You can now start using the classes in the Google Analytics SDK for Android.

Tip
You may also need to create a Proguard Exception to your application to prevent ProGuard from removing classes that are required during compilation. To learn more about what lines you should include, see the following: *http://d.android.com/google/play-services/setup .html#Proguard.*

Collecting Data from Your Applications

Now that you've created an account and added the Google Play services library to your project, you're ready to start using Google Analytics to track events and other information in your application. To start tracking in an `Activity` class, retrieve an instance of `GoogleAnalytics`. You typically want to start tracking in the `onCreate()` method of your `Activity`, track various events throughout your `Activity` lifecycle, and stop tracking in your `onDestroy()` method. To start tracking, supply your UA- account number and an interval (seconds) at which to dispatch events to the server, such as this:

```
GoogleAnalytics analytics = GoogleAnalytics.getInstance(this);
mTracker = analytics.newTracker("UA-1234567-89");
analytics.reportActivityStart(this);
```

When you're done tracking, stop the tracker:

```
analytics.reportActivityStop(this);
```

Stopping a tracking session is commonly performed in the `onDestroy()` callback method of your `Activity` class.

Logging Different Events

Now that you've got the SDK set up and working with your application, you want to look into the different types of events you can log with the Google Analytics SDK for Android. You can log page views, events, e-commerce events, and other useful information. The logging methods are flexible enough that you can adapt them to your needs.

During a valid tracking session, you can track events by supplying the category, action, label, and value (all developer-defined fields) of an event like so:

```
buttonEvent = new EventBuilder();
buttonEvent.setCategory("Click");
buttonEvent.setAction("Press");
buttonEvent.setLabel("Button");
buttonEvent.setValue(0);
mTracker.send(buttonEvent.build());
```

Using the Google Analytics Dashboard

After users begin to use your application, the statistics are collected for each of the event hooks you have put in place in your application. This data is then sent to the Google Analytics servers, and it's time to head over to the Google Analytics Dashboard and interpret the results.

Tip

Luckily, some of the statistics collected by Google Analytics are now shown in real time. Earlier versions had up to a 24-hour delay between when an event was logged and when it showed up in the data on the Dashboard. Real-time statistics are still in beta at the time of this writing.

When your data has been collected and run through the Google Analytics servers, your Dashboard should show the data on the Home screen overview, as shown in Figure 20.4.

You can review the Users Overview details by clicking on the Reporting tab and choosing Audience, Overview, as shown in Figure 20.5.

You can drill down to the individual button click events by clicking on the Reporting tab and choosing Behavior, Events, Overview, and then drilling down by clicking on the Top Events, Event Label link. This displays the button click events, as shown in Figure 20.6.

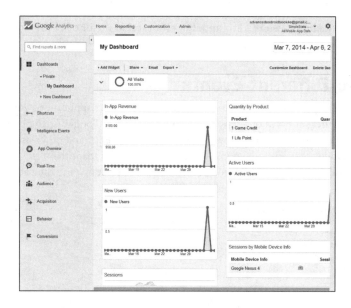

Figure 20.4   The Google Analytics Dashboard.

Figure 20.5   A Google Analytics Users Overview report.

Figure 20.6   A Google Analytics Event Overview report.

The Google Analytics Dashboard has a variety of useful features. We recommend reading through the documentation and messing around with where you put your event hooks in the application prior to publication, as you may want to adjust your analysis strategy to get the reports you desire.

Gathering E-commerce Information

You can also use the Google Analytics SDK for Android to track e-commerce data. This data includes store transactions, purchase data, and other useful information for e-commerce services, which can just as easily include tracking in-app billing data or virtual purchases in a game.

> **Note**
>
> This type of tracking is not enabled by default. You need to log in to your Google Analytics Dashboard and enable e-commerce tracking under the profile settings of your specific account.

Logging E-commerce Events in Your Applications

To start tracking e-commerce information, you must still instantiate the tracker as with other types of events. Then, when you are processing in-app payments or the like, you can use the `TransactionBuilder` class to log information about a user purchase. Basically, think of a `TransactionBuilder` as a shopping cart instance; the `ItemBuilder` class is used to specify the individual items purchased in the cart. Here is the sample code necessary to build a transaction with two items for purchase:

```
String orderID = "1001" + new Date().toString();

transactionEvent = new TransactionBuilder();
transactionEvent.setTransactionId(orderID);
transactionEvent.setAffiliation("My Game Store");
transactionEvent.setShipping(0);
transactionEvent.setRevenue(2.99);
transactionEvent.setTax(0);
transactionEvent.setCurrencyCode("USD");

mTracker.send(transactionEvent.build());
```

Both the `Transaction` and `Item` classes have helper `Builder` classes:

```
// Item #1
item1Event = new ItemBuilder();

item1Event.setTransactionId(orderID);
item1Event.setName("1 Game Credit");
item1Event.setSku("SKU_123");
item1Event.setPrice(1.99);
item1Event.setQuantity(1);
item1Event.setCategory("LIFE POINTS");
item1Event.setCurrencyCode("USD");
```

```
mTracker.send(item1Event.build());

// Item #2
item2Event = new ItemBuilder();

item2Event.setTransactionId(orderID);
item2Event.setName("1 Game Credit");
item2Event.setSku("SKU_456");
item2Event.setPrice(0.99);
item2Event.setQuantity(1);
item2Event.setCategory("Game Credit");
item2Event.setCurrencyCode("USD");

mTracker.send(item2Event.build());
```

When you're ready to commit the event and dispatch the results to the Google Analytics servers, simply use the send() method of the Tracker class, including the parameters of the event that you are tracking:

```
mTracker.send(eventToTrack.build());
```

Reviewing E-commerce Reports

After you have logged some e-commerce events, you can check out the reports on the Google Analytics Dashboard (assuming you enabled e-commerce tracking in your profile). You can find these reports on the Reporting tab, under the Conversions, Ecommerce section. Figure 20.7 shows an Ecommerce Overview report after multiple clicks

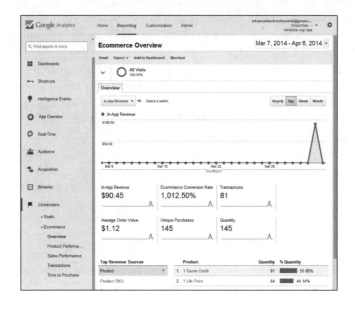

Figure 20.7   A Google Analytics Ecommerce Overview report.

of the Buy button in the sample application running the `TransactionBuilder` code shown earlier.

Tracking Ad and Market Referrals

The SDK supports several types of campaign tracking, which allow you to keep track of installation referrals through the Android Market and otherwise. To participate in Google Play campaign tracking, see the online documentation: *https://developers.google.com/analytics/devguides/collection/android/v4/campaigns*.

Gathering Statistics

Now let's talk about some strategies, as well as tips and tricks, for gathering relevant, useful statistics with Google Analytics. Much of the "magic" involves dropping statistics-gathering hooks at clever places in your specific applications. The trick is to place your event hooks at exactly the places in your application that mean something to you, the developer. Place the hooks in the wrong code locations, and you're going to generate erroneous statistics. It's a bit of an art to do this well, and it's not really something we can give you examples for, but we can talk about some commonsense approaches. For example:

- Develop, document, and test your event-tracking strategy and make it consistent. When you track events, you can provide a category, action, label, and value. Use these features consistently throughout your application so that the creation of reports is done in a similar fashion, regardless of who added the event hooks in that part of the application. We see a lot of tracking solutions that generate tons of data but little of real value.

- Know all your application entry points. Most users will launch your application from the application tray, but you might have other entry points as well, via notifications or live folders and other intents. If you're trying to log application launches, you need to log each entry point to get an accurate result.

- Remember your application, `Activity`, and `Fragment` lifecycle events. You might want to log each time an `Activity` or `Fragment` runs. Make sure you do this in a callback that runs only once per `Activity` or `Fragment`, such as the `onCreate()` callback. You probably want to avoid logging `onResume()`, as it may be called repeatedly during the lifetime of an `Activity` or `Fragment`. Even so, keep in mind that something as simple as rotating the screen will result in a new call to `onCreate()`.

- Gather only the statistics you need, and don't store them if you can avoid it. Gathering excessive information from the user creates and exacerbates a number of issues regarding performance and privacy.

- Consider tracking behavior rather than page views. For example, you can rank the difficulty of a game by tracking the actions of restarting, dying, quitting frequently, opening help or forum links, and so on. Higher frequencies of these compared to a "completion" action might indicate a higher level of difficulty. In a newsreader application, tracking views that last longer than 30 seconds or involve scrolling down to more content might be more useful than just tracking the number of times an article is loaded. In fact, behavior is often what analytics tries to glean from page views. You're writing a full application and can more directly indicate behavior through careful creation of tracking events.

- Always verify your assumptions that any data you use is unique. Timestamps are not globally unique. Handset device identifiers are available on smartphones, but not tablets and other types of devices.

Protecting Users' Privacy

When you collect user statistics, you need to make sure that the users are aware of your activities, so that privacy concerns are addressed. The Google Analytics Terms of Service require that you indicate to your application users that you reserve the right to anonymously track and report a user's activity inside of your application. By signing up for a Google Analytics account, you agree to these terms. Send only anonymous information that can be aggregated to the Google Analytics servers. Do not send private user information. This isn't the only item you must comply with in the terms of service, of course. Be sure to read and understand them before adding instrumentation to your code with many calls.

Summary

The Google Analytics SDK for Android is an effective way to generate helpful information about how users are using your applications. It's flexible, powerful, and easy to integrate into your applications. As with any logging, you should always inform your users that you are tracking their behavior in the application and have a well-understood privacy policy. How you take advantage of the Google Analytics SDK for Android depends on what you're hoping to determine from your users. Heavy analytics may be appropriate for beta projects, whereas lightweight informational logging might be more appropriate for published applications.

Quiz Questions

1. True or false: To track your application, you must use the Analytics ID created during the Google Analytics application setup process.

2. What letters are used at the beginning of the tracking ID of a Google Analytics application?

3. What library project must you include in your application to leverage the Google Analytics version 4 SDK for Android?

4. What two `android.permission` values are required to use the Google Analytics SDK for Android?

5. True or false: The `commit()` method of the `Tracker` class is used to submit events to the Google Analytics servers.

Exercises

1. Use the Google Analytics SDK for Android documentation to determine how you would send social interactions to Google Analytics.

2. Use the Google Analytics SDK for Android documentation to determine how you would perform automatic session management.

3. Create an application that is capable of sending a screen view to Google Analytics.

References and More Information

Google Analytics documentation:
  http://code.google.com/apis/analytics/
Google Analytics account signup (requires a Google account):
  http://www.google.com/analytics/sign_up.html
Google Analytics documentation for event tracking:
  https://developers.google.com/analytics/devguides/collection/android/v4/events
Google Analytics documentation for e-commerce tracking:
  https://developers.google.com/analytics/devguides/collection/android/v4/ecommerce
Google Analytics documentation on tracking campaigns:
  https://developers.google.com/analytics/devguides/collection/android/v4/campaigns
"Best Practices for Mobile App Analytics Setup":
  https://support.google.com/analytics/answer/2587087

21

An Overview of Google
Play Game Services

Good game design and development require features to make your game viral, engaging, and monetize-able. Google Play game services provide many of the features to help your game go viral by allowing players to invite their friends to join in on the game play. In addition, there are also features available that make it easier to keep players coming back for more, increasing engagement with your game, with other players, and with their friends. Finally, the ability to monetize your content while preventing piracy is a key aspect of building a long-lasting and successful game.

> **Note**
> We believe that game design is an art form, so we will not be going into the many different aspects of it. The main focus of this chapter is to introduce the features of Google Play game services for Android that have been designed for improving the game play of applications.

If you are developing a gaming application for the Android platform, Google Play game services is definitely worth a look. Google Play game services provide cross-platform SDKs for adding achievements and leaderboards, backing up progress, integrating social and multiplayer features, and securing your game with antipiracy abilities. There is a Java SDK available for Android, in addition to an Objective-C SDK for iOS, a browser client-side JavaScript SDK, server-side SDKs, and a C++ SDK for easing portability across Android and iOS. In this chapter, we introduce many of the features of Google Play game services that are available to Android application game developers.

Getting Up and Running with Google Play Game Services

To get started with Google Play game services for Android, you need to create a new application in your IDE, and you need to make sure that you have already created a Google Play Developer Console account. The Google Play Developer Console is where you will incorporate and manage some of the many features of the Google Play Game Services for your application.

Once you have created your application in your IDE and once your application has been added into the Google Play Developer Console, the development process for integrating with Google Play game services is as follows:

1. Select one of the tabs for the available Google Play game services features within the Google Play Developer Console.

2. Add the appropriate metadata for a particular Google Play game services feature from the Google Play Developer Console.

3. Implement the Google Play game services features within your application.

4. Test your game on a real Android device to make sure everything works as expected.

Tip

The Google Play game services documentation makes many sample games available for download that demonstrate many different capabilities of game services, implemented for many different platforms. There is a great write-up that uses one of the sample games for Android to walk you through the entire process of setting up an application for game services, and it even walks you through configuring the game from the Google Play Developer Console. For a complete walk-through, see the "Getting Started for Android Game Development" section of the Google Play game services documentation found here: *https://developers.google.com/games/services/android/quickstart*.

Note

Make sure to read through the Google Play game services API Terms of Service found here: *https://developers.google.com/games/services/terms*. The terms cover various rules that game developers must follow when leveraging Google Play game services.

Incorporating Google Play Game Services into Your Applications

There are two different ways to integrate Google Play game services into your application. The first way is by using the provided BaseGameActivity class rather than just a standard Activity. This class can be found by downloading the BaseGameUtils library provided here: *https://github.com/playgameservices/android-samples*. You then need to import the BaseGameActivity class from the com.google.example.games .basegameutils package. The second way is by using a GameHelper class. You would use the GameHelper class only if you are subclassing an Activity directly rather than subclassing the BaseGameActivity class.

To make use of the BaseGameActivity class, you first need to import the entire gms.common.api package. You also need a reference to the GoogleApiClient object for communicating with the Google Play game services API from your application. You access the `GoogleApiClient` object by calling the `getApiClient()` method any time after invoking the `onCreate()` method of an `Activity`.

> **Tip**
>
> The `BaseGameActivity` class provides access to the Google Play game services APIs, but not to other Google Play services APIs. If you would like your application to be able to make use of other Google Play services such as Google+, in the `onCreate()` method of your application, before calling `super.onCreate()`, you may set the `setRequestedClients()` to include the flags for the services you would like to access.
>
> The Google+ API flag is `CLIENT_PLUS`, the Games API flag is `CLIENT_GAMES`, the App State API is `CLIENT_APPSTATE`, and for accessing all of these APIs together, use the `CLIENT_ALL` flag.

Understanding Achievements

Achievements are a great tool for increasing engagement within your game. An achievement is used to motivate players to continue playing your game until they have achieved the achievement. An achievement is a goal that you set, so once players achieve the set goal, you are able to reward them with the recognition that they accomplished that particular goal.

An achievement is composed of the following data:

- **ID:** Generated by the Google Developer Console, and unique for each achievement
- **Name:** Name of the achievement, less than 100 characters
- **Description:** Description of the achievement, less than 500 characters
- **Icon:** 512 × 512 PNG or JPG file, recommended not to include any text or localized content
- **Incremental achievements:** A setting to determine if this achievement builds on another required achievement
- **State:** One of hidden, revealed, or unlocked
- **Points:** A value between 5 and 200, in multiples of 5
- **List order:** The index of where the achievement will be displayed in the list of game achievements

There are a few different ways of working with achievements. You may `increment()`, `reveal()`, `setSteps()`, or `unlock()` them by using those methods from the `Games.Achievements` class.

Warning

When making calls to the Google Play Game Services APIs, you need to be aware that your application must remain within the quota allocated and may not exceed the available rate limit. To understand more about these limits imposed on applications, see "Managing Quota and Rate Limiting" found here: *https://developers.google.com/games/services/quota*. If your application requires a quota increase, you may request one from the Google Play Developer Console.

Note

In order for your application to be published in the Google Play Developer Console, you must create at least five achievements.

Understanding Leaderboards

Leaderboards are a great way to encourage competition among players, either through social leaderboards (competitive ranking among a user's circles) or a public leaderboard (competitive ranking among all players who share their game play activity publicly). In addition, Google Play game services creates daily, weekly, and all-time leaderboards for each and every leaderboard that you create without any additional coding required on your part, with a maximum of 70 leaderboards for a particular application.

A leaderboard is composed of the following data:

- **ID:** Generated by the Google Developer Console, and unique for each leaderboard
- **Name:** Name of the leaderboard, less than 100 characters
- **Score formatting:** Presenting to a user in one of the following formats: numeric, time, currency, or custom units
- **Icon:** 512 × 512 PNG or JPG file, recommended not to include any text or localized content
- **Ordering:** One of "Larger is better" or "Smaller is better"
- **List order:** The index of where the leaderboard will be displayed in the list of game leaderboards
- **Limits:** The lower and upper limits of leaderboard scores to prevent users from trying to submit falsified scores

To update a player's score for a particular leaderboard, use the `submitScore()` method of the `Games.Leaderboards` class and pass in the score and the leaderboard ID.

Warning

The Google Play game services SDK is in charge of displaying leaderboard data for you. If you would like to display the leaderboard data in your own custom UI you may do so, but be aware that Unicode characters may appear in player names, so you will have to handle formatting of player names manually.

Saving Game Data with Cloud Save

Google Cloud Save is a service that allows developers to configure their applications to save user data on Google's servers. For an Android game, this service would allow a player to save game progress on a phone; later, when using an Android tablet, the player would be able to resume that same game at exactly the same place.

To work with Google Cloud Save, first you need to add a `<meta-data>` tag inside the `<application>` tag of your manifest file and include a `name` attribute of `com.google.android.gms.appstate.APP_ID` and the appropriate `value` attribute. Then you need to retrieve a `GoogleApiClient` object for passing in to the `update()`, `load()`, and `resolve()` methods of the `AppStateManager` class, along with passing in other required information to those methods.

Note

The Google Cloud Save service is intended to be used only for storing small amounts of data, such as the current level or a player's score. You are able to store 4-byte arrays worth of 256 kilobytes of data, totaling 1024 kilobytes.

Introducing Multiplayer Gaming

The Google Play game services APIs include features for two types of multiplayer gaming: real-time multiplayer and turn-based multiplayer. The real-time multiplayer APIs leverage Google servers to connect multiple players into a single game session for communicating with other players without significant development on your part. The turn-based multiplayer APIs also leverage Google servers for easy implementation of asynchronous game play in a turn-based fashion. These features allow you to integrate ways for players to invite their friends or allow players to find others who have made their presence public.

Tip

To learn about all of the Google Play game services features available for real-time multiplayer gaming, see *https://developers.google.com/games/services/common/concepts/realtimeMultiplayer*. To learn about all of the Google Play game services features available for turn-based multiplayer gaming, see *https://developers.google.com/games/services/common/concepts/turnbasedMultiplayer*.

Understanding Antipiracy

Many sophisticated users will try to circumvent the Google Play store to install your game, especially if the application requires purchasing. To prevent users from installing unauthorized copies of your game, the antipiracy features of Google Play game services may be turned on from within the Google Play Developer Console. Once they are turned on, your game will communicate with the game services API to

determine if a particular user has a game license. If not, the API call will return a
`LICENSE_CHECK_FAILED`.

Note
Android games are the only class of applications that are able to make use of the antipiracy
features. Installing the application from Google Play is the only way to create the user
license for your game.

Summary

The many features of Google Play game services allow you to quickly build advanced
gaming features with very easy-to-use APIs. Building ways to make your application go
viral are easy with the multiplayer gaming APIs. Further, the leaderboards and achievements APIs provide many ways to encourage players to keep playing. Finally, to make
sure you are not losing out on revenue from piracy, use the antipiracy features.

Quiz Questions

1. Where do you manage and configure metadata for Google Play game services
   features?

2. True or false: The `GameHelperActivity` class should be used when integrating
   with Google Play game services.

3. What is the Google+ API flag for requesting access in the `setRequested`
   `Clients()` method?

4. What does the incremental achievement setting of an achievement from within the
   Google Developer Console determine?

5. What is the maximum amount of data that you are able to store for your game with
   Google Cloud Save?

6. True or false: The antipiracy features are available to all applications, not just games.

Exercises

1. Read through the Google Play game services quality checklist (*https://developers
   .google.com/games/services/checklist*) documentation to learn best practices for how to
   increase the quality of your game.

2. Read through the "Google Play Game Services Branding Guidelines" (*https://
   developers.google.com/games/services/branding-guidelines*) to make sure you understand
   how you may use the Google branding elements within your game.

3. Log in to the Google Play Developer Console and go through the "Getting Started
   for Android Game Development" (*https://developers.google.com/games/services/
   android/quickstart*) guide to become familiar with how to work with Google Play
   game services.

References and More Information

Android Google Services: "Google Play Game Services":
  http://d.android.com/google/play-services/games.html
Google Products: "Google Play Game Services":
  https://developers.google.com/games/services/
Google Play Game Services: "Getting Started for Android Game Development":
  https://developers.google.com/games/services/android/quickstart
Android Google Services: "Package Index":
  https://developer.android.com/reference/gms-packages.html
Google Play Game Services: "Game Engine Integrations with Google Play Games
  Services":
  https://developers.google.com/games/services/integration/
Google Play Game Services: "Quality Checklist for Google Play Games Services":
  https://developers.google.com/games/services/checklist
Google Play Game Services: "Google Play Games Services Branding Guidelines":
  https://developers.google.com/games/services/branding-guidelines
Google Permissions: "Getting Permission to Use Google's Brand Features":
  http://www.google.com/intl/en/permissions/
Google Play Game Services: "Downloads":
  https://developers.google.com/games/services/downloads/
Google Play Game Services: "Google Play Game Services Terms of Service":
  https://developers.google.com/games/services/terms

V

Drawing, Animations, and Graphics Programming with Android

22
Developing Android 2D Graphics Applications

In *Introduction to Android™ Application Development: Android Essentials*, we talked about layouts and the various `View` classes available in Android to make screen design simple and efficient. Now we must think at a slightly lower level and talk about drawing objects on the screen. This chapter covers the two-dimensional drawing features built into the Android platform, including creating custom `View` classes and working with `Canvas` and `Paint` to draw shapes and text. You will also learn about working with bitmaps and how to use the hardware acceleration features of the Android platform.

Drawing on the Screen

With Android, we can display images such as PNG and JPG graphics as well as text and primitive shapes to the screen. We can paint these items with various colors, styles, and gradients and modify them using standard image transforms. We can even animate objects to give the illusion of motion.

Tip

Many of the code examples provided in this chapter are taken from the SimpleDrawing application. The source code for this application is provided for download on the book's website.

Working with Canvases and Paints

To draw to the screen, you need a valid `Canvas` object. Typically, we get a valid `Canvas` object by extending the `View` class for our own purposes and implementing the `onDraw()` method.

For example, here's a simple `View` subclass called `ViewWithRedDot`. We override the `onDraw()` method to dictate what the `View` looks like; in this case, it draws a red circle on a black background.

```
private static class ViewWithRedDot extends View {
    public ViewWithRedDot(Context context) {
        super(context);
    }
```

```
@Override
protected void onDraw(Canvas canvas) {
    canvas.drawColor(Color.BLACK);
    Paint circlePaint = new Paint();
    circlePaint.setColor(Color.RED);
    canvas.drawCircle(canvas.getWidth()/2,
        canvas.getHeight()/2,
        canvas.getWidth()/3, circlePaint);
}
}
```

We can then use this View like any other layout. For example, we might override the onCreate() method in our Activity with the following:

```
setContentView(new ViewWithRedDot(this));
```

The resulting screen looks something like Figure 22.1.

Figure 22.1   The ViewWithRedDot view draws
a red circle on a black background.

Understanding the `Canvas` Object

The `Canvas` (`android.graphics.Canvas`) object holds the draw calls, in order, for a rectangle of space. There are methods available for drawing images, text, and shapes and support for clipping regions.

The dimensions of the `Canvas` are bound by the container `View`. You can retrieve the size of the `Canvas` using the `getHeight()` and `getWidth()` methods.

Understanding the `Paint` Object

In Android, the `Paint` (`android.graphics.Paint`) object stores far more than a color. The `Paint` class encapsulates the style and complex color and rendering information that can be applied to a drawable such as a graphic, shape, or piece of text in a given `Typeface`.

Working with `Paint` Color

You can set the color of the `Paint` using the `setColor()` method. Standard colors are predefined in the `android.graphics.Color` class, an integer value can be used, and a helper method called `setARGB()` can be used when you don't have the integer value for the color. For example, the following code sets the paint color to red:

```
Paint redPaint = new Paint();
redPaint.setColor(Color.RED);
```

Working with `Paint` Anti-aliasing

Anti-aliasing makes many graphics—whether they are shapes or typefaces—look smoother on the screen. This property is set in the `Paint` of an object.

For example, the following code instantiates a `Paint` object with anti-aliasing enabled:

```
Paint aliasedPaint = new Paint(Paint.ANTI_ALIAS_FLAG);
```

Working with `Paint` Styles

`Paint` styles control how an object is filled with color. For example, the following code instantiates a `Paint` object and sets the `Style` to `STROKE`, which signifies that the object should be painted as a line drawing and not filled (the default):

```
Paint linePaint = new Paint();
linePaint.setStyle(Paint.Style.STROKE);
```

Working with `Paint` Gradients

You can create a gradient of colors using one of the gradient subclasses. The different gradient classes (see Figure 22.2), including `LinearGradient`, `RadialGradient`, and `SweepGradient`, are available under the superclass `android.graphics.Shader`.

All gradients need at least two colors—a start color and an end color—but might contain any number of colors. The types of gradients are differentiated by the direction in which the gradient "flows." Gradients can be set to mirror and repeat as necessary.

You can set the `Paint` gradient using the `setShader()` method.

Working with Linear Gradients

A *linear gradient* is one that changes colors along a single straight line. The top-left circle in Figure 22.2 is a linear gradient between black and red, which is mirrored.

You can achieve this by creating a `LinearGradient` and setting the `Paint` method `setShader()` before drawing on a `Canvas`, as follows:

```
import android.graphics.Canvas;
import android.graphics.Color;
import android.graphics.LinearGradient;
import android.graphics.Paint;
import android.graphics.Shader;
...
Paint circlePaint = new Paint(Paint.ANTI_ALIAS_FLAG);
LinearGradient linGrad = new LinearGradient(0, 0, 25, 25,
    Color.RED, Color.BLACK,
    Shader.TileMode.MIRROR);
circlePaint.setShader(linGrad);
canvas.drawCircle(100, 100, 100, circlePaint);
```

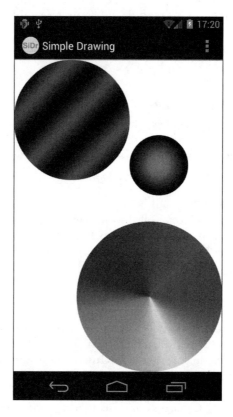

Figure 22.2   Examples of a `LinearGradient` (top),
a `RadialGradient` (right), and a `SweepGradient` (bottom).

Working with Radial Gradients

A *radial gradient* is one that changes colors starting at a single point and radiates outward in a circle. The smaller circle on the right in Figure 22.2 is a radial gradient between green and black.

You can achieve this by creating a `RadialGradient` and setting the `Paint` method `setShader()` before drawing on a `Canvas`, as follows:

```
import android.graphics.Canvas;
import android.graphics.Color;
import android.graphics.RadialGradient;
import android.graphics.Paint;
import android.graphics.Shader;
...
Paint circlePaint = new Paint(Paint.ANTI_ALIAS_FLAG);
RadialGradient radGrad = new RadialGradient(250,
    175, 50, Color.GREEN, Color.BLACK,
    Shader.TileMode.MIRROR);
circlePaint.setShader(radGrad);
canvas.drawCircle(250, 175, 50, circlePaint);
```

Working with Sweep Gradients

A *sweep gradient* is one that changes colors in the shape of slices of a pie. This type of gradient is often used for a color chooser. The large circle at the bottom of Figure 22.2 is a sweep gradient between red, yellow, green, blue, and magenta.

You can achieve this by creating a `SweepGradient` and setting the `Paint` method `setShader()` before drawing on a `Canvas`, as follows:

```
import android.graphics.Canvas;
import android.graphics.Color;
import android.graphics.SweepGradient;
import android.graphics.Paint;
import android.graphics.Shader;
...
Paint circlePaint = new Paint(Paint.ANTI_ALIAS_FLAG);
SweepGradient sweepGrad = new
    SweepGradient(canvas.getWidth()-125,
    canvas.getHeight()-125,
    new int[] { Color.RED, Color.YELLOW, Color.GREEN,
    Color.BLUE, Color.MAGENTA, Color.RED }, null);

circlePaint.setShader(sweepGrad);
canvas.drawCircle(canvas.getWidth()-125,
    canvas.getHeight()-125, 125,
    circlePaint);
```

Working with `Paint` Utilities for Drawing Text

The `Paint` class includes a number of utilities and features for rendering text to the screen in different typefaces and styles. Now is a great time to start drawing some text to the screen.

Working with Text

Android provides several default font typefaces and styles. Applications can also use custom fonts by including font files as application assets and loading them using the `AssetManager`, much as one would use resources.

Using Default Fonts and Typefaces

By default, Android uses the Sans Serif typeface, but Monospace and Serif typefaces are also available. The following code excerpt draws some anti-aliased text in the default typeface (Sans Serif) to a `Canvas`:

```
import android.graphics.Canvas;
import android.graphics.Color;
import android.graphics.Paint;
import android.graphics.Typeface;
...
Paint mPaint = new Paint(Paint.ANTI_ALIAS_FLAG);
Typeface mType;

mPaint.setTextSize(16);
mPaint.setTypeface(null);

canvas.drawText("Default Typeface", 20, 20, mPaint);
```

You can instead load a different typeface, such as Monospace:

```
Typeface mType = Typeface.create(Typeface.MONOSPACE, Typeface.NORMAL);
```

Perhaps you would prefer italic text, in which case you can simply set the style of the typeface and the font family:

```
Typeface mType = Typeface.create(Typeface.SERIF, Typeface.ITALIC);
```

Warning

Not all typeface styles are supported by all typeface families. You need to test to make sure the desired typeface and style exist on the device.

You can set certain properties of a typeface such as anti-aliasing, underlining, and strike-through using the `setFlags()` method of the `Paint` object:

```
mPaint.setFlags(Paint.UNDERLINE_TEXT_FLAG);
```

Figure 22.3 shows some of the typeface families and styles available by default on Android.

Using Custom Typefaces

You can easily use custom typefaces with your application by including the font files as application assets and loading them on demand. Fonts might be used for a custom look and feel, for implementing language symbols that are not supported natively, or for custom symbols.

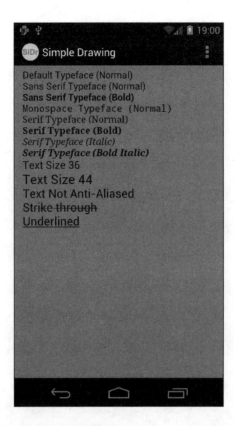

Figure 22.3 Some typefaces and typeface styles available on Android.

For example, you might want to use a handy chess font to implement a simple, scalable chess game. A chess font includes every symbol needed to implement a chessboard, including the board and the pieces. Hans Bodlaender has kindly provided a free chess font called Chess Utrecht. Using the Chess Utrecht font, the letter Q draws a black queen on a white square, whereas a *q* draws a white queen on a white square, and so on. This nifty font is available at *http://www.chessvariants.com/d.font/utrecht.html* as `chess1.ttf`.

To use a custom font such as Chess Utrecht, simply download the font from the website and copy the `chess1.ttf` file from your hard drive to the project directory `/assets/fonts/`.

Now you can load the `Typeface` object programmatically much as you would any resource:

```
import android.graphics.Typeface;
import android.graphics.Color;
import android.graphics.Paint;
...
```

Figure 22.4   Using the Chess Utrecht font to draw a chessboard.

```
Paint mPaint = new Paint(Paint.ANTI_ALIAS_FLAG);
Typeface mType = Typeface.createFromAsset(getContext().getAssets(),
    "fonts/chess1.ttf");
```

You can then use the Chess Utrecht typeface to "draw" a chessboard (see Figure 22.4) using the appropriate character sequences.

Measuring Text Screen Requirements

You can measure how large text with a given `Paint` is and how big a rectangle you need to encompass it using the `measureText()` and `getTextBounds()` methods.

Working with Bitmaps

You can find lots of goodies for working with graphics such as bitmaps (including `NinePatch`) in the `android.graphics` package. The core class for bitmaps is `android.graphics.Bitmap`.

Drawing `Bitmap` Graphics on a `Canvas`

You can draw bitmaps onto a valid `Canvas`, such as in the `onDraw()` method of a `View`, using one of the `drawBitmap()` methods. For example, the following code loads a `Bitmap` resource and draws it on a `Canvas`:

```
import android.graphics.Bitmap;
import android.graphics.BitmapFactory;
...
Bitmap pic = BitmapFactory.decodeResource(getResources(), R.drawable.bluejay);
canvas.drawBitmap(pic, 0, 0, null);
```

Scaling `Bitmap` Graphics

Perhaps you want to scale your graphic to a smaller size. In this case, you can use the `createScaledBitmap()` method, like this:

```
Bitmap sm = Bitmap.createScaledBitmap(pic, 50, 75, false);
```

You can preserve the aspect ratio of the `Bitmap` by checking the `getWidth()` and `getHeight()` methods and scaling appropriately.

Transforming Bitmaps Using Matrixes

You can use the helpful `Matrix` class to perform transformations on a `Bitmap` graphic (see Figure 22.5). Use the `Matrix` class to perform tasks such as mirroring and rotating graphics, among other actions.

The following code uses the `createBitmap()` method to generate a new `Bitmap` that is a mirror of an existing `Bitmap` called `pic`:

```
import android.graphics.Bitmap;
import android.graphics.Matrix;
...
Matrix mirrorMatrix = new Matrix();
mirrorMatrix.preScale(-1, 1);

Bitmap mirrorPic = Bitmap.createBitmap(pic, 0, 0,
    pic.getWidth(), pic.getHeight(), mirrorMatrix, false);
```

You can perform a 30-degree rotation in addition to mirroring by using this `Matrix` instead:

```
Matrix mirrorAndTilt30 = new Matrix();
mirrorAndTilt30.preRotate(30);
mirrorAndTilt30.preScale(-1, 1);
```

You can see the results of different combinations of tilt and mirror `Matrix` transforms in Figure 22.5. When you're no longer using a `Bitmap`, you can free its memory using the `recycle()` method:

```
pic.recycle();
```

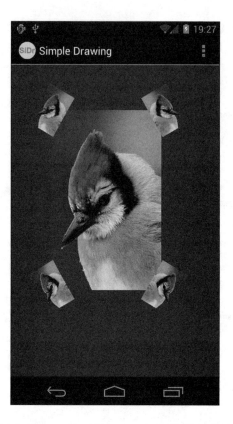

Figure 22.5   A single-source bitmap: scaled, tilted, and mirrored using
Android `Bitmap` classes.

There are a variety of other `Bitmap` effects and utilities available as part of the Android
SDK, but they are numerous and beyond the scope of this book. See the `android`
`.graphics` package for more details.

`Bitmap` Performance Optimizations

When displaying images in an application, one gotcha that developers tend to overlook
is the amount of memory allocated for the application. A really large image could end up
consuming all of the available memory before the application is fully loaded into memory,
causing the application to run out of memory and resulting in the `OutOfMemoryError`.

If your application loads multiple images at once, and you do not take care how
you manage the images within the application, even if the images are able to load, your

application will become slow and feel unresponsive, resulting in a poor user experience that may cause users to uninstall the application.

Luckily, there are a few best practices for working with bitmaps. The following list gives a few suggestions for managing bitmaps:

- Load images at the same resolution as you will display them, rather than display them at their source resolution. This can be achieved by using a `BitmapFactory` `.Options` object and setting the `inSampleSize` parameter for a given image, which allows you to sample the original image by making it smaller in width and height and reduces the number of pixels based on powers of 2.

- Load images concurrently, in the background and off the main UI thread, using an `AsyncTask` object.

- Leverage the memory cache for temporarily storing bitmaps in your application's available memory allotment so images don't need to be re-created every time they are needed, and allocate a portion of your application's `LruCache` for `Bitmap` caching.

API Level 19 introduced a few new `Bitmap` methods that are useful for managing the performance of bitmaps that you should be aware of. `getAllocationByteCount()` will help you to determine the memory consumption of a particular `Bitmap`. `reconfigure()` allows you to re-initialize a `Bitmap` to a new configuration without affecting the memory allocated for a particular `Bitmap`.

Tip

To learn more about how to optimize your application for working with bitmaps, read the Training guide found within the Android documentation found here: *http://d.android.com/ training/building-graphics.html.*

Working with Shapes

You can define and draw primitive shapes such as rectangles and ovals using the `Shape` `Drawable` class in conjunction with a variety of specialized `Shape` classes. You can define `Paintable` drawables as XML resource files, but more often, especially with more complex shapes, this is done programmatically.

Tip

Many of the code examples provided in this section are taken from the SimpleShapes application. The source code for this application is provided for download on the book's website.

Defining Shape Drawables as XML Resources

You can define primitive shapes such as rectangles using specially formatted XML files in the `/res/drawable/` resource directory, as discussed in *Introduction to Android Application*

Development: Android™ Essentials, Fourth Edition. The following resource file called
`/res/drawable/green_rect.xml` describes a simple green rectangle shape `Drawable`:

```
<?xml version="1.0" encoding="utf-8"?>
<shape xmlns:android="http://schemas.android.com/apk/res/android"
    android:shape="rectangle">
    <solid
        android:color="#0f0"/>
</shape>
```

You can then load the shape resource and set it as the `Drawable` as follows:

```
ImageView iView = (ImageView)findViewById(R.id.ImageView1);
iView.setImageResource(R.drawable.green_rect);
```

You should note that many `Paint` properties can be set via XML as part of the `Shape`
definition. For example, the following `Oval` shape is defined with a linear gradient (red to
white) and stroke style information:

```
<?xml version="1.0" encoding="utf-8"?>
<shape xmlns:android="http://schemas.android.com/apk/res/android"
    android:shape="oval">
    <solid
        android:color="#f00"/>
    <gradient
        android:startColor="#f00"
        android:endColor="#fff"
        android:angle="180"/>
    <stroke
        android:width="3dp"
        android:color="#00f"
        android:dashWidth="5dp"
        android:dashGap="3dp"/>
</shape>
```

Defining Shape Drawables Programmatically

You can also define these `ShapeDrawable` instances programmatically. The different
shapes are available as classes in the `android.graphics.drawable.shapes` package. For
example, you can programmatically define the aforementioned green rectangle as follows:

```
import android.graphics.drawable.ShapeDrawable;
import android.graphics.drawable.shapes.RectShape;
...
ShapeDrawable rect = new ShapeDrawable(new RectShape());
rect.getPaint().setColor(Color.GREEN);
```

You can then set the `Drawable` for the `ImageView` directly:

```
ImageView iView = (ImageView)findViewById(R.id.ImageView1);
iView.setImageDrawable(rect);
```

The resulting green rectangle is shown in Figure 22.6.

Figure 22.6   A green rectangle ShapeDrawable drawn to the View.

Drawing Different Shapes

Some of the different shapes available in the android.graphics.drawable.shapes
package include the following:

- Rectangles (and squares)
- Rectangles with rounded corners
- Ovals (and circles)
- Arcs and lines
- Other shapes defined as paths

You can create and use these shapes as Drawable resources directly in ImageView
views, or you can find corresponding methods for creating these primitive shapes in a
Canvas.

Drawing Rectangles and Squares

Drawing rectangles and squares (rectangles with equal height/width values) is simply a matter of creating a `ShapeDrawable` from a `RectShape` object. The `RectShape` object has no dimensions but is bound by the container object—in this case, the `ShapeDrawable`. You can set some basic properties of the `ShapeDrawable`, such as the `Paint` color and the default size.

For example, here we create a magenta-colored rectangle that is 100 pixels long and 2 pixels wide, which looks like a straight, horizontal line. We then set the shape as the `Drawable` for an `ImageView` so the shape can be displayed:

```
import android.graphics.drawable.ShapeDrawable;
import android.graphics.drawable.shapes.RectShape;
...
ShapeDrawable rect = new ShapeDrawable(new RectShape());
rect.setIntrinsicHeight(2);
rect.setIntrinsicWidth(100);
rect.getPaint().setColor(Color.MAGENTA);

ImageView iView = (ImageView)findViewById(R.id.ImageView1);
iView.setImageDrawable(rect);
```

Drawing Rectangles with Rounded Corners

You can create rectangles with rounded corners, which can be nice for making custom buttons. Simply create a `ShapeDrawable` from a `RoundRectShape` object. The `RoundRectShape` requires an array of eight float values, which signify the radii of the rounded corners. For example, the following creates a simple cyan-colored, rounded-corner rectangle:

```
import android.graphics.drawable.ShapeDrawable;
import android.graphics.drawable.shapes.RoundRectShape;
...
ShapeDrawable rndrect = new ShapeDrawable(
    new RoundRectShape(new float[] { 5, 5, 5, 5, 5, 5, 5, 5 },
                       null, null));

rndrect.setIntrinsicHeight(50);
rndrect.setIntrinsicWidth(100);
rndrect.getPaint().setColor(Color.CYAN);
ImageView iView = (ImageView)findViewById(R.id.ImageView1);
iView.setImageDrawable(rndrect);
```

The resulting round-corner rectangle is shown in Figure 22.7.

You can also specify an inner-rounded rectangle within an outer rectangle, if you choose. The following creates an inner rectangle with rounded edges within an outer white rectangle with rounded edges:

```
import android.graphics.drawable.ShapeDrawable;
import android.graphics.drawable.shapes.RoundRectShape;
...
float[] outerRadii = new float[]{ 6, 6, 6, 6, 6, 6, 6, 6 };
RectF insetRectangle = new RectF(8, 8, 8, 8);
float[] innerRadii = new float[]{ 6, 6, 6, 6, 6, 6, 6, 6 };
```

Figure 22.7   A cyan rectangle `ShapeDrawable` with rounded corners drawn to the `View`.

```
ShapeDrawable rndrect = new ShapeDrawable(
    new RoundRectShape(outerRadii, insetRectangle, innerRadii));
rndrect.setIntrinsicHeight(50);
rndrect.setIntrinsicWidth(100);
rndrect.getPaint().setColor(Color.WHITE);
ImageView iView = (ImageView)findViewById(R.id.ImageView1);
iView.setImageDrawable(rndrect);
```

The resulting round rectangle with an inset rectangle is shown in Figure 22.8.

Drawing Ovals and Circles

You can create ovals and circles (which are ovals with equal height/width values) by creating a `ShapeDrawable` using an `OvalShape` object. The `OvalShape` object has no dimensions but is bound by the container object—in this case, the `ShapeDrawable`. You can set some basic properties of the `ShapeDrawable`, such as the `Paint` color and the

Figure 22.8   A white rectangle `ShapeDrawable` with rounded corners
with an inset rounded rectangle drawn to the `View`.

default size. For example, here we create a red oval that is 40 pixels high and 100 pixels wide, which looks like a Frisbee:

```
import android.graphics.drawable.ShapeDrawable;
import android.graphics.drawable.shapes.OvalShape;
...
ShapeDrawable oval = new ShapeDrawable(new OvalShape());
oval.setIntrinsicHeight(40);
oval.setIntrinsicWidth(100);
oval.getPaint().setColor(Color.RED);
ImageView iView = (ImageView)findViewById(R.id.ImageView1);
iView.setImageDrawable(oval);
```

The resulting red oval is shown in Figure 22.9.

Drawing Arcs

You can draw arcs, which look like pie charts or Pac-Man, depending on the sweep angle you specify. You can create arcs by creating a `ShapeDrawable` using an `ArcShape`

Figure 22.9   A red oval ShapeDrawable drawn to the View.

object. The ArcShape object requires two parameters: a startAngle and a sweepAngle. The startAngle begins at 3 o'clock. Positive sweepAngle values sweep clockwise; negative values sweep counterclockwise. You can create a circle by using the values 0 and 360.

The following code creates an arc that looks like a magenta Pac-Man:

```
import android.graphics.drawable.ShapeDrawable;
import android.graphics.drawable.shapes.ArcShape;
...
ShapeDrawable pacMan = new ShapeDrawable(new ArcShape(45, 270));
pacMan.setIntrinsicHeight(100);
pacMan.setIntrinsicWidth(100);
pacMan.getPaint().setColor(Color.MAGENTA);
ImageView iView = (ImageView)findViewById(R.id.ImageView1);
iView.setImageDrawable(pacMan);
```

The resulting arc is shown in Figure 22.10.

Figure 22.10   A magenta arc `ShapeDrawable` of 270 degrees,
starting at 45 degrees (resembling Pac-Man or a pie chart
with 75 percent showing), drawn to the `View`.

Drawing Paths

You can specify any shape you want by breaking it down into a series of points along a path. The `android.graphics.Path` class encapsulates a series of lines and curves that make up some larger shape.

For example, the following `Path` defines a rough five-point star shape:

```
import android.graphics.Path;
...
Path p = new Path();
p.moveTo(50, 0);
p.lineTo(25,100);
p.lineTo(100,50);
p.lineTo(0,50);
p.lineTo(75,100);
p.lineTo(50,0);
```

You can then encapsulate this star `Path` in a `PathShape`, create a `ShapeDrawable`, and paint it yellow:

```
import android.graphics.drawable.ShapeDrawable;
import android.graphics.drawable.shapes.PathShape;
...
ShapeDrawable star = new ShapeDrawable(new PathShape(p, 100, 100));
star.setIntrinsicHeight(100);
star.setIntrinsicWidth(100);
star.getPaint().setColor(Color.YELLOW);
```

By default, this generates a star shape filled with the `Paint` color yellow (see Figure 22.11).

Figure 22.11   A yellow star `ShapeDrawable` drawn to the `View`.

Figure 22.12   A yellow star `ShapeDrawable` using
the `STROKE` style of `Paint` drawn to the `View`.

Or, you can set the `Paint` style to `STROKE` for a line drawing of a star:

```
star.getPaint().setStyle(Paint.Style.STROKE);
```

The resulting star would look something like Figure 22.12.

Tip

The graphics support available in the Android SDK could be the subject of an entire book. After you have familiarized yourself with the basics, we recommend that you check out the APIDemos application provided with the Android SDK legacy samples.

Leveraging Hardware Acceleration Features

Just about every Android application draws on the screen in some form or another. Whether you're using standard `View` controls or custom drawing, 2D hardware acceleration can improve your application. Android developers can easily harness the built-in hardware acceleration features added to the Android platform in Android 3.0 from within their applications. These newer versions of the Android platform boast an improved OpenGL rendering pipeline for common 2D graphics operations.

There's little reason not to leverage hardware acceleration for a smoother, more responsive experience for your users. You can simply take advantage of the default features, or you can fine-tune your application graphics acceleration at the application, `Activity`, `Window`, or `View` level, if required.

Controlling Hardware Acceleration

Hardware acceleration is available on devices running Android 3.0 and higher. In fact, if your application has a `minSdkVersion` or `targetSdkVersion` set to API Level 14 or greater, hardware acceleration is enabled for all windows. You may still want to control acceleration in your application, though. This can be done directly in the manifest file in the `<application>` and `<activity>` tags. Set the `android:hardwareAccelerated` attribute to `true` or `false`, depending on your needs. To control acceleration at the `Window` or even for a specific `View` instance, you need to do this programmatically. For the `Window`, use the `setFlags()` method with `WindowManager.LayoutParams` `.FLAG_HARDWARE_ACCELERATED` to enable acceleration. There is no programmatic way to disable acceleration. For a `View` control, use the `setLayerType()` method with the appropriate layer type, such as `View.LAYER_TYPE_HARDWARE`. For more information on layers, see the Android documentation at *http://d.android.com/guide/topics/graphics/hardware-accel.html#layers*.

Fine-Tuning Hardware Acceleration

If you've got custom drawing operations or work with the `Canvas` and `Paint` classes in your application, you need to pay attention to which features are available in Android hardware acceleration at this time. Certain `Canvas` and `Paint` operations are not currently supported, whereas others behave differently depending on hardware versus software acceleration. Notably, the methods `clipPath()`, `clipRegion()`, `drawPicture()`, `drawVertices()`, `drawPosText()`, and `drawTextOnPath()` are not supported in the `Canvas` class. In the `Paint` class, `setLinearText()`, `setMaskFilter()`, and `setRasterizer()` are not supported. The Android documentation has a list of specific drawing operations not fully supported by hardware acceleration at this time, available at *http://d.android.com/guide/topics/graphics/hardware-accel.html#unsupported*.

Test your app thoroughly, and if you run into problems, you've got a couple of options. You can work around any problems by re-implementing your drawing code using supported functionality. You can also turn off hardware acceleration on that `Activity`, `Window`, or specific `View` control and rely on the default software acceleration instead.

Tip

You can determine whether a `View` is leveraging hardware acceleration at runtime using the `View.isHardwareAccelerated()` method. You can disable hardware acceleration on a specific `View` control at runtime using the following method call:

```
setLayerType(View.LAYER_TYPE_SOFTWARE, null);
```

For more details about hardware acceleration on the Android platform, see the references section at the end of this chapter.

Summary

The Android SDK comes with the `android.graphics` package, which includes powerful classes for drawing graphics and text to the screen in a variety of different ways. Some features of the graphics library include `Bitmap` graphics utilities, `Typeface` and font style support, `Paint` colors and styles, different types of gradients, and a variety of primitive and not-so-primitive shapes that can be drawn to the screen. You also learned different ways of working with and optimizing bitmaps in your applications. Hardware acceleration is now enabled on the platform and may affect drawing operations.

Quiz Questions

1. True or false: One way to retrieve a valid `Canvas` object is by extending the `View` class and implementing the `onDraw()` method.

2. What are the two methods used for retrieving the size of a `Canvas` object?

3. What does anti-aliasing do to a graphic and how do you perform anti-aliasing to a `Paint` object?

4. True or false: The `reconfigure()` method allows you to re-initialize a `Bitmap` to a new configuration without affecting the memory allocated for a particular `Bitmap`.

5. What are the different layers for which you are able to control hardware acceleration in your application?

Exercises

1. Use the Android documentation to determine the variety of forms that drawables may take.

2. Modify the `DrawBitmapActivity` of the SimpleDrawing application that accompanies this chapter so that the `Bitmap` is loaded off the UI thread.

3. Modify the sample applications that accompany this chapter so that they make use of the hardware acceleration features of Android.

References and More Information

Android SDK Reference documentation for the `android.graphics` package:
   http://d.android.com/reference/android/graphics/package-summary.html
Android SDK Reference documentation for the `Bitmap` class:
   http://d.android.com/reference/android/graphics/Bitmap.html
YouTube Android Developers Channel: "DevBytes: Bitmap Allocation":
   http://www.youtube.com/watch?v=rsQet4nBVi8
YouTube Android Developers Channel: "Bitmap Scaling":
   http://www.youtube.com/watch?v=12cB7gnL6po
Android API Guides: "Hardware Acceleration":
   http://d.android.com/guide/topics/graphics/hardware-accel.html

23

Working with Animation

In this chapter we talk about the different animation features built into Android. Here, we cover everything from using animated GIF and drawable animation (for frame-by-frame animations) to using view animation (for tweens) and the more robust property animation features that were added in later versions of the Android SDK. We also look at new APIs such as the `android.transition` framework.

Animating Your Applications

The Android platform supports several types of graphics animation:

- Animated GIF images
- Drawable animation (frame-by-frame animation)
- View animation (tweened animation)
- Property animation

Animated GIFs store the animation frames in the image, and you simply include these GIFs as you would any other graphic-drawable resource. For drawable animation (frame-by-frame animation), the developer must provide all graphic frames of the animation. However, with view animation (or tweened animation), only a single graphic is needed, to which transforms can be programmatically applied. Property animation, or the modification of any object property over a certain time duration, was added in Android 3.0. The Android animation framework also supports numerous interpolators for different animation effects.

Tip

Many of the code examples provided in this chapter are taken from the ShapeShifter application. The source code for this application is provided for download on the book's website.

Working with Drawable Animation

You can think of drawable animation as a digital flipbook in which a series of similar images display on the screen in a sequence, each subtly different from the last. When you

Figure 23.1   Three frames for an animation of a genie juggling.

display these images quickly, they give the illusion of movement. This technique is called frame-by-frame animation and is often used on the Web in the form of animated GIF images.

Frame-by-frame animation is best used for complicated graphics transformations that are not easily implemented programmatically.

For example, we can create the illusion of a genie juggling gifts using a sequence of three images, as shown in Figure 23.1.

In each frame, the genie remains fixed, but the gifts are repositioned slightly. The smoothness of the animation is controlled by providing an adequate number of frames and choosing the appropriate speed with which to swap them.

The following code demonstrates how to load three `Bitmap` resources (our three genie frames) and create an `AnimationDrawable`. We then set the `AnimationDrawable` as the background resource of an `ImageView` and start the animation:

```
ImageView img = (ImageView)findViewById(R.id.ImageView1);

BitmapDrawable frame1 = (BitmapDrawable)getResources().
    getDrawable(R.drawable.f1);
BitmapDrawable frame2 = (BitmapDrawable)getResources().
    getDrawable(R.drawable.f2);
BitmapDrawable frame3 = (BitmapDrawable)getResources().
    getDrawable(R.drawable.f3);

int reasonableDuration = 250;
AnimationDrawable mFrameAnimation = new AnimationDrawable();

mFrameAnimation.addFrame(frame1, reasonableDuration);
mFrameAnimation.addFrame(frame2, reasonableDuration);
mFrameAnimation.addFrame(frame3, reasonableDuration);

img.setBackground(mFrameAnimation);
```

`setBackground()` was added in API Level 16 and is used for adding the frame animation as the background.

To make the animation loop continuously, we can call the `setOneShot()` method:

```
mAnimation.setOneShot(false);
```

To begin the animation, we call the `start()` method:

```
mAnimation.start();
```

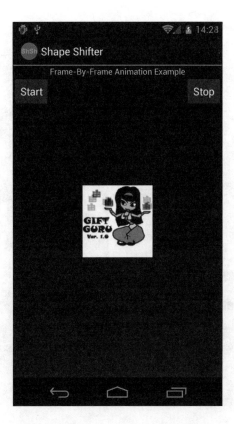

Figure 23.2   The genie animation in the Android emulator.

We can end our animation at any time using the stop() method:

```
mAnimation.stop();
```

Although we used an ImageView background in this example, you can use a variety of different View controls for animations. For example, you can instead use the Image Switcher view and change the displayed Drawable resource using a timer. This sort of operation is best done on a separate thread. The resulting animation might look something like Figure 23.2—you just have to imagine it moving.

Working with View Animations

With view animations (also called tween animations), you can provide a single Drawable resource as a Bitmap graphic (see Figure 23.3, left), a ShapeDrawable, a TextView (see Figure 23.3, right), or any other type of View object and the system will automatically render the intermediate frames of the animation. Android provides tweening support for several common image transformations, including alpha, rotate, scale, and translate

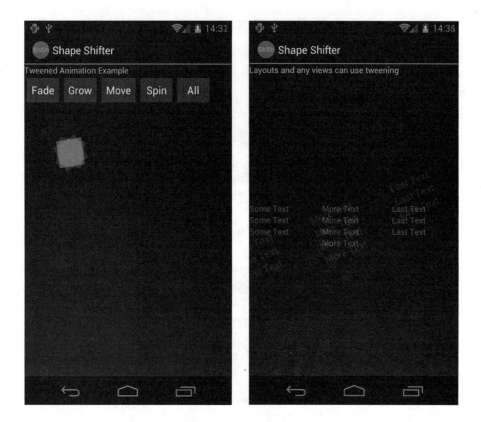

Figure 23.3   Rotating a green rectangle `ShapeDrawable` (left)
and a `TableLayout` (right).

animations. You can apply tweened animation transformations to any `View`, whether it is
an `ImageView` with a `Bitmap`, a `ShapeDrawable`, or a layout such as a `TableLayout`.

Defining Tweening Transformations

You can define tweening transformations as XML resource files or programmatically. All
tweened animations share some common properties, including when to start, how long
to animate, and whether to return to the starting state upon completion.

Defining Tweened Animations as XML Resources

You can store animation sequences as specially formatted XML files in the
`/res/animator/` resource directory. For example, the following resource file called
`/res/animator/spin.xml` describes a simple 5-second rotation:

```
<?xml version="1.0" encoding="utf-8" ?>
<set xmlns:android="http://schemas.android.com/apk/res/android"
    android:shareInterpolator="false">
```

```
    <rotate
        android:fromDegrees="0"
        android:toDegrees="360"
        android:pivotX="50%"
        android:pivotY="50%"
        android:duration="5000" />
</set>
```

Defining Tweened Animations Programmatically

You can programmatically define these animations. The different types of transformations are available as classes in the `android.view.animation` package. For example, you can define the aforementioned rotation animation as follows:

```
import android.view.animation.RotateAnimation;
...
RotateAnimation rotate = new RotateAnimation(
    0, 360, RotateAnimation.RELATIVE_TO_SELF, 0.5f,
    RotateAnimation.RELATIVE_TO_SELF, 0.5f);

rotate.setDuration(5000);
```

Defining Simultaneous and Sequential Tweened Animations

Animation transformations can happen simultaneously or sequentially when you set the `startOffset` and `duration` properties, which control when an animation starts and how long it takes to complete. You can combine animations into the <set> tag (programmatically, using `AnimationSet`) to share properties.

For example, the following animation resource file `/res/animator/grow.xml` includes a set of two scale animations. First, we take 2.5 seconds to double in size, and then at 2.5 seconds, we start a second animation to shrink back to our starting size:

```
<?xml version="1.0" encoding="utf-8" ?>
<set xmlns:android=http://schemas.android.com/apk/res/android
    android:shareInterpolator="false">
    <scale
        android:pivotX="50%"
        android:pivotY="50%"
        android:fromXScale="1.0"
        android:fromYScale="1.0"
        android:toXScale="2.0"
        android:toYScale="2.0"
        android:duration="2500" />
    <scale
        android:startOffset="2500"
        android:duration="2500"
        android:pivotX="50%"
        android:pivotY="50%"
        android:fromXScale="1.0"
        android:fromYScale="1.0"
        android:toXScale="0.5"
        android:toYScale="0.5" />
</set>
```

Loading Animations

Loading animations is made simple using the `AnimationUtils` helper class. The following code loads an animation XML resource file called `/res/animator/grow.xml` and applies it to an `ImageView` whose source resource is a green rectangle `ShapeDrawable`:

```
import android.view.animation.Animation;
import android.view.animation.AnimationUtils;
...
ImageView iView = (ImageView)findViewById(R.id.ImageView1);
iView.setImageResource(R.drawable.green_rect);
Animation an = AnimationUtils.loadAnimation(this, R.anim.grow);
iView.startAnimation(an);
```

We can listen for `Animation` events, including the animation start, end, and repeat events, by implementing an `AnimationListener` class, such as the `MyAnimation Listener` class shown here:

```
class MyAnimationListener implements Animation.AnimationListener {
    public void onAnimationEnd(Animation animation) {
        // Do at end of animation
    }

    public void onAnimationRepeat(Animation animation) {
        // Do each time the animation loops
    }

    public void onAnimationStart(Animation animation) {
        // Do at start of animation
    }
}
```

You can then register your `AnimationListener` as follows:

```
an.setAnimationListener(new MyAnimationListener());
```

Exploring the Four Different Tweening Transformations

Now let's look at each of the four types of tweening transformations individually. These types are:

- Transparency changes (alpha)
- Rotations (rotate)
- Scaling (scale)
- Movement (translate)

Working with Alpha Transparency Transformations

Transparency is controlled using alpha transformations. Alpha transformations can be used to fade objects in and out of view or to layer them on the screen.

Alpha values range from 0.0 (fully transparent or invisible) to 1.0 (fully opaque or visible). Alpha animations involve a starting transparency (`fromAlpha`) and an ending transparency (`toAlpha`).

The following XML resource file excerpt defines a transparency-change animation, taking 5 seconds to fade in from fully transparent to fully opaque:

```
<alpha
    android:fromAlpha="0.0"
    android:toAlpha="1.0"
    android:duration="5000">
</alpha>
```

Programmatically, you can create this same animation using the `AlphaAnimation` class within the `android.view.animation` package.

Working with Rotating Transformations

You can use rotation operations to spin objects clockwise or counterclockwise around a pivot point in the object's boundaries.

Rotations are defined in terms of degrees. For example, you might want an object to make one complete clockwise rotation. To do this, you set the `fromDegrees` property to 0 and the `toDegrees` property to 360. To rotate the object counterclockwise instead, you set the `toDegrees` property to −360.

By default, the object pivots around the (0,0) coordinate, or the top-left corner of the object. This is great for rotations such as those of a clock's hands, but much of the time, you want to pivot from the center of the object. You can do this easily by setting the pivot point, which can be a fixed coordinate or a percentage.

The following XML resource file excerpt defines a rotation animation, taking 5 seconds to make one full clockwise rotation, pivoting from the center of the object:

```
<rotate
    android:fromDegrees="0"
    android:toDegrees="360"
    android:pivotX="50%"
    android:pivotY="50%"
    android:duration="5000" />
```

Programmatically, you can create this same animation using the `RotateAnimation` class in the `android.view.animation` package.

Working with Scaling Transformations

You can use scaling operations to stretch objects vertically and horizontally. Scaling operations are defined as relative scales. Think of the scale value of 1.0 as 100 percent, or full size. To scale to half size, or 50 percent, set the target scale value to 0.5.

You can scale horizontally and vertically on different scales or on the same scale (to preserve aspect ratio). You need to set four values for proper scaling: starting scale (`fromXScale`, `fromYScale`) and target scale (`toXScale`, `toYScale`). Again, you can use a pivot point to stretch your object from a specific (x,y) coordinate such as the center or another coordinate.

The following XML resource file excerpt defines a scaling animation, taking 5 seconds to double an object's size, pivoting from the center of the object:

```
<scale
    android:pivotX="50%"
    android:pivotY="50%"
    android:fromXScale="1.0"
    android:fromYScale="1.0"
    android:toXScale="2.0"
    android:toYScale="2.0"
    android:duration="5000" />
```

Programmatically, you can create this same animation using the `ScaleAnimation` class within the `android.view.animation` package.

Working with Moving Transformations

You can move objects around using translate operations. Translate operations move an object from one position on the (x,y) coordinate to another position.

To perform a translate operation, you must specify the change, or delta, in the object's coordinates. You can set four values for translations: starting position (`fromXDelta`, `fromYDelta`) and relative target location (`toXDelta`, `toYDelta`).

The following XML resource file excerpt defines a translate animation, taking 5 seconds to move an object up (negative) by 100 on the y axis. We also set the `fillAfter` property to be `true`, so the object doesn't "jump" back to its starting position when the animation finishes:

```
<translate
    android:toYDelta="-100"
    android:fillAfter="true"
    android:duration="2500" />
```

Programmatically, you can create this same animation using the `TranslateAnimation` class in the `android.view.animation` package.

Working with Property Animation

Introduced in Android API Level 11 and refined in Android API Level 12, property animation is the capability to animate any object property over time. The property animation system is much more flexible and robust than the features available in view animations. Unlike view animations, when property animation is used, the properties of the object (such as a `View` control) are actually modified over the course of time, as opposed to just drawn with the underlying object remaining unchanged.

Property animation can be configured in the following ways:

- Animations can be applied to value or object types.
- Animations can use the various interpolators available on the platform.

- Animations can be defined in sets, with multiple attributes changing simultaneously or in sequence.

- Animations are created separately from the target objects to which they are applied, and they can be reused.

- Animation duration, repeat count (a number or infinite), repeat behavior (repeat from the beginning or reverse), and other animation characteristics can be set as needed.

Tip

The code examples provided in this section are taken from the SimplePropertyAnimation application. The source code for this application is provided for download on the book's website.

There are several important classes you'll want to be aware of for property animation:

- The `ValueAnimator` class (`android.animation.ValueAnimator`) is the base class for all property animations.

- The `ObjectAnimator` class (`android.animation.ObjectAnimator`) is the convenience class for animating a specific target object and property. This is the class you will use most frequently for animating properties on objects like `View` controls.

- The `ViewPropertyAnimator` class (`android.view.ViewPropertyAnimator`) enables optimized and easy animation for `View` objects. The `animate()` method of `View` objects provides access to this class, and its performance may be better than that of alternative methods. In fact, the results may be hardware accelerated.

- The `Animator.AnimatorPauseListener` interface was added in API Level 19 and is used for receiving animation notifications. The `onAnimationPause()` method responds to paused animations, and the `onAnimationResume()` method responds to resumed animations.

- The `RectEvaluator` class, added in API Level 18, is used to interpolate coordinates of a rectangle.

- There are a number of evaluator classes (`android.animation.*`), such as `IntEvaluator`, `FloatEvaluator`, `ArgbEvaluator`, and `TimeAnimator`. These enable you to animate any type of property an object can have by defining how to calculate changes in the property over time.

In addition to these classes, which are specific to property animation, you also use the standard `AnimationSet` and interpolator classes.

Defining Property Animations as XML Resources

Property animation sets can be configured via XML, much like view animations. You can store property animation sequences as specially formatted XML files in the `/res/animator/` resource directory.

Tip

Although you can save your animation resources wherever you like, it is recommended in Android 3.1+ that property animation resources be stored in the `/res/animator/` resource directory instead of the `/res/anim` directory so that the Android IDE can find them.

A property animation has a number of attributes, including:

- **A duration:** The amount of time it takes, in milliseconds, for the animation to complete. This value is set with the `android:duration` attribute.

- **A property name:** The name of the property to be modified in the animation. This value is set with the `android:propertyName` attribute. Only properties with getter/setter methods that return `int` or `float` should be used, such as `set<propertyName>` or `get<propertyName>`.

- **The repeat count:** The number of times this animation should take place. This value is set with the `android:repeatCount` attribute. If you want the animation to repeat without stopping, use −1.

- **The repeat mode:** The way the animation repeats. This value is set with the `android:repeatMode` attribute. If you want the animation to repeat by resetting and starting from the beginning, use repeat. If you want the animation to reverse and go back to where it started, use reverse.

- **The value start and stop points:** The range of values between which to animate the value of the property. These values are set with the `android:valueFrom` and `android:valueTo` attributes. If you want to animate from the current value of the property, you need not specify it with the `android:valueFrom` attribute.

- **The value type:** This is the data type of the property being animated on. This value is set with the `android:valueType` attribute. XML files support both `intType` and `floatType`. Other types, such as color values, can be set programmatically.

For example, the following resource file called `/res/animator/blinky_anim.xml` describes a simple property animation set that modifies the `alpha` and `backgroundColor` properties of an object over time:

```
<?xml version="1.0" encoding="utf-8" ?>
<set xmlns:android="http://schemas.android.com/apk/res/android"
    android:ordering="together" >
    <objectAnimator
        android:duration="2500"
        android:propertyName="alpha"
        android:repeatCount="-1"
        android:repeatMode="reverse"
        android:valueFrom="0"
        android:valueTo="1"
        android:valueType="floatType" />
    <objectAnimator
        android:duration="7500"
        android:propertyName="backgroundColor"
```

```
            android:repeatCount="-1"
            android:repeatMode="reverse"
            android:valueFrom="#2E0854"
            android:valueTo="#BF5FFF" />
</set>
```

This animation set contains two animations that are performed simultaneously. The first animates the `alpha` property, causing the object to fade in and out of view over the course of 5 seconds, indefinitely, because a `repeatCount` of −1 means to animate continuously and the `repeatMode` causes the animation to reverse itself each time. The second animation happens more slowly, changing the `backgroundColor` attribute of the object between two purple colors, as specified in the `valueFrom` and `valueTo` attributes of the animation configuration.

Defining and Modifying Property Animations Programmatically

You can also programmatically define property animations. The property animation classes are available in the `android.animation` package. There are also times when you may need to modify an animation defined in XML. For example, here we load the animation set that was defined earlier in XML and set the value type of the `object Animator` for the `backgroundColor` attribute to an `ArgbEvaluator`, which can't be defined via XML:

```
AnimatorSet set = (AnimatorSet) AnimatorInflater.loadAnimator(this,
             R.animator.blinky_anim);

ArrayList<Animator> animations = set.getChildAnimations();

for (Animator animator : animations) {
    if (animator instanceof ObjectAnimator) {
        ObjectAnimator anim = (ObjectAnimator) animator;

        if (anim.getPropertyName().compareTo("backgroundColor") == 0) {
            anim.setEvaluator(new ArgbEvaluator());
        }
    }
}
set.setInterpolator(new LinearInterpolator());
```

Starting Property Animations Programmatically

To use a property animation, you must attach it to an object of your choice. For example, we can attach the property animation we just created to a `TextView` control (defined in the layout) and start the animation as follows:

```
TextView tv = (TextView) findViewById(R.id.myText);
set.setTarget(tv);
set.start();
```

Here, we attach the property animation to a `View` using the `setTarget()` method and then begin animating with the `start()` method.

When you are just animating properties of a `View` control, it is often more efficient and usually easier to use the `animate()` method. Starting with API Level 12, all `View` objects have an `animate()` method that returns a `ViewPropertyAnimator` object. Through this object, a subset of properties can be animated easily and efficiently. For example:

```
tv.animate().translationXBy(75f).rotationXBy(720).setDuration(1250);
layout.animate().scaleX(0.5f)
        .scaleY(0.5f)
        .setInterpolator(new BounceInterpolator())
        .setDuration(1500);
```

The first one shows a `TextView` being moved horizontally by 75 pixels and rotated around the *x* axis, both of which take place over 1250 milliseconds. The rotation around the *x* axis is, indeed, a three-dimensional rotation. The second example shows an entire layout—including all buttons, images, text, indeed, all children—being scaled to 50 percent of its original size with a bounce interpolator, over a duration of 1500 milliseconds.

For more examples of programmatic property animation, see the sample application provided. We recommend running it so you can see what the animations do; print does not treat animations well (Figure 23.4). You can also find numerous property animation

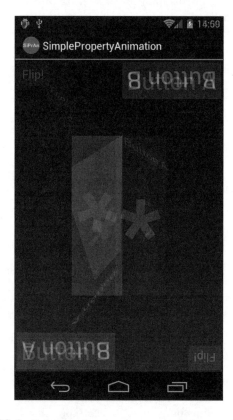

Figure 23.4   Example of a `ViewPropertyAnimator` in action.

examples in the `Animations.zip` (*http://developer.android.com/shareables/training/ Animations.zip*) download found at the online Android documentation Training section listed under "Building Android Apps with Graphics and Animation: Adding Animations."

Working with Different Interpolators

The interpolator determines the rate at which an animation happens in time. Interpolators apply to both view and property animations. A number of different interpolators are provided as part of the Android SDK framework. Some of these interpolators include:

- `AccelerateDecelerateInterpolator`: Animation starts slowly, speeds up, and ends slowly.
- `AccelerateInterpolator`: Animation starts slowly and then accelerates.
- `AnticipateInterpolator`: Animation starts backward, and then flings forward.
- `AnticipateOvershootInterpolator`: Animation starts backward, flings forward, overshoots its destination, and then settles at the destination.
- `BounceInterpolator`: Animation "bounces" into place at its destination.
- `CycleInterpolator`: Animation is repeated a certain number of times, smoothly transitioning from one cycle to the next.
- `DecelerateInterpolator`: Animation begins quickly and then decelerates.
- `LinearInterpolator`: Animation speed is constant throughout.
- `OvershootInterpolator`: Animation overshoots its destination, and then settles at the destination.

You can specify the interpolator used by an animation programmatically using the `setInterpolator()` method or in the animation XML resource using the `android:interpolator` attribute. For more information, check out the `Interpolator` class (`android.view.animation.Interpolator`) and its subclasses.

Animating `Activity` Launch

API Level 16 introduced the new `ActivityOptions` class which allows you to animate an `Activity` launch using custom or zoom animations. There are three animation methods available for this class: `makeCustomAnimation()`, `makeScaleUpAnimation()`, and `makeThumbnailScaleUpAnimation()`. The custom method allows you to use an animation resource file for controlling the animation. The scale-up method allows you to choose the location on the screen where you want the animation to originate from, and the thumbnail scale-up method allows you to choose a `Bitmap` object to scale up from a particular location on the screen.

State Animations with Scenes and Transitions

Many applications require different UI states at particular usability points within an application. Certain visual components of a particular state are frequently reused throughout the user flow within the application, but not all components are needed across different states.

The new `android.transition` framework, introduced with Android KitKat (API Level 19), is a way to define different scene states of your UI, and to animate between those defined states using definable transitions. Scene state transitions are generally accomplished in the following manner:

1. Begin with a UI component state `ViewGroup` that needs animating.
2. Determine the next `Scene` layout to transition to.
3. Determine the transition type for the animation such as `Fade` or `ChangeBounds` and use a `TransitionManager` to manage the scene transition.
4. Perform the transition using the `go()` or `transitionTo()` method and include the `Scene` for transitioning to.

You may also define transitions using XML files included within your resources directory. These files would reside under `res/transition` and require including `<transition>` and `<transitionManager>` tag elements for controlling the state animations between scenes.

Summary

The Android SDK supports several different types of animation. All versions of the Android SDK support drawable (frame-by-frame) animation, animated GIF files, and view (tween) animation. Android 3.0 added a much more robust animation framework that supports property animation that leverages the hardware acceleration features built into newer versions of the Android platform. Property animation allows developers to animate any object attribute over time, be it a `View` control or something else. The new `Transition` framework allows you to create sophisticated and controlled state transitions among various UI components for different usability points within your application.

Quiz Questions

1. What is another term for a `Drawable` animation?
2. What are the four types of tweening transformations?
3. True or false: The `Animator.AnimatorPauseListener` interface was added in API Level 18.

4. Name the animation interpolator that starts backward and then flings forward.

5. What is the name of the framework for defining different scene states of your application UI and animating between those states?

Exercises

1. Use the Android documentation to determine the default duration of a property animation.

2. Create an application that animates an `Activity` launch.

3. Create an application that makes use of the `Transition` framework.

References and More Information

Android SDK Reference documentation on the `android.animation` package:
http://d.android.com/reference/android/animation/package-summary.html

Android SDK Reference documentation on the `android.view.animation` package:
http://d.android.com/reference/android/view/animation/package-summary.html

Android API Guides: "Animation and Graphics":
http://developer.android.com/guide/topics/graphics/index.html

Android Training: "Adding Animations":
http://developer.android.com/training/animation/index.html

Android SDK Reference documentation on the `ActivityOptions` package:
http://d.android.com/reference/android/app/ActivityOptions.html

Android SDK Reference documentation on the `TransitionManager` package:
http://d.android.com/reference/android/transition/TransitionManager.html

Android SDK Reference documentation on the `Transition` package:
http://d.android.com/reference/android/transition/Transition.html

YouTube Android Developers Channel: "DevBytes: ListView Expanding Cells Animation":
http://www.youtube.com/watch?v=mwE61B56pVQ

24

Developing Android 3D Graphics Applications

The world around us is not two-dimensional but rich with depth. Although Android device displays are flat surfaces, presenting games and applications with visual depth has long been a way to enhance and add realism to them. For this purpose, developers can use the OpenGL ES framework provided in the Android SDK.

Working with OpenGL ES

Before 1992, Silicon Graphics (SGI) had a proprietary graphics standard called Integrated Raster Imaging System Graphics Library (IRIS GL) that was known typically as just GL (Graphics Library). In 1992, to clean up the code and make GL more maintainable, SGI created OpenGL and set up a consortium of companies to maintain the open-standard form of GL. Today, this consortium is known as the nonprofit Khronos Group, with more than 100 member companies. OpenGL ES was developed in the early 2000s to extend this open library to embedded devices. OpenGL ES is a subset of OpenGL. EGL (Embedded-System Graphics Library) was developed shortly thereafter to provide a common interface layer to native platform graphics.

In the interfaces, OpenGL is simply referred to as GL. This is true for OpenGL ES, as well. In the text of this chapter, GL typically refers to the underlying objects and interfaces in OpenGL to be consistent with the naming conventions in the code. OpenGL ES typically refers to the Android implementation of the OpenGL ES subset of OpenGL. Finally, OpenGL is used in a more generic fashion to refer to the generic concept or library.

Note

This chapter discusses how to use OpenGL ES in the Android SDK. Familiarity with OpenGL concepts can be helpful. This chapter does not teach you OpenGL, but it shows you how to perform a variety of common tasks with OpenGL ES on Android devices. These include configuring EGL and GL, drawing objects, animating objects and scenes, lighting a scene, and texturing objects.

Leveraging OpenGL ES in Android

OpenGL ES is a graphics API for embedded systems based on the OpenGL desktop standard. It is popular on wireless platforms and is supported on all major mobile phone platforms, including Windows Mobile, Symbian, MeeGo, BREW, Apple iOS, Palm WebOS, and Android. Android devices support different versions of OpenGL ES depending on the platform version.

Android developers can implement 3D graphics applications that leverage OpenGL ES in two ways:

- The Android SDK provides OpenGL ES functionality in the `android.opengl` package in conjunction with the Khronos `javax.microedition.khronos` `.opengles` and `javax.microedition.khronos.egl` packages.

- The Android NDK can be used to leverage OpenGL ES 1.1, 2.0, and 3.0 native libraries for optimum performance.

Note

In this chapter, we focus on how to use the Android SDK to develop OpenGL ES applications. We discuss the Android NDK in Chapter 25, "Using the Android NDK."

The Android SDK has support for different versions of OpenGL ES, depending on the API level or platform version:

- OpenGL ES 1.0 functionality (`android.opengl`) is fully supported on devices running Android 1.0 (API Level 1) and higher.

- OpenGL ES 1.1 (`android.opengl.GLES11`) is fully supported on devices running Android 1.6 (API Level 4) and higher.

- OpenGL ES 2.0 (`android.opengl.GLES20`) is fully supported on devices running Android 2.2 (API Level 8) and higher.

- OpenGL ES 3.0 (`android.opengl.GLES30`) is fully supported on devices running Android 4.3 (API Level 18) and higher.

Ensuring Device Compatibility

Applications that require OpenGL functionality should declare this fact in the Android manifest file using the `<uses-feature>` tag with the `android:glEsVersion` attribute. This enables stores like Google Play to filter the application and provide it only to devices that support the OpenGL version required by the application. The `android:glEsVersion` attribute is a 32-bit number where the high bits specify the major version and the low bits specify the minor version.

- If the application requires OpenGL ES 1.0, you do not need to declare any `<uses-feature>` tag, as this is the default for all applications. All Android devices support OpenGL ES 1.0.

- If the application requires OpenGL ES 1.1, you should declare a `<uses-feature>` tag as follows: `<uses-feature android:glEsVersion="0x00010001" />`.

- If the application requires OpenGL ES 2.0, you should declare a `<uses-feature>` tag as follows: `<uses-feature android:glEsVersion="0x00020000" />`.
- If the application requires OpenGL ES 3.0, you should declare a `<uses-feature>` tag as follows: `<uses-feature android:glEsVersion="0x00030000" />`.

Only one OpenGL ES version should be listed in the Android manifest file. Applications that can function using different versions of OpenGL ES by checking for the supported graphics libraries at runtime should specify the lowest version supported by their application. It's also safe to assume that if a platform supports a newer version of OpenGL ES, such as 3.0, it also supports all older versions (such as 2.0, 1.1, and 1.0).

Using OpenGL ES APIs in the Android SDK

Using OpenGL ES on Android is a mix of using Android `View` object concepts and regular OpenGL ES concepts. There are a number of different ways to initialize and use the OpenGL ES functionality provided as part of the Android SDK:

- Developers can implement their own OpenGL ES solutions, handling the initialization of EGL and GL, managing a separate worker thread for OpenGL ES calls, and drawing on a `SurfaceView` control.
- As of Android API Level 3, developers can take advantage of the `GLSurfaceView` and `GLSurfaceView.Renderer` classes to help handle EGL initialization and threading. Calls are made into a user-defined `Renderer` class. The `Renderer` class handles the drawing and GL initialization and is run outside of the UI thread.

In this chapter, we give examples of both of these methods. Although the second method (using `GLSurfaceView`) is indeed simpler, you gain a more complete understanding of the fundamentals of Android OpenGL ES by following along as we describe the "manual" way first. In addition, many developers port their code over from a platform where they normally go through this configuration and might have the need to customize many pieces. Therefore, we start with the "manual" method so that we can review the steps necessary to set up, draw, and tear down OpenGL ES correctly. The concepts and classes used for both methods are similar, though, making this discussion useful even if you choose to use only the included `GLSurfaceView` method for your projects.

Tip

Many of the code examples provided in this chapter are taken from the SimpleOpenGL application. The source code for this application is provided for download on the book's website.

Handling OpenGL ES Tasks Manually

We have provided a custom implementation leveraging OpenGL without using `GLSurfaceView` for users who need to develop for Android versions previous to Android 1.5 or who have a need for tighter control of the rendering pipeline and initialization. The following steps to initialize OpenGL ES enable you to start drawing on the screen via the OpenGL interface:

1. Initialize `SurfaceView` with a surface of type `SURFACE_TYPE_GPU`.
2. Start a thread for OpenGL; all OpenGL calls are performed on this thread.
3. Initialize EGL.
4. Initialize GL.
5. Start drawing!

Warning

When OpenGL ES is initialized on a particular thread of your application, all subsequent calls must be on this same thread; otherwise, they will fail. You should not use your application's main thread for OpenGL ES calls, as the extra processing and loops can cause your application to become less responsive. This does introduce some thread synchronization consequences that you must handle, and we discuss those later in this chapter.

Creating a `SurfaceView`

The first step to drawing fancy 3D graphics on the screen is to create your `SurfaceView`. This involves extending `SurfaceView` and implementing callbacks for `SurfaceHolder`. `Callback`. The following is an empty implementation that we will complete shortly:

```
private class BasicGLSurfaceView
    extends SurfaceView
    implements SurfaceHolder.Callback {

    SurfaceHolder mAndroidHolder;

    BasicGLSurfaceView(Context context) {
        super(context);
        mAndroidHolder = getHolder();
        mAndroidHolder.addCallback(this);
    }

    public void surfaceChanged(SurfaceHolder holder,
        int format, int width, int height) {}

    public void surfaceCreated(SurfaceHolder holder) {}

    public void surfaceDestroyed(SurfaceHolder holder) {}
}
```

First, in the constructor, the `getHolder()` method is called to get and store the `SurfaceHolder`. Because the `SurfaceView` implements the `SurfaceHolder.Callback` interface, this `SurfaceView` is assigned for receiving callbacks for those events. This class is initialized and set as the content `View` for the `Activity` as follows:

```
protected void onCreate(Bundle savedInstanceState) {
    super.onCreate(savedInstanceState);
    mAndroidSurface = new BasicGLSurfaceView(this);
    setContentView(mAndroidSurface);
}
```

Although setting the `SurfaceView` as the entire content `View` works fine, it isn't flexible if you want other functionality on the screen besides the 3D area. One way to place the `SurfaceView` on your screen and still have the benefits of using an XML layout file is to use one of the container widgets, such as `FrameLayout`, and add this `View` to it. For instance, consider this `FrameLayout` definition, which can exist anywhere in a layout:

```
<FrameLayout
    android:id="@+id/gl_container"
    android:layout_height="100dp"
    android:layout_width="100dp" />
```

This puts a 100 x 100 density-independent pixel square container somewhere on the screen, depending on the rest of the layout. Now, the following code uses the identifier for this `FrameLayout` to place the child `SurfaceView` in the `FrameLayout`:

```
mAndroidSurface = new TextureGLSurfaceView(this);
setContentView(R.layout.constrained);
FrameLayout v = (FrameLayout) findViewById(R.id.gl_container);
v.addView(mAndroidSurface);
```

In this example, `R.layout.constrained` is our layout resource, which contains the `FrameLayout` with the particular identifier we used. You will see why this works regardless of what is drawn in the OpenGL surface as we continue through the initialization of OpenGL ES on Android.

Starting Your OpenGL ES Thread

In Android, you can update the screen only from the main thread of your application, sometimes referred to as the UI thread. The `SurfaceView` widget, however, is used so that we can offload graphics processing to a secondary thread, which can update this part of the screen. This is our OpenGL thread. Like updating the screen from the UI thread, all OpenGL calls must be in the same thread.

Recall that the `SurfaceView` presented also implemented the `SurfaceHolder` `.Callback` interface. You can access the underlying surface of the `SurfaceView` only after calling `surfaceCreated()` and before calling `surfaceDestroyed()`. Between these two calls is the only time that we have a valid surface for our OpenGL instance to draw to.

As such, we won't bother creating the OpenGL thread until `surfaceCreated()` is called. The following is an example implementation of `surfaceCreated()`, which starts up the OpenGL thread:

```
public void surfaceCreated(SurfaceHolder holder) {
    mGLThread = new BasicGLThread(this);
    mGLThread.start();
}
```

As promised, little more than launching the thread takes place here. The `SurfaceView` is passed to the thread. This is done because the OpenGL calls need to know which `SurfaceView` to draw upon.

The `BasicGLThread` class is an implementation of a `Thread` that contains the code we run in the OpenGL thread described. The following code block shows which functionality is placed where. The `BasicGLThread` is placed as a private member of the `Activity` class.

```
private class BasicGLThread extends Thread {
    SurfaceView sv;
    BasicGLThread(SurfaceView view) {
        sv = view;
    }

    private boolean mDone = false;
    public void run() {
        initEGL();
        initGL();
        while (!mDone) {
            // drawing code
        }
    }

    public void requestStop() {
        mDone = true;
        try {
            join();
        } catch (InterruptedException e) {
            Log.e("GL", "failed to stop gl thread", e);
        }
        cleanupGL();
    }

    public void cleanupGL() {}
    public void initGL() {}
    public void initEGL() {}

    // main OpenGL variables
}
```

During creation, the `SurfaceView` is saved for later use. In the `run()` method, EGL and GL are initialized, which we describe later in this chapter. Then, the drawing code is executed either once or, as shown here, in a loop. Finally, the thread can safely be stopped from outside the thread with a call to the `requestStop()` method. This also cleans up the OpenGL resources. More on this is found in the "Cleaning Up OpenGL ES" section later in this chapter.

Initializing EGL

Up to this point, the application has a `SurfaceView` with a valid `Surface` and an OpenGL thread that has just been launched. The first step with most OpenGL implementations is to initialize EGL, or the native hardware. You do this in basically the same way each time, and this is a good block of code to write once and reuse. The following steps must be performed to initialize EGL on Android:

1. Get the EGL object.
2. Initialize the display.

3. Get a configuration.

4. Link the `EGLSurface` to an Android `SurfaceView`.

5. Create the EGL context.

6. Tell EGL which display, surface, and context to use.

7. Get our GL object for use in rendering.

The Android SDK provides some utility classes for use with OpenGL ES. The first of these is the `GLDebugHelper` class. OpenGL calls don't directly return errors. Instead, they set an error internally that can be queried. You can use the `GLDebugHelper` class to wrap all EGL and GL calls and have the wrapper check for errors and throw an exception. The first call for getting the EGL object uses this wrapper, as shown here:

```
mEGL = (EGL10) GLDebugHelper.wrap(
    EGLContext.getEGL(),
    GLDebugHelper.CONFIG_CHECK_GL_ERROR |
    GLDebugHelper.CONFIG_CHECK_THREAD,
    null);
```

Here, the `EGL10` object is retrieved and wrapped. Turning on the `CONFIG_CHECK_GL_ERROR` flag checks for all GL errors. In addition, the wrapper makes sure all our GL and EGL calls are made from the correct thread because `CONFIG_CHECK_THREAD` is enabled.

Now we can proceed with initializing the display, as shown here:

```
mGLDisplay = mEGL.eglGetDisplay(EGL10.EGL_DEFAULT_DISPLAY);
```

The default display, `EGL10.EGL_DEFAULT_DISPLAY`, is configured by the internals of the Android implementation of OpenGL ES. Now that we have the display, we can initialize EGL and get the version of the implementation:

```
int[] curGLVersion = new int[2];
mEGL.eglInitialize(mGLDisplay, curGLVersion);
```

The current GL version varies by device. With the display initialized, we can request which configuration is closest to the one we require:

```
int[] mConfigSpec = { EGL10.EGL_RED_SIZE, 5,
                      EGL10.EGL_GREEN_SIZE, 6,
                      EGL10.EGL_BLUE_SIZE, 5,
                      EGL10.EGL_DEPTH_SIZE, 16,
                      EGL10.EGL_NONE };
EGLConfig[] configs = new EGLConfig[1];
int[] num_config = new int[1];
mEGL.eglChooseConfig(mGLDisplay, mConfigSpec, configs, 1, num_config);
mGLConfig = configs[0];
```

The preceding configuration works on the emulator and the current hardware. If you are unsure that the configuration you've chosen works with your application's target platforms, this is a good way to check the resulting list of configurations.

Now we can create the EGL surface based on this configuration:

```
mGLSurface = mEGL.eglCreateWindowSurface(mGLDisplay,
    mGLConfig, sv.getHolder(), null);
```

Recall that we stored our `SurfaceView` for use later. Here, we use it to pass the native Android surface to EGL so they can be linked correctly. We still need to get the EGL context before we can finalize and get our instance of the GL object.

```
mGLContext = mEGL.eglCreateContext(mGLDisplay,
    mGLConfig, EGL10.EGL_NO_CONTEXT, null);
```

Now that we have our display, surface, and context, we can get our GL object:

```
mEGL.eglMakeCurrent(mGLDisplay, mGLSurface, mGLSurface, mGLContext);
mGL = (GL10) GLDebugHelper.wrap(
    mGLContext.getGL(),
    GLDebugHelper.CONFIG_CHECK_GL_ERROR |
    GLDebugHelper.CONFIG_CHECK_THREAD, null);
```

Once again, we use `GLDebugHelper` to wrap the GL object so that it checks errors and confirms the thread for us. This completes the initialization of EGL on Android. Next, we can initialize GL to set up our projection and other rendering options.

Initializing GL

Now the fun begins. We have EGL fully initialized, and we have a valid GL object, so we can initialize our drawing space. For this example, we won't be drawing anything complex. We leave most options at their default values.

Typically, one of the first calls made to initialize GL is to set the viewport. Here is an example of how to set the viewport to the same dimensions as our `SurfaceView`:

```
int width = sv.getWidth();
int height = sv.getHeight();
mGL.glViewport(0, 0, width, height);
```

The location of the surface on the screen is determined internally by EGL. We also use the following width and height of the `SurfaceView` to determine the aspect ratio for GL to render in. In the following code, we complete the configuration of a basic GL projection setup:

```
mGL.glMatrixMode(GL10.GL_PROJECTION);
mGL.glLoadIdentity();
float aspect = (float) width/height;
GLU.gluPerspective(mGL, 45.0f, aspect, 1.0f, 30.0f);
mGL.glClearColor(0.5f, 0.5f, 0.5f, 1);
```

The Android SDK provides a few helpers similar to those found in GLUT (OpenGL Utility Toolkit). Here, we use one of them to define a perspective in terms of the vertical angle of view, aspect ratio, and near and far clipping planes. The `gluPerspective()` method is useful for configuring the projection matrix, which transforms the 3D scene into a flat surface. Finally, we clear the screen to gray.

Drawing on the Screen

Now that EGL and GL are initialized, objects can be drawn to the screen. For this example, to demonstrate that we've set up everything to actually draw, we put a simple three-vertex flat surface (in layman's terms, a triangle) on the screen. Here is some sample code to do this:

```
mGL.glMatrixMode(GL10.GL_MODELVIEW);
mGL.glLoadIdentity();
GLU.gluLookAt(mGL, 0, 0, 10f, 0, 0, 0, 0, 1, 0f);
mGL.glColor4f(1f, 0f, 0f, 1f);
while (!mDone) {
    mGL.glClear(GL10.GL_COLOR_BUFFER_BIT |
        GL10.GL_DEPTH_BUFFER_BIT);
    mGL.glRotatef(1f, 0, 0, 1f);
    triangle.draw(mGL);
    mEGL.eglSwapBuffers(mGLDisplay, mGLSurface);
}
```

If it looks like something is missing, you are correct. This code doesn't actually show the draw command for the triangle. However, it does use an Android SDK utility method to transform the model view matrix with the intuitive `gluLookAt()` method. Here, it sets the eye point 10 units away from the origin and looks toward the origin. The up value is, as usual, set to the positive y axis. In the loop, notice that the identity matrix is not assigned. This gives the `glRotatef()` method a compounding effect, causing the triangle to rotate in a counterclockwise direction. In the next section, "Drawing 3D Objects," we discuss the details of drawing with OpenGL ES in Android.

When launched, a screen similar to that in Figure 24.1 should display.

You now have a working OpenGL ES environment in the Android SDK. We continue from this point to talk more about drawing in the environment.

Drawing 3D Objects

Now that you have the OpenGL ES environment working within Android, it's time to do some actual drawing. This section leads you through a number of examples, each building upon the previous one. In doing so, these examples introduce new Android-specific concepts with OpenGL ES.

Drawing Your Vertices

OpenGL ES supports two primary drawing calls, `glDrawArrays()` and `glDraw Elements()`. Both of these methods require the use of a vertex buffer assigned through

Figure 24.1   A red triangle rendered using OpenGL ES
on the Android emulator.

a call to `glVertexPointer`. Because Android runs on top of Java, though, an arbitrary array cannot be passed in as the array contents might move around in memory. Instead, we have to use a `ByteBuffer`, `FloatBuffer`, or `IntBuffer` so the data stays at the same location in memory. Converting various arrays to buffers is common, so we have implemented some helper methods. Here is one for converting a float array into a `FloatBuffer`:

```
FloatBuffer getFloatBufferFromFloatArray(float array[]) {
    ByteBuffer tempBuffer = ByteBuffer.allocateDirect(array.length * 4);
    tempBuffer.order(ByteOrder.nativeOrder());
    FloatBuffer buffer = tempBuffer.asFloatBuffer();
    buffer.put(array);
    buffer.position(0);
    return buffer;
}
```

This creates a buffer of 32-bit float values with a stride of 0. You can then store the resulting `FloatBuffer` and assign it to OpenGL calls. Here is an example of doing this, using the triangle we showed previously in this chapter:

```
float[] vertices = {
    -0.559016994f, 0, 0,
    0.25f, 0.5f, 0f,
    0.25f, -0.5f, 0f
};
mVertexBuffer = getFloatBufferFromFloatArray(vertices);
```

With the buffer assigned, we can now draw the triangle, as shown here:

```
void drawTriangle(GL10 gl) {
    gl.glEnableClientState(GL10.GL_VERTEX_ARRAY);
    gl.glVertexPointer(3, GL10.GL_FLOAT, 0, mVertexBuffer);
    gl.glDrawArrays(GL10.GL_TRIANGLES, 0, 3);
}
```

We have to enable the GL_VERTEX_ARRAY state, though you can do this in GL configuration, as it is required to draw anything with OpenGL ES. We then assign the vertex buffer through a call to `glVertexPointer()`, also telling GL that we're using float values. Fixed-point values, through GL_FIXED, can also be used and might be faster with some Android implementations. Finally, a call to `glDrawArrays()` is made to draw the triangles using three vertices from the vertex buffer. The result of this can be seen in Figure 24.1.

Coloring Your Vertices

In OpenGL ES, you can use an array of colors to individually assign colors to each vertex that is drawn. This is accomplished by calling the `glColorPointer()` method with a buffer of colors. The following code sets up a small buffer of colors for three vertices:

```
float[] colors = {
    1f, 0, 0, 1f,
    0, 1f, 0, 1f,
    0, 0, 1f, 1f
    };
mColorBuffer = getFloatBufferFromFloatArray(colors);
```

With the buffer available, we can now use it to color our triangle, as shown in the following code:

```
void drawColorful(GL10 gl) {
    gl.glEnableClientState(GL10.GL_COLOR_ARRAY);
    gl.glColorPointer(4, GL10.GL_FLOAT, 0, mColorBuffer);
    draw(gl);
    gl.glDisableClientState(GL10.GL_COLOR_ARRAY);
}
```

First, the client state for GL_COLOR_ARRAY is enabled. Then, calling the `glColor Pointer` method sets the preceding color buffer created. The call to `draw()` draws the triangle like the colorful one seen in Figure 24.2.

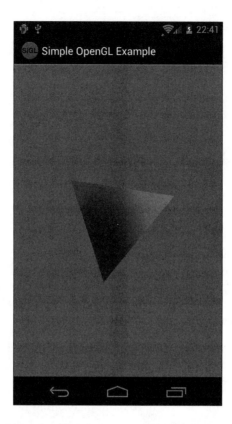

Figure 24.2   A triangle with red, green, and blue vertices smoothly blended.

Drawing More Complex Objects

A standard cube has eight vertices. However, in OpenGL ES, each of the six faces needs to be drawn with two triangles. Each of these triangles needs three vertices. That's a total of 36 vertices to draw an object with just eight of its own vertices. There must be a better way.

OpenGL ES supports index arrays. An index array is a list of vertex indices from the current vertex array. The index array must be a buffer, and in this example, we use a ByteBuffer because we don't have many vertices to indicate. The index array lists the order in which the vertices should be drawn when used with glDrawElements(). Note that the color arrays (and normal arrays that we will get to shortly) are still relative to the vertex array and not the index array. Here is some code that draws an OpenGL cube using just eight defined vertices:

```
float vertices[] = {
    -1,1,1,  1,1,1,  1,-1,1,  -1,-1,1,
    1,1,-1,  -1,1,-1,  -1,-1,-1,  1,-1,-1
};
```

```
byte indices[] = {
    0,1,2,  2,3,0,  1,4,7,  7,2,1,  0,3,6,  6,5,0,
    3,2,7,  7,6,3,  0,1,4,  4,5,0,  5,6,7,  7,4,5
};
FloatBuffer vertexBuffer = getFloatBufferFromFloatArray(vertices);
ByteBuffer indexBuffer = getByteBufferFromByteArray(indices);
gl.glVertexPointer(3, GL10.GL_FLOAT, 0, vertexBuffer);
gl.glDrawElements(GL10.GL_TRIANGLES, indices.length,
    GL10.GL_UNSIGNED_BYTE, indexBuffer);
```

The vertices define the typical shape for a cube. Then, however, we use the index array to define in what order the vertices are drawn to create the cube out of the 12 triangles that we need (recalling that OpenGL ES does not support quads). Now you have a red shape on your screen that looks like Figure 24.3 (left). It doesn't actually look much like a cube, though, does it? Without some shading, it looks too much like a random polygon. If, however, you switch the glDrawElements() to GL_LINE_LOOP instead of GL_TRIANGLES, you see a line-drawing version of the shape, such as Figure 24.3 (right).

Figure 24.3   A solid cube with no shading (left)
and the same cube with only lines (right).

Now you can see that it is a cube. You can reuse the vertex buffer with different index buffers, too. This is useful if you can define multiple shapes using the same set of vertices and then draw them in their own locations with transformations.

Lighting Your Scene

The last 3D object that we drew was a cube that looked like some strange polygon on the flat 2D screen. The colors of each face could be made different by applying coloring between each call to draw a face. However, that still produces a fairly flat-looking cube. Instead, why not shine some light on the scene and let the lighting give the cube some additional depth?

Before you can provide lighting on a scene, each vertex of each surface needs a vector applied to it to define how the light reflects and, thus, how it is rendered. Although this vector can be anything, most often it is perpendicular to the surface defined by the vertices; this is called the normal of a surface. Recalling our cube from the preceding example, we see now that a cube can't actually be created out of eight vertices as each vertex can carry only one normal array, and we would need three per vertex because each vertex belongs to three faces. Instead, we have to use a cube that does, in fact, contain the entire lot of 24 vertices. (Technically, you can define a bunch of index arrays and change the normal array between calls to each face, but it's more commonly done with a large list of vertices and a single list of normal vectors.)

Like the color array, the normal array is applied to each vertex in the vertex array in order. Lighting is a fairly complex topic; if you're unfamiliar with it, check out the "References and More Information" section at the end of this chapter to learn more. For now, we just give an example of how to use the lighting features of OpenGL ES in Android.

Here is some code for enabling simple lighting:

```
mGL.glEnable(GL10.GL_LIGHTING);
mGL.glEnable(GL10.GL_LIGHT0);
mGL.glLightfv(GL10.GL_LIGHT0, GL10.GL_AMBIENT,
    new float[] {0.1f, 0.1f, 0.1f, 1f}, 0);
mGL.glLightfv(GL10.GL_LIGHT0, GL10.GL_DIFFUSE,
    new float[] {1f, 1f, 1f, 1f}, 0);
mGL.glLightfv(GL10.GL_LIGHT0, GL10.GL_POSITION,
    new float[] {10f, 0f, 10f, 1f}, 0);
mGL.glEnable(GL10.GL_COLOR_MATERIAL);
mGL.glShadeModel(GL10.GL_SMOOTH);
```

This code enables lighting, enables GL_LIGHT0, and then sets the color and brightness of the light. Finally, the light is positioned in 3D space. In addition, we enable GL_COLOR_MATERIAL so the color set for drawing the objects is used with the lighting. We also enable the smooth shading model, which helps remove the visual transition between triangles on the same face. You can use color material definitions for fancier lighting and more realistic-looking surfaces, but that is beyond the scope of this book.

Here is the drawing code for our cube, assuming we now have a full vertex array of all 24 points and an index array defining the order in which they should be drawn:

```
gl.glEnableClientState(GL10.GL_NORMAL_ARRAY);
gl.glVertexPointer(3, GL10.GL_FLOAT, 0, mVertexBuffer);
gl.glNormalPointer(GL10.GL_FLOAT, 0, mNormalBuffer);
gl.glDrawElements(GL10.GL_TRIANGLES, indices.length,
GL10.GL_UNSIGNED_BYTE, mIndexBuffer);
```

Notice that the normal array and normal mode are now turned on. Without this, the lighting won't look right. As with the other arrays, this has to be assigned through a fixed buffer in Java, as this code demonstrates:

```
float normals[] = {
    // front
    0, 0, 1, 0, 0, 1, 0, 0, 1, 0, 0, 1,
    // back
    0, 0, -1, 0, 0, -1, 0, 0, -1, 0, 0, -1,
    // top
    0, 1, 0, 0, 1, 0, 0, 1, 0, 0, 1, 0,
    // bottom
    0, -1, 0, 0, -1, 0, 0, -1, 0, 0, -1, 0,
    // right
    1, 0, 0, 1, 0, 0, 1, 0, 0, 1, 0, 0,
    // left
    -1, 0, 0, -1, 0, 0, -1, 0, 0, -1, 0, 0 };
mNormalBuffer = getFloatBufferFromFloatArray(normals);
```

The preceding code uses one of the helper methods we talked about previously to create a `FloatBuffer`. We use a floating-point array for the `normals`. This also shows the `normals` and how each vertex must have one. (Recall that we now have 24 vertices for the cube.) You can create various lighting effects by making the `normals` not actually perpendicular to the surface, but for more accurate lighting, it's usually better to just increase the polygon count of your objects or add textures. Figure 24.4 shows the solid cube, now shaded to show depth better.

Texturing Your Objects

Texturing surfaces, or putting images on surfaces, is a rather lengthy and complex topic. It's enough for our purposes to focus on learning how to texture with Android, so we will use the previously lit and colored cube and texture it.

First, texturing needs to be enabled, as shown in the following code:

```
mGL.glEnable(GL10.GL_TEXTURE_2D);
int[] textures = new int[1];
mGL.glGenTextures(1, textures, 0);
```

Figure 24.4   A cube with a light shining from the right to shade it.

This code enables texturing and creates an internally named slot for one texture. We use this slot to tell OpenGL what texture we operate on in the next block of code:

```
gl.glBindTexture(GL10.GL_TEXTURE_2D, textures[0]);
Bitmap bitmap = BitmapFactory.decodeResource(c.getResources(),
    R.drawable.android);
Bitmap bitmap256 = Bitmap.createScaledBitmap(bitmap, 256, 256, false);
GLUtils.texImage2D(GL10.GL_TEXTURE_2D, 0, bitmap256, 0);
bitmap.recycle();
bitmap256.recycle();
```

You've probably begun to wonder what happened to Android-specific code. Well, it's back. OpenGL ES needs bitmaps to use as textures. Luckily for us, Android comes with a `Bitmap` class that can read in nearly any format of image, including PNG, GIF, and JPG files. You can do this straight from a `Drawable` resource identifier, too, as demonstrated in the preceding code. OpenGL requires that textures be square and have sides that are powers of 2, such as 64 x 64 or 256 x 256. Because the source image might or might not be in one of these exact sizes, we scale it again with just a single Android method call. If the source image isn't square, though, the original aspect ratio is not kept. Sometimes it is easier to scale down with the original aspect ratio and add colored padding around the edges of the image instead of stretching it, but this is beyond the scope of this example.

Finally, `GLUtils.texImage2D()` assigns an Android `Bitmap` to an OpenGL texture. OpenGL keeps the image internally, so we can clean up the `Bitmap` objects with a call to the `recycle()` method.

Now that OpenGL ES knows about the texture, the next step is to tell it where to draw the texture. You can accomplish this by using a texture coordinate buffer. This is similar to all the other buffer arrays in that it must be assigned to a fixed Java buffer and enabled. Here is the code to do this with our cube example:

```
float texCoords[] = {
    1,0, 1,1, 0,1, 0,0,
    1,0, 1,1, 0,1, 0,0,
    1,0, 1,1, 0,1, 0,0,
    1,0, 1,1, 0,1, 0,0,
    1,0, 1,1, 0,1, 0,0,
    1,0, 1,1, 0,1, 0,0,
    };
mCoordBuffer = getFloatBufferFromFloatArray(texCoords);
gl.glEnableClientState(GL10.GL_TEXTURE_COORD_ARRAY);
gl.glTexCoordPointer(2, GL10.GL_FLOAT, 0, mCoordBuffer);

draw(gl);
```

As promised, this code creates a fixed buffer for the texture coordinates. We set the same ones on each face of the cube, so each vertex has a texture coordinate assigned to it (0,0 is the lower-left portion of the texture and 1,1 is the upper-right). Next, we enable the GL_TEXTURE_COORD_ARRAY state and then tell OpenGL which buffer to use. Finally, we draw the cube. Now, we left the code the same as before, which produces the output you see in Figure 24.5 (left). The coloring does still apply, even with textures. If coloring is not applied, the output looks like what you see in Figure 24.5 (right).

Figure 24.5   A red-colored cube with texture (left)
and the same cube without red coloring (right).

Interacting with Android Views and Events

Now that you have gone through this introduction to OpenGL ES on Android, you have
seen how to draw 3D objects on the screen. Actually, these 3D objects are drawn on a
SurfaceView, which has all the typical Android attributes found on View widgets. We
now use these attributes to interact with the rest of the application.

First, we show you how to send information from the OpenGL thread back to the
main thread to monitor performance. Then, we give an example of how to forward
key events from the main thread to the OpenGL thread to control the animation on the
screen.

Enabling the OpenGL Thread to Talk to the Application Thread

The Android SDK provides a helper class for running code on another thread. The
Handler class can allow a piece of code to run on a target thread—the thread that the

`Handler` was instantiated in. For the purpose of this example, you do this in the `Activity` class:

```
public final Handler mHandler = new Handler();
```

This enables the OpenGL thread to execute code on the `Activity` thread by calling the `post()` method of the `Handler`. This enables us to act on other `View` objects on the screen that we can't act on from outside of the `Activity` thread on the OpenGL thread. For this example, the frame rate of the scene rendered is calculated in the OpenGL thread and then posted back to the `Activity` thread. Here is a method that does just that:

```
public void calculateAndDisplayFPS() {
    if (showFPS) {
        long thisTime = System.currentTimeMillis();
        if (thisTime - mLastTime < mSkipTime) {
            mFrames++;
        } else {
            mFrames++;
            final long fps = mFrames / ((thisTime-mLastTime)/1000);
            mFrames = 0;
            mLastTime = thisTime;
            mHandler.post(new Runnable() {
                public void run() {
                    mFPSText.setText("FPS = " + fps);
                }
            });
        }
    }
}
```

The `calculateAndDisplayFPS()` method is called from within the animation loop of the OpenGL thread. The math is fairly straightforward: the number of frames divided by the duration of those frames in seconds. Then, we take that and post it to the `Handler` for the `Activity` thread by creating a new `Runnable` object that applies a `String` to the `TextView` that holds the current frame rate.

However, doing this for every iteration causes performance to drop substantially. Instead, a counter tracks the number of frames drawn, and we do the calculation and display every time the duration of `mSkipTime` has gone by. A value of 5000 milliseconds has worked well to avoid influencing the performance too much by simply measuring the performance. Figure 24.6 shows the display with the frame rate.

Enabling the Application Thread to Talk to the OpenGL Thread

Now let's look at the reverse situation. We want the main application thread to communicate with the OpenGL thread. We can use a `Handler` to post code to the OpenGL thread for execution. However, if we are not going to execute any OpenGL code, we aren't required to run it in the OpenGL thread context. Instead, we can add a key event handler to the `SurfaceView` to either speed up or stop the animation in the OpenGL thread.

Figure 24.6   A textured, lit, shaded cube with the frame rate displayed.

A `SurfaceView` needs to be the current focus before it receives key events. A couple of method calls configure this:

```
setFocusable(true);
setFocusableInTouchMode(true);
```

Setting focusable for both touch modes enables key events to come in regardless of the mode. Now, within the `SurfaceView`, key event handlers need to be implemented. First, we implement a handler for toggling the frame rate on and off. The following is a sample implementation of the `onKeyDown()` method override:

```
public boolean onKeyDown(int keyCode, KeyEvent event) {
    switch (keyCode) {
        case KeyEvent.KEYCODE_F:
            mGLThread.toggleFPSDisplay();
            return true;
    }
    return super.onKeyDown(keyCode, event);
}
```

When the user presses the F key, a call to the `toggleFPSDisplay()` method of the OpenGL ES thread is made. This merely changes the state of the `boolean` flag and then updates the text field status. The `onKeyDown()` method is called multiple times if the key is held, toggling the display until the key is released. There are multiple methods to prevent this, such as just handling it within `onKeyUp()` or using different keys to enable and disable the state.

The next control we provide to the user is the ability to pause the animation while the P key is held down. Add the following case statement to `onKeyDown()`:

```
case KeyEvent.KEYCODE_P:
    mGLThread.setAnim(false);
    return true;
```

Here, the state is forced to `false` regardless of how many times `onKeyDown()` is called. Next, an implementation of `onKeyUp()` is needed to resume the animation when the user lifts his or her finger:

```
public boolean onKeyUp(int keyCode, KeyEvent event) {
    switch (keyCode) {
        case KeyEvent.KEYCODE_P:
            mGLThread.setAnim(true);
            return true;
    }
    return super.onKeyUp(keyCode, event);
}
```

Again, the value is forced and set to `true` so that when the user lifts his or her finger off the key, the animation resumes regardless of the current state. An `if` statement around the inner part of the entire `while()` animation loop can pause the entire rendering in this example.

In these examples, the code does not actually run in the OpenGL thread to change the state of the flags. This is acceptable for the following reasons:

- The values are set in this way exclusively (no concurrency problems).
- The exact state of the flags is unimportant during the loop.
- No calls to OpenGL are made.

The first two reasons mean that we don't have to perform thread synchronization for the functionality to work acceptably and safely. The last reason means that we don't need to create a `Handler` on the OpenGL thread to execute OpenGL calls in the proper thread. There are many circumstances where changing the state of the flags requires running in the OpenGL thread. Discussing thread synchronization is not within the scope of this chapter, however. Standard Java methods are available for doing this.

Cleaning Up OpenGL ES

It is necessary for your application to clean up OpenGL when your application is done using it. This happens when the application quits or the `Activity` has changed in some way. The recommended process for gracefully shutting down OpenGL is to reset the surface and context, destroy the surface and context you configured, and then terminate the EGL instance. You can do this with the following code:

```
private void cleanupGL() {
    mEGL.eglMakeCurrent(mGLDisplay, EGL10.EGL_NO_SURFACE,
        EGL10.EGL_NO_SURFACE, EGL10.EGL_NO_CONTEXT);
    mEGL.eglDestroySurface(mGLDisplay, mGLSurface);
    mEGL.eglDestroyContext(mGLDisplay, mGLContext);
    mEGL.eglTerminate(mGLDisplay);
}
```

First, `eglMakeCurrent()` removes the surface and context that were used. Next, `eglDestroySurface()` and `eglDestroyContext()` release any resources held by OpenGL for the surface and the context. Finally, OpenGL is terminated through a call to `eglTerminate()`. If OpenGL runs in a separate thread, the thread can now be terminated as well.

It is up to the application to clean up OpenGL properly. There are no helper methods available for managing all of it automatically in the Android lifecycle as there are with `Cursor` objects and the like.

Using `GLSurfaceView` (Easy OpenGL ES)

Several new classes were introduced with Android 1.5 (API Level 3) that you can use to simplify application OpenGL ES implementation. The `GLSurfaceView` and `GLSurface View.Renderer` classes effectively require less code to write so that you can focus on the actual GL drawing process instead of the implementation details and upkeep necessary to handle OpenGL ES calls. Essentially, the `GLSurfaceView` class handles the EGL initialization, threading, and calls into a user-defined `Renderer` class. The `Renderer` class handles the drawing and GL initialization.

Tip

The code examples provided in this section are taken from the `ShowAndroidGLActivity` `.java` class in the SimpleOpenGL application. The source code for this application is provided for download on the book's website.

To use the `GLSurfaceView` class, you must either extend it or instantiate it directly. Either way, you then need to provide an implementation of a `GLSurfaceView` `.Renderer` class. The `Renderer` class must contain appropriate callbacks for drawing and GL initialization. Additionally, the `Activity` must pass `onPause()` and `onResume()` events on to the `GLSurfaceView`. The EGL initialization is handled by the `GLSurface View` object, and threading is used to offload the processing away from the main thread.

The following code demonstrates an entire `Activity` that duplicates the colorful triangle we drew earlier in this chapter, shown in Figure 24.2:

```
public class AndroidOpenGL extends Activity {
CustomSurfaceView mAndroidSurface = null;
```

```
protected void onPause() {
    super.onPause();
    mAndroidSurface.onPause();
}

protected void onResume() {
    super.onResume();
    mAndroidSurface.onResume();
}

protected void onCreate(Bundle savedInstanceState) {
    super.onCreate(savedInstanceState);

    mAndroidSurface = new CustomSurfaceView(this);
    setContentView(mAndroidSurface);
}

private class CustomSurfaceView extends GLSurfaceView {
    final CustomRenderer mRenderer = new CustomRenderer();

    public CustomSurfaceView(Context context) {
        super(context);
        setFocusable(true);
        setFocusableInTouchMode(true);
        setRenderer(mRenderer);
    }

    public boolean onKeyDown(int keyCode, KeyEvent event) {
        switch (keyCode) {
        case KeyEvent.KEYCODE_P:
            queueEvent(new Runnable() {
                public void run() {
                    mRenderer.togglePause();
                }
            });
            return true;
        }
        return super.onKeyDown(keyCode, event);
    }
}

private class CustomRenderer implements GLSurfaceView.Renderer {
    TriangleSmallGLUT mTriangle = new TriangleSmallGLUT(3);
    boolean fAnimPaused = false;

    public void onDrawFrame(GL10 gl) {
        if (!fAnimPaused) {
            gl.glClear(GL10.GL_COLOR_BUFFER_BIT |
                GL10.GL_DEPTH_BUFFER_BIT);
            gl.glRotatef(1f, 0, 0, 1f);

            if (mTriangle != null) {
                mTriangle.drawColorful(gl);
            }
        }
    }
```

```
public void togglePause() {
    if (fAnimPaused == true) {
        fAnimPaused = false;
    } else {
        fAnimPaused = true;
    }
}

public void onSurfaceChanged(GL10 gl, int width, int height) {
    gl.glViewport(0, 0, width, height);

    // configure projection to screen
    gl.glMatrixMode(GL10.GL_PROJECTION);
    gl.glLoadIdentity();
    gl.glClearColor(0.5f, 0.5f, 0.5f, 1);
    float aspect = (float) width / height;
    GLU.gluPerspective(gl, 45.0f, aspect, 1.0f, 30.0f);
}

public void onSurfaceCreated(GL10 gl, EGLConfig config) {
    gl.glEnableClientState(GL10.GL_VERTEX_ARRAY);

    // configure model space
    gl.glMatrixMode(GL10.GL_MODELVIEW);
    gl.glLoadIdentity();
    GLU.gluLookAt(gl, 0, 0, 10f, 0, 0, 0, 0, 1, 0f);
    gl.glColor4f(1f, 0f, 0f, 1f);
}
}}
```

As you can see, this code demonstrates creating a new GLSurfaceView and a new
GLSurfaceView.Renderer. The end result, with proper implementation of the triangle
drawing class (included with the book code and discussed earlier in this chapter), is a
spinning triangle that the user can pause with the press of the P key. The GLSurface
View implementation contains its own Renderer, which is less generic than assigning
it externally, but with the key handling we implemented. The two classes must work
closely together.

The GLSurfaceView implements key handling by overriding the onKeyDown()
method of the regular View class. The action is passed on to the Renderer through a
helper method called queueEvent(). The queueEvent() method passes the Runnable
object on to the Renderer thread held by the GLSurfaceView.

Next, the Renderer implementation provides the drawing in the onDrawFrame()
method. This is either called continuously or on demand, depending on the render mode
set via a call to the GLSurfaceView.setRenderMode() method. The implementation
of onSurfaceChanged() is now where we set up the screen projection—an appropriate
place because this method is called on orientation or size changes of the surface. Then, in
onSurfaceCreated(), the basic GL configuration is performed, including setting client
states and static data, such as the model view.

All EGL configuration is now performed internally to GLSurfaceView, so the application need not worry about it. If, however, the application needs to perform custom

configuration of the EGL, the EGLConfig object is passed to the onSurfaceCreated() method and is used to perform such custom configuration.

If you choose to use this method to bring up a GL surface on Android, the implementation of the rendering code doesn't need to change at all.

Using OpenGL ES 2.0

Android began supporting Open GL ES 2.0 in Android 2.2 (API Level 8), although applications that leveraged the Android NDK can use 2.0 features as early as API Level 5 with NDK release 3. In this section, we discuss the Android Java API support for OpenGL ES 2.0. Support also remains for OpenGL ES 1.x and for good reason. Open GL ES 2.0 is not backward compatible with OpenGL ES 1.x. The different OpenGL ES versions provide different methods of handling 3D graphics:

- OpenGL ES 1.x provides a fixed-function rendering and texturing pipeline. That is to say, the math used to transform, light, and color a scene is all the same—fixed functions.

- OpenGL ES 2.0 replaced the fixed functions with vertex and fragment shader programs written, of course, by you, the developer. Writing the shader programs provides much more flexibility but does incur a bit more overhead on the development side.

The choice of which version of OpenGL ES to use is yours. In this section, we show you how to initialize and get a basic OpenGL ES 2.0 program up and running. Using the NDK method is discussed in Chapter 25, "Using the Android NDK."

Tip

Many of the code examples provided in this section are taken from the SimpleOpenGL2 application. The source code for this application is provided for download on the book's website.

Configuring Your Application for OpenGL ES 2.0

If you're going to use the Android OpenGL ES 2.0 APIs and aren't planning on supporting alternate code paths, you need to specify two items in your manifest file: your application requires Android 2.2 or higher using the <uses-sdk> tag, and it requires OpenGL ES 2.0 using the <uses-feature> tag:

```
<uses-sdk
    android:targetSdkVersion="19"
    android:minSdkVersion="8" />
<uses-feature
    android:glEsVersion="0x00020000" />
```

Requesting an OpenGL ES 2.0 Surface

Start by creating your custom `SurfaceView`, which you usually do within the `Activity` class `onCreate()` method, as follows:

```
mAndroidSurface = new CustomGL2SurfaceView(this);
setContentView(mAndroidSurface);
```

Of course, you need to implement the `CustomGL2SurfaceView` class. In our sample project, we did this as an inner class of the `Activity`, for convenience:

```
private class CustomGL2SurfaceView extends GLSurfaceView {
    final CustomRenderer renderer;

    public CustomGL2SurfaceView(Context context) {
        super(context);
        setEGLContextClientVersion(2);
        renderer = new CustomRenderer();
        setRenderer(renderer);
    }
}
```

The most important line of code here is the call to the `setEGLContextClient Version()` method. This call is made in order to request an EGL context for OpenGL ES 1.x (when the parameter is 1) or OpenGL ES 2.x (when the parameter is 2). Then the custom `Renderer` is set.

Although it might seem confusing, the `Renderer` methods take `GL10` objects. How, then, are you to make OpenGL ES 2.0 calls? The answer turns out to be simple: the `GLES20` class is entirely static. Just ignore the `GL10` parameters and make calls directly to the `GLES20` class.

The `CustomRenderer` class starts out by initializing the vertices, much as we did earlier. Then, when the `onSurfaceCreate()` method is called, we can initialize the shader program as follows:

```
@Override
public void onSurfaceCreated(GL10 unused, EGLConfig unused2) {
    try {
        initShaderProgram(R.raw.simple_vertex, R.raw.simple_fragment);
        initialized = true;
    } catch (Exception e) {
        Log.e(DEBUG_TAG, "Failed to init GL");
    }
}
```

The two resource identifiers, `simple_vertex` and `simple_fragment`, simply reference two text files stored as raw resources. Now, let's look at the initialization of the shaders:

```
private int shaderProgram = 0;
private void initShaderProgram(int vertexId,
    int fragmentId) throws Exception {
        int vertexShader =
            loadAndCompileShader(GLES20.GL_VERTEX_SHADER, vertexId);
```

```
        int fragmentShader =
            loadAndCompileShader(GLES20.GL_FRAGMENT_SHADER, fragmentId);
    shaderProgram = GLES20.glCreateProgram();
    if (shaderProgram == 0) {
        throw new Exception("Failed to create shader program");
    }
    // attach the shaders to the program
    GLES20.glAttachShader(shaderProgram, vertexShader);
    GLES20.glAttachShader(shaderProgram, fragmentShader);
    // bind attribute in our vertex shader
    GLES20.glBindAttribLocation(shaderProgram, 0, "vPosition");
    // link the shaders
    GLES20.glLinkProgram(shaderProgram);
    // check the linker status
    int[] linkerStatus = new int[1];
    GLES20.glGetProgramiv(shaderProgram, GLES20.GL_LINK_STATUS,
        linkerStatus, 0);
    if (GLES20.GL_TRUE != linkerStatus[0]) {
        Log.e(DEBUG_TAG, "Linker Failure: "
            + GLES20.glGetProgramInfoLog(shaderProgram));
        GLES20.glDeleteProgram(shaderProgram);
        throw new Exception("Program linker failed");
    }
    GLES20.glClearColor(0.5f, 0.5f, 0.5f, 1);
}
```

This process does not change substantially for different shaders. Recall that
OpenGL ES 2.0 requires both a vertex shader and a fragment shader. First, we load the
text for each shader and compile both of them. Then, we create a new shader program
reference, attach both shaders to it, assign an attribute position to our only input parameter, and link the program. Finally, checks are made to confirm that the program linked
successfully.

The loading of each shader is handled by our `loadAndCompileShader()` method.
Here is a sample implementation of this method:

```
private int loadAndCompileShader(int shaderType,
    int shaderId) throws Exception {
    InputStream inputStream =
        AndroidGL2Activity.this.getResources().openRawResource(shaderId);
    String shaderCode = inputStreamToString(inputStream);
    int shader = GLES20.glCreateShader(shaderType);
    if (shader == 0) {
        throw new Exception("Can't create shader");
    }
    // hand the code over to GL
    GLES20.glShaderSource(shader, shaderCode);
    // compile it
    GLES20.glCompileShader(shader);
    // get compile status
    int[] status = new int[1];
    GLES20.glGetShaderiv(shader, GLES20.GL_COMPILE_STATUS, status, 0);
    if (status[0] == 0) {
        // failed
        Log.e(DEBUG_TAG, "Compiler Failure: "
```

```
        + GLES20.glGetShaderInfoLog(shader));
    GLES20.glDeleteShader(shader);
    throw new Exception("Shader compilation failed");
    }
    return shader;
}
```

The `loadAndCompileShader()` method reads in the raw resource as a string. Then the source is handed over to `GLES20` via a call to the `glShaderSource()` method. Finally, the shader is compiled with a call to `glCompileShader()`. The result is checked to make sure the compile was successful. OpenGL ES 2.0 holds the binary results internally so that they can be used later during linking.

The `onSurfaceChanged()` method should look quite familiar—it changes little. The viewport is reconfigured for the new display metrics and then the clear color is set. Note again that you can simply use the static `GLES20` calls rather than the `GL10` parameter.

```
@Override
public void onSurfaceChanged(GL10 unused, int width, int height) {
    Log.v(DEBUG_TAG, "onSurfaceChanged");
    GLES20.glViewport(0, 0, width, height);
    GLES20.glClearColor(0.5f, 0.5f, 0.5f, 1);
}
```

Finally, we're ready to render the triangle. The scene is rendered each time the system calls our `onDrawFrame()` implementation.

```
@Override
public void onDrawFrame(GL10 unused) {
    if (!initialized) {
        return;
    }
    GLES20.glClear(GLES20.GL_COLOR_BUFFER_BIT);
    GLES20.glUseProgram(shaderProgram);
    GLES20.glVertexAttribPointer(0, 3, GLES20.GL_FLOAT, false, 12,
        verticesBuffer);
    GLES20.glEnableVertexAttribArray(0);
    GLES20.glDrawArrays(GLES20.GL_TRIANGLES, 0, 3);
}
```

At this point, the code should also appear familiar. The primary difference here is the call to the `glUseProgram()` method, where we must pass in the numeric identifier of the program we compiled and linked. The final result is simply a static (motionless) triangle on the screen. It's not very exciting, considering the amount of code required. The flexibility of the shaders is powerful, but many applications don't need the extra flexibility that comes with using OpenGL ES 2.0, either.

By now, you might be wondering what the shaders look like. Because the resource system of Android just uses the part of the filename before the extension, we decided to name our shader files very clearly so we could easily tell what they were: `simple_vertex.shader` and `simple_fragment.shader`. These are two of the simplest shaders one can define.

First, let's look at the vertex shader because it's first in the pipeline:

```
attribute vec4 vPosition;
void main() {
    gl_Position = vPosition;
}
```

This has a single input, vPosition, which is simply assigned to the output. No transformations are applied, and we're not doing any texturing. Now let's turn our attention to the fragment shader:

```
precision mediump float;
void main() {
    gl_FragColor = vec4(0.0, 1.0, 0.0, 1.0);
}
```

This shader is even simpler. It's assigning a fixed color to the output. In this case, it's assigning green to the output.

Shader definitions can be quite complex. Implementing lighting, texturing, fog effects, and other interesting OpenGL ES 2.0 features that can't be fashioned using the fixed pipeline of OpenGL ES 1.x is far beyond the scope of this book. However, we recommend picking up a book on OpenGL ES 2.0, such as *OpenGL ES 2.0 Programming Guide* by Aaftab Munshi, Dan Ginsburg, and Dave Shreiner (Addison-Wesley, 2008, ISBN 0321502795) or *OpenGL SuperBible* by Graham Sellers, Richard S. Wright, Jr., and Nicholas Haemel (Addison-Wesley, 2014, ISBN 0321902947), or finding resources online.

Exploring OpenGL ES 3.0

Android 4.3 (API Level 18) introduced the OpenGL ES 3.0 specification. Currently there are a limited number of devices on the market that support this newer version of OpenGL ES. As with version 2.0, you are able to make use of the OpenGL ES 3.0 specification APIs through the Android SDK and the NDK.

Optimizations that OpenGL ES 3.0 brings to the Android platform are advancements to gradient rendering fidelity and texture management for hardware-accelerated 2D rendering. OpenGL ES 3.0 also includes the following new features:

- Advanced visual effects acceleration
- High-quality texture compression (ETC2/EAC)
- GLSL ES shading language (supporting integer and 32-bit floating points)
- Texture rendering (advanced)
- Render buffer formats and texture size standardizations

When designing your application and using OpenGL ES 3.0, you may want to be able to fall back to version 2.0 in case the version 3.0 API is not available. There is a great write-up within the Android documentation on which version of OpenGL ES your application should use depending on what version a given device supports: *http://d.android.com/guide/topics/graphics/opengl.html#compatibility*.

Note

Previous editions of this book provided code samples demonstrating how to use OpenGL ES using the `RenderScript` graphics engine. As of Android 4.1 (API Level 16), OpenGL ES support for `RenderScript` has been deprecated and removed completely from newer versions of Android.

Summary

In this chapter, you learned the basics of using OpenGL ES from within an Android application. You also learned about the different versions of OpenGL ES supported by the Android platform.

You learned about several ways to use OpenGL ES in your Android applications. You learned how to initialize OpenGL ES in its own thread. Then you learned how to draw, color, and light objects using a variety of OpenGL and Android helper methods. You then learned how your application thread and the OpenGL thread can interact with each other. Finally, you learned how to clean up OpenGL.

Creating fully functional 3D applications and games is a vast topic, more than enough to fill entire books. You have learned enough to get started drawing in three dimensions on Android and can use the knowledge to apply general OpenGL concepts to Android. The reference section at the end of the chapter contains links to more information to help you deepen your OpenGL ES knowledge.

Quiz Questions

1. What must you declare in your manifest file to support OpenGL ES 2.0?
2. True or false: If a device supports OpenGL ES 3.0, it will no longer support older versions of OpenGL ES, such as versions 2.0, 1.1, and 1.0.
3. What are the different types of views you can use to draw OpenGL graphics on the screen?
4. True or false: It is not possible to draw 3D graphics with OpenGL ES APIs.
5. True or false: `RenderScript` support for graphics has been removed from recent Android APIs.

Exercises

1. Use the Android documentation to determine how to declare texture compression support in your manifest file.
2. Use the Android documentation to determine what percentage of devices support OpenGL ES 2.0.
3. Create a simple OpenGL ES 3.0 application that displays a blue square.

References and More Information

Khronos OpenGL ES overview:
http://www.khronos.org/opengles/
OpenGL ES 1.1 API documentation:
http://www.khronos.org/opengles/sdk/1.1/docs/man/
OpenGL ES 2.0 API documentation:
http://www.khronos.org/opengles/sdk/2.0/docs/man/
OpenGL ES 3.0 API documentation:
http://www.khronos.org/opengles/sdk/docs/man3/
OpenGL ES information:
http://www.opengl.org
Android Training: "Displaying Graphics with OpenGL ES":
http://d.android.com/training/graphics/opengl/index.html
Android API Guides: "OpenGL ES":
http://d.android.com/guide/topics/graphics/opengl.html
Android Dashboards: "Platform Versions":
http://d.android.com/about/dashboards/index.html#OpenGL
Android SDK Reference documentation for the `android.opengl` package:
http://d.android.com/reference/android/opengl/package-summary.html
Android SDK Reference documentation for the `javax.microedition.khronos.egl` package:
http://d.android.com/reference/javax/microedition/khronos/egl/package-summary.html
Android SDK Reference documentation for the `javax.microedition.khronos.opengles` package:
http://d.android.com/reference/javax/microedition/khronos/opengles/package-summary.html

## 25

Using the Android NDK

Although Android applications are primarily written in Java, there are times when developers need or prefer to leverage native C or C++ libraries. The Android Native Development Kit (NDK) provides the tools necessary to include and use native libraries in Android applications. In this chapter, you will learn under what circumstances the Android NDK should be considered and how to configure and use it.

Determining When to Use the Android NDK

Most Android applications are written solely in Java using the Android SDK and run within the Dalvik virtual machine (VM). Most applications run smoothly and efficiently in this fashion. However, there are situations when calling in to native code from Java can be preferable. The Android NDK provides tool-chain support for compiling and using native C and C++ libraries in conjunction with Android Java applications. This is usually done for one of two reasons:

- To perform processor-intensive operations such as complex physics, which can be implemented more efficiently in C and C++, offering substantial performance improvements.
- To leverage existing code, usually in the form of shared or proprietary C or C++ libraries, when rewriting is not ideal. This is often the case when trying to support multiple platforms with a single code base.

Warning
The native libraries created by the Android NDK can be used only on devices running Android 1.5 and higher. You cannot develop applications that use the Android NDK for older platform versions. Currently Android NDK can be used only on Google TV devices based on Android 4.2.2. Devices running Honeycomb and older are not compatible with the NDK.

Calling in to native code from Java involves some trade-offs. Application developers must consider their application design carefully, weighing the benefits of using the NDK versus the drawbacks, which include:

- Increased code complexity
- Increased debugging complexity

- Performance overhead for each native code call
- More complex build process
- Developers required to be versed in Java, C/C++, and JNI concepts

Although developers can write entire applications in C or C++, not all of the Android APIs are available directly in native code. If your application requires complex math, physics, graphics algorithms, or other intensive operations, the Android NDK might be right for your project. Your libraries can take advantage of a number of stable native C and C++ APIs, including:

- C library headers (libc)
- Math library headers (libm)
- The zlib compression library headers (libz)
- 3D graphics library headers (OpenGL ES 1.1, 2.0, and 3.0)
- Multimedia and sound libraries (OpenMAX AL and OpenSL ES)
- A CPU features library for detecting device CPU features at runtime
- Other headers for C++, logging, JNI, and more

The full list of stable APIs that your code can take advantage of is found in the documentation downloaded with the NDK in the STABLE-APIS.HTML file.

Installing the Android NDK

You can install the Android NDK on Windows, Mac OS X, or Linux operating systems that have the Android SDK and tools properly installed. You also need to install or have already installed:

- GNU Make 3.81 or later (*http://www.gnu.org/software/make/*)
- GNU Awk (Gawk) or Nawk (*http://www.gnu.org/software/gawk/*)
- Cygwin 1.7 or later (Windows only, *http://www.cygwin.com*)

You can download the Android NDK from the Android developer website at *http://d.android.com/tools/sdk/ndk/index.html*. As of Android NDK r7, the Windows installer contains everything needed to perform all NDK operations, except ndk-gdb, without the need for Cygwin. ndk-gdb.py is an experimental Python implementation of the debugger, which requires a Python installation, if you do not want to install Cygwin on your machine. That is to say, if you don't need to debug (for instance, on a build machine) or don't need the use of gdb, no additional tools need to be installed on Windows machines.

Exploring the Android NDK Sample Application

The Android NDK contains a number of different tools and files, specifically:

- Native system libraries and headers that are forward compatible with the Android platform (1.5 and beyond)
- Tools for compiling and linking native libraries for ARMv5TE, ARMv7-A, and x86 devices
- Build files for embedding native libraries into Android applications
- Native debugging using `ndk-gdb`
- NDK documentation in the `/docs` subdirectory
- NDK sample applications in the `/samples` subdirectory

The best way to familiarize yourself with the Android NDK is to build one of the sample applications provided, such as `hello-jni`. To do this, take the following steps:

1. Build the `hello-jni` native library, located in the NDK `/samples/hello-jni` subdirectory, by typing the following on the command line: `ndk-build`.
2. In the Android IDE, import the existing project from the `/samples/hello-jni` subdirectory of the NDK installation directory by choosing New, Android Project from Existing Code, and then choosing Browse to locate the root directory of the project; then click Finish. Do a clean build on the project.
3. Create a Debug Configuration for the project.
4. Create an appropriate AVD if necessary. Run the application as normal.
5. If you get errors, you might need to do a "Clean project" in the Android IDE after running an `ndk-build clean` and `ndk-build` again. It's not uncommon for the Android IDE's state to get out of sync with the build status of the native library.

Creating Your Own NDK Project

Now let's look at an example of how to set up and use the NDK for your own Android applications using the Android IDE. To create a new Android application that calls into native code, take the following steps:

1. Create a new Android project in the Android IDE.
2. Navigate to your project directory and create a subdirectory called `/jni`. Inside this directory, place two C files: `native_basics.c` and `native_opengl2.c`.

3. In the /jni subdirectory, create a file called Android.mk. A sample Android.mk file might look like this, the one used in our sample application:

```
LOCAL_PATH := $(call my-dir)
include $(CLEAR_VARS)
LOCAL_LDLIBS := -llog -lGLESv2
APP_ABI := all
LOCAL_MODULE    := simplendk
LOCAL_SRC_FILES := native_basics.c native_opengl2.c
include $(BUILD_SHARED_LIBRARY)
```

4. Edit the Android.mk file and make any build changes necessary. By default, only the ARMv5TE instruction set will be targeted. For our sample, this is not necessary. You might want to target a narrower number of devices, but use ARMv7 code to gain native floating-point operations to possibly improve math performance. The value of all for APP_ABI also currently includes x86 architecture targets.

5. Build the native library and embed it in your Android application by navigating back to the project directory and running the ndk-build script. You might need to set up the path to this batch file; the ndk-build script is located in the ndk install directory.

6. In the Android IDE, update your application manifest file. Be sure to set the <uses-sdk> tag with its android:minSdkVersion attribute set to a value of 3 or higher. In our sample, we ultimately add OpenGL ES 2.0, so we've set this value to 8.

7. Create an Android IDE Debug Configuration and any necessary AVDs as normal.

Tip

Many of the code examples provided in this chapter are taken from the SimpleNDK application. The source code for this application is provided for download on the book's website.

Calling Native Code from Java

There are three main steps necessary to add a call from Java to native code, as follows:

1. Add a declaration for the new function in your Java class file as a native type.

2. Add a static initializer for the library that the native function will be compiled into.

3. Add the function of the appropriate name, following a specific naming scheme, to the native source file.

This isn't as complex as it sounds, but we'll go through each step now. The Simple NDK project has a class called NativeBasicsActivity.java. Let's start there by adding the declaration for the native function. The following declaration must be added to the class:

```
private native void basicNativeCall();
```

Now, make sure that the native library with this function is loaded. This doesn't need to happen for every call, just for each library. In the `Android.mk` file, we identified the library as simplendk (the value of `LOCALE_MODULE`), so we load that library. Add this static initializer to the `NativeBasicsActivity` class:

```
static {
    System.loadLibrary("simplendk");
}
```

Finally, the function needs to be added to the `native_basics.c` file in the native library that's being compiled. Each function must follow a specific naming convention. Instead of dots, each part of the function name is separated using an underscore, as follows:

```
Java_package_name_ClassName_functionName
(JNIEnv *env, jobject this, your vars...);
```

For the example, that means our function looks like this:

```
void Java_com_advancedandroidbook_simplendk_NativeBasicsActivity_basicNativeCall
    (JNIEnv *env, jobject this) {
    // do something interesting here
}
```

That's a lengthy function name, but your code will not work if you name it incorrectly. This function is now called whenever the Java method declared as `basicNative Call()` is invoked. But how will you know? Add the following line to the function and then make sure to include `"android/log.h"` in the `native_basics.c` file:

```
__android_log_print(ANDROID_LOG_VERBOSE, DEBUG_TAG, "Basic call");
```

And there you have it—your first call from Android Java to native C! If you're familiar with JNI, you might realize that it's mostly the same. The main difference is which libraries are available. If you're familiar with JNI, you should find using the NDK fairly straightforward.

Handling Parameters and Return Values

Now that you can make a basic native call, let's pass some parameters in to C and then return something. We make a simple little C function that takes a format string that works with the `stdio sprintf()` call and two numbers to add. The numbers are added and placed in the format string, and a new string is returned. Although simplistic, this demonstrates the handling of Java objects and reminds us that we need to manage memory properly in native C code.

```
jstring
Java_com_advancedandroidbook_simplendk_NativeBasicsActivity_formattedAddition
    (JNIEnv *env, jobject this, jint number1,
            jint number2, jstring formatString) {
    // get a C string from a Java string object
    jboolean fCopy;
    const char * szFormat = (*env)->GetStringUTFChars(env,
```

```
          formatString, &fCopy);
    char * szResult;
    // add the two values
    jlong nSum = number1 + number2;
    // make sure there's ample room for nSum
    szResult = malloc(sizeof(szFormat)+30);
    // make the call
    sprintf(szResult, szFormat, nSum);
    // get a Java string object
    jstring result = (*env)->NewStringUTF(env, szResult);

    // free the C strings
    free(szResult);
    (*env)->ReleaseStringUTFChars(env, formatString, szFormat);
    // return the Java string object
    return(result);
}
```

The JNI environment object is used for interacting with Java objects. Regular C functions are used for regular C memory management.

Using Exceptions with Native Code

Native code can throw exceptions that the Java side can catch as well as check for exceptions when making calls to Java code. This makes heavy use of the JNIEnv object and might be familiar to those with JNI experience. The following native function throws an exception if the input number parameter isn't a certain value:

```
void Java_com_advancedandroidbook_simplendk_NativeBasicsActivity_throwsException
    (JNIEnv * env, jobject this, jint number) {
    if (number < NUM_RANGE_MIN || number > NUM_RANGE_MAX) {
        // throw an exception
        jclass illegalArgumentException =
            (*env)->FindClass(env, "java/lang/IllegalArgumentException");
        if (illegalArgumentException == NULL) {
            return;
        }
        (*env)->ThrowNew(env, illegalArgumentException,
            "What an exceptional number.");
    } else {
        __android_log_print(ANDROID_LOG_VERBOSE, DEBUG_TAG,
            "Nothing exceptional here");
    }
}
```

The Java declaration for this, as you might expect, needs a throws clause:

```
private native void throwsException(int num)
    throws IllegalArgumentException;
```

Basically, the exception class is found through reflection. Then, the ThrowNew() method of the JNIEnv object is used to do the actual throwing of the exception.

To show how to check for an exception in native C code, we need to also show how to call a Java method from C. The following block of code does just that:

```
void Java_com_advancedandroidbook_simplendk_NativeBasicsActivity_checksException
    (JNIEnv * env, jobject this, jint number) {
    jthrowable exception;
    jclass class = (*env)->GetObjectClass(env, this);
    jmethodID fnJavaThrowsException =
        (*env)->GetMethodID(env, class, "javaThrowsException", "(I)V");
    if (fnJavaThrowsException != NULL) {
        (*env)->CallVoidMethod(env, this, fnJavaThrowsException, number);
        exception = (*env)->ExceptionOccurred(env);
        if (exception) {
            (*env)->ExceptionDescribe(env);
            (*env)->ExceptionClear(env);
            __android_log_print(ANDROID_LOG_ERROR,
                DEBUG_TAG, "Exception occurred. Check LogCat.");
        }
    } else {
        __android_log_print(ANDROID_LOG_ERROR,
            DEBUG_TAG, "No method found");
    }
}
```

The call to the `GetMethodID()` function is best looked up in your favorite JNI reference or online. It's basically a reflective way of getting a reference to the method, but the fourth parameter must be supplied correctly. In this case, it takes a single integer and returns a void.

Because the method returns a void, use the `CallVoidMethod()` function to actually call it and then use the `ExceptionOccurred()` function to check to see whether the method threw an exception. If it did, the `ExceptionDescribe()` function actually writes the exception out to LogCat, but it looks slightly different from a normal exception output. Then the exception is cleared so it doesn't go any further.

The Java method being called, `javaThrowsException()`, is defined as follows:

```
@SuppressWarnings("unused") // is called from native
private void javaThrowsException(int num)
    throws IllegalArgumentException {
    if (num == 42) {
        throw new IllegalArgumentException("Anything but that number!");
    } else {
        Log.v(DEBUG_TAG, "Good choice in numbers.");
    }
}
```

The use of the `@SuppressWarnings` option is due to the fact that the method is never called directly from Java, only from native code. You can also use this process of calling Java methods for Android SDK methods. However, remember that the idea of using NDK is generally to improve performance. If you find yourself doing many Android calls, the performance might be improved by simply staying on the Java side of things and leaving algorithmically heavy functionality on the native side.

Using Native Activities

While most uses of Android NDK involve calling native code through JNI, it is possible to build a fully native `Activity` and, indeed, a fully native application. This is useful for applications that don't use the Android APIs much, such as ports of existing games. Many APIs are available, however. Read more about creating a fully native application in the NDK documentation file `NATIVE_ACTIVITY.HTML`.

Improving Graphics Performance

One of the most common reasons to use the Android NDK is to leverage the OpenGL ES 1.1, 2.0, and 3.0 native libraries to perform complex math calculations that benefit from native code and speed up the porting process. Although you can use the Java APIs in the Android SDK to provide OpenGL ES support, some developers with core graphics libraries built in C or C++ might prefer to use the NDK. Here are some tips for developing and using graphics libraries provided with the Android NDK:

- OpenGL ES 1.1 native libraries are guaranteed on Android 1.6 (API Level 4) and higher; OpenGL ES 2.0 native libraries are guaranteed on Android 2.0 (API Level 5) and higher; OpenGL ES 3.0 native libraries are guaranteed on Android 4.3 (API Level 18) and higher. Make sure you include "GLES2/gl2.h" or "GLES3/gl3.h" and, optionally, "GLES2/gl2ext.h" or "GLES3/gl3ext.h" to get access to the functions. They are named in the standard OpenGL way (for example, `glClearColor`).

- Use the `<uses-sdk>` manifest tag to enforce the minimum SDK supported by the OpenGL ES version your application leverages.

- Use the `<uses-feature>` manifest tag to specify which version of OpenGL ES your application leverages so that the Android Market can filter your application and provide it only to compatible devices.

For example, the following block of code is how the `drawFrame()` method from Chapter 24, "Developing Android 3D Graphics Applications," would look in the NDK. You can find this code in the SimpleNDK project:

```
const GLfloat gVertices[] = {
    0.0f, 0.5f, 0.0f,
    -0.5f, -0.5f, 0.0f,
    0.5f, -0.5f, 0.0f
};

void Java_com_advancedandroidbook_simplendk_NativeOpenGL2Activity_drawFrame
    (JNIEnv * env, jobject this, jint shaderProgram) {
    glClear(GL_COLOR_BUFFER_BIT);
    glUseProgram(shaderProgram);
    glVertexAttribPointer(0, 3, GL_FLOAT, GL_FALSE, 12, gVertices);
    glEnableVertexAttribArray(0);
    glDrawArrays(GL_TRIANGLES, 0, 3);
}
```

This is called from the `onDrawFrame()` method of our `CustomRenderer` class. Because this is the code that runs in a tight loop, it makes sense to implement it with native code. Of course, this particular implementation doesn't benefit at all, but if we had done a bunch of complex math, transformations, and other algorithmically heavy code, it could possibly be faster. Only testing on actual devices can determine for each case what is or isn't faster, though.

Comparing `RenderScript` to the NDK

`RenderScript` is a set of high-performance computation APIs that was introduced in Android 3.0 (API Level 11). `RenderScript` uses a C language (C99, specifically) for writing scripts. Through intermediate compilation, `RenderScript` is designed to run on a variety of processor architectures, providing a means of writing performance-critical code that the system later compiles to native code for the processor it can run on. This can be the device CPU, a multicore CPU, GPU, or even DSPs.

Computing with `RenderScript`

`RenderScript` is based on the C programming language. If you're not familiar with C, we recommend that you get familiar with it before trying to use `RenderScript`. Using `RenderScript` for heavy computation might be faster to develop and it might perform better than similar NDK solutions (due to automatic distribution across hardware cores). Unlike developing with the Android NDK, you don't have to worry about the underlying hardware architecture. In fact, when it comes to NDK limitations, such as no Honeycomb support for Google TV, `RenderScript` has fewer. It does work on Google TV.

`RenderScript` is used for computational purposes. As one of the reasons for using Android NDK is also for computational purposes, there is some overlap. However, `RenderScript` has a couple of advantages that are compelling when you're not using existing C code.

First, unlike NDK code, `RenderScript` code is compiled for the target device once on the device. This means you don't have to worry about new CPU architectures that come out. Second, `RenderScript` makes it easy to leverage multiple cores. Many calls do this automatically, but there are explicit calls for dividing work. Combined, if all you're looking for from native code is a performance boost, `RenderScript` might be an excellent choice.

Native `RenderScript`

Android KitKat 4.4 (API Level 19) introduced a new native C++ API for using `Render Script` with the NDK, and any `RenderScript` code written using the NDK will work on devices with Android 2.2 or higher. Handling performance-intensive tasks from your native code is now possible by using the native `RenderScript` APIs.

Tip

The Android documentation provides a great introduction to computation with RenderScript found here: *http://d.android.com/guide/topics/renderscript/index.html*. The Android SDK also comes with a few great sample applications demonstrating RenderScript. You can find these samples in the /sdk/samples/android-19/renderscript folder if you are interested in learning more.

Summary

The Android NDK provides helpful tools that enable developers to call into native C and C++ libraries on devices running Android 1.5 and higher. Installing the Android NDK toolset is a relatively straightforward process. Using the Android NDK involves creating build scripts in order to include shared native libraries in your Android application package files. Although the Android NDK is not necessary for every application, certain types of applications might benefit greatly from its use. Android KitKat 4.4 introduced RenderScript APIs accessible through the Android NDK.

Quiz Questions

1. True or false: You should use the NDK when performing memory-intensive operations.
2. What language options are available for programming with the Android NDK?
3. What is the name of the native debugging tool provided with the NDK?
4. What command-line script is used to compile NDK applications?
5. True or false: RenderScript is based on the C++ programming language.

Exercises

1. Read the ANDROID-MK.HTML documentation that comes with the NDK toolkit to determine the three types of source modules you are able to create.
2. Use the NDK documentation to determine what the ndk-depends tool is used for.
3. Write an application that makes use of a native Activity.

References and More Information

Android Tools: "Android NDK":
  http://d.android.com/tools/sdk/ndk/index.html
Android Developers Blog: NDK label:
  http://android-developers.blogspot.com/search/label/NDK

YouTube Android Developers Channel: "DevBytes: Play Games and the NDK—Part 1: Setting Up":
http://www.youtube.com/watch?v=dxI5bReatJw

YouTube Android Developers Channel: "DevBytes: Play Games and the NDK—Part 2: Achievements and Leaderboards":
http://www.youtube.com/watch?v=zst3R1OP6Y0

YouTube Android Developers Channel: "DevBytes: Play Games and the NDK—Part 3: Threading and Lifecycle":
http://www.youtube.com/watch?v=K3BKlczc8bU

Google discussion group: "Android NDK":
http://groups.google.com/group/android-ndk

JNI reference book:
http://docs.oracle.com/javase/6/docs/technotes/guides/jni/spec/jniTOC.html

Android API Guides: "Computation":
http://d.android.com/guide/topics/renderscript/index.html

Android Developers Blog: RenderScript label:
http://android-developers.blogspot.com/search/label/Renderscript

Android SDK Reference documentation on the `RenderScript` API:
http://d.android.com/reference/android/renderscript/RenderScript.html

VI

Maximizing Android's Unique Features

26

Extending Android Application Reach

Android applications can be extended far beyond traditional functional boundaries to integrate tightly with the rest of the operating system. Developers can use a number of other platform features to improve the usefulness of an application. In this chapter, you will learn about the various ways to enhance your applications and extend their reach, making them even more powerful and compelling to your users.

Enhancing Your Applications

One of Android's most compelling features as a platform is its approach to application interoperability. Unlike the mobile development platforms of the past, which allowed each simple application to run in its own little bubble, Android allows applications to share data and functionality with other applications and the rest of the operating system in a secure and reasonable fashion. After you've developed your core application, it's time to give some thought to how to extend the application's reach beyond the traditional use case, which is:

1. User launches the app.
2. User runs the app.
3. User closes the app.

Although it's certainly necessary to support that particular scenario, it's not the only way that users can interact with an app or its features. The Android framework includes a number of ways to move beyond this paradigm. You can extend and enhance Android applications in a variety of ways, including:

- Exposing small segments of application functionality in the form of App Widgets, which can reside on the user's Home screen or on the Lock screen.
- Providing users with an interactive background associated with your application in the form of a live wallpaper.

- Displaying an interactive screen saver while the device is plugged into a charger or residing in a dock in the form of a Daydream.

- Making application content searchable across the device, as discussed in Chapter 27, "Enabling Application Search."

- Enabling your application to act as a content type handler, exposing the capability to process common types of data such as pictures or videos.

- Enabling different application entry points using intent filters above and beyond the default `Activity` to launch.

- Having your application act as a content provider, exposing internal data for use by other applications, and taking advantage of other content providers to enhance your application. See Chapter 4, "Building Android Content Providers," for more details.

- Enabling your application to act as a broadcast receiver to react to important events that occur and to broadcast application events of interest to other applications. See Chapter 5, "Broadcasting and Receiving Intents," for more details.

- Having your application act as a `Service`, providing data services and special functionality to other applications, as discussed in Chapter 2, "Working with Services."

This is where we encourage you to think outside the box and consider how to extend the reach of your applications. By doing so, you keep your application fresh in your users' minds so they continually rely on your application and don't forget about it. Now let's look at some of the options listed in more detail.

Working with App Widgets

Introduced in API Level 3, the App Widget provides a level of application integration with the Android operating system that was previously not available to mobile developers. Applications that publish App Widgets are called App Widget providers. A component that can contain an App Widget is called an App Widget host. An App Widget is a lightweight, simply featured application (such as a desktop plug-in) that can be installed on a host such as the Home screen.

An App Widget is normally tied back to some underlying application. For example, a calendar application might have an App Widget that shows the current date and enables the user to view the scheduled events of the day. Clicking on a specific event might launch the full calendar application to that date, enabling the user to access the full range of application features. Similarly, a music application might provide a simple set of controls within an App Widget, enabling the user to easily start and stop music playback from the Home screen. We provide a simple App Widget implementation as part of the code that accompanies this book; this App Widget displays information about the United States Homeland Security Advisory System's threat level (imminent and elevated); this type of App Widget might be appropriate for a travel application.

An App Widget can be updated at regular intervals with fresh content. This makes App Widgets ideal for secondary application features, whereas notifications that launch into the full application functionality might be more appropriate for events that require a speedy user response.

Tip

As of Android 4.2 (API Level 17), App Widgets may now be added to a user's Lock screen. This makes an App Widget available for view while the user is locked out of the phone, similar to the Clock application found on many Android devices.

Creating an App Widget

Consider whether or not your application should include App Widget functionality. Although App Widgets are small in size and light on functionality, they allow the user to access application functionality straight from the Home screen. App Widgets also serve to keep users using the application by reminding them that they installed it. Some applications allow only one instance of an App Widget to run (such as the music player), whereas others might allow multiple instances of the same App Widget to be placed simultaneously, though generally showing different content (such as a picture frame).

You need to make the following changes to your application to support App Widgets:

- Provide an XML App Widget configuration.
- Determine whether the App Widget requires a configuration `Activity`.
- Provide an `AppWidgetProvider` class implementation.
- Provide a `Service` class implementation to handle App Widget content updates, as needed.
- Update the application Android manifest file to register the App Widget provider information and any information about the update `Service`.

Now let's look at some of these requirements in greater detail.

Tip

The code examples provided in this section are taken from the SimpleAppWidget application. The source code for this application is provided for download on the book's website.

Creating an App Widget Configuration

First, your application must provide an XML App Widget definition. You can store this definition in the project's resources in the `/res/xml` directory. Let's take a closer look at an example of an App Widget definition, as defined in `res/xml/simple_widget_info.xml`:

```xml
<?xml version="1.0" encoding="utf-8"?>
<appwidget-provider
    xmlns:android="http://schemas.android.com/apk/res/android"
    android:minWidth="146dp"
    android:minHeight="72dp"
    android:updatePeriodMillis="28800000"
```

```
   android:initialLayout="@layout/widget"
   android:previewImage="@drawable/widgetPreview" >
</appwidget-provider>
```

This simple App Widget definition is encapsulated in the `<appwidget-provider>` XML tag. The `minWidth` and `minHeight` attributes dictate the size of the App Widget (a dimension, here in `dp`), and the `updatePeriodMillis` attribute is used to define how often the App Widget content is refreshed (using the App Widget update `Service`)—in this case, once every eight hours. The App Widget layout definition is referenced using the `initialLayout` attribute—we talk more about this layout file in a few moments. Finally, a preview of the App Widget is provided with the `previewImage` field. This is useful in Android 3.0 and later where selecting images is done from the preview image rather than a list.

Note

An App Widget cannot be updated more frequently than every 30 minutes (1,800,000 milliseconds). Ensure that the `updatePeriodMillis` attribute of your App Widget provider reflects this limitation. This limit has testing implications. You might consider a tool to force an update or some sort of Refresh button that users might benefit from, as well.

If your widget must break this limit, which you should do only for a very good reason, you must implement the timer yourself. Keep in mind the effect on battery life and performance this decision might have.

To draw nicely on the Home screen, the App Widget dimensions must follow certain guidelines. The Home screen is divided into cells of a particular size. When the user attempts to install an App Widget, the system checks to make sure there is enough space (as dictated by the minimum width and height values of the App Widget).

Tip

The basic formula for determining the size of an App Widget is to multiply the number of cells you want by 70, and then subtract 30. In our case, we want an App Widget two cells high and two cells wide. Therefore, we use a size of ((70*2) – 30) or 110. This formula has changed a few times in the past, so make sure to check the documentation for the current formula to calculate the appropriate size for your App Widget. For a nice write-up on App Widget design guidelines, see the Android website at *http://d.android.com/guide/ practices/ui_guidelines/widget_design.html*.

There are a number of other attributes available in the `<appwidget-provider>` tag. For example, you can specify the `Activity` class used to configure the App Widget using the `configure` attribute, which is especially useful when you support multiple simultaneous App Widget instances. For a complete list of available App Widget provider configuration details, see the class documentation for the `android.appwidget` `.AppWidgetProviderInfo` class.

Determining Whether the App Widget Requires a Configuration `Activity`

Generally speaking, if there is more than one instance of an App Widget, each instance should look or behave differently. This isn't a strict requirement; if each instance of the App Widget looks and acts the same, users quickly catch on and install only one instance at a time.

However, if you want to differentiate between App Widget instances, you need to provide each with settings, and thus you must create a configuration `Activity`. This configuration `Activity` is a normal `Activity`, but it will read in certain `Intent` extras upon launch. The configuration `Activity` must be defined in the App Widget XML configuration.

Each time a new App Widget instance is created, the configuration `Activity` is launched. The `Activity` is launched with the unique App Widget identifier, passed in via the launch `Intent`'s `EXTRA_APPWIDGET_ID` extra. The `Activity`, on completion, must set this value back in the result `Intent` along with result status, such as `RESULT_OK`.

The configuration `Activity` should not only let the user configure options on this particular App Widget instance, but it should also update the `RemoteViews` object, as the App Widget will not receive an update event when it's first created with a configuration `Activity` set in the XML configuration. Subsequent updates receive the update event, though.

Creating an App Widget Provider

An App Widget is basically a `BroadcastReceiver` that handles particular actions. As with a broadcast receiver, the primary interaction with an App Widget happens through the `onReceive()` method. However, the default `AppWidgetProvider` class handles `onReceive()` and, in turn, delegates operations to its other methods, which you then implement.

Implementing the `AppWidgetProvider` Class

The `AppWidgetProvider` class simplifies the handling of these actions by providing a framework for developers to implement App Widgets. An `AppWidgetProvider` implementation requires the following methods:

- The `onEnabled()` method is called when the App Widget is created. This is a good place to perform any configuration shared for the entire widget provider. This method is called once for the first App Widget instance added to the widget host (usually the Home screen).

- The `onDisabled()` method is called when the App Widget is disabled. This method is called only after all App Widget instances for this provider are removed from the App Widget host. For example, if there were five App Widgets for this provider on the Home screen, this method would be called only after the user removed the fifth and final App Widget.

- The `onUpdate()` method is called at regular intervals, depending on the update frequency specified in the App Widget configuration file. This frequency uses an in-exact timer, so do not rely on this frequency being precise. If you need precision updates, consider scheduling updates using the `AlarmManager` class. This method is called with a list of widget identifiers. Each identifier references a unique App Widget instance in the App Widget host. The App Widget provider implementation must differentiate between each instance and, typically, store different configuration values for each as well.

▪ The `onDeleted()` method is called when a particular instance of this App Widget is deleted.

Using Remote Views

Android App Widgets do not run in the application process, but in the host's process. Therefore, the App Widget uses the `RemoteViews` class to define its user interface. The `RemoteViews` class supports a subset of the overall `View` hierarchy, for display in another process. Generally speaking, you want to configure the `RemoteViews` object and send it to the App Widget Manager during the `onUpdate()` method. However, you also need to update it when an instance is created and a configuration `Activity` exists.

`View` hierarchies defined using `RemoteViews` can contain only a limited set of controls, including `Button`, `ImageButton`, `ImageView`, `TextView`, `AnalogClock`, `Chronometer`, `ProgressBar`, `ListView`, `GridView`, `StackView`, `ViewFlipper`, and `AdapterViewFlipper` controls and only in `FrameLayout`, `LinearLayout`, `RelativeLayout`, or `GridLayout` layouts. Objects derived from these controls cannot be used, either. The `RemoteViews` configuration should be kept as simple as possible because access to its `View` hierarchy is controlled through helper methods, such as `setImageViewResource()`, `setTextViewText()`, `setProgressBar()`, `setShort()`, `setString()`, `setChronometer()`, and `setRemoteAdapter()`. In short, you can generate an XML layout definition for an App Widget, but you must be careful to use only controls that are supported by the `RemoteViews` class.

Let's look at the incredibly simple layout definition used by the threat level App Widget, as defined in the resource file `/res/layout/widget.xml`:

```xml
<?xml version="1.0" encoding="utf-8"?>
<RelativeLayout
    xmlns:android="http://schemas.android.com/apk/res/android"
    android:layout_height="match_parent"
    android:layout_width="match_parent"
    android:id="@+id/widget_view">
    <TextView
        android:layout_width="wrap_content"
        android:layout_height="wrap_content"
        android:id="@+id/widget_text_threat"
        android:layout_centerInParent="true">
    </TextView>
</RelativeLayout>
```

Nothing too complex in this layout, eh? A single `TextView` control, which displays the threat level information, is encapsulated in a `RelativeLayout` control. Now your layout can be loaded programmatically into a `RemoteViews` object for use in the App

Widget provider. Don't worry; things get more complex when we cram that layout into a `RemoteViews` object and act upon it across processes.

To load a layout resource (such as `widget.xml`, defined earlier) into a `RemoteViews` object, you can use the following code:

```
RemoteViews remoteView =
    new RemoteViews(context.getPackageName(), R.layout.widget);
```

When you want to update the text in that layout's `TextView` control, you need to use the `setTextViewText()` method of the `RemoteViews` class, like this:

```
remoteView.setTextViewText(R.id.widget_text_threat, "Red alert!");
```

If you want the user to be able to click in the `RelativeLayout` control of the App Widget display and to launch the underlying application, use the `setOnClickPending Intent()` method of the `RemoteViews` class. For example, the following code creates a pending `Intent` that can launch the `SimpleAppWidgetActivity` activity:

```
Intent launchAppIntent =
    new Intent(context, SimpleAppWidgetActivity.class);
PendingIntent launchAppPendingIntent = PendingIntent.getActivity(
    context, 0, launchAppIntent,
    PendingIntent.FLAG_UPDATE_CURRENT);
remoteView.setOnClickPendingIntent
    (R.id.widget_view, launchAppPendingIntent);
```

Finally, when the `RemoteViews` object is all set up, the App Widget provider needs to tell the App Widget Manager about the updated `RemoteViews` object:

```
ComponentName simpleWidget = new ComponentName(context,
    SimpleAppWidgetProvider.class);
AppWidgetManager appWidgetManager =
    AppWidgetManager.getInstance(context);
appWidgetManager.updateAppWidget(simpleWidget, remoteView);
```

To update the appropriate App Widget, the `AppWidgetManager` object requires its component name. The App Widget Manager then updates the content of the specific named App Widget using the contents of the `RemoteViews` object you provide in the `updateAppWidget()` method. Each time the `RemoteViews` object is updated, it is rebuilt. Although this usually happens infrequently, keep the `RemoteViews` simple for good performance.

Note

Unfortunately, the complete implementation of the `AppWidgetProvider` class provided in SimpleAppWidget is too lengthy for print. See the `SimpleAppWidgetProvider` class in the sample project for the full details of how the threat level App Widget works.

Updating an App Widget

When the `onUpdate()` method of the App Widget provider is called, a list of identifiers is passed in. Each identifier references a particular App Widget instance for this provider. That is, a user can add any number of App Widgets of a particular kind to a host. It's up to you, though, how they differ. During the update event, each identifier must be iterated over and each of the `RemoteViews` objects updated individually (that is, if you support different instances simultaneously).

An App Widget must be responsive during the update event because it is being executed from the UI thread of the host process. When the updates are done, there is no guarantee that the App Widget provider object stays around. Therefore, if an App Widget refresh requires any lengthy blocking operations, it must use a `Service` so that it can create a thread to perform these operations in the background.

In our threat level App Widget example, we already have a `Service` that performs some network operations to download updated threat level data. This `Service` is perfect for the needs of an App Widget and the application, so they can share it. Convenient, huh?

Creating an App Widget Update `Service`

Most App Widgets do not contain static content but are updated from time to time. Normally, an Android `Service` is used to enable App Widget content updates. The `Service` performs any necessary update-related tasks, including spawning threads, connecting to the Internet, and so on. The App Widget provider's `onUpdate()` method, which is called at the App Widget update interval, is a great place to start this update `Service`. After the `Service` has done its job, it should shut itself down until the next time fresh content is needed. Let's revisit the threat level App Widget, which uses two services:

- The `SimpleDataUpdateService` class runs at the App Widget update interval (started in the `onUpdate()` method of the App Widget provider). The `Service` connects to the Internet, checks the current threat level, and stores the result in the application's shared preferences. Finally, the `Service` shuts itself down. It might be helpful to consider the application as the "owner" of this `Service`—it provides information for both the application and the App Widget by saving data to the shared preferences.

- The `PrefListenerService` class listens for changes in the application's shared preferences. In addition to using the `onUpdate()` method, this `Service` is started when the App Widget is enabled, thus allowing it to be updated whenever the data changes (for example, when the underlying application modifies the shared preferences by checking the threat level itself). When the threat level preference changes, this `Service` triggers a call to the `updateAppWidget()` method of the App Widget provider, which updates the `RemoteViews` object for the App Widget—bypassing the frequency limitations of the App Widget Manager. It might be helpful to consider the App Widget as the "owner" of this `Service`—it runs in the App Widget lifecycle and exists only to update the content of the App Widget.

Certainly, there are simpler ways to update your App Widget. For example, the App Widget can use its one `Service` to do the work of downloading the threat level data and updating the App Widget content, but then the application is left to do its own thing. The method described here illustrates how you can bypass some of the update frequency limitations of App Widgets and still share content between App Widgets and their underlying applications.

Tip

Updating the RemoteViews object need not happen from within the App Widget provider. It can be called directly from the application, too. In this example, the Service created for downloading the threat level data is used by the application and App Widget alike. Using a Service for downloading online data is a good practice for a number of reasons. However, if there was no download Service to leverage, we could have gotten away with just one Service. In this Service, fully controlled by the App Widget, we would have not only done the download but also then updated the RemoteViews object directly. Doing this would have eliminated the need for listening to changes of the shared preferences from the App Widget Service, too.

Configuring the Android Manifest File for App Widgets

For the Android system to know about your application's App Widget, you must include a <receiver> tag in the application's Android manifest file to register it as an App Widget provider. App Widgets often use services, and these services must be registered in the Android manifest file with a <service> tag like any other Service. Here is an excerpt of the Android manifest file from the SimpleAppWidget project:

```
<receiver android:name="SimpleAppWidgetProvider"
    android:label="@string/widget_desc"
    android:icon="@drawable/threat_levels_descriptions">
    <intent-filter>
        <action android:name=
            "android.appwidget.action.APPWIDGET_UPDATE" />
    </intent-filter>
    <meta-data
        android:name="android.appwidget.provider"
        android:resource="@xml/simple_widget_info" />
</receiver>
<service android:name="SimpleDataUpdateService" />
<service android:name="SimpleAppWidgetProvider$PrefListenerService" />
```

Notice that, unlike a typical <receiver> definition, a <meta-data> section references an XML file resource. The <receiver> tag includes several bits of information about the App Widget configuration, including a label and icon for the App Widget, which is displayed on the App Widget picker (where the user chooses from available App Widgets on the system). The <receiver> tag also includes an intent filter to handle the android.appwidget.action.APPWIDGET_UPDATE action, as well as a <meta-data> tag that references the App Widget configuration file stored in the XML resource directory. Finally, the services used to update the App Widget are registered.

Installing an App Widget to the Home Screen

After your application has implemented App Widget functionality, a user (who has installed your application) can install it to the Home screen using the following steps:

1. From the Home screen, click to the button to show all applications.

2. Choose the Widgets tab, as shown in Figure 26.1.

3. From the Widget menu, choose the App Widget you want to include by pressing and holding. Users can see the preview image here. Set the preview to something useful—generally what the widget will look like in a typical situation.

4. Drag the App Widget to the place you want it and release, as shown in Figure 26.2.

Figure 26.1   Using the Widget picker to install
an App Widget on the Home screen.

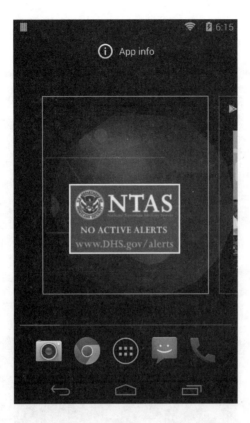

Figure 26.2   A simple App Widget that displays NTAS alerts
being placed on the Home screen.

Becoming an App Widget Host

Although somewhat less common, applications might also become App Widget hosts.
App Widget hosts (android.appWidget.AppWidgetHost) are simply containers that
can embed and display App Widgets. The most commonly used App Widget host is the
Home screen. Creating an App Widget host is not a trivial process and usually requires
trial and error. For more information on developing an App Widget host, see the
Android SDK documentation.

Introducing Lock Screen App Widgets

Android API Level 17 introduced a new type of App Widget configuration for the Lock
screen. Lock screen App Widgets function the same as Home screen App Widgets; they

just appear on a user's Lock screen. To add Lock screen support to an App Widget, simply add the android:widgetCategory attribute to the <appwidget-provider> tag, and assign a value of keyguard. By default, the <appwidget-provider> is set to the value of home_screen. You should also set the attribute android:initialKeyGuardLayout with a layout value for the Lock screen. To add Lock screen support to our App Widget, update the <appwidget-provider> XML file with the following:

```
<appwidget-provider xmlns:android="http://schemas.android.com/apk/res/android"
    android:initialLayout="@layout/widget"
    android:initialKeyguardLayout="@layout/widget"
    android:minHeight="72dp"
    android:minWidth="146dp"
    android:previewImage="@drawable/widget_preview"
    android:updatePeriodMillis="28800000"
    android:widgetCategory="keyguard|home_screen" >
</appwidget-provider>
```

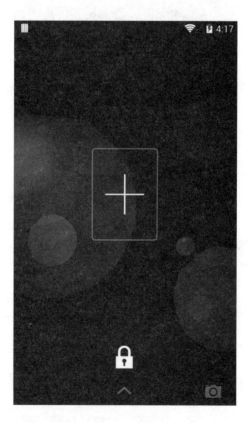

Figure 26.3   An empty Lock screen prompting
the user to add an App Widget.

Installing an App Widget to the Lock Screen

Installing to the Lock screen is similar to installing on the Home screen with some small differences. A user can install an App Widget to the Lock screen with the following steps:

1. From the Lock screen, swipe left (or right) until you reveal an empty Lock screen page.

2. Press the big plus button in the middle of the screen, as shown in Figure 26.3. After pressing the plus button, you will be asked to enter your screen lock passphrase (if one has been set on the device).

3. After successfully entering your screen lock passphrase, from the Widget menu, choose the App Widget you want to include by pressing and holding.

4. Drag the App Widget to the place you want it and release, as shown in Figure 26.4.

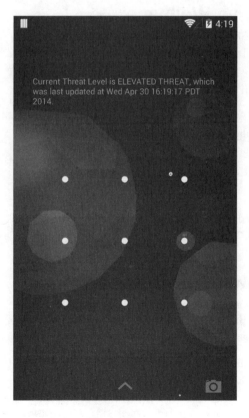

Figure 26.4   A simple App Widget that displays NTAS alerts
being placed on the Lock screen.

Working with Live Wallpapers

In addition to still image wallpapers, Android supports the notion of a live wallpaper. Instead of displaying a static background image on the Home screen, the user can set an interactive, or live, wallpaper that can display anything that can be drawn on a surface, such as graphics and animations. Live wallpapers were introduced in Android 2.1 (API Level 7).

Your applications can provide live wallpapers that use 3D graphics and animations as well as display interesting application content. Some examples of live wallpapers include:

- A 3D display showing an animated scene portraying abstract shapes
- A `Service` that animates between images found on an online image-sharing service
- An interactive pond with water that ripples with touch
- Wallpapers that change based on the actual season, weather, and time of day

Creating a Live Wallpaper

A live wallpaper is similar to an Android `Service`, but its result is a surface that the host can display. You need to make the following changes to your application in order to support live wallpapers:

- Provide an XML wallpaper configuration.
- Provide a `WallpaperService` implementation.
- Update the application Android manifest file to register the wallpaper `Service` with the appropriate permissions.

Now let's look at some of these requirements in greater detail.

Tip

The code examples provided in this section are taken from the SimpleLiveWallpaper application. The source code for this application is provided for download on the book's website.

Creating a Live Wallpaper `Service`

The guts of the live wallpaper functionality are provided as part of a `WallpaperService` implementation, and most of the live wallpaper functionality is driven by its `WallpaperService.Engine` implementation.

Implementing a Wallpaper `Service`

Your application needs to extend the `WallpaperService` class. The most important method the class needs to override is the `onCreateEngine()` method. Here is a sample implementation of a wallpaper `Service` called `SimpleDroidWallpaper`:

```
public class SimpleDroidWallpaper extends WallpaperService {
    private final Handler handler = new Handler();
```

```
@Override
public Engine onCreateEngine() {
    return new SimpleWallpaperEngine();
}
class SimpleWallpaperEngine extends WallpaperService.Engine {
    // Your implementation of a wallpaper service engine here...
}
}
```

There's not much to this wallpaper `Service`. The `onCreateEngine()` method simply returns your application's custom wallpaper engine, which provides all the functionality for a specific live wallpaper. You can also override the other wallpaper `Service` methods, as necessary. A `Handler` object is initialized for posting wallpaper draw operations.

Implementing a Wallpaper `Service` Engine

Now let's take a closer look at the wallpaper `Service` engine implementation. The wallpaper `Service` engine handles all the details regarding the lifecycle of a specific instance of a live wallpaper. Much like the graphics examples used in Chapter 24, "Developing Android 3D Graphics Applications," live wallpaper implementations use a `Surface` object to draw to the screen.

There are a number of callback methods of interest in the wallpaper `Service` engine:

- You can override the `onCreate()` and `onDestroy()` methods to set up and tear down the live wallpaper. The `Surface` object is not valid during these parts of the lifecycle.

- You can override the `onSurfaceCreated()` and `onSurfaceDestroyed()` methods (convenience methods for the `Surface` setup and teardown) to set up and tear down the `Surface` used for live wallpaper drawing.

- You should override the `onVisibilityChanged()` method to handle live wallpaper visibility. When invisible, a live wallpaper must not remain running. This method should be treated much like an `Activity` pause or resume event.

- The `onSurfaceChanged()` method is another convenience method for `Surface` management.

- You can override the `onOffsetsChanged()` method to enable the live wallpaper to react when the user swipes between Home screens.

- You can override the `onTouchEvent()` method to handle touch events. The incoming parameter is a `MotionEvent` object—we talk about the `MotionEvent` class in detail in the "Working with Gestures" section of Chapter 8, "Handling Advanced User Input." You also need to enable touch events (off by default) for the live wallpaper using the `setTouchEventsEnabled()` method.

The implementation details of the live wallpaper are up to the developer. Often, a live wallpaper implementation uses OpenGL ES calls to draw to the screen. For example, the sample live wallpaper project included with this book includes a live wallpaper `Service` that creates a `Bitmap` graphic of a bug droid that floats around the screen, bouncing off the edges of the wallpaper boundaries. It also responds to touch events by changing its drift direction. Its wallpaper engine uses a thread to manage drawing operations, posting them back to the system using the `Handler` object defined in the wallpaper `Service`.

Tip

Your live wallpaper can respond to user events, such as touch events. It can also listen for events when the user drops items on the screen. For more information, see the documentation for the `WallpaperService.Engine` class.

Note

Unfortunately, the wallpaper engine implementation of the sample application, SimpleLiveWallpaper, is far too lengthy for print due to all the OpenGL ES drawing code. However, you can see its implementation as part of the sample code provided for download on the book's website. Specifically, check the `SimpleDroidWallpaper` class.

Warning

You should take into account device responsiveness and battery life when designing live wallpapers. Unlike your application where you can simply perform lengthy operations off the main thread, live wallpapers take away performance from the Home screen and use battery life regardless of what thread the operation takes place in.

Creating a Live Wallpaper Configuration

Next, your application must provide an XML wallpaper definition. You can store this definition in the project's resources in the `/res/xml` directory. For example, here is a simple wallpaper definition called `/res/xml/droid_wallpaper.xml`:

```xml
<?xml version="1.0" encoding="utf-8"?>
<wallpaper xmlns:android="http://schemas.android.com/apk/res/android"
    android:thumbnail="@drawable/live_wallpaper_android"
    android:description="@string/wallpaper_desc" />
```

This simple wallpaper definition is encapsulated in the `<wallpaper>` XML tag. The description and thumbnail attributes are displayed on the wallpaper picker, where the user is prompted to select a specific wallpaper to use.

Configuring the Android Manifest File for Live Wallpapers

Finally, you need to update the application's Android manifest file to expose the live wallpaper `Service`. Specifically, the `WallpaperService` needs to be registered using the `<service>` tag. The `<service>` tag must include several important bits of information:

- The `WallpaperService` class
- The `BIND_WALLPAPER` permission

- An intent filter for the `WallpaperService` action
- Wallpaper metadata to reference the live wallpaper configuration

Let's look at an example. Here is the `<service>` tag implementation for a simple live wallpaper:

```
<service
    android:label="@string/wallpaper_name"
    android:name="SimpleDroidWallpaper"
    android:permission="android.permission.BIND_WALLPAPER">
    <intent-filter>
        <action
            android:name="android.service.wallpaper.WallpaperService" />
    </intent-filter>
    <meta-data
        android:name="android.service.wallpaper"
        android:resource="@xml/droid_wallpaper" />
</service>
```

In addition to the `Service` definition, you also need to limit installation of your application to API Level 7 and higher (where support for live wallpapers exists) using the `<uses-sdk>` manifest tag:

```
<uses-sdk android:minSdkVersion="7" android:targetSdkVersion="19" />
```

Keep in mind that your live wallpaper might use APIs (such as OpenGL ES 2.0 APIs) that require a higher `minSdkVersion` than API Level 7. You might also want to use the `<uses-feature>` tag to specify that your application includes live wallpaper support for use in Google Play filters:

```
<uses-feature android:name="android.software.live_wallpaper" />
```

Installing a Live Wallpaper

After you've implemented live wallpaper support in your application, you can set a live wallpaper on your Home screen using the following steps:

1. Long-press on the Home screen.
2. From the menu, choose the Live Wallpapers option, as shown in Figure 26.5 (left).
3. From the Live Wallpaper menu, choose the live wallpaper you want to include, as shown in Figure 26.5 (right). Here you can see the values you configured in `droid_wallpaper.xml`. Make these indicative of what the wallpaper is and does.
4. After you've chosen a wallpaper, it is shown in preview mode. Simply choose the Set Wallpaper button to confirm you want to use that live wallpaper. The live wallpaper is now visible on your Home screen, as shown in Figure 26.6.

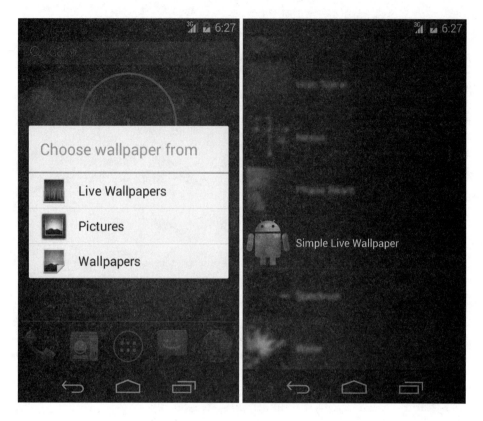

Figure 26.5   Installing a live wallpaper on the Home screen.

Introducing Daydream

New in Android 4.2 (API Level 17) is an interactive screen saver feature called Day-dream. A Daydream occurs when a device is charging. This allows you to package up particular features of your application for presenting to users when their device is charging, acting as another point of interactivity. Here are two very important points to think about when planning your Daydream:

- **Privacy:** A Daydream is presented on top of the keyguard or Lock screen, so make sure you take care not to reveal any information a user would not want visible to others.

- **Power:** A Daydream works only when a device is charging or docked, so if your Daydream consumes considerable power while running, a user's device might take a long time to charge, or maybe won't even charge at all.

Figure 26.6   A simple live wallpaper on the Home screen background that bounces a colorful bug droid around.

To select a default Daydream to run, the user navigates to the Settings app, chooses Display, then Daydream (the feature should be turned on if it is off), then selects the Daydream he or she wishes to have as the default. Users may even customize the settings of a particular Daydream provided the developer allows for configuration changes to be made. Finally, users are able to select when they would like a Daydream to occur by choosing the When to daydream button. They are presented with three options: While docked, While charging, and Either (see Figure 26.7).

Implementing a Daydream is like implementing a `Service` and is done by extending the `DreamService` class of the `android.service.dreams` package. You also need to include a `<service>` tag in your Android manifest file while including an `<intent-filter>` for the `<service>` tag that defines an `<action>` tag with the name attribute value set to `android.service.dreams.DreamService`. Optionally, you may include a `<meta-data>` tag specifying a resource file for linking to a settings `Activity` for managing the settings of the Daydream.

Figure 26.7   The Daydream settings dialog for selecting when to daydream.

Acting as a Content Type Handler

Your application can act as a content type filter—that is, handle common Intent actions such as VIEW, EDIT, or SEND for specific MIME types.

Tip
See the android.content.Intent class for a list of standard Activity actions.

A photo application might act as a content type handler for VIEW actions for any graphic formats, such as JPG, PNG, or RAW image file MIME types. Similarly, a social networking application might want to handle Intent SEND actions when the underlying data has a MIME type associated with typical social content (for example, text, graphics, or video). This means that any time the user tries to send data (with the MIME types that the social networking application was interested in) from an Android application using an Intent with action SEND, the social networking application is listed as a choice for completing the SEND action request. If the user chooses to send the content using the social networking application, that application has to launch an `Activity` to handle the request (for example, an `Activity` that uploads the content to the social networking website to share).

Finally, content type handlers make it easier to extend the application to act as a content provider, provide search capabilities, or include App Widget features. Define data records using custom MIME types, so that no matter how an `Intent` fires (inside or outside the application), the action is handled by the application in a graceful fashion.

To enable your application to act as a content type handler, you need to make several changes to your application:

- Determine which `Intent` actions and MIME types your application needs to be able to handle.

- Implement an `Activity` that can process the `Intent` action or actions that you want to handle.

- Register that `Activity` in your application's Android manifest file using the `<activity>` tag as you normally would. You then need to configure an `<intent-filter>` tag for that `Activity` in your application's Android manifest file, providing the appropriate `Intent` action and MIME types your application can process.

Determining `Intent` Actions and MIME Types

Let's look at a simple example. For the remainder of this chapter, we make various modifications to a simple field notes application that uses a content provider to expose African game animal field notes; each note has a title and text body (the content itself comes from field notes on African game animals that we wrote up years ago on our nature blog, which is very popular with grade-schoolers). Throughout these examples, the application acts as a content type handler for `VIEW` requests for data with a custom MIME type:

`vnd.android.cursor.item/vnd.advancedandroidbook.live.fieldnotes`

Tip

MIME types come in two forms. Most developers are familiar with MIME types, such as `text/plain` or `image/jpeg` (as defined in RFC 2045 and RFC 2046, which are standards used globally). The Internet Assigned Numbers Authority (IANA, at *http://www.iana.org*) manages these global MIME types.

Developers frequently need to create their own MIME types, without the need for them to become global standards. These types must still be sufficiently unique that MIME type namespace collisions do not occur. When you're dealing with Android content providers, there are two well-defined prefixes that you can use for creating MIME types. The `ContentResolver.CURSOR_DIR_BASE_TYPE` prefix (`"vnd.android.cursor.dir"`) is for use with directories or folders of items. The `ContentResolver.CURSOR_ITEM_BASE_TYPE` prefix (`"vnd.android.cursor.item"`) is for use with a single type. The part after the slash must then be unique. It's not uncommon to pattern MIME types after package names or other such unique qualifiers.

Implementing the `Activity` to Process the Intents

Next, the application needs an `Activity` class to handle the `Intent` objects it receives. For the sample, we simply need to load a page capable of viewing a field note. Here is a sample implementation of an `Activity` that can parse the `Intent` data and show a screen to display the field note for a specific animal:

```
public class SimpleViewDetailsActivity extends Activity {
    @Override
    protected void onCreate(Bundle savedInstanceState) {
        super.onCreate(savedInstanceState);
        setContentView(R.layout.details);
        try {
            Intent launchIntent = getIntent();
            Uri launchData = launchIntent.getData();
            String id = launchData.getLastPathSegment();
            Uri dataDetails = Uri.withAppendedPath
                (SimpleFieldnotesContentProvider.CONTENT_URI, id);
            CursorLoader loader = new CursorLoader(this, dataDetails,
                                          null, null, null, null);
            Cursor cursor = loader.loadInBackground();
            cursor.moveToFirst();
            String fieldnoteTitle = cursor.getString(cursor
                .getColumnIndex(SimpleFieldnotesContentProvider
                .FIELDNOTES_TITLE));
            String fieldnoteBody = cursor.getString(cursor
                .getColumnIndex(SimpleFieldnotesContentProvider
                .FIELDNOTES_BODY));
            TextView fieldnoteView = (TextView)
                findViewById(R.id.text_title);
            fieldnoteView.setText(fieldnoteTitle);
            TextView bodyView = (TextView) findViewById(R.id.text_body);
            bodyView.setLinksClickable(true);
            bodyView.setAutoLinkMask(Linkify.ALL);
            bodyView.setText(fieldnoteBody);
        } catch (Exception e) {
            Toast.makeText(this, "Failed.", Toast.LENGTH_LONG).show();
        }
    }
}
```

The `SimpleViewDetailsActivity` class retrieves the `Intent` that was used to launch the `Activity` using the `getIntent()` method. It then inspects the details of that `Intent`, extracting the specific field note identifier using the `getLastPathSegment()` method. The rest of the code simply involves querying the underlying content provider for the appropriate field note record and displaying it using a layout.

Registering the Intent Filter

Finally, the `Activity` class must be registered in the application's Android manifest file, and the intent filter must be configured so that the application accepts only intents for specific actions and specific MIME types. For example, the SimpleViewDetails Activity would be registered as follows:

```
<activity
    android:name="SimpleViewDetailsActivity">
    <intent-filter>
        <action
            android:name="android.intent.action.VIEW" />
            <category
                android:name="android.intent.category.DEFAULT" />
            <data android:mimeType=
                "vnd.android.cursor.item/
                        vnd.advancedandroidbook.live.fieldnotes" />
    </intent-filter>
</activity>
```

The <activity> tag remains the same as any other. The <intent-filter> tag is what's interesting here. First, the <action> tag defines the matching criteria an Intent object will need to specify in order to be handled by this application. The name property of the <action> tag specifies the type of action, in this case the VIEW action. The <category> tag is set to DEFAULT, which is most appropriate, and finally, the <data> tag is used to filter VIEW intents further to only those of the custom MIME type associated with field notes.

Summary

The Android platform provides a number of ways to integrate your applications tightly into the operating system, enabling you to extend your reach beyond traditional application boundaries. In this chapter, you learned how to extend your application by creating App Widgets, live wallpapers, Daydreams, and more. The Android APIs provide many ways that applications can integrate into the system and take part in the user experience at many levels.

Quiz Questions

1. What changes do you need to make to your application to support App Widgets?

2. What attributes of the <appwidget-provider> tag are used to define the size of an App Widget?

3. True or false: An App Widget cannot be updated more frequently than every 15 minutes.

4. What is the formula for determining the size of an App Widget?

5. True or false: To make an App Widget available to the Lock screen, you must set the <appwidget-provider> tag attribute android:widgetCategory to the value of lock_screen.

6. What changes do you need to make to your application to support a live wallpaper?

7. What `Service` permission must you include in the Android manifest file to support a live wallpaper?

8. What Google Play filter would you include to notify users that your application supports live wallpaper?

Exercises

1. Use the Android documentation to determine what the `<appwidget-provider>` tag `configure` attribute is defined for.

2. Use the Android documentation to determine the intents your application may monitor for receiving App Widget broadcasts.

3. Create a new Daydream application that presents a new text-based affirmation every minute. Include five different affirmations for the application to rotate through.

References and More Information

Android API Guides: "App Widgets":
  http://d.android.com/guide/topics/appwidgets/index.html
Android API Guides: "App Widget Host":
  http://d.android.com/guide/topics/appwidgets/host.html
Android API Guides: "App Widget Design Guidelines":
  http://d.android.com/guide/practices/ui_guidelines/widget_design.html
Android Design: "Widgets":
  http://d.android.com/design/patterns/widgets.html
Android Developers Blog: "Daydream: Interactive Screen Savers":
  http://android-developers.blogspot.com/2012/12/daydream-interactive-screen-savers.html
Android SDK Reference documentation on the `DreamService` class:
  http://d.android.com/reference/android/service/dreams/DreamService.html

## 27

Enabling Application Search

Android devices boast powerful search features, thanks to the search framework that was built into the Android SDK from the beginning. Application developers can enable search features in their applications in a variety of ways, including exposing app data on device-wide searches, providing relevant search suggestions, enabling voice search, and more. In this chapter, you will become familiar with some of the most common ways apps can leverage the Android search framework.

Making Application Content Searchable

If your application is content rich, either with content created by users or with content provided by you, the developer, integrating with the search capabilities of Android can provide many benefits and add value to the user. The application data becomes part of the overall device experience and is more accessible, and your application can be presented to users in more cases than just when they launch it.

Developers can implement powerful search features in their applications using the Android framework. There are two ways that search capabilities are generally added to Android applications:

- Applications implement a search framework that enables their activities to react to the user pressing the Search button, requesting a search, and performing searches on data within that application.

- Applications can expose their content for use in global, system-wide searches that include application and web content.

Search framework features include the capability to search for and access application data as search results, as well as the ability to provide suggestions as the user types search criteria. Applications can also provide an `Intent` to launch when a user selects specific search suggestions.

Tip

The code examples provided in this section are taken from the SimpleSearchIntegration application. The source code for this application is provided for download on the book's website.

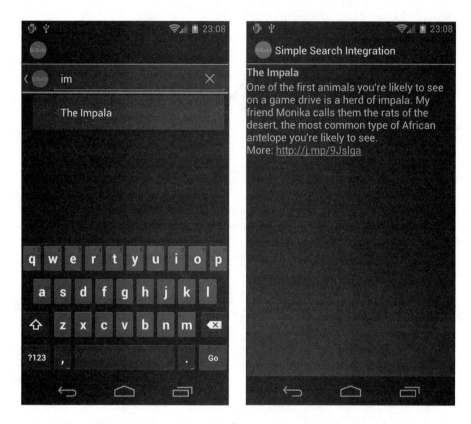

Figure 27.1   Handling in-application searches and search suggestions.

Let's revisit the African field notes application we discussed in the previous chapter. This application uses a simple content provider to supply information about game animals. Enabling search support in this application seems rational; it enables the user to quickly find information about a specific animal simply by pressing the Search button or using a search widget. When a result is found, the application needs to be able to apply an `Intent` for launching the appropriate screen to view that specific field note—the perfect time to implement a simple content type handler that enables the application to handle "view field note" actions, as shown in Figure 27.1.

Enabling Searches in Your Application

You need to make a number of changes in your application to enable searches. Although these changes might seem complex, the good news is that if you do them right, enabling global searches later is simple. Searching content generally necessitates that your application expose a content provider or, at the very least, that it has some sort of underlying database that can be searched in a systematic fashion.

Note

The search framework provided by the `SearchManager` class (`android.app.Search Manager`) does not actually perform the search queries—that is up to you, the developer. The `SearchManager` class simply manages search services and the search dialog controls. How and what data is searched and which results are returned are implementation details.

To enable in-application searches, you need to:

- Develop an application with data, ideally exposed as a content provider
- Create an XML search configuration file
- Implement an `Activity` class to handle searches
- Configure the application's Android manifest file for searches

Now let's look at each of these requirements in more detail.

Creating a Search Configuration

Creating a search configuration for your application simply means that you need to create an XML file with special search tags. This search configuration file is normally stored in the XML resource directory (for example, `/res/xml/searchable.xml`) and referenced in the searchable application's Android manifest file.

Enabling Basic Searches

The following is a sample search configuration that the field notes application might use, stored as an application resource file:

```xml
<?xml version="1.0" encoding="utf-8"?>
<searchable
    xmlns:android="http://schemas.android.com/apk/res/android"
    android:label="@string/app_name"
    android:hint="@string/search_hint"
    android:searchSettingsDescription="@string/search_settings_help">
</searchable>
```

The basic attributes of the search configuration are fairly straightforward. The `label` attribute is generally set to the name of your application (the application providing the search result). The `hint` attribute is the text that shows in the `EditText` control of the search box when no text has been entered—a prompt. You can further customize the search dialog by customizing the search button text and input method options, if desired.

Enabling Search Suggestions

If your application acts as a content provider and you want to enable search suggestions—those results provided in a list below the search box as the user types in search criteria—you must include several additional attributes in your search configuration. You need to specify information about the content provider used to supply the search suggestions, including its authority, path information, and the query to use to return search suggestions. You also need to provide information for the `Intent` to trigger when a user clicks on a specific suggestion.

Again, let's go back to the field notes example. Here are the search configuration attributes required to support search suggestions that query field note titles:

```
android:searchSuggestAuthority =
    "com.advancedandroidbook.simplesearchintegration.
        SimpleFieldnotesContentProvider"
android:searchSuggestPath="fieldnotes"
android:searchSuggestSelection="fieldnotes_title LIKE ?"
android:searchSuggestIntentAction="android.intent.action.VIEW"
android:searchSuggestIntentData=
    "content://com.advancedandroidbook.simplesearchintegration.
        SimpleFieldnotesContentProvider/fieldnotes"
```

The first attribute, `searchSuggestAuthority`, sets the content provider to use for the search suggestion query. The second attribute defines the path appended to the `Authority` and right before `SearchManager.SUGGEST_URI_PATH_QUERY` is appended to the `Authority`. The third attribute supplies the SQL WHERE clause of the search query (here, only the field note titles, not their bodies, are queried to keep search suggestion performance reasonably fast). Next, an `Intent` action is provided for when a user clicks a search suggestion, and then finally the `Uri` used to launch the `Intent` is defined.

You can also set a threshold (`android:searchSuggestThreshold`) on the number of characters the user needs to type before a search suggestion query is performed. Consider setting this value to a reasonable number like three or four characters to keep queries to a minimum (the default is 0). At a value of zero, even an empty search field shows suggestions—but these are not filtered at all.

Each time the user begins to type in search criteria, the system performs a content provider query to retrieve suggestions. Therefore, the application's content provider interface needs to be updated to handle these queries. In order to make this all work properly, you need to define a projection in order to map the content provider data columns to those that the search framework expects to use to fill the search suggestion list with content. For example, the following code defines a project to map the field note unique identifiers and titles to the `_ID`, `SUGGEST_COLUMN_TEXT_1`, and `SUGGEST_COLUMN_INTENT_DATA_ID` fields for the search suggestions:

```
private static final HashMap<String, String>
FIELDNOTES_SEARCH_SUGGEST_PROJECTION_MAP;
static {
    FIELDNOTES_SEARCH_SUGGEST_PROJECTION_MAP =
        new HashMap<String, String>();
    FIELDNOTES_SEARCH_SUGGEST_PROJECTION_MAP.put(_ID, _ID);
    FIELDNOTES_SEARCH_SUGGEST_PROJECTION_MAP.put(
        SearchManager.SUGGEST_COLUMN_TEXT_1, FIELDNOTES_TITLE + " AS "
        + SearchManager.SUGGEST_COLUMN_TEXT_1);
```

```
FIELDNOTES_SEARCH_SUGGEST_PROJECTION_MAP.put(
    SearchManager.SUGGEST_COLUMN_INTENT_DATA_ID, _ID + " AS "
    + SearchManager.SUGGEST_COLUMN_INTENT_DATA_ID);
}
```

Each time search suggestions need to be displayed, the system executes a query using the `Uri` provided as part of the search configuration. Don't forget to define this `Uri` and register it in the content provider's `UriMatcher` object (using the `addURI()` method). For example, the field notes application used the following URI for search suggestion queries:

```
content://com.advancedandroidbook.simplesearchintegration.
    SimpleFieldnotesContentProvider/fieldnotes/search_suggestion_query
```

By providing a special search suggestion `Uri` for the content provider queries, you can simply update the content provider's `query()` method to handle the specialized query, including building the projection, performing the appropriate query, and returning the results. Let's take a closer look at the field notes content provider `query()` method:

```
@Override
public Cursor query(Uri uri, String[] projection, String selection,
    String[] selectionArgs, String sortOrder) {
    SQLiteQueryBuilder queryBuilder = new SQLiteQueryBuilder();
    queryBuilder.setTables(SimpleFieldnotesDatabase.FIELDNOTES_TABLE);
    int match = sURIMatcher.match(uri);
    switch (match) {
    case FIELDNOTES_SEARCH_SUGGEST:
        selectionArgs = new String[] { "%" + selectionArgs[0] + "%" };
        queryBuilder.setProjectionMap(
            FIELDNOTES_SEARCH_SUGGEST_PROJECTION_MAP);
        break;
    case FIELDNOTES:
        break;
    case FIELDNOTE_ITEM:
        String id = uri.getLastPathSegment();
        queryBuilder.appendWhere(_ID + "=" + id);
        break;
    default:
        throw new IllegalArgumentException("Invalid URI: " + uri);
    }
    SQLiteDatabase sql = database.getReadableDatabase();
    Cursor cursor = queryBuilder.query(sql, projection, selection,
        selectionArgs, null, null, sortOrder);
    cursor.setNotificationUri(getContext().getContentResolver(), uri);
    return cursor;
}
```

This `query()` method implementation handles both regular content queries and special search suggestion queries (those that come in with the search suggestion `Uri`). When the search suggestion query occurs, we wrap the search criteria in wildcards and use the handy `setProjectionMap()` method of the `QueryBuilder` object to set and execute the query as normal. Because we want to return results quickly, we search only for titles matching the search criteria for suggestions, not the full text of the field notes.

Tip

Instead of using wildcards and a slow LIKE expression in SQLite, we could have used the SQLite FTS3 extension, which enables fast full-text queries. With a limited number of rows of data, this is not strictly necessary in our case, and it requires creating tables in a different and much less relational way. Indices are not supported, so query performance might suffer. See the SQLite FTS3 documentation at *http://www.sqlite.org/fts3.html*.

Enabling Voice Search

You can also add voice search capabilities to your application. This enables the user to speak the search criteria instead of type them. There are several attributes you can add to your search configuration to enable voice searches. The most important attribute is voice SearchMode, which enables voice searches and sets the appropriate mode. The showVoice SearchButton value enables the little voice recording button to display as part of the search dialog, the launchRecognizer value tells the Android system to use voice recording activity, and the launchWebSearch value initiates the special voice web search activity.

To add voice support to the field notes sample application, add the following line to the search configuration:

```
android:voiceSearchMode="showVoiceSearchButton|launchRecognizer"
```

Other voice search attributes you can set include the voice language model (free-form or web search), the voice language, the maximum voice results, and a text prompt for the voice recognition dialog.

Requesting a Search

Up until Android API Level 11, most Android devices had a physical Search button. From within your application, this button can be pressed and the search dialog comes up (Figure 27.1, left). The search dialog can also be triggered by calling the onSearchRequested() method of the Activity class.

With API Level 11 and later, the Search button is gone. Instead, developers must add a Search button to their applications. The best way to do this is with the SearchView class. With this class, an expandable search area can easily be added to the action bar. Take, for example, the following implementation of onCreateOptionsMenu(), found in the sample app:

```
@Override
public boolean onCreateOptionsMenu(Menu menu) {
    MenuInflater inflater = getMenuInflater();
    inflater.inflate(R.menu.menu, menu);

    SearchManager searchManager =
        (SearchManager) getSystemService(Context.SEARCH_SERVICE);
    SearchView searchView = (SearchView) menu.findItem(R.id.menu_search)
        .getActionView();
    searchView.setSearchableInfo(searchManager
        .getSearchableInfo(new ComponentName(this,
            SimpleSearchableActivity.class)));
    searchView.setIconifiedByDefault(true);
    return true;
}
```

Here's the corresponding menu resource file:

```xml
<?xml version="1.0" encoding="utf-8"?>
<menu xmlns:android="http://schemas.android.com/apk/res/android" >
    <item
        android:id="@+id/menu_search"
        android:actionViewClass="android.widget.SearchView"
        android:icon="@drawable/ic_menu_search"
        android:showAsAction="ifRoom|collapseActionView"
        android:title="@string/menu_search"/>
</menu>
```

The result of this `SearchView` configuration is shown in Figure 27.2. The action bar receives the menu item with the search icon (Figure 27.2, left). When the search item is clicked, the search field appears right in the action bar, and the suggestions appear below it (Figure 27.2, right).

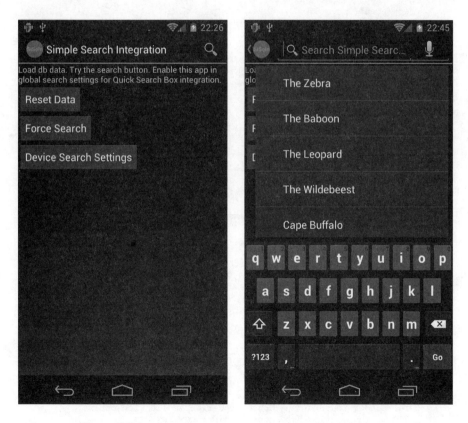

Figure 27.2   Use `SearchView` to search from the action bar.

Creating a Search `Activity`

Next, you need to implement an `Activity` class that actually performs the requested searches. This `Activity` is launched whenever your application receives an `Intent` with the action value of `ACTION_SEARCH`.

The search request contains the search string in the extra field called `SearchManager` `.QUERY`. The `Activity` takes this value, performs the search, and then responds with the results.

Let's look at the search `Activity` from our field notes example. You can implement its search `Activity`, `SimpleSearchableActivity`, as follows:

```
public class SimpleSearchableActivity extends ListActivity {
    @Override
    protected void onCreate(Bundle savedInstanceState) {
        super.onCreate(savedInstanceState);
        Intent intent = getIntent();
        checkIntent(intent);
    }

    @Override
    protected void onNewIntent(Intent newIntent) {
        // update the activity launch intent
        setIntent(newIntent);
        // handle it
        checkIntent(newIntent);
    }

    private void checkIntent(Intent intent) {
        String query = "";
        String intentAction = intent.getAction();
        if (Intent.ACTION_SEARCH.equals(intentAction)) {
            query = intent.getStringExtra(SearchManager.QUERY);
            Toast.makeText(this,
                "Search received: " + query, Toast.LENGTH_LONG)
                .show();
        } else if (Intent.ACTION_VIEW.equals(intentAction)) {
            // pass this off to the details view activity
            Uri details = intent.getData();
            Intent detailsIntent =
                new Intent(Intent.ACTION_VIEW, details);
            startActivity(detailsIntent);
            finish();
            return;
        }
        fillList(query);
    }

    private void fillList(String query) {
        String wildcardQuery = "%" + query + "%";
        CursorLoader loader = new CursorLoader(getApplicationContext(),
            SimpleFieldnotesContentProvider.CONTENT_URI, null,
            SimpleFieldnotesContentProvider.FIELDNOTES_TITLE +
            " LIKE ? OR " +
            SimpleFieldnotesContentProvider.FIELDNOTES_BODY + " LIKE ?",
            new String[] { wildcardQuery, wildcardQuery }, null);
```

```
        Cursor cursor = loader.loadInBackground();
        ListAdapter adapter = new SimpleCursorAdapter(this,
                android.R.layout.simple_list_item_1, cursor,
                new String[] { SimpleFieldnotesContentProvider.
                        FIELDNOTES_TITLE },
                new int[] { android.R.id.text1 });

        setListAdapter(adapter);
    }

    @Override
    protected void onListItemClick(
        ListView l, View v, int position, long id) {
        Uri details = Uri.withAppendedPath(
            SimpleFieldnotesContentProvider.CONTENT_URI, "" + id);
        Intent intent =
            new Intent(Intent.ACTION_VIEW, details);
        startActivity(intent);
    }
}
```

Both the onCreate() and onNewIntent() methods are implemented because the Activity is flagged with a launchMode set to singleTop. This Activity is capable of bringing up the search dialog when the user presses the Search button, like the rest of the activities in this example. When the user performs a search, the system launches the SimpleSearchableActivity—the same Activity the user was already viewing. We don't want to create a huge stack of search result activities, so we don't let it have more than one instance on top of the stack—thus the singleTop setting.

Handling the search is fairly straightforward. We use the search term provided for us to create a CursorLoader. Using the loader.loadInBackground() call, the results are obtained as a Cursor object that is then used with the SimpleCursorAdapter object to fill the ListView control of the Activity class.

For list item click handling, the implementation here simply creates a new VIEW intent and, effectively, lets the system handle the item clicking. In this case, the details Activity handles the displaying of the proper field note. Why do this instead of launching the class Activity directly? No reason other than it's simple and it's well tested from other uses of this launch style.

When a user clicks on a suggestion in the list, instead of an ACTION_SEARCH, this Activity receives the usual ACTION_VIEW. Instead of handling it here, though, it's passed on to the details view Activity as that Activity is already designed to handle the drawing of the details for each item—there's no reason to implement it twice.

Configuring the Android Manifest File for Search

Now it's time to register your searchable Activity class in the application manifest file, including configuring the intent filter associated with the ACTION_SEARCH action. You also need to mark your application as searchable using a <meta-data> manifest file tag.

Here is the Android manifest file excerpt for the searchable `Activity` registration:

```
<activity
    android:name="SimpleSearchableActivity"
    android:launchMode="singleTop">
    <intent-filter>
        <action android:name="android.intent.action.SEARCH" />
    </intent-filter>
    <intent-filter>
        <action android:name="android.intent.action.VIEW" />
    </intent-filter>
    <meta-data
        android:name="android.app.searchable"
        android:resource="@xml/searchable" />
</activity>
```

The main difference between this `<activity>` tag configuration and a typical `Activity` is the addition of the intent filter for intents with an action type of `SEARCH`. In addition, some metadata is provided so that the system knows where to find the search configuration details.

Next, let's look at an example of how to enable the Search button for all activities in the application. This `<meta-data>` block needs to be added to the `<application>` tag, outside any `<activity>` tags:

```
<meta-data
    android:name="android.app.default_searchable"
    android:value =
        "com.advancedandroidbook.simplesearchintegration.
            SimpleSearchableActivity" />
```

This `<meta-data>` tag configures the default `Activity` that handles the search results for the entire application. This way, pressing the Search button brings up the search dialog from any `Activity` in the application. If you don't want this functionality in every `Activity`, you need to add this definition to each `Activity` for which you do want the Search button enabled.

Note

Not all Android devices have a Search button. If you want to guarantee search abilities within the application, consider adding other ways to initiate a search, such as adding a Search button to the application screen or providing the search option on the options menu.

Enabling Global Search

After you have enabled your application for searches, you can make it part of the global device search feature with a few extra steps. Global searches are often invoked using the Quick Search Box. In order to enable your application for global search, you need to:

- Begin with an application that already has in-application search capabilities as described earlier
- Update the search configuration file to enable global searches
- Include your application in global searches by updating the Search settings of the device

Now let's look at these requirements in a bit more detail. Let's assume we're working with the same sample application—the field notes.

Updating a Search Configuration for Global Searches

Updating an existing search configuration is simple. All you need to do is add the `include InGlobalSearch` attribute in your configuration and set it to `true` as follows:

```
android:includeInGlobalSearch="true"
```

At this point, you should also ensure that your application is acting as a content type handler for the results you provide as part of global searches (if you haven't already). That way, users can select search suggestions provided by your application. Again, you probably want to leverage the content type handler functionality again, in order to launch the application when a search suggestion is chosen.

Tip

You can initiate a global search using the `SearchManager.INTENT_ACTION_GLOBAL_SEARCH` intent.

Updating Search Settings for Global Searches

However, the user has ultimate control over what information is included as part of the global search. Your applications are not included in global searches by default. The user must include applications explicitly. For your application to show up as part of global searches, the user must adjust the device Search settings. The user makes this configuration from the device Search settings page.

If your application is appropriate for global searches, you might want to include a shortcut to these settings so that users can easily navigate to them without feeling like they've left your application. The `SearchManager` class has an `Intent` called `INTENT_ACTION_SEARCH_SETTINGS` for this purpose:

```
Intent intent = new Intent(SearchManager.INTENT_ACTION_SEARCH_SETTINGS);
startActivity(intent);
```

This `Intent` launches the Settings application on the Search settings screen. As you can see, searches—whether they are in-application searches or global searches—allow applications and content to be exposed in new and interesting ways so that the user's data is always just a few keystrokes (or spoken words) away.

Tip

Each device may have a different way of navigating to the Search settings screen, so you may need to browse through your device manual to learn how to reach these settings. One possible way to reach these settings is to navigate to the Google account settings you configured for your device and look for Search settings there.

Summary

The Android search framework enables applications to expose their data so that the user can find information easily and efficiently through a consistent interface. Applications can enable in-application searches, search suggestions, voice searching, and more. Often, applications with content providers and application databases are the simplest to enable for search, so using these common design practices will work to your advantage.

Quiz Questions

1. True or false: The `<searchable>` attribute `searchSuggestAuthority` sets the content provider to use for a search suggestion query.

2. What `<searchable>` attribute would you set to require a certain number of characters to be typed by the user before a search suggestion query is performed?

3. How would you add voice support to the field notes sample application with web search?

4. True or false: The `SearchButton` class is used to add a Search button to an application.

5. What `<searchable>` attribute and value must you declare to include your application in global search?

Exercises

1. Use the Android documentation to determine what type of `Cursor` you would use if your search suggestions are not stored in a SQLite table or table format.

2. Use the Android documentation to determine what `<path-permission>` you would need to set if your content provider requires a read permission.

References and More Information

Android Training: "Adding Search Functionality":
   http://d.android.com/training/search/index.html
Android API Guides: "Search Overview":
   http://d.android.com/guide/topics/search/index.html
Android SDK Reference documentation on the `SearchManager` class:
   http://d.android.com/reference/android/app/SearchManager.html
Android SDK Reference documentation on the `SearchView` class:
   http://d.android.com/reference/android/widget/SearchView.html
Android SDK Reference documentation on the `SearchRecentSuggestions` class:
   http://d.android.com/reference/android/provider/SearchRecentSuggestions.html

## 28

Managing User Accounts and Synchronizing User Data

Android is cloud friendly. Android applications can integrate tightly with remote services, helping users transition seamlessly. Android applications can synchronize data with remote cloud-based (Internet) services using sync adapters. Developers can also take advantage of Android's cloud-based backup service to protect and migrate application data safely and effectively. In this chapter, you will learn about the account and synchronization features used to sync data to built-in applications and how to protect application data using the backup and restore features available in Android.

Managing Accounts with the Account Manager

From a user perspective, the Android 2.0 platform introduced many exciting new device features. For instance, the user can register and use multiple accounts for email and contact management. This feature was provided through a combination of new synchronization and account services that are also available to developers. Although you can use the account and synchronization packages with any kind of data, the intention seems to be to provide a way for developers and companies to integrate their business services with the system that synchronizes data to the built-in Android applications.

Android user accounts are manipulated using the classes available in the `android.accounts` package. This functionality is primarily designed for accounts with services that contain contact, email, or other such information. A good example of this type of online service is a social networking application that contains friends' contact information, as well as other relevant information such as their statuses. This information is often delivered and used on an Android device using the synchronization service (we talk more about synchronization later in the chapter).

First, we talk about accounts. Accounts registered with the Android account manager should provide access to the same sort of information—contact information, for the most part. Different accounts can be registered for a given user using the Android `AccountManager` class. Each account contains authentication information for a service, usually credentials for a server account somewhere online. Android services, such as the synchronization services built into the platform, can access these accounts, mining them for the appropriate types of information (again, primarily contact details, but also other bits of data such as social networking status).

Let's look at how using account information provided via the `AccountManager` and `Account` classes works. An application that needs to access the server can request a list of accounts from the system. If one of the accounts contains credentials for the server, the application can request an authentication token (auth token, for short) for the account. The application would then use this token as a way to log in to the remote server to access its services. This keeps the user credentials secure and private while also providing a convenience to users in that they need to provide their credentials only once, regardless of how many applications use the information. All these tasks are achieved using the `AccountManager` class. A call to the `getAccountByType()` method retrieves a list of accounts, and then a call to the `getAuthToken()` method retrieves the token associated with a specific account, which the application can use to communicate with a password-protected resource, such as a web service.

On the other side of this process, authenticating credentials against the back-end server are the account providers, that is, the services that provide users with accounts and with which user information is authenticated so the applications can get the auth tokens. In order to do all of this (handle system requests to authenticate an `Account` object against the remote server), the account provider must implement an account authenticator. Through the authenticator, the account provider requests appropriate credentials and then confirms them with whatever account authentication operations are necessary—usually an online server. To implement an account authenticator, you need to make several modifications to your application. Begin by implementing the `AbstractAccountAuthenticator` class. You also need to update the application's Android manifest file, provide an authenticator configuration file (XML), and provide an authenticator preference screen configuration in order to make the authentication experience as seamless as possible for the user.

Tip

Learn more about creating system-wide accounts in the Android SDK documentation for the `AbstractAccountAuthenticator` class. Learn more about using accounts in the Android SDK documentation for the `AccountManager` class. Also see the Google Play services documentation on "Authorization" (*http://d.android.com/google/play-services/ auth.html*).

Multiple Users, Restricted Profiles, and Accounts

Android 4.2 (API Level 17) added the ability to create multiple user spaces on Android devices. This allows each user of a particular device to have his or her own separate area where applications, accounts, data, and other information are stored. There are no changes to make within your application for managing accounts when working with multiple users.

In addition to multiple users, Android 4.3 (API Level 18) introduced what is known as restricted profiles for tablets. A restricted profile is a configurable profile based on the primary user of the device, allowing for setting restrictions such as limiting access to certain applications, or even more fine-grained control such as restricting certain features within a particular application. If your application requires access to accounts, keep the following in mind:

- If you would like to access the primary user's account from within a restricted profile, add the `android:restrictedAccountType` attribute to the `<application>` tag in the Android manifest. Understand that this setting grants access to the primary user's accounts from the restricted profile, so care must be taken not to expose personally identifiable information in cases where a restricted profile may be for a user other than the primary user.

- If you are not able to access any existing accounts on the device or are unable to create your own account for the restricted profile, make sure to disable features within your application that require account access; that way other features of your application will still be available to the restricted profile.

- If you are not able to access private accounts on the device, add the `android:requiredAccountType` attribute to the `<application>` tag in the Android manifest. Understand that this will prevent your application from being available to restricted profiles.

Synchronizing Data with Sync Adapters

The synchronization feature available in the Android SDK requires the use of the accounts classes we talked about earlier. This service is principally designed to enable syncing of contact, email, and calendar data to the built-in applications from a back-end data store—you're "adapting" back-end server data to the existing content providers. In other words, the service is not generally used for syncing data specific to your typical Android application. In theory, applications can use this service to keep generic data in sync, but they might be better served by implementing synchronization internally. You can do this using the `AlarmManager` class to schedule systematic data synchronization via the network, perhaps using an Android `Service`.

If, however, you are working with data that is well suited to syncing to the internal applications, such as contacts or calendar information that you want to put in the built-in applications and content providers, implementing a sync adapter makes sense. This enables the Android system to manage synchronization activities.

The account service must provide the sync adapter by extending the `AbstractThreadedSyncAdapter` class. When the sync occurs, the `onPerformSync()` method of the sync adapter is called. The parameters to this method tell the adapter what account (as defined by the `Account` parameter) is being used, thus providing necessary auth tokens for accessing protected resources without having to ask the user for credentials. The adapter is also told which content provider to write the data to and to which authority, in the content provider sense, the data belongs.

In this way, synchronization operations are performed on their own thread at a time requested by the system. During the sync, the adapter gets updated information from the server and synchronizes it to the given content provider. The implementation details for this are flexible and up to the developer.

Tip

Learn more about creating sync adapters by checking out the "Creating a Sync Adapter" Training guide on the Android developer website: *http://d.android.com/training/ sync-adapters/creating-sync-adapter.html.*

Using Backup Services

Android backup services were introduced in Android 2.2 (API Level 8). Applications can use the backup system service to request that application data such as shared preferences and files be backed up or restored. The backup service handles things from there, sending the appropriate backup archives to a remote backup service or retrieving them from the service.

Backup services should not be used for syncing application content. Backup and restore operations do not occur on demand. Use a synchronization strategy such as the sync adapter discussed earlier in this chapter in this case. Use Android backup services only to back up important application data.

Tip

Many of the code examples provided in this section are taken from the SimpleBackup application. The source code for this application is provided for download on the book's website. Also, you need to use the `adb bmgr` command to force backups and restores to occur. For more information on `adb`, see Appendix A, "Quick-Start Guide: Android Debug Bridge."

Choosing a Remote Backup Service

One of the most important decisions when it comes to backing up application data is where to back it up to. The remote backup service you choose should be secure, reliable, and always available. Many developers will likely choose the solution provided by Google: Android Backup Service.

Note

Other third-party remote backup services might be available. If you want complete control over the backup process, you might want to consider creating your own. However, that is beyond the scope of this book.

For your application to use Android Backup Service, you must register your application with Google and acquire a unique backup service key for use within the application's manifest file. You can sign up for Google's backup service at the Android Backup Service website: *https://developer.android.com/google/backup/signup.html.*

Warning

Backup services are available on most, but not all, Android devices running Android 2.2 and higher. The underlying implementation might vary. Also, different remote backup services might impose additional limitations on the devices supported. Test your specific target devices and backup solution thoroughly to determine that backup services function properly with your application.

Registering with Android Backup Service

After you have chosen a remote backup service, you might need to jump through a few more hoops. With Google's Android Backup Service, you need to register for a special key to use. After you've acquired this key, you can use it in your application's manifest file using the `<meta-data>` tag in the `<application>` block, like this:

```
<meta-data android:name="com.google.android.backup.api_key"
    android:value="KEY HERE" />
```

Implementing a Backup Agent

The backup system service relies on an application's backup agent to determine what application data should be archived for backup and restore purposes.

Providing a Backup Agent Implementation

Now it's time to implement the backup agent for your particular application. The backup agent determines what application data to send to the backup service. If you want to back up only shared preference data and application files, you can simply use the `BackupAgent Helper` class.

Tip

If you need to customize how your application backs up its data, you need to extend the `BackupAgent` class, which requires you to implement two callback methods. The `onBackup()` method is called when your application requests a backup and provides the backup service with the appropriate application data to back up. The `onRestore()` method is called when a restore is requested. The backup service supplies the archived data, and the `onRestore()` method handles restoring the application data.

Here is a sample implementation of a backup agent class:

```
public class SimpleBackupAgent extends BackupAgentHelper {
    @Override
    public void onCreate() {
        // Register helpers here
    }
}
```

Your application's backup agent needs to include a backup helper for each type of data it wants to back up.

Implementing a Backup Helper for Shared Preferences

To back up shared preferences files, you need to use the `SharedPreferencesBackup Helper` class. Adding support for shared preferences is straightforward. Simply update the backup agent's `onCreate()` method, create a valid `SharedPreferencesBackupHelper` object, and use the `addHelper()` method to add it to the agent:

```
SharedPreferencesBackupHelper prefshelper =
      new SharedPreferencesBackupHelper(this,
PREFERENCE_FILENAME);
addHelper(BACKUP_PREFERENCE_KEY, prefshelper);
```

This particular helper backs up all shared preferences by name. In this case, the `addHelper()` method takes two parameters:

- A unique name for this helper (in this case, the backup key is stored as a `String` variable called `BACKUP_PREFERENCE_KEY`)

- A valid `SharedPreferencesBackupHelper` object configured to control backups and restores on a specific set of shared preferences by name (in this case, the preference filename is stored in a `String` variable called `PREFERENCE_FILENAME`)

That's it. In fact, if your application is backing up only shared preferences, you don't even need to implement the `onBackup()` and `onRestore()` methods of your backup agent class.

Tip

Got more than one set of preferences? No problem. The constructor for `SharedPreferencesBackupHelper` can take any number of preference filenames. You still need only one unique name key for the helper.

Implementing a Backup Helper for Files

To back up application files, use the `FileBackupHelper` class. Files are a bit trickier to handle than shared preferences because they are not thread-safe. Begin by updating the backup agent's `onCreate()` method, create a valid `FileBackupHelper` object, and use the `addHelper()` method to add it to the agent:

```
FileBackupHelper filehelper = new FileBackupHelper(this, APP_FILE_NAME);
addHelper(BACKUP_FILE_KEY, filehelper);
```

The file helper backs up specific files by name. In this case, the `addHelper()` method takes two parameters:

- A unique name for this helper (in this case, the backup key is stored as a `String` variable called `BACKUP_FILE_KEY`)

- A valid `FileBackupHelper` object configured to control backups and restores on a specific file by name (in this case, the filename is stored in a `String` variable called `APP_FILE_NAME`)

> **Tip**
>
> Got more than one file to back up? No problem. The constructor for `FileBackupHelper` can take any number of filenames. You still need only one unique name key for the helper. The services were designed to back up configuration data, not necessarily all files or media. There are currently no guidelines for the size of the data that can be backed up. For instance, a book reader application might back up book titles and reading states, but not the book contents. Then, after a restore, the data can be used to download the book contents again. To the user, the state appears the same. This type of backup is intended for state and configuration files, not large data files, though.

You also need to make sure that all file operations in your application are thread-safe as it's possible a backup will be requested while a file is being accessed. The Android website suggests the following method for defining a lock from a simple `Object` array within an `Activity`:

```
static final Object[] fileLock = new Object[0];
```

Use this lock each and every time you perform file operations, either in your application logic or in the backup agent. For example:

```
synchronized(fileLock){
    // Do app logic file operations here
}
```

Finally, you need to override the `onBackup()` and `onRestore()` methods of your backup agent, if only to make sure all file operations are synchronized using your lock for thread-safe access. Here we have the full implementation of a backup agent that backs up one set of shared preferences called `AppPrefs` and a file named `appfile.txt`:

```
public class SimpleBackupAgent extends BackupAgentHelper {
    private static final String PREFERENCE_FILENAME = "AppPrefs";
    private static final String APP_FILE_NAME = "appfile.txt";
    static final String BACKUP_PREFERENCE_KEY = "BackupAppPrefs";
    static final String BACKUP_FILE_KEY = "BackupFile";

    @Override
    public void onCreate() {
        SharedPreferencesBackupHelper prefshelper = new
            SharedPreferencesBackupHelper(this,
            PREFERENCE_FILENAME);
        addHelper(BACKUP_PREFERENCE_KEY, prefshelper);
        FileBackupHelper filehelper =
            new FileBackupHelper(this, APP_FILE_NAME);
        addHelper(BACKUP_FILE_KEY, filehelper);
    }
    @Override
    public void onBackup(ParcelFileDescriptor oldState,
        BackupDataOutput data, ParcelFileDescriptor newState)
        throws IOException {
            synchronized (SimpleBackupActivity.fileLock) {
                super.onBackup(oldState, data, newState);
            }
    }
```

```
    @Override
    public void onRestore(BackupDataInput data, int appVersionCode,
        ParcelFileDescriptor newState) throws IOException {
            synchronized (SimpleBackupActivity.fileLock) {
                super.onRestore(data, appVersionCode, newState);
            }
    }
}
```

To make the onBackup() and onRestore() methods thread-safe, we simply wrapped the superclass call with a synchronized block using a file lock.

Registering the Backup Agent in the Application Manifest File

Finally, you need to register your backup agent class in your application's manifest file using the android:backupAgent attribute of the <application> tab. For example, if your backup agent class is called SimpleBackupAgent, you register it using its fully qualified path name as follows:

```
<application
    android:icon="@drawable/icon"
    android:label="@string/app_name"
    android:backupAgent=
        "com.advancedandroidbook.simplebackup.SimpleBackupAgent">
```

Backing Up and Restoring Application Data

The BackupManager system service manages backup and restore requests. This service works in the background, on its own schedule. Applications that implement a backup agent can request a backup or restore, but the operations might not happen immediately. To get an instance of the BackupManager, simply create one in your Activity class, as follows:

```
BackupManager mBackupManager = new BackupManager(this);
```

Requesting a Backup

An application can request a backup using the dataChanged() method. Generally, this method should be called any time application data that is to be archived changes. It can be called any number of times, but when it's time to back up, the backup takes place only one time, regardless of how many times dataChanged() was called before the backup.

```
mBackupManager.dataChanged();
```

Normally, the user does not initiate a backup. Instead, whenever important application data changes, the dataChanged() method should be called as part of the data-saving process. At some point in the future, a backup is performed "behind the scenes" by the backup manager.

Warning

Avoid backing up sensitive data to remote servers. Ultimately, you, the developer, are responsible for securing user data, not the backup service you employ. Although some services might encrypt data for you, if the data is sensitive to you or your users, you can always add a layer of encryption yourself.

Requesting a Restore

Restore operations occur automatically when a user resets his or her device or upgrades after "accidentally" dropping the old one in a hot tub or running it through the washing machine (it happens more often than you'd think). When a restore occurs, the user's data is fetched from the remote backup service, and the application's backup agent refreshes the data used by the application, overwriting any data that was there.

An application can directly request a restore using the `requestRestore()` method as well. The `requestRestore()` method takes one parameter: a `RestoreObserver` object. The following code illustrates how to request a restore:

```
RestoreObserver obs = new RestoreObserver(){
    @Override
    public void onUpdate(int nowBeingRestored, String currentPackage) {
        Log.i(DEBUG_TAG, "RESTORING: " + currentPackage);
    }

    @Override
    public void restoreFinished(int error) {
        Log.i(DEBUG_TAG, "RESTORE FINISHED! (" + error +")");
    }

    @Override
    public void restoreStarting(int numPackages) {
        Log.i(DEBUG_TAG, "RESTORE STARTING...");
    }
};

try {
    mBackupManager.requestRestore(obs);
} catch (Exception e) {
    Log.i(DEBUG_TAG,
        "Failed to request restore. Try adb bmgr restore...");
}
```

Tip

Testing of backup services is best done on a device running Android 2.2 or later, in conjunction with the `adb bmgr` command, which can force an immediate backup or restore to occur.

Summary

Android applications do not exist in a vacuum. Users demand that their data be accessible (securely, of course) across any and all technologies they use regularly. Phones fall into hot tubs (more often than you'd think), and users upgrade to newer devices. The Android platform provides services for keeping local application data synchronized with remote cloud services and for protecting application data using remote backup and restore services.

Quiz Questions

1. True or false: Use the `AccountManager` class to register different accounts for a given user.

2. What Android manifest `<application>` tag attribute do you need to include to disable your application from accessing the primary user account?

3. What class do you extend for implementing a sync adapter?

4. What methods do you need to override for implementing a `BackupAgentHelper` class?

5. True or false: You must define the `android:backupAgent` attribute in the `<activity>` tag of your application's manifest file.

Exercises

1. Create an application that creates a user account for the device.

2. Create an application that supports accounts in a restricted profile environment following the considerations recommended in this chapter.

3. Read the Android documentation to determine how you would override the aborting of a restore operation when an application version is detected that is newer than what was originally backed up.

References and More Information

Wikipedia on cloud computing:
http://en.wikipedia.org/wiki/Cloud_computing

Android Reference documentation on the `AccountManager` class:
http://d.android.com/reference/android/accounts/AccountManager.html

Android Google Services: "Authorization":
http://d.android.com/google/play-services/auth.html

Android Training: "Creating a Sync Adapter":
http://d.android.com/training/sync-adapters/creating-sync-adapter.html

Android Training: "Running a Sync Adapter":
http://d.android.com/training/sync-adapters/running-sync-adapter.html

Android Training: "Using the Backup API":
http://d.android.com/training/cloudsync/backupapi.html

Android API Guides: "Data Backup":
http://d.android.com/guide/topics/data/backup.html

Android Google Services: "Android Backup Service":
http://d.android.com/google/backup/index.html

VII

Advanced Topics in Application Publication and Distribution

29

Internationalizing
Your Applications

There are now hundreds of Android devices on the market worldwide. In this chapter, you will learn how to design and develop Android applications for foreign users and markets. This involves following design principles that make for easy internationalization, such as using alternative string resources for different languages and leveraging locale-aware classes for format-sensitive data such as date and time formats. Finally, we talk a bit about publishing applications in foreign countries.

Localizing Your Application's Language

Android users hail from many different parts of the world. They speak different languages, use different currencies, and format their dates in different ways—just to name a few examples. Android application internationalization generally falls into three categories:

- Providing alternative resources such as strings or graphics for use when the application runs in different languages
- Implementing locale-independent or locale-specific code and other programmatic concerns
- Configuring your application for sale in foreign markets

We already discussed how to use alternative resources in *Introduction to Android Application Development: Android Essentials, Fourth Edition*, but perhaps another example is in order. Let's look at an application that loads resources based upon the device language settings. Specifically, let's consider a simple application that loads different string and graphic resources based on the language and region settings of the device.

Internationalization Using Alternative Resources

Let's look at two examples of how to use alternative resources—this time, to localize an application for a variety of different languages and locales. By language, we mean the linguistic variety such as English, French, Spanish, German, Japanese, and so on. By locale, we are getting more specific, such as English (United States) versus English (United Kingdom) or English (Australia). There are times when you can get away with just providing language resources (English is English is English, right?) and times when this just won't work.

Our first example is theoretical. If you want your application to support both English and French strings (in addition to the default strings), you can simply create two additional resource directories called /res/values-en (for the English strings.xml) and /res/values-fr (for the French strings.xml). Within the strings.xml files, the resource names are the same. For example, the /res/values-en/strings.xml file can look like this:

```
<?xml version="1.0" encoding="utf-8"?>
<resources>
    <string name="hello">Hello in English!</string>
</resources>
```

Whereas the /res/values-fr/strings.xml file would look like this:

```
<?xml version="1.0" encoding="utf-8"?>
<resources>
    <string name="hello">Bonjour en Français!</string>
</resources>
```

A default layout file in the /res/layout directory that displays the string refers to the string by the variable name @string/hello, without regard to which language or directory the string resource is in. The Android operating system determines which version of the string (French, English, or default) to load at runtime. A layout with a TextView control to display the string might look like this:

```
<?xml version="1.0" encoding="utf-8"?>
<LinearLayout
    xmlns:android="http://schemas.android.com/apk/res/android"
    android:orientation="vertical"
    android:layout_width="match_parent"
    android:layout_height="match_parent">
    <TextView
        android:layout_width="match_parent"
        android:layout_height="match_parent"
        android:text="@string/hello" >
</LinearLayout>
```

The string is accessed programmatically in the normal way:

```
String str = getString(R.string.hello);
```

It's as easy as that. So, we move on to a more complex example, which illustrates how you can organize alternative application resources to provide functionality based on the device language and locale.

Tip

The code examples provided in this section are taken from the SimpleInternationalization application. The source code for this application is provided for download on the book's website.

Again, this application has no real code to speak of. Instead, all interesting function-ality depends upon the judicious and clever use of resource folder qualifiers to specify resources to load. These resources are:

- The default resources for this application include the application icon stored in the /res/drawable directory, the layout file stored in the /res/layout directory, and the strings.xml string resources stored in the /res/values directory. These resources are loaded whenever there isn't a more specific resource available to load. They are the fallbacks.

- There are English string resources stored in the /res/values-en directory. If the device language is English, these strings load for use in the default layout.

- There are French Canadian string resources stored in the /res/values-fr-rCA directory. If the device language and locale are set to French (Canada), these strings load for use within the layout. But wait! There's also an alternative layout stored in the /res/layout-fr-rCA directory, and this alternative layout uses a special draw-able graphic (the Quebec flag) stored in the /res/drawable-fr-rCA directory.

- Finally, there are French string resources stored in the /res/values-fr directory. If the device language is French (any locale except Canada), these strings load for use in the default layout.

In this way, the application loads different resources based on the language and locale information, as shown in Figure 29.1. This figure shows the project layout, in terms

Figure 29.1   Using alternative resources for different language string resources. Locales set to (clockwise from top left) English (any), French (any but Canadian), anything but French or English, and French Canadian.

of resources, and what the screen might look like when the device settings are set to different languages and locales.

Changing the Language Settings

Generally, a device ships in a default language. In the United States, this language is English (United States). Users who purchase devices in France, however, are likely to have a default language setting of French (France), while those in Britain and many British territories would likely have the language set to English (United Kingdom)—that said, Australia and New Zealand have their own English settings and Canada has both an English (Canada) language option and a French (Canada) option.

To change the locale setting on the emulator or the device, you need to perform the following steps:

1. Navigate to the Home screen.
2. Press the All Apps button.
3. Choose the Settings option.
4. Scroll down and choose the Language & input settings.
5. Choose the Language option (see Figure 29.2, top).
6. Select the locale you want to change the system to, for example, French (France), English (United States), or English (United Kingdom) (see Figure 29.2, bottom).

Make sure you memorize the steps (and related icons) required to change the language settings, as you need to navigate back to this screen in that foreign language in order to change the settings back. Figure 29.3 shows the Language Settings menu in French (Canada). If you do not remember the steps you took to change the language, you may have a hard time understanding how to change the language back to your own.

Tip

You can also create custom locales for testing using the Custom Locale application, available on the Android emulator. For example, you might want to create a Spanish locale for Mexico. When you use a custom locale, the emulator displays in its default language, but the current locale is detected as your custom locale, allowing you to localize your application.

Internationalization forces design choices on the development team. For example, will you build one big project for all languages, or will you break the applications up by region? For some projects with light internationalization, you might be able to get away with one project with all internationalized resources. For deep internationalization, you might need to reorganize projects so that no application becomes too large or cumbersome for the user.

Because much of the work for application localization revolves around alternative resources, this means that this work might fall not to a developer who knows how to use the Android IDE and the Android tools well, but to a designer who needs some training on

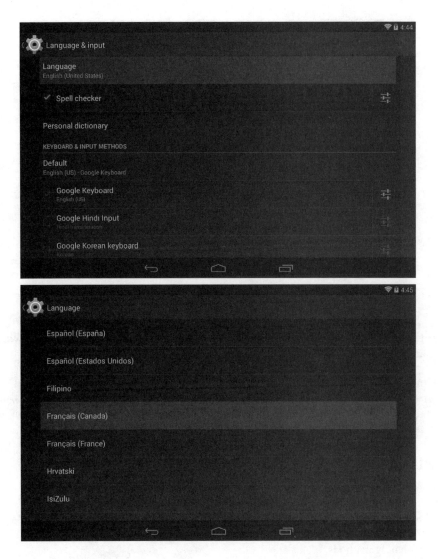

Figure 29.2   Changing device language settings
from English to French (Canada).

how Android internationalization works, how resources can be layered, and the drawbacks
of over-internationalizing (resulting in large package files with many graphics and such). On
the plus side, this leaves developers free to do what they do best: developing code.

Finally, you've likely noticed that the Android alternative resource structure isn't
perfect—especially for countries with multiple official (and unofficial) languages. It is possible to work around these issues, when necessary, by loading graphics programmatically

Figure 29.3   The Language Settings menu in French.

based on the current locale setting on the device, but this should be attempted only when absolutely necessary.

Tip

While testing on real hardware is the only way to be sure that your internationalization works the way you expect, the Graphical Layout designer in the Android IDE allows you to preview alternative resources.

Implementing Locale Support Programmatically

There are times when you should ensure that your application code is "locale aware." Often, this means writing code that is flexible enough to run smoothly regardless of the locale. However, when your application needs to be locale aware—for example, to download appropriate content from a remote application server—you should rely on locale-friendly methods.

Tip

To determine the device locale, developers can use the `getDefault()` method of the `java.util.Locale` class. Similarly, you can use the `getAvailableLocales()` method to retrieve a list of locales available on the device. Not all locales are supported on all devices; device manufacturers and operators might include only a subset of all locales supported by the Android operating system. For example, you might see devices sold in the United States that support only English and Spanish. You might also want to check out the `android.content.res.Configuration` class for more information on device configuration, including locale settings.

Here are some pointers for developing applications that work in a variety of locales:

- Begin by accepting that different parts of the world have different ways of expressing common information. Respect these differences and support them when feasible.

- Apply standard methods for internationalizing Java applications.

- Most localization issues with application code revolve around the use and formatting of strings, numbers, currencies, dates, and times. Audio and video containing speech are also routinely localized.

- Don't make assumptions about character encodings or what locale your application runs in.

- Always use locale-friendly methods when they are available. Often, a class has two versions of a method: one that uses the current locale and another that includes a `Locale` parameter that you can use when necessary to override behavior.

Tip

There are a number of utility classes and methods provided in the Android SDK for a locale- and region-specific string (start with the `String.format()` method), date manipulation (start with the `java.text.DateFormat` utility class), and phone number formatting (start with the `android.telephony.PhoneNumberUtils` class). Note also that many classes have methods that take a `Locale` parameter, enabling the developer to override behavior for other than the current locale.

Right-to-Left Language Localization

Android 4.2 (API Level 17) introduced a new set of APIs for supporting layouts and languages that are read from right to left (RTL), such as Hebrew and Arabic. RTL layouts are easy to add by setting the `android:supportsRtl` attribute to `true` for the `<application>` tag in your manifest file. When this attribute is set to `true`, various UI components that were previously displayed on the left side will now appear on the right, such as the application icon and title displayed within the action bar, in addition to reversing any `View` classes within your layout.

Further enhancements were added in Android 4.3 (API Level 18) for cases where mixed-direction text needs to be displayed, to ensure proper formatting. Information such as street addresses was difficult to display properly in an RTL layout, so the `Bidi Formatter` utility class was added to help with the directionality of text displayed partially in a left-to-right manner mixed with right-to-left text.

Translation Services through Google Play

The more language translations your application supports, the more users your application will be able to reach. Unless you are able to speak many languages, chances are that you require help translating your application into languages other than what you know.

Fortunately, Google added some great features to the Developer Console to make the process of translating applications much smoother, as part of a new pilot program Google is testing.

Using the Developer Console

To make use of the translation services, you must be using the ADT Bundle which includes the ADT Translation Manager Plugin. Once your development environment is configured, you will then be able to purchase professional translation services through the Google Play Developer Console. Google provides links to many third-party service providers who are able to assist with translation services for a fee, and the good thing is that these vendors have been prequalified.

From within the Android IDE, all you have to do is click the upload strings for translation (⬆) toolbar button to start the localization process, or click the download translated strings (⬇) toolbar button to complete the process once the files have been translated.

Publishing Applications for Foreign Users

After you've designed and developed an application that targets different locales, you need to make sure you can distribute the application to them easily. Google Play has fairly sophisticated settings available for publishing and selling applications in a variety of countries around the world. This is due to the fact that Google Wallet has worked out the tax and export situations with these countries. Developers can create application listings in a variety of languages and easily target the users they desire. Other markets, such as the Amazon Appstore, are available to a much more limited set of users. See the specific publication channels you wish to use for details about where they distribute applications.

Summary

By internationalizing your Android applications, you enable them to reach the maximum number of users. Internationalization requires a multifaceted approach and is best done as part of the application design process. Application assets like strings should be organized by language or region in the appropriate alternative resource directories. You also want to ensure that locale-dependent information such as dates, times, and currencies is displayed appropriately. Finally, be aware that once you internationalize your applications, you must still manage their internationalized application profiles on various publication channels, such as Google Play.

Quiz Questions

1. True or false: The /res/values-fr/strings.xml file should be used to store French string translations.

2. What directory would you use for French layout files?

3. What directory would you use to store French Canadian graphic files?

4. True or false: The Custom Locale emulator application is used for creating custom locales for Android applications.

5. How would you add support for RTL layouts to your Android application?

Exercises

1. Use the Android documentation to determine how you would programmatically perform a manual locale lookup in your application.

2. Use the Android documentation to determine how you would change the locale of an emulator using adb from the command line.

References and More Information

Android API Guides: "Providing Alternative Resources":
   http://d.android.com/guide/topics/resources/providing-resources.html#AlternativeResources
Android API Guides: "Localizing with Resources":
   http://d.android.com/guide/topics/resources/localization.html
Android API Guides: "How Android Finds the Best-Matching Resource":
   http://d.android.com/guide/topics/resources/providing-resources.html#BestMatch
Android SDK Reference documentation for the BidiFormatter class:
   http://d.android.com/reference/android/text/BidiFormatter.html
Android Tools: "Installing the Eclipse Plugin":
   http://d.android.com/sdk/installing/installing-adt.html
Android Distribute: "Publishing: Localization Checklist":
   http://d.android.com/distribute/googleplay/publish/localizing.html
ISO 639.2:
   http://www.loc.gov/standards/iso639-2/php/code_list.php
Country Codes—ISO 3166:
   http://www.iso.org/iso/country_codes/iso_3166_code_lists/country_codes

30

Protecting Applications from Software Piracy

Android application developers face numerous threats to success in the real world. Apps can be illegally copied and made available for download in alternative locations. A free application might be exploited, causing damage to a brand and leveraging valuable product resources like server bandwidth. All apps are vulnerable to hacking, resulting in rogue downloads with embedded malware, or using knowledge learned to hack a server or other underlying service. Unfortunately, this malicious behavior does happen. Protecting yourself is an ongoing battle; the opposition is constantly improving its methods, and you need to stay a step ahead. In this chapter, we talk about some of the ways you can protect yourself from becoming a victim of software piracy.

All Applications Are Vulnerable

Perhaps you've heard some of the startlingly high statistics about the number of mobile applications that are illegally downloaded each year. For the application developer, this loss in revenue, in addition to the other ramifications of software piracy, is staggering; most developers try to take some steps to protect their intellectual property.

All applications deserve protection whether they are paid or free. Just because you're giving away the software doesn't mean that it doesn't contain valuable intellectual property or revenue-making content that you should protect. The last thing you want is for your awesome technology to be copied, misused, or misrepresented simply because you left your work unprotected. This applies to your brand and professional reputation as well. They are all pieces in this puzzle.

The truth is, there is no such thing as a truly invulnerable app (or developer), but you can make your app a hard target. There are various actions Android developers can take to help protect their applications from exploitation. Some of these methods include:

- Use secure coding practices.
- Obfuscate your binary code using ProGuard.
- Leverage the License Verification Library (LVL).

Let's talk about each of these methods in more detail.

Using Secure Coding Practices

As usual, the first step in developing and publishing secure applications is to make security a priority and use common sense. Take a hard look at your application design; look for its vulnerabilities. Where is data stored? How is it accessed? What is plaintext and readable? How would you exploit your application?

Begin by battening down the hatches. Keep developer keys and digital signatures safe so that your development identity cannot be easily exploited. Make sure the passwords that protect these assets are not "password." The same goes for application server accounts and credentials.

Applications that send data over the network can be exploited in a variety of ways. Start by ensuring that your application servers are secure; use strong passwords and all the safeguards you should to protect any network resource. Network sniffing can be a problem, so it's important to safeguard any communication between your application and its server. Here are some tips for protecting network communications and resources:

- Don't send any information across the network unless it's absolutely necessary.
- Don't store any private user information remotely unless it's absolutely necessary.
- Don't use predictable or spoofable network communication protocols.
- Use secure network protocols, such as HTTPS and SSL (or TLS), even when data is not sensitive.

Warning

In a game, someone might be able to gain points, levels, experience, swords of smiting, or anything else that is useful simply by performing the same or similar network commands multiple times. If the method for performing the action is easily determined through sniffing, smart users might decide to write a script to do the work for them, regardless of whether the network content is encrypted or not. Although they have a valid account, and have possibly even paid for the game, they will have an unfair advantage over other users. Some cheaters simply do this for their own benefit, while other more entrepreneurially minded cheaters may monetize their findings and provide them to others. Make sure your network communication is sufficiently unpredictable to avoid these repeat offenders.

Obfuscating with ProGuard

Android applications are written in Java. Java is especially susceptible to reverse engineering due to the fact that it supports reflection, or the capability to look up code objects at runtime by name. These labels are kept when the application is compiled. When someone has knowledge of what your application does and the ability to systematically inspect the elements of your code in a human-readable fashion, it takes only a short amount of time to unwind your hard work and exploit it.

Android developers can use the ProGuard tool to make code more difficult to interpret and understand. ProGuard obfuscates, shrinks, and optimizes your code. The end result is a smaller, more secure application package file. Enabling ProGuard is simple in the Android IDE. For Android developers, there's little excuse not to provide at least this moderate level of protection for application source code.

Tip

Using ProGuard changes the code inside the packages and may have implications for how your application works. Be sure to thoroughly test the release version of your application prior to release.

ProGuard processing occurs when you export a signed or unsigned APK file using the Android tools in the Android IDE. Besides the added protection of obfuscation, package files are often reduced in size. We routinely see package size reductions of around 25 percent. Surely users will appreciate the faster downloads and having more free space on their devices.

Configuring ProGuard for Your Android Applications

ProGuard is an open-source tool for compacting and obfuscating compiled Java code. From a protection point of view, the resulting binary files are much harder, but not impossible, to reverse engineer. Android projects created with the Android IDE include a default ProGuard configuration file, called `proguard-project.txt`. To enable ProGuard, add the following configuration line to the `project.properties` file:

```
proguard.config=proguard-project.txt
```

Note

The `project.properties` file says not to make changes, otherwise they'll be erased. Don't worry. This change won't be erased even if you edit the Android settings for the project. At least, it never has been for us, and this is the way suggested by the Android team.

ProGuard is now enabled, but only when you use the Android Developer Tools to export a signed or unsigned package with a release version of the application. However, there are several common scenarios when the default ProGuard configuration file doesn't work. During the export process, ProGuard may display some errors. One common error looks like this:

```
[2014-03-10 16:52:07 - SampleFragments] Warning: android.support.v4.app
.ActivityCompat: can't find referenced method 'void invalidateOptionsMenu()'
in class android.app.Activity
[2014-03-10 16:52:07 - SampleFragments] Warning: android.support.v4.app
.ActivityCompat: can't find referenced method 'void dump(java.lang.String,java
.io.FileDescriptor,java.io.PrintWriter,java.lang.String[])' in class android.app
.Activity
[2014-03-10 16:52:07 - SampleFragments] Warning: android.support.v4.view
.MenuCompat: can't find referenced method 'void setShowAsAction(int)' in class
android.view.MenuItem
```

The error messages go on to talk about how the classes are inconsistent. This might happen when you try to use ProGuard on a project using the Android compatibility library. The warnings, all of which end in Compat, are for compatibility classes that are used to call the compatibility versions of methods. This happens only when they are available when compiling to previous SDK versions, as you probably are with the compatibility library. You can safely ignore these warnings by adding the following warning suppression line to your ProGuard configuration file (proguard.cfg):

```
-dontwarn **Compat
```

Then, in a manner similar to the existing -keep statements that exist in the file by default, you'll want to include classes that you use. For instance, if you're using fragments, you should add this line:

```
-keep public class * extends android.support.v4.app.Fragment
```

This keeps any unreferenced class that extends the Fragment class. If you've referenced only your fragments through XML, this is absolutely required.

After you have edited the proguard.cfg file to suit your project, you're ready to test your application thoroughly. Going through the trouble of configuring ProGuard will help protect your application from tampering and reverse engineering, regardless of your distribution method.

Dealing with Error Reports after Obfuscation

Now that your Android application source code is obfuscated, your error reports will also be obfuscated, making debugging release builds difficult by design. Luckily, the ProGuard tool outputs a file named mapping.txt that can later be used to de-obfuscate the error report. In the SDK tools directory, there is a directory named /proguard. In a subdirectory, you'll find a tool called retrace. This tool takes an obfuscated stack trace and makes it readable again. The mapping.txt file is stored in a directory named /proguard, which is found in the root of your project.

There's one important caveat, though. Every time you make a release, the mapping.txt file is re-created. It's not necessarily the same every time. This means that each time you actually release an application to users, you need to keep track of which mapping.txt file goes with which release. Otherwise, stack traces are basically useless to you. Needless to say, keep your mapping.txt files secure so they are not exploited either.

Leveraging the License Verification Library

Let's look at another scenario. Let's imagine that you have developed a killer application and published it a month ago to Google Play. So far it has been downloaded 25,000 times. But wait! There are 100,000 unique users according to your server logs. Welcome to the world of software piracy. One solution is to live with it and be happy that your application is good enough that people took the time to steal it. Another solution is to fight back; you can start by using the License Verification Library (LVL) to further protect your application from piracy.

Tip

The LVL verifies only Google Play paid applications and free apps that include APK expansion files. LVL is not a solution for developers who have published free apps without APK expansion files, including those with in-app billing or those using alternative markets.

The LVL is available for download through the Android SDK Manager. The library works only with Google Play and is meant for paid applications or free applications that include APK expansion files. If you distribute your application through other means, you need to use a separate licensing scheme, and you might need to provide separate binaries to support these differing means.

It's up to you to determine whether it's worth the effort to use LVL with your specific project. Unlike ProGuard, the LVL is not a turnkey solution; it takes time and effort to get it set up, integrated with your application, and working properly. You have to manage keys, policies, and testing. In addition, even the LVL itself is prone to exploitation. As a public shared library, LVL code compiles the same way against all applications. While obfuscation through ProGuard does help, even that leaves similar patterns for pirates to look for and take advantage of. Identical Java code through ProGuard turns into identical obfuscated code and, ultimately, identical binary. A person looking to crack the licensing can do so much faster if multiple apps use the exact same code patterns; thus, you'll want to modify what you can.

The consensus is that modifying the LVL code base to make it different from all other implementations used by other parties, while keeping the functionality, is your best defense. For that reason, we aren't going to provide code examples here; you'd just have to change them. Instead, we recommend that if you think the LVL is right for you, consult the documentation provided, available at *http://d.android.com/guide/publishing/licensing.html*.

Other Antipiracy Tips

If piracy is a huge concern for you or your company, there are other methods to help protect your applications. Although piracy can never be stopped completely, here are a few things you might be able to do to combat it:

- Use in-app billing on a free app. Careful control over features that can be enabled through in-app billing allows more users to try your app for free, while the features that must be paid for are protected by requiring accurate billing information. The leak of your compiled binary will no longer be devastating.

- Update your application with great features frequently. Creating an awesome application means supporting your application and adding new features. If this is done frequently, you create more work for those trying to pirate your app while giving an incentive to people to pay for and get updates more frequently.

- Block old versions of your application from accessing server resources. If you know a particular version has been pirated and you provide free updates (as most mobile apps do), simply push out an update and provide a message to users of the old version that they must update to continue.

- Price your services and apps appropriately. If your application is overpriced for what it is, it's more likely to be pirated by people who won't pay that amount. If it's priced correctly, people will be happy to pay for it.

- Provide free trial versions of your app or, if your app is highly valuable and priced correctly, provide cheap trial editions. Without any way to evaluate a paid app, users who actually do want to evaluate the app first may search for a pirated version. If that version actually works, there's little incentive for them to go out and buy the full version.

Although none of these methods are foolproof, the point is to provide a great experience to the user that will bring in more paying users in total. Make people want to pay for what you're offering rather than want to find a workaround to not pay.

Summary

In this chapter, you have learned a variety of straightforward methods to protect your Android applications from theft and tampering. Although no method is perfect, there's no reason to be an easy target. Use commonsense techniques for securing your applications, protect your network communication from cheaters, obfuscate with ProGuard, and consider validating application licensing with the LVL. The longer it takes for your application to be cracked and stolen, the more likely it is that those software pirates will simply turn to easier prey.

Quiz Questions

1. What are some ways to prevent software piracy?
2. True or false: ProGuard is a tool for preventing hackers from installing malware into your application's code.
3. How do you enable ProGuard to your project?
4. True or false: The -stopwarn flag is used to suppress warnings in your ProGuard configuration file.
5. What is the name of the file that ProGuard outputs to de-obfuscate the error report?

Exercises

1. Use the online documentation to determine the name of the ProGuard file that lists the classes and members that are not obfuscated after running ProGuard.

2. Use the online documentation to help you configure an application for license verification and use an `Activity` to perform a license check.

3. Use the online documentation to determine which LVL classes and interfaces are used for data obfuscation.

References and More Information

Android Training: "Security Tips":
  http://d.android.com/training/articles/security-tips.html
Android Tools: "ProGuard":
  http://developer.android.com/tools/help/proguard.html
ProGuard Manual:
  http://proguard.sourceforge.net/index.html#manual/introduction.html
Android Google Services: "App Licensing":
  http://developer.android.com/google/play/licensing/index.html
Android Developers Blog article on securing Android LVL applications:
  http://android-developers.blogspot.com/2010/09/securing-android-lvl-applications.html
YouTube Android Developers Channel: "Google I/O 2011: Evading Pirates and Stopping Vampires":
  http://www.youtube.com/watch?v=TnSNCXR9fbY

VIII

Preparing for Future
Android Releases

Introducing the
L Developer Preview

At Google I/O 2014, the Android team released the L Developer Preview, or Android L (API Level 20). In the past, if you wanted to get your application working on the latest version of Android, you had to wait until the official release was generally available. The new L Developer Preview releases the upcoming version of Android to early adopter developers and testers, allowing them to get a head start porting their applications to the newest version of Android. Not only are you able to get an early look at the latest APIs and features with the preview, you may even be able to influence the direction of Android by providing feedback to the Android team. This chapter introduces you to the L Developer Preview release of the Android SDK and many of the preview's newest features.

Tip

To get started using the L Developer Preview, you first need to set up the SDK. The Android documentation provides an article titled "Setting Up the Preview SDK," found at *http://d.android.com/preview/setup-sdk.html*, which walks you through the steps of downloading the preview SDK, setting up your development environment, and creating your first project.

Exploring the L Developer Preview

The Android L Developer Preview comes with many enhancements to previous features and many new capabilities. Over 5000 new APIs have been added to the L Developer Preview; it probably would require multiple books to cover all of them, so we will narrow our focus in this chapter to some of the most compelling additions to this preview release.

Tip

For a more complete overview of the APIs that can be found in the L Developer Preview, see the "API Overview" Android documentation found here: *http://d.android.com/preview/api-overview.html*.

Warning

Because this is a preview release of the Android SDK, the APIs are subject to change, as the preview is still a work in progress. You must download a zip file to access the preliminary reference documentation and learn how the APIs are implemented. You can download the zip file here: *http://storage.googleapis.com/androiddevelopers/preview/ l-developer-preview-reference.zip.*

Improving Performance

One of the goals of the Android team for the L Developer Preview was to improve performance. This preview release is packed with performance enhancements, features, and tools that make creating performant applications much easier than in the past. In this section, we discuss some of those additions.

ART Runtime

The L Developer Preview replaced the Dalvik runtime with a new runtime called ART (**A**ndroid **R**untime), which was originally released in the 4.4 release as an optional and experimental feature. Some of the benefits of ART are:

- It supports ahead-of-time (AOT) compilation in addition to just-in-time (JIT) compilation, many times resulting in a 2X performance improvement over the Dalvik runtime without requiring a single change to application code for most applications.

- Garbage collection (GC) pauses have been reduced from two to one, while running parallel processes during the pause, many times reducing garbage collection times from 10 milliseconds to 2 to 4 milliseconds.

- There are debug tracing improvements during application execution with a dedicated sampling profiler without causing significant performance degradation, including many new debugging options and more information detailing exceptions and crash reports.

Warning

You should always test your applications before release to ensure that they work with ART. Most developers will not have to make any changes to their code, but if you are using JNI bindings and native code, or use nonstandard code obfuscation, you may run into issues that require code modification. If you are using JNI bindings and you run into bugs, you should look into using the `CheckJNI` tool. There is a great blog post about debugging with `CheckJNI` here: *http://android-developers.blogspot.com/2011/07/debugging-android-jni-with-checkjni.html.*

Graphics

Support for OpenGL ES 3.1 has been added to the L Developer Preview with both native and Java support, in addition to the Android Extension pack, which brings advanced OpenGL ES 3.1 graphics capabilities. To add support for OpenGL ES 3.1, you need to add the following line of code to your manifest file:

```
<uses-feature android:glEsVersion="0x00030001" />
```

These OpenGL ES 3.1 Java interfaces are included with GLES31 and GLES31Ext.

Project Volta

The L Developer Preview introduced an initiative called Project Volta, which aims to provide the necessary tools to help developers optimize battery performance. Some of these features include the following:

- A new JobScheduler API allows you to implement jobs to be performed upon certain conditions occurring, such as when charging or when connected to Wi-Fi, and even allows you to schedule jobs to execute as a batch to increase efficiency.

- The dumpsys batterystats developer tool can be run from the ADB shell command line and is useful for generating statistics about usage of the battery on the device.

- The Battery Historian (historian.par) developer tool can be run from the command line and used for generating an HTML visualization of the device's power consumption.

Improving the User Experience

Another goal of the Android team for the L Developer Preview was to improve the user experience. This preview release is full of capabilities that make it simple to create visually appealing applications while providing a high-quality user experience. We will be talking about two of the most profound additions to the L Developer Preview: the new material design and enhanced notifications.

Material Design

The first user experience improvement is a new design guideline referred to as material design. The material design guidelines are an attempt to create a seamless experience across all devices, regardless of the form factor or platform, with a mobile-first focus—Android to the Web. These guidelines are founded on a set of principles for improving motion, visual, and interaction design. In addition, the L Developer Preview has also introduced many APIs for implementing these newfound best practices.

Tip
Google provides a fantastic resource for learning about the material design guidelines that will most likely evolve over time, so be sure to check these documents frequently for the latest updates and information. You can learn more here: *http://www.google.com/design/spec/material-design/introduction.html*.

Material Theme

A new material theme has been added to the L Developer Preview which provides an easy way to apply these new styles to your application. Both a light material theme and a dark material theme have been provided. In addition, new color attributes have been defined, the `colorPrimary` and `colorPrimaryDark` style attributes. These are useful for defining a light and dark primary color for an application. For example, if you wanted to apply the new material light theme with a dark action bar and two primary colors, you would define the following style and items in your `/res/values-v21/styles.xml` file:

```
<style name="Theme.AdvancedAndroid"
    parent="@android:style/Theme.Material.Light/DarkActionBar">
    <item name="android:colorPrimary">
        @color/advanced
    </item>
    <item name="android:colorPrimaryDark">
        @color/advanced_dark
    </item>
</style>
```

Tip

You are now able to recolor drawable resources at runtime either by specifying a tint using the `setTint()` method in your application code or by defining the `android:tint` attribute of a `<bitmap>` tag within a layout.

Complex Views, Animations, and Shadows

Two new `View` widgets have been added to the L Developer Preview: the `RecyclerView` and `CardView`. The `RecyclerView` is a new type of widget that you should consider using in place of a `GridView` or a `ListView`. This `View` allows for more layout flexibility when displaying items in a list, is better performing, and is much easier to use. When using the `RecyclerView`, you need to define both a `LayoutManager` and an `Adapter`. In addition, `RecyclerView` animations are provided for adding and removing items, which definitely makes this new widget worth using.

The `CardView` is a way to present information in a widget that has the appearance of a card. You are able to define attributes such as the card's corner radius or the card's background color. You are even able to define a new *z* axis value by defining an `elevation` and `translationZ` value, and when these two values—added together—equal 0 under an orthographic projection, the card will have the appearance of rising above other views on the *z* axis.

Defining the `elevation` attribute will also add a shadow to the card, and the higher the elevation, the larger the shadow. As a matter of fact, you are able to define the `elevation` and `translationZ` values on all views within Android. Figure 31.1 shows the Google-provided ElevationBasic L Developer Preview sample application (*https://github.com/googlesamples/android-ElevationBasic*), which implements a *z* axis for a circle and a square, and when the square is touched, its *z* axis value changes in relation to the circle.

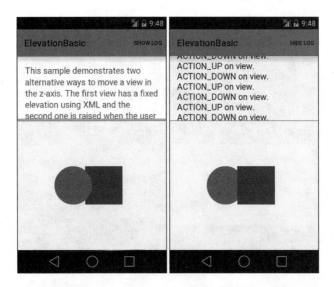

Figure 31.1   The ElevationBasic sample application with a changing *z* axis
value for the square, before touch (left) and after touch (right).

Enhanced Notifications

Since notifications are such an important part of the Android experience, it's no wonder
that the L Developer Preview introduces many improvements to notifications. Here is a
list of the changes made to notifications:

- Material design improvements have been added to notifications to enhance
  their visual appearance. If you have already created notifications using the
  `Notification.Builder` class, there are really no changes you need to make as
  Android handles the style differences automatically.

- Heads-up notifications are a new type of notification introduced for delivering
  high-priority messages to users while they are performing other tasks on the device.

- The Lock screen is a new integration point for displaying notifications. You can
  define visibility levels for these notifications to ensure that sensitive information is
  protected. Figure 31.2 shows a Lock screen notification created from the
  CustomNotifications sample application included with the Android SDK.

- You can sync your notifications across devices through the cloud, and when you
  dismiss a notification on one device, that notification will be dismissed on all your
  devices.

Figure 31.2   A notification created from the CustomNotifications
sample application included with the Android SDK,
displayed in the expanded system bar (left) and displayed
in collapsed mode on the Lock screen (right).

Introducing Android TV

In Chapter 10, "Development Best Practices for Tablets, TVs, and Wearables," we discussed Google TV, which has been around since 2010. Although Google TV is based on Android, the L Developer Preview released a new version of Android for TVs—Android TV.

Included in the L Developer Preview is the v17 leanback library, which is an Android TV support library. This support library is optional for including in your application, but it contains many APIs designed specifically for TVs. In order to include the v17 leanback library, you must also include the v4 support library—v17 depends on v4. The v17 leanback library has special fragments that have been created for TV: the `SearchFragment`, `BrowseFragment`, and `DetailsFragment`.

Tip

To learn more about Android TV for the L Developer Preview, visit the following URL: *http://d.android.com/preview/tv/index.html.*

Understanding Android TV Development Requirements

Included with the L Developer Preview are two Android TV system images. These system images are all you need to get started developing for Android TV. You should always test your applications on real hardware. In order to do so, you need to have access to the ADT-1 Developer Kit, which at the time of this writing is available only upon approved request from Google. This is currently a limitation, as not everyone who requests access will be approved. To apply for access to the ADT-1 Developer Kit, visit *https://support .google.com/googleplay/android-developer/contact/adt_request* and submit the requested information.

Understanding TV Application Hardware Limitations

TVs do not typically have access to certain hardware that would be included in a phone or tablet. You need to keep this in mind when developing your applications for Android TV, and if for some reason your application uses such hardware when running on other device form factors, you need to make sure that you check for the availability of a particular feature and handle cases where it is not supported. Hardware that is usually not present on a TV includes:

- Telephony
- GPS
- Touchscreen
- Camera
- NFC
- Microphone

Summary

The L Developer Preview is a new version of Android that has been released so that application developers can have a head start on getting their applications working on the newest version of Android before its official release. You have learned about the performance and user experience improvements included in the preview. In addition, you have also learned that APIs for the new Android TV are included in this exciting new preview.

Quiz Questions

1. True or false: There are over 5000 new APIs included with the L Developer Preview.
2. What does ART stand for?
3. What feature should you add to your manifest to begin working with OpenGL ES 3.1?
4. True or false: The `JobScheduler` API currently does not support executing jobs in batches.
5. What attribute should you define on a `View` to have a shadow added?

Exercises

1. Use the reference found below—"Setting Up the Preview SDK"—and set up the SDK.
2. Use the Android documentation to determine how to include a `CardView` in your layout.

References and More Information

Android L Developer Preview: "Setting Up the Preview SDK":
   http://d.android.com/preview/setup-sdk.html
Android L Developer Preview: "API Overview":
   http://d.android.com/preview/api-overview.html
YouTube Google Developers Channel: "Google I/O 2014—The ART Runtime":
   https://www.youtube.com/watch?v=EBlTzQsUoOw
YouTube Google Developers Channel: "Using the Android Job Scheduler":
   https://www.youtube.com/watch?v=QdINLG5QrJc
YouTube Google Developers Channel: "Google I/O 2014—Introduction to Project Volta":
   https://www.youtube.com/watch?v=KzSKIpJepUw
Android L Developer Preview: "Material Design":
   http://d.android.com/preview/material/index.html
Google Design Spec: "Material Design":
   http://www.google.com/design/spec/material-design/introduction.html
YouTube Google Developers Channel: "Google I/O 2014—Material Science: Developing Android Applications with Material Design":
   https://www.youtube.com/watch?v=lSH9aKXjgt8
Android L Developer Preview: "Design for Notifications":
   http://d.android.com/preview/notifications.html
Android L Developer Preview: "Samples":
   http://d.android.com/preview/samples.html
Android L Developer Preview: "Reference":
   http://d.android.com/preview/reference.html
Android L Developer Preview: "Support":
   http://d.android.com/preview/support.html
Android L Developer Preview: "License Agreement":
   http://d.android.com/preview/license.html

IX

Appendixes

A
Quick-Start Guide: Android Debug Bridge

The Android Debug Bridge (ADB) is a client-server tool that interacts directly with Android devices and emulators using a command-line interface. You can use this tool, which is provided as part of the Android SDK, to manage and interact with emulator and device instances connected to a development machine and view logging and debugging information. ADB also provides the underpinnings for other tools, such as the Android ADT Bundle and Dalvik Debug Monitor Service (DDMS). This Quick-Start Guide is not intended to completely document the ADB functionality. Instead, it is designed to get you up and running with common tasks. See the ADB documentation provided with the Android SDK for a complete list of features.

Much of the functionality provided by the ADB (such as the LogCat Android logging utility or pushing and pulling files using the File Explorer) is closely integrated into the development environment through DDMS and ADT. Developers might prefer to use these friendly methods to interact with devices and emulators; however, you can use ADB for automation and scripting purposes. You can also use ADB to customize functionality, instead of relying on the defaults exposed through secondary tools.

Listing Connected Devices and Emulators

You can use ADB to list all Android devices and emulator instances connected to a development machine. To do this, simply use the `devices` command of the `adb` command line. For example:

```
adb devices
```

This command lists the emulators and devices attached to this machine by their serial number and state (offline or device). For emulator instances, the serial number is based on their unique port numbers. For example, in this case, we have one emulator instance (port 5554) and one Android device:

```
C:\>adb devices
List of devices attached
emulator-5554   device
HT841LC1977     device
```

Directing ADB Commands to Specific Devices

When you know the serial number of the device you want to connect to, you can issue commands as follows:

```
adb -s <serial number> <command>
```

For example, to get the state of a specific device, type

```
adb -s emulator-5554 get-state
```

Instead of using the -s flag with a unique serial number, you can use the -d flag to direct a command to the *only* device instance connected or the -e flag to direct a command to the *only* emulator instance, provided you have only one of each type connected. For example, if we have only one Android phone connected, we can query its serial number as follows:

```
adb -d get-serialno
```

Starting and Stopping the ADB Server

Sometimes you might need to manually restart the ADB server process. We have needed to do this, for example, when we've had an emulator instance running for a long time and have repeatedly connected and disconnected the debugger, eventually resulting in a loss of LogCat logging. In this case, you might want to kill and restart the ADB server (and perhaps the Android IDE).

Stopping the ADB Server Process

To terminate the ADB server process, use the kill-server command. For example, type

```
adb kill-server
```

Starting and Checking the ADB Server Process

You can start the ADB server using the start-server command:

```
adb start-server
```

You can also use the start-server command to check whether the server is running. If the server isn't running when other commands are issued, it is started automatically.

Listing ADB Commands

To get a list of all ADB commands, type

```
adb help
```

You can also simply type adb without any arguments to get a list of all other commands available through the ADB shell.

Issuing Shell Commands

ADB includes a shell interface where you can interact directly with the device and issue commands and run binaries. The shell has your typical file access commands, such as pwd and ls.

Issuing a Single Shell Command

You can issue a single shell command without starting a shell session using the following command:

```
adb shell <command>
```

For example, to list all the files in the /sdcard/download directory on the emulator, type

```
adb -e shell ls /sdcard/download
```

Using a Shell Session

Often you might want to issue more than one command. In this case, you might want to start a shell session. To do so, simply type

```
adb shell
```

For example, to connect to a specific device instance by serial number and start a shell session, type

```
adb -s emulator-5554 shell
# <type commands here>
# exit
```

You can then issue commands. Ending your session is as easy as typing exit.

Tip

If you connect to a device instead of the emulator, you might see a $ as a prompt instead of a # prompt. This indicates user-level access, but the commands, such as logcat and monkey, work as described.

Using the Shell to Start and Stop the Emulator

Stopping the emulator makes it stop responding, although it still displays on your development machine. To stop the emulator, you can issue the stop command in the ADB shell:

```
adb -s emulator-5554 shell stop
```

You can then restart the emulator using the `start` command:

```
adb -s emulator-5554 shell start
```

You could also perform these commands from within a shell session, like this:

```
adb -s emulator-5554 shell
# stop
# start
```

Tip

You can also use the shell interface to run built-in command-line programs such as `sqlite3` to examine SQLite application databases and `monkey` to stress test an application. You can also install custom binaries on the emulator or device. We talk more about this later in the appendix. That said, you can run `sqlite3` on the device shell only if the device is rooted, which we do not recommend, although many people do it.

Copying Files

You can use the ADB command line to copy files to and from your hard drive to an Android device. You need to know the full path to the file you want to copy. File operations are subject to your user permissions (locally and remotely).

Sending Files to a Device or Emulator

You can copy files to the device using the `push` command, as follows:

```
adb push <local file path> <remote file path on device>
```

For example, to copy the file `Pic.jpg` from the local hard drive to a device's SD card download directory, use the following command:

```
adb -s HT841LC1977 push c:\Pic.jpg /sdcard/download/Pic.jpg
```

Retrieving Files from a Device or Emulator

You can copy files from the device using the `pull` command, as follows:

```
adb pull <remote file path on device> <local file path>
```

For example, to copy the file `Lion.jpg` to your local hard drive from a device's SD card download directory, use the following command:

```
adb -s HT841LC1977 pull /sdcard/download/Lion.jpg C:\Lion.jpg
```

Tip

If you put picture files onto your SD card—virtual or otherwise—using this method, you might need to force the Android operating system to refresh using the Media Provider (available in the DevTools application on the emulator).

Installing and Uninstalling Applications

You can use ADB to install and uninstall packages (applications) on a given Android device or emulator. Although the ADT Bundle does this for developers automatically, this functionality is useful for developers who are not using the Android IDE and for those developers and testers who want to create automated build procedures and testing environments. ADB can also be used to install third-party application packages, including those that are self-distributed and not found on application stores such as Google Play.

Note

All Android applications are installed as packages created with the Android Asset Packaging Tool (aapt). This is the tool used by the ADT Bundle as well.

Installing Applications

To install applications, first create an Android package (.apk) file, and then use the `install` command:

```
adb install <apk file path>
```

For example, to install the sample application Snake on the emulator, you can use the following command:

```
adb -e install C:\AndroidEnv\sdk\samples\android-19\legacy\Snake\bin\Snake.apk
821 KB/s (17656 bytes in 0.021s)
        pkg: /data/local/tmp/Snake.apk
Success
```

Reinstalling Applications

You can use the `-r` command flag to reinstall the application package without overwriting its data. For example, you can now reinstall the Snake application without losing your data by using the following command:

```
adb -e install -r C:\AndroidEnv\sdk\samples\android-19\legacy\Snake\bin\Snake.apk
```

Uninstalling Applications

To uninstall an Android application, you need to know the name of its package:

```
adb uninstall <package>
```

For example, to uninstall the MyFirstAndroidApp application from the emulator, you can use the following command:

```
adb -e uninstall com.advancedandroidbook.myfirstandroidapp
```

Tip

You might use this command often if you switch between computers and, thus, switch signatures frequently.

Working with LogCat Logging

Android logging information is accessible through the LogCat utility. This utility is integrated into DDMS and the Android IDE, but you can also access it directly from the ADB command line using the following command:

```
adb logcat <option> <filter>
```

This type of command is best done from within the ADB shell.

Displaying All Log Information

For example, you can display all LogCat logging information from the emulator instance by opening the shell and typing the `logcat` command:

```
adb -e shell
# logcat
```

By default, the logging mode is set to brief. For example, the following is an Informational (I) log message (brief mode) from the debug tag called `AppLog` from process ID 20054:

```
I/AppLog(20054): An Informational Log message.
```

Including Date and Time with Log Data

Another useful mode is the `time` mode, which includes the date and time the log message was invoked. To change the logging mode, use the `-v` flag and specify the format. For example, to change to `time` mode, use the following ADB shell command:

```
# logcat -v time
```

The resulting log messages are formatted with the date and time, followed by the event severity, tag, process ID, and log message:

```
01-05 21:52:22.465 I/AppLog(20054): Another Log Message.
```

Filtering Log Information

The log information available through the LogCat tool can be overwhelmingly verbose. Most of the time, a filter or two is required to sift out only the messages you want to view. Filters are formatted tags and event priority pairs. The format for each filter is:

```
<Tag Name>:<Lowest Event Priority to Print>
```

For example, a filter to display Informational log messages (and higher-priority messages including Warnings, Errors, and Fatal messages) from log messages tagged with the string `AppLog` would look like this:

```
AppLog:I
```

Tip

You can also use the asterisk (*), which means "all." So if you use an asterisk on the Tag side of the filter, it means "All tags." If you put it on the Event Priority side, it's much like using the V priority—the lowest priority—so all messages display.

Filtering by Event Severity

You can create filters to display only log events of a certain severity. The severity types (from lowest priority or most verbose to highest priority or least verbose) are:

- Verbose (V)
- Debug (D)
- Info (I)
- Warning (W)
- Error (E)
- Fatal (F)
- Silent (S)

For example, the following shell command displays all Errors and Fatal errors but suppresses Warnings, Informational messages, Debug messages, and Verbose messages:

```
# logcat *:E
```

Tip

In API Level 8, a new type of error was created called a `wtf` error. These errors are generated using the `Log.wtf()` method. In this case, `wtf` supposedly stands for "What a terrible failure." This log method should be used to report events that should never happen. See the `Log` class documentation for more details.

Filtering by Tag

You can use multiple filters, ending with a catch-all. Perhaps you want to see all messages from a specific application (a specific tag) and no others. In this case, you want to create a filter to show all messages for a given tag and another filter to suppress all other tags. We also change into `time` mode, so we get the date and time of the logged events messages. The following shell command displays all `AppLog`-tagged logging information and suppresses all other tags:

```
# logcat -v time AppLog:V *:S
```

This filter is roughly equivalent to this other command line:

```
# logcat -v time AppLog:* *:S
```

The resulting log messages are formatted with the date and time, followed by the event severity, tag, process ID, and message:

```
01-05 21:52:22.465 I/AppLog(20054): Another Log Message.
```

Clearing the Log

You can clear the emulator log using the -c flag:

```
adb -e logcat -c
```

Or, you can clear it from the ADB shell like this:

```
# logcat -c
```

Redirecting Log Output to a File

You can redirect log output to a file on the device using the -f flag. For example, to direct all Informational logging messages (and those of higher priority) from the emulator to the file mylog.txt in the sdcard directory, you can use the following ADB shell command:

```
# logcat -f /sdcard/mylog.txt *:I
```

Note

This file is stored on the emulator or device. You need to pull it onto your desktop using either ADB or the DDMS File Explorer.

Accessing the Secondary Logs

Android has several different logs. By default, you look at the main log. However, an events log and a radio log also exist. You can connect to the other log buffers using the -b flag. For example, to connect to the events log to review events, type

```
# logcat -b events
```

The radio log is similarly accessed as follows:

```
# logcat -b radio
```

Controlling the Backup Service

Android 2.2 introduced a backup service that applications can use to archive important data in case of a factory reset or lost device. This service normally runs in the background, backing up data and restoring it on its own schedule. However, you can use the bmgr shell tool to prompt the backup service to do its thing, which is helpful for testing backup functionality. You can check to see whether the Backup Manager is enabled using the following ADB shell command:

```
# bmgr enabled
Backup Manager currently disabled
```

You can enable the Backup Manager from the ADB shell as follows:

```
# bmgr enable true
Backup Manager now enabled
```

Tip

The user can enable and disable the Backup Manager on a specific device by navigating to the backup settings, accessed via Settings, Backup & reset.

Forcing Backup Operations

From the ADB shell, you can schedule a backup using the following command:

```
# bmgr backup <package>
```

For example, you can schedule a backup of the SimpleBackup application data as follows:

```
# bmgr backup com.advancedandroidbook.simplebackup
```

The previous commands schedule the backup to occur only at some point in the future. You can trigger all scheduled backup tasks with the following command:

```
# bmgr run
```

Forcing Restore Operations

From the ADB shell, you can force a restore using the following command:

```
# bmgr restore <package>
```

For example, you can force a restore of the SimpleBackup application data as follows:

```
# bmgr restore com.advancedandroidbook.simplebackup
```

Unlike the `backup` command, the `restore` command immediately causes a restore operation.

Wiping Archived Data

From the ADB shell, you can wipe archived data for a specific application using the following command:

```
# bmgr wipe <package>
```

For example, you would wipe out all archived backup data from the SimpleBackup application as follows:

```
# bmgr wipe com.advancedandroidbook.simplebackup
```

Generating Bug Reports

You can create a rather verbose bug report to attach to application defects using the `bugreport` command. For example, to print the debug information for the sole emulator instance running on your development machine, use:

```
adb -e bugreport
```

To print the debug information for the sole phone connected via USB, you issue this command instead:

```
adb -d bugreport
```

Using the Shell to Inspect SQLite Databases

You can use the standard `sqlite3` database tool from within the ADB shell. This tool enables you to inspect and interact directly with a SQLite database on the emulator. For a thorough explanation of the `sqlite3` tool, see Appendix B, "Quick-Start Guide: SQLite."

Using the Shell to Stress Test Applications

You can use the Exerciser Monkey tool from within the ADB shell to send random user events to a specific application. Think of it as handing your phone (or emulator) to a monkey (or a baby, or a baby monkey) and letting it push random keys, causing random events on the phone—events that can crash your application if it doesn't handle them correctly. If your application crashes, the monkey application stops and reports the error, making this a useful tool for quality assurance.

Letting the Monkey Loose on Your Application

To launch the `monkey` tool, use the following ADB shell command:

```
# monkey -p <package> <options> <event count>
```

For example, to have the `monkey` tool generate five random events in the PetTracker application in the emulator, do the following:

```
adb -s emulator-5554 shell
# monkey -p com.advancedandroidbook.pettracker 5
```

Listening to Your Monkey

You can watch each event generated by using the verbose flag -v. For example, to see which events you send to the PetTracker application, use this command:

```
adb -s emulator-5554 shell
# monkey -p com.advancedandroidbook.pettracker -v 5
```

Here is the important output from this command:

```
:SendKey: 21    // KEYCODE_DPAD_LEFT
:Sending Trackball ACTION_MOVE x=-4.0 y=2.0
:Sending Trackball ACTION_UP x=0.0 y=0.0
:SendKey: 82    // KEYCODE_MENU
:SendKey: 22    // KEYCODE_DPAD_RIGHT
:SendKey: 23    // KEYCODE_DPAD_CENTER
:Dropped: keys=0 pointers=0 trackballs=0
// Monkey finished
```

You can tell from the verbose logging that the monkey application sent five events to the PetTracker application: a navigation event (left), two trackball events, the Menu button, and then two more navigation events (right, center).

Directing Your Monkey's Actions

You can specify the types of events generated by the monkey application. You basically give weights (percentages) to the different types of events. The event types available are shown in Table A.1.

Table A.1 **Monkey Event Types**

Event Type	Description	Default Percentage	Command-Line Flag	Event ID (As Shown in Verbose Mode)
Touch	Up/Down event on a single screen location	15%	--pct-touch	0
Motion	Down event on a single location, followed by some movement; then an Up event in a different screen location	10%	--pct-motion	1
Trackball	Trackball events, which are sometimes followed by a Click event	15%	--pct-trackball	2
Basic Navigation	Up, Down, Left, Right	25%	--pct-nav	3
Major Navigation	Menu, Back, Center of D-pad, and such	15%	--pct-majornav	4
System Key	Home, Volume, Send, End, and such	2%	--pct-syskeys	5
Activity Switch	Randomly switch to other activities	2%	--pct-appswitch	6
Other Events	Key presses, other buttons	16%	--pct-anyevent	7

To use a different mix of events, you need to include the event type's command-line flag as listed in Table A.1, followed by the desired percentage:

```
# monkey [<command line flag> <percentage>...] <event count>
```

For example, to tell the monkey tool to use only touch events, use the following command:

```
# monkey -p com.advancedandroidbook.pettracker -pct-touch 100 -v 5
```

Or, let's say you want just Basic and Major navigation events (50%/50%):

```
# monkey -p com.advancedandroidbook.pettracker -pct-nav 50 -pct-majornav 50 -v 5
```

You get the picture.

Training Your Monkey to Repeat His Tricks

For random yet reproducible results, you can use the seed option. The seed feature enables you to modify the events that are produced as part of the event sequence, yet you can rerun the sequence in the future (and verify bug fixes, for example). To set a seed, use the -s flag:

```
# monkey -p <package> -s <seed> -v <event count>
```

For example, in the command we used previously, we can change the five events by setting a different starting seed. In this case, we set a seed of 555:

```
# monkey -p com.advancedandroidbook.pettracker -s 555 -v 5
```

Changing the seed changes the event sequence sent by the monkey, so as part of a stress test, you might want to consider generating random seeds, sending them to the monkey, and logging the results. When the application fails on a given seed, keep that seed (and any other command-line options, such as event type percentages) when you log the bug and rerun the test later to verify the bug fix.

Keeping the Monkey on a Leash

By default, the monkey generates events as rapidly as possible. However, you can slow down this behavior using the throttle option, as follows:

```
# monkey -throttle <milliseconds> <event count>
```

For example, to pause for 1 second (1000 milliseconds) between each of the five events issued to the PetTracker application, use the following command:

```
# monkey -p com.advancedandroidbook.pettracker -v -throttle 1000 5
```

Learning More about Your Monkey

For more information about the monkey commands, see the Android SDK Tools website at *http://developer.android.com/tools/help/monkey.html.* You can also get a list of commands by typing monkey without any command options, like this:

```
adb -e shell monkey
```

Installing Custom Binaries via the Shell

You can install custom binaries on the emulator or device. For example, if you spend a lot of time working in the shell, you might want to install BusyBox, which is a free and useful set of command-line tools available under the GNU General Public License and has been called "The Swiss Army Knife of Embedded Linux" (thanks, Wikipedia, for that little fact). BusyBox provides a number of helpful and familiar UNIX utilities, all packaged in a single binary—for example, utilities such as find and more. BusyBox provides many useful functions (although some might not apply or be permissible on Android), such as the following:

```
[, [[, addgroup, adduser, adjtimex, ar, arp, arping, ash, awk, basename,
bunzip2, bzcat, bzip2, cal, cat, catv, chattr, chgrp, chmod, chown, chpasswd,
chpst, chroot, chrt, chvt, cksum, clear, cmp, comm, cp, cpio, crond, crontab,
cryptpw, cut, date, dc, dd, deallocvt, delgroup, deluser, df, dhcprelay,
diff, dirname, dmesg, dnsd, dos2unix, du, dumpkmap, dumpleases, echo, ed,
egrep, eject, env, envdir, envuidgid, ether-wake, expand, expr, fakeidentd,
false, fbset, fdflush, fdformat, fdisk, fgrep, find, fold, free, freeramdisk,
fsck, fsck.minix, ftpget, ftpput, fuser, getopt, getty, grep, gunzip,
gzip, halt, hdparm, head, hexdump, hostid, hostname, httpd, hwclock, id,
ifconfig, ifdown, ifup, inetd, init, insmod, install, ip, ipaddr, ipcalc,
ipcrm, ipcs, iplink, iproute, iprule, iptunnel, kbd_mode, kill, killall,
killall5, klogd, last, length, less, linux32, linux64, linuxrc, ln, loadfont,
loadkmap, logger, login, logname, logread, losetup, ls, lsattr, lsmod,
lzmacat, makedevs, md5sum, mdev, mesg, microcom, mkdir, mkfifo, mkfs.minix,
mknod, mkswap, mktemp, modprobe, more, mount, mountpoint, mt, mv, nameif,
nc, netstat, nice, nmeter, nohup, nslookup, od, openvt, passwd, patch, pgrep,
pidof, ping, ping6, pipe_progress, pivot_root, pkill, poweroff, printenv,
printf, ps, pscan, pwd, raidautorun, rdate, readlink, readprofile, realpath,
reboot, renice, reset, resize, rm, rmdir, rmmod, route, rpm, rpm2cpio,
run-parts, runlevel, runsv, runsvdir, rx, sed, seq, setarch, setconsole,
setkeycodes, setlogcons, setsid, setuidgid, sh, sha1sum, slattach, sleep,
softlimit, sort, split, start-stop-daemon, stat, strings, stty, su, sulogin,
sum, sv, svlogd, swapoff, swapon, switch_root, sync, sysctl, syslogd,
tail, tar, taskset, tcpsvd, tee, telnet, telnetd, test, tftp, time, top,
touch, tr, traceroute, true, tty, ttysize, udhcpc, udhcpd, udpsvd, umount,
uname, uncompress, unexpand, uniq, unix2dos, unlzma, unzip, uptime, usleep,
uudecode, uuencode, vconfig, vi, vlock, watch, watchdog, wc, wget, which,
who, whoami, xargs, yes, zcat, zcip
```

All you need to do is install the binary (which is available online) using the following steps:

1. Download the `BusyBox` binary (at your own risk, or compile it for yourself). You can find the binary online at *http://benno.id.au/blog/2007/11/14/android-busybox*, where Benno has kindly hosted it for you. (Thanks, Benno!)

2. Make a directory called `/data/local/busybox/` on your emulator using the ADB shell; for example, `adb -e shell mkdir /data/local/busybox/`.

3. Copy the `BusyBox` binary to the directory you created; for example,
   `adb -e push C:\busybox /data/local/busybox/busybox`.

4. Launch the ADB shell; for example, `adb -e shell`.

5. Navigate to the `BusyBox` directory; for example, `#cd /data/local/busybox`.

6. Change the permissions on the `BusyBox` file; for example, `#chmod 777 busybox`.

7. Install `BusyBox`; for example, `#./busybox -install`.

8. Export the path for ease of use. Note: You need to reset the `PATH` for each session; for example, `#export PATH=/data/busybox:$PATH`.

You can find out more about `BusyBox` at *http://www.busybox.net*.

Summary

In this appendix, we covered the Android Debug Bridge (ADB). We started by showing how to list your connected devices and emulators, start and stop the ADB server, and direct commands to specific devices. You should now be comfortable listing ADB and issuing shell commands, copying files to and from your device, and installing and uninstalling applications to your devices and emulators, all from a command line. Further, we covered how to work with LogCat logging, looked at controlling the backup service, and generated bug reports, along with various other features of ADB. You should now be well equipped to manage your devices and emulators from the command line.

Quiz Questions

1. What is the `adb` command for listing the attached devices?

2. True or false: `adb start` is the command for starting the ADB server.

3. What is the command-line flag for directing a command to the only device connected to ADB?

4. True or false: It is not possible to install an Android application from the command line.

5. What is the shell command for backing up a package?

Exercises

1. Use the online documentation to make a list of the debugging command flags you may use with the `monkey` command-line tool.

2. Use the online documentation to learn how to use the `screenrecord` utility for recording the display of devices.

3. Use the online documentation to determine what command to issue for running the package manager tool, and then make a list of the package manager commands.

References and More Information

Android Developer Tools: "Android Debug Bridge":
http://developer.android.com/tools/help/adb.html
Android Developer Tools: "logcat":
http://developer.android.com/tools/help/logcat.html
Android Developer Tools: "bmgr":
http://developer.android.com/tools/help/bmgr.html
Android Developer Tools: "UI/Application Exerciser Monkey":
http://developer.android.com/tools/help/monkey.html

B
Quick-Start Guide: SQLite

The Android system allows individual applications to have private SQLite databases in which to store their application data. This Quick-Start Guide is not a complete documentation of the SQLite commands. Instead, it is designed to get you up and running with common tasks. The first part of this appendix introduces the features of the `sqlite3` command-line tool. We then provide an in-depth database example using many common SQLite commands. See the online SQLite documentation (*http://www.sqlite.org*) for a complete list of features, functionality, and limitations of SQLite.

Exploring Common Tasks with SQLite

SQLite is a lightweight and compact, yet powerful, embedded relational database engine available in the public domain. It is fast and has a small footprint, making it perfect for phone system use. Unlike the heavyweight server-based databases such as Oracle and Microsoft SQL Server, each SQLite database is a self-contained single file on disk.

Android applications store their private databases (SQLite or otherwise) under a special application directory:

```
/data/data/<application package name>/databases/<databasename>
```

For example, the database for the PetTracker application provided in this book is found at:

```
/data/data/com.advancedandroidbook.PetTracker/databases/pet_tracker.db
```

The database file format is standard and can be moved across platforms. You can use the Dalvik Debug Monitor Service (DDMS) File Explorer to pull the database file and inspect it with third-party tools such as SQLite Database Browser 2.0, if you like.

Tip

Application-specific SQLite databases are private files accessible only from within that application. To expose application data to other applications, the application must become a content provider.

Using the `sqlite3` Command-Line Interface

In addition to programmatic access to create and use SQLite databases from within your applications, you can also interact with the database using the familiar command-line `sqlite3` tool, which is accessible via the Android Debug Bridge (ADB) remote shell.

The command-line interface for SQLite, called `sqlite3`, is exposed using the ADB tool, which we covered in Appendix A, "Quick-Start Guide: Android Debug Bridge."

Launching the ADB Shell

You must launch the ADB shell interface on the emulator or device (if it is rooted) to use the `sqlite3` commands. If only one Android device (or emulator) is running, you can connect by simply typing

```
c:\>adb shell
```

If you want to connect to a specific instance of the emulator, you can connect by typing

```
adb -s <serialNumber> shell
```

For example, to connect to the emulator at port 5554, you would use the following command:

```
adb -s emulator-5554 shell
```

Connecting to a SQLite Database

Now you can connect to the Android application database of your choice by name. For example, to connect to the database we created with the PetTracker application, we would connect like this:

```
c:\> adb -e shell
# sqlite3 /data/data/com.advancedandroidbook.pettracker/databases/pet_tracker.db
SQLite version 3.6.22
Enter ".help" for instructions
sqlite>
```

Now we have the `sqlite3` command prompt, where we can issue commands. You can exit the interface at any time by typing

```
sqlite>.quit
```

Or, type

```
sqlite>.exit
```

Commands for interacting with the `sqlite3` program start with a dot (.) to differentiate them from SQL commands you can execute directly from the command line. This syntax might be different from that of other programs you are familiar with (for example, MySQL commands).

Warning
Most Android devices don't allow running the `sqlite3` command as emulators do. Rooted devices do allow this command.

Exploring Your Database

You can use the `sqlite3` commands to explore what your database looks like and interact with it. You can:

- List available databases
- List available tables
- List indices of a given table
- List the database schema of a table
- List the database schema of a database

Listing Available Databases

You can list the names and file locations attached to this database instance. Generally, you have your main database and a temp database, which contains temp tables. You can list this information by typing

```
sqlite> .databases
seq name file
--- ---- -------------------------------------------------
0   main /data/data/com.advancedandroidbook.PetTracker/databases/...
1   temp
sqlite>
```

Listing Available Tables

You can list the tables in the database you connect to by typing

```
sqlite> .tables
android_metadata table_pets table_pettypes
sqlite>
```

Listing Indices of a Table

You can list the indices of a given table by typing

```
sqlite>.indices table_pets
```

Listing the Database Schema of a Table

You can list the schema of a given table by typing

```
sqlite>.schema table_pets
CREATE TABLE table_pets (_id INTEGER PRIMARY KEY
AUTOINCREMENT,pet_name TEXT,pet_type_id INTEGER);
sqlite>
```

Listing the Database Schema of a Database

You can list the schema for the entire database by typing

```
sqlite>.schema
CREATE TABLE android_metadata (locale TEXT);
CREATE TABLE table_pets (_id INTEGER PRIMARY KEY
AUTOINCREMENT,pet_name TEXT,pet_type_id INTEGER);
CREATE TABLE table_pettypes (_id INTEGER PRIMARY KEY
AUTOINCREMENT,pet_type TEXT);
sqlite>
```

Importing and Exporting the Database and Its Data

You can use the `sqlite3` commands to import and export database data and the schema;
you can also interact with it. You can:

- Send command output to a file instead of stdout (the screen)
- Dump the database contents as a SQL script (so you can re-create it later)
- Execute SQL scripts from files
- Import data into the database from a file

Note

The file paths are on the Android device, not your computer. You need to find a directory on
the Android device in which you have permission to read and write files. For example,
`/data/local/tmp/` is a shared directory.

Sending Output to a File

Often, you want the `sqlite3` command results to pipe to a file instead of to the screen.
To do this, you can type the `output` command followed by the file path to which the
results should be written on the Android system. For example:

```
sqlite>.output /data/local/tmp/dump.sql
```

Dumping Database Contents

You can create a SQL script to create tables and their values by using the `dump` command. The `dump` command creates a transaction that includes calls to `CREATE TABLE` and
`INSERT` to populate the database with data. This command can take an optional table
name or dump the whole database.

Tip

The `dump` command is a great way to do a full archival backup of your database.

For example, the following commands pipe the `dump` output for the `table_pets`
table to a file, and then set the output mode back to the console:

```
sqlite>.output /data/local/tmp/dump.sql
sqlite>.dump table_pets
sqlite>.output stdout
```

You can then use DDMS and the File Explorer to pull the SQL file off the Android file system. The resulting `dump.sql` file looks like this:

```
BEGIN TRANSACTION;
CREATE TABLE table_pets (
_id INTEGER PRIMARY KEY AUTOINCREMENT,
pet_name TEXT,
pet_type_id INTEGER);

INSERT INTO "table_pets" VALUES(1,'Rover',9);
INSERT INTO "table_pets" VALUES(2,'Garfield',8);
COMMIT;
```

Executing SQL Scripts from Files

You can create SQL script files and run them through the console. These scripts must be on the Android file system. For example, let's put a SQL script called `myselect.sql` in the `/data/local/tmp/` directory of the Android file system. The file has two lines:

```
SELECT * FROM table_pettypes;
SELECT * FROM table_pets;
```

We can then run this SQL script by typing

```
sqlite>.read /data/local/tmp/myselect.sql
```

You see the query results on the command line.

Importing Data

You can import formatted data using the `import` and `separator` commands. Files such as CSV use commas for delimiters, but other data formats might use spaces or tabs. You specify the delimiter using the `separator` command. You specify the file to import using the `import` command.

For example, put a CSV script called `some_data.csv` in the `/data/local/tmp/` directory of the Android file system. The file has four lines. It is a comma-delimited file of pet type IDs and pet type names:

```
18,frog
19,turkey
20,piglet
21,great white shark
```

You can then import this data into the `table_pettypes` table, which has two columns: an `_id` column and a `pet_type` descriptor. To import this data, type the following command:

```
sqlite>.separator ,
sqlite>.import /data/local/tmp/some_data.csv table_pettypes
```

Now, if you query the table, you see it has four new rows.

Executing SQL Commands on the Command Line

You can also execute raw SQL commands on the command line. Simply type the SQL command, making sure it ends with a semicolon (;). If you use queries, you might want to change the output mode to column so that query results are easier to read (in columns) and the headers (column names) are printed. For example:

```
sqlite> .mode column
sqlite> .header on
sqlite> select * from table_pettypes WHERE _id < 11;
_id         pet_type
----------  ----------
8           bunny
9           fish
10          dog
sqlite>
```

You're not limited to queries, either. You can execute any SQL command you see in a SQL script on the command line if you like.

Tip

We've found it helpful to use the sqlite3 command line to test SQL queries if our Android SQL queries with QueryBuilder are not returning the results as expected. This is especially true of more complicated queries.

You can also control the width of each column (so text fields don't truncate) using the width command. For example, the following command prints query results with the first column five characters wide (often an ID column such as _id), followed by a second column 50 characters wide (text column):

```
sqlite> .width 5 50
```

Warning

SQLite keeps the database schema in a special table called sqlite_master. You should consider this table read-only. SQLite stores temporary tables in a special table called sqlite_temp_master, which is also a temporary table.

Using Other sqlite3 Commands

A complete list of sqlite3 commands is available by typing

```
sqlite> .help
```

Understanding SQLite Limitations

SQLite is powerful, but it has several important limitations compared to traditional SQL Server implementations, such as the following:

- SQLite is not a substitute for a high-powered, server-driven database.
- Being file based, the database is meant to be accessed in a serial, not a concurrent, manner. Think "single user"—the Android application. It has some concurrency features, but they are limited.

- Access control is maintained by file permissions, not database user permissions.

- Referential integrity is not maintained. For example, foreign key constraints are parsed (for example, in CREATE TABLE) but not enforced automatically. However, using trigger functions can enforce them.

- ALTER TABLE support is limited. You can use only RENAME TABLE and ADD COLUMN. You may not drop or alter columns or perform any other such operations. This can make database upgrades a bit tricky.

- Trigger support is limited. You cannot use FOR EACH STATEMENT or INSTEAD OF. You cannot create recursive triggers.

- You cannot nest transaction operations.

- Views are read-only.

- You cannot use RIGHT OUTER JOIN or FULL OUTER JOIN.

- SQLite does not support stored procedures or auditing.

- The built-in functions of the SQL language are limited.

- See the SQLite documentation for limitations on the maximum database size, table size, and row size. The Omitted SQL page is helpful (*http://www.sqlite .org/omitted.html*), as is the Unsupported SQL wiki (*http://www.sqlite.org/cvstrac/ wiki?p=UnsupportedSql*).

Learning by Example: A Student Grade Database

Let's work through a student Grades database to show standard SQL commands to create and work with a database. Although you can create this database from the command line using sqlite3, we suggest using the Android application to create the empty Grades database, so that it is created in a standard "Android" way.

The purpose of the database is to keep track of each student's test results for a specific class. In this example, grades are calculated from each student's individual performance on the following:

- Four quizzes (each weighted as 10 percent of the overall grade)
- One midterm (weighted as 25 percent of the overall grade)
- One final (weighted as 35 percent of the overall grade)

All tests are graded on a scale of 0–100.

Designing the Student Grade Database Schema

The Grades database has three tables: Students, Tests, and TestResults.

The Students table contains student information. The Tests table contains information about each test and how much it counts toward the student's overall grade. Finally, all students' test results are stored in the TestResults table.

Setting Column Data Types

`sqlite3` has support for the following common data types for columns:

- `INTEGER` (signed integers)
- `REAL` (floating-point values)
- `TEXT` (UTF-8 or UTF-16 string; encoded using database encoding)
- `BLOB` (data chunk)

Tip

Do not store files such as images in the database. Instead, store images as files in the application file directory and store the filename or URI path in the database.

Creating Simple Tables with `AUTOINCREMENT`

First, let's create the Students table. We want a student `id` to reference each student. We can make this the primary key and set its `AUTOINCREMENT` attribute. We also want the first and last name of each student, and we require these fields (no nulls). Here's our SQL statement:

```
CREATE TABLE Students (
id INTEGER PRIMARY KEY AUTOINCREMENT,
fname TEXT NOT NULL,
lname TEXT NOT NULL );
```

For the Tests table, we want a test `id` to reference each test or quiz, much like the Students table. We also want a friendly name for each test and a weight value for how much each test counts for the student's final grade (as a percentage). Here's our SQL statement:

```
CREATE TABLE Tests (
id INTEGER PRIMARY KEY AUTOINCREMENT,
testname TEXT,
weight REAL DEFAULT .10 CHECK (weight<=1));
```

Inserting Data into Tables

Before we move on, let's look at several examples of how to add data to these tables. To add a record to the Students table, you need to specify the column names and the values in order. For example:

```
INSERT into Students (fname, lname) VALUES ('Harry', 'Potter');
```

Now, we're going to add a few more records to this table for Ron and Hermione. At the same time, we need to add a bunch of records to the Tests table. First, we add the Midterm, which counts for 25 percent of the grade:

```
INSERT into Tests (testname, weight) VALUES ('Midterm', .25);
```

Then we add a couple of Quizzes, which use the default weight of 10 percent:

```
INSERT into Tests (testname) VALUES ('Quiz 1');
```

Finally, we add a Final test worth 35 percent of the total grade:

```
INSERT into Tests (testname, weight) VALUES ('Final', .35);
```

Querying Tables for Results with SELECT

How do we know the data we've added is in the table? Well, that's easy. We simply query for all rows in a table using a SELECT:

```
SELECT * FROM Tests;
```

This returns all records in the Tests table:

```
id     testname          weight
-----  ----------------  ------
1      Midterm           0.25
2      Quiz 1            0.1
3      Quiz 2            0.1
4      Quiz 3            0.1
5      Quiz 4            0.1
6      Final             0.35
```

Now, ideally, we want the weights to add up to 1.0. Let's check using the SUM aggregate function to sum all the weight values in the table:

```
SELECT SUM(weight) FROM Tests;
```

This returns the sum of all weight values in the Tests table:

```
SUM(weight)
-----------
1.0
```

We can also create our own columns and alias them. For example, we can create a column alias called fullname that is a calculated column: it's the student's first and last name concatenated using the || concatenation.

```
SELECT fname||' '|| lname AS fullname, id FROM Students;
```

This gives us the following results:

```
fullname          id
-----------       --
Harry Potter      1
Ron Weasley       2
Hermione Granger  3
```

Using Foreign Keys and Composite Primary Keys

Now that we have our students and tests all set up, let's create the TestResults table. This is a more complicated table. It's a list of student-test pairings, along with the score.

The TestResults table pairs up student IDs from the Students table with test IDs from the Tests table. Columns, which link to other tables in this way, are often called *foreign keys*. We want unique student-test pairings, so we create a composite primary key from the student and test foreign keys. Finally, we enforce that the scores are numbers between 0 and 100. No extra credit or retaking tests in this class!

```
CREATE TABLE TestResults (
studentid INTEGER REFERENCES Students(id),
testid INTEGER REFERENCES Tests(id),
score INTEGER CHECK (score<=100 AND score>=0),
PRIMARY KEY (studentid, testid));
```

Tip

SQLite does not enforce foreign key constraints, but you can set them up anyway and enforce the constraints by creating triggers. For an example of using triggers to enforce foreign key constraints in SQL, check out the SimpleDatabase project provided on the book's website for Chapter 3.

Now it's time to insert some data into this table. Let's say Harry Potter received an 82 percent on the midterm exam:

```
INSERT into TestResults (studentid, testid, score) VALUES (1,1,82);
```

Now let's input the rest of the students' scores. Harry is a good student. Ron is not a good student, and Hermione aces every test (of course). When they're all added, we can list them. We can do a SELECT * to get all columns, or we can specify the columns we want explicitly like this:

```
SELECT studentid, testid, score FROM TestResults;
```

Here are the results from this query:

studentid	testid	score
1	1	82
1	2	88
1	3	78
1	4	90
1	5	85
1	6	94
2	1	10
2	2	90
2	3	50
2	4	55
2	5	45
2	6	65
3	6	100
3	5	100
3	4	100
3	3	100
3	2	100
3	1	100

Altering and Updating Data in Tables

Ron's not a good student, and yet he received a 90 percent on Quiz 1. This is suspicious, so as the teacher, we check the actual paper test to see if we made a recording mistake. He actually earned 60 percent. Now we need to update the table to reflect the correct score:

```
UPDATE TestResults SET score=60 WHERE studentid=2 AND testid=2;
```

You can delete rows from a table using the DELETE function. For example, to delete the record we just updated, use the following:

```
DELETE FROM TestResults WHERE studentid=2 AND testid=2;
```

You can delete all rows in a table by not specifying the WHERE clause:

```
DELETE FROM TestResults;
```

Querying Multiple Tables Using JOIN

Now that we have all our data in our database, it is time to use it. The preceding listing was not easy for a human to read. It would be much nicer to see a listing with the names of the students and names of the tests instead of their IDs.

Combining data is often handled by performing a JOIN with multiple table sources; there are different kinds of JOIN operations. When you work with multiple tables, you need to specify which table a column belongs to (especially with all these different id columns). You can refer to columns by their column name or by their table name, then a dot (.), and then the column name.

Let's list the grades again, only this time, we include the name of the test and the name of the student. Also, we limit our results only to the score for the Final (testid 6):

```
SELECT
Students.fname||' '|| Students.lname AS StudentName,
Tests.testname,
TestResults.score
FROM TestResults
JOIN Students
     ON (TestResults.studentid=Students.id)
JOIN Tests
     ON (TestResults.testid=Tests.id)
WHERE testid=6;
```

This gives us the following results (you could leave off the WHERE to get all tests):

```
StudentName          testname        score
------------------   --------------   -----
Harry Potter         Final            94
Ron Weasley          Final            65
Hermione Granger     Final            100
```

Using Calculated Columns

Hermione always likes to know where she stands. When she comes to ask what her final grade is likely to be, we can perform a single query to show all her results and calculate the weighted scores:

```
SELECT
Students.fname||' '|| Students.lname AS StudentName,
Tests.testname,
Tests.weight,
TestResults.score,
(Tests.weight*TestResults.score) AS WeightedScore
FROM TestResults
JOIN Students
      ON (TestResults.studentid=Students.id)
JOIN Tests
      ON (TestResults.testid=Tests.id)
WHERE studentid=3;
```

This gives us predictable results:

```
StudentName         testname weight score WeightedScore
----------------    -------- ------ ----- -------------
Hermione Granger    Midterm  0.25   100        25.0
Hermione Granger    Quiz 1   0.1    100        10.0
Hermione Granger    Quiz 2   0.1    100        10.0
Hermione Granger    Quiz 3   0.1    100        10.0
Hermione Granger    Quiz 4   0.1    100        10.0
Hermione Granger    Final    0.35   100        35.0
```

We can just add up the Weighted Scores and be done, but we can also do it via this query:

```
SELECT
Students.fname||' '|| Students.lname AS StudentName,
SUM((Tests.weight*TestResults.score)) AS TotalWeightedScore
FROM TestResults
JOIN Students
      ON (TestResults.studentid=Students.id)
JOIN Tests
      ON (TestResults.testid=Tests.id)
WHERE studentid=3;
```

Here we get a nice consolidated listing:

```
StudentName       TotalWeightedScore
----------------  ------------------
Hermione Granger 100.0
```

If we wanted to get all our students' grades, we need to use the GROUP BY clause. Also, let's order them so the best students are at the top of the list:

```
SELECT
Students.fname||' '|| Students.lname AS StudentName,
SUM((Tests.weight*TestResults.score)) AS TotalWeightedScore
FROM TestResults
JOIN Students
      ON (TestResults.studentid=Students.id)
```

```
JOIN Tests
       ON (TestResults.testid=Tests.id)
GROUP BY TestResults.studentid
ORDER BY TotalWeightedScore DESC;
```

This makes our job as teacher almost too easy, but at least we're saving trees by using a digital grade book.

```
StudentName              TotalWeightedScore
------------------------ ------------------
Hermione Granger         100.0
Harry Potter             87.5
Ron Weasley              46.25
```

Using Subqueries for Calculated Columns

You can also include queries within other queries. For example, you can list each student and a count of how many tests he or she passed, where a passing score means higher than 60, as in the following:

```
SELECT
Students.fname||' '|| Students.lname AS StudentName,
Students.id AS StudentID,
(SELECT COUNT(*)
FROM TestResults
WHERE TestResults.studentid=Students.id
AND TestResults.score>60)
AS TestsPassed
FROM Students;
```

Again, we see that Ron needs a tutor:

```
StudentName      StudentID TestsPassed
-----------      --------- -----------
Harry Potter     1         6
Ron Weasley      2         1
Hermione Granger 3         6
```

Deleting Tables

You can always delete tables using the DROP TABLE command. For example, to delete the TestResults table, use the following SQL command:

```
DROP TABLE TestResults;
```

Summary

In this appendix we began by exploring common SQLite tasks and introduced using the sqlite3 command-line interface. You should now be comfortable connecting to a SQLite database, querying the data, importing and exporting data to and from the database, and executing various other commands. We also covered some of the SQLite limitations and provided an example student grade database schema to work with. Further, you should now understand how to partition your data into tables, use foreign and composite primary keys, perform table joins, and other features common to SQL databases. In all, you should be well on your way to building a data-backed application for the Android platform.

Quiz Questions

1. Where on the Android file system is an application's private SQLite database stored?
2. True or false: The command for listing available databases is `databases`.
3. What is the SQLite command for listing the database schema of a table?
4. What are the data types for columns that `sqlite3` supports?
5. True or false: The command for deleting all rows in a table is `DELETE TABLE <tablename>`.

Exercises

1. Create a simple database schema for storing a user's social networking application data locally, and include information on who the user's friends are and what messages have been exchanged between friends.
2. Create a simple database schema for managing a list of a user's favorite restaurants and include information about the address, category, and rating.
3. Create a simple database schema appropriate for a student application where students are able to manage their course work. Include information about teachers, class by subject, and homework assignments for each class.

References and More Information

Android Developer Tools: "`sqlite3`":
   http://developer.android.com/tools/help/sqlite3.html

C

Java for Android Developers

This appendix contains examples of a number of Java techniques frequently used in Android applications and by seasoned Java developers but not always found in beginner Java books and tutorials. If you are new to Java, this information, used in conjunction with a good Java reference, can help you develop Android applications quickly and effectively.

Learning the Java Programming Language

Android applications are written in Java, so learn Java first—it's essential. This appendix does not teach you standard Java syntax or object-oriented programming and how the object hierarchy works. For that, you should get good reference materials such as books or websites that work for you and, if necessary, take some classes. (It should go without saying that learning programming fundamentals comes first, but experience has shown us that many people try to write Android apps without doing so. Learning programming language syntax, such as Java, is not the same as learning how to program.) Without basic Java skills, you're going to have trouble developing good Android applications. It's like asking someone to write a poem in a foreign language without first learning how to speak the language . . . or learning what a poem is.

We, the authors, believe that the Android platform is a good way to learn Java development. This works only if you are either under the instruction of a teacher who is guiding you through programming and application development topics simultaneously, or you are a real self-starter who looks up things as you go and pulls together information from a variety of sources outside this book.

 Tip
A great resource for learning Java is the online documentation found here: *http://docs .oracle.com/javase/tutorial/tutorialLearningPaths.html*.

Learning the Java Development Tools

Once you've begun learning the basics of Java programming, you've got to learn to use the tools associated with development. Many Android developers use the free Android IDE (a version of the Eclipse IDE) included with the Android Developer Tools (ADT) Bundle for Android development. Others use their own copy of the Eclipse IDE with the ADT Plugin. Android Studio, based on ItelliJ IDEA, has been released as another development environment for Android.

This book uses the Android IDE from the ADT Bundle in its examples. Get familiar with the tool so that you can easily debug your applications, or at least read the errors generated by them. We frequently receive emails from frustrated beginners who have no idea why their applications are not compiling but would have been able to figure it out themselves if only they had looked at the errors generated by the Android IDE, for simple mistakes like missing semicolons, mismatched brackets, or undefined variables. The Android IDE spits out errors on the Problems tab at the bottom of the screen.

Familiarizing Yourself with Java Documentation

Javadocs are automatically generated Java class documentation files created from the source code. All the Java references associated with the Android SDK are available for download through the Android SDK Manager and online at *http://d.android.com/reference/* (the Reference tab on the website). This book refers to various Android SDK classes and interfaces, but if we were to reproduce the class documentation for the entire Android SDK, the book would need to be many, many volumes.

Understand that this book, and any other book on Android development for that matter, must be used along with the full class documentation. Android developers must constantly refer to the class documentation to choose the right methods and supply the correct parameters. Do not make the mistake of thinking you can develop applications without this core documentation. You'll become familiar with the most commonly used class documentation as you get up to speed, but with new classes and methods being added all the time, it's not practical to even attempt to memorize all of it.

Understanding Java Shorthand

Now let's talk about some of the less common Java syntax you frequently see used in Android applications for one reason or another. These are techniques and shorthand that are often seen in the field but rarely covered in your typical Java class or beginner's reference, yet you find them in the simplest of examples on the Android Developers website, in our books, and in other references.

Java shorthand is rarely shown in books, which tend to want to spell out each individual coding step, often on its own line, for readability. Some Java professionals prefer that style, whereas others strive to make the perfect, terse line of code that does everything, often at the expense of readability. Here are some examples of Java shorthand you're likely to see in Android applications.

Chaining Methods and Unnecessary Temp Variables

Java developers often want to avoid creating unnecessary variables, especially temp variables that are used once to store the result of a calculation, either in the middle of a larger calculation, or for a return value. Therefore, you are likely to see statements evaluated as return values, like this:

```
int sum(int a, int b)
{
    return (a+b);
}
```

This is equivalent to a longer method with a temp variable, as in the following:

```
int sumVerbose(int a, int b)
{
    int temp = a + b;
    return temp;
}
```

Android developers often take these Java features to the extreme in what is called *method chaining*. This means that the interim return values of the methods are not stored in their own named variables but are simply used "on the fly." Here is a typical method chaining example:

```
InputStream isIconData = getResources().openRawResource(R.drawable.icon);
```

This is equivalent to the following:

```
Resources myAppResources = this.getResources();
InputStream isIconData = myAppResources.openRawResource(R.drawable.icon);
```

Note that the `this` keyword has also been dropped. You often see method chaining in builder-style classes. For example, with the Android `AlertDialog` classes, you can either construct a new `AlertDialog` class and call a bunch of setter methods, or use the `AlertDialog.Builder` class to chain all of the setter methods together, ending with a call to the builder's `create()` method that ultimately returns an `AlertDialog` (not an `AlertDialog.Builder` class, which is used only for chaining). Although you don't have to use method chaining, you should recognize what it is and how to read it, because the Android SDK sample applications (and our books) use this technique frequently.

Looping Infinitely

In Java, you can have empty statements simply by terminating a blank line of code with a semicolon. This trick is often used to specify `for` loop conditionals to create an infinite loop, like this:

```
for (;;) {
    // Loop
}
```

Each of the `for` loop components is an empty statement. This evaluates to be `true` and therefore the loop continues indefinitely. As with any code design, make sure any infinite loops you create have reasonable exit cases.

There's also a `for-each` syntax you might see with arrays and classes that implement the `Iterable` interface. To use the `for-each` loop syntax, you need to define your loop variable, then put a colon, and then specify the name of your array or class. For example:

```
int aNums[] = { 2, 4, 6 };
for (int num : aNums) {
    String strToPrint = num;
}
```

This is equivalent to the following:

```
int aNums[] = { 2, 4, 6 };
for (int i = 0; i < aNums.length; i++) {
    String strToPrint = aNums[i];
}
```

Note that we've also been lazy about the automatic `toString()` conversion done on the `int` values when assigned to the `String` variables.

Working with Unary and Ternary Operators

Java supports unary operations, which allow developers to easily increment or decrement variable values by 1 using ++ and --. For example:

```
int counter = 1;
counter++;
counter--;
```

This code is equivalent to the following:

```
int counter = 1;
counter = counter + 1;
counter = counter - 1;
```

Unary operators can appear before (prefix) or after (postfix) the variable. The location of the operator dictates whether the operation happens before or after the rest of the expression is evaluated. For example, the following code shows how unary operators work by manipulating a variable called `counter` using Android logging:

```
int counter = 0;
Log.i(DEBUG_TAG, "The counter value is =" + counter++);     // prints 0
Log.i(DEBUG_TAG, "The counter value is =" + counter);       // prints 1
Log.i(DEBUG_TAG, "The counter value is =" + counter--);     // prints 1
Log.i(DEBUG_TAG, "The counter value is =" + counter);       // prints 0
Log.i(DEBUG_TAG, "The counter value is =" + (++counter));   // prints 1
Log.i(DEBUG_TAG, "The counter value is =" + --counter);     // prints 0
```

There are also a number of other operators, such as +=, -=, *=, /=, %=, ^=, >>=, <<=, &=, |=.

Java also supports ternary operators for `if-else` shorthand. You might see conditional statements followed by a question mark (?), then a statement to evaluate whether the conditional is true, then a colon (:) and another statement to evaluate whether the conditional is false. The result of a ternary operator is the value of the evaluated statement. Here's an example of a ternary operator in use in a simple conditional evaluation:

```
int lowNum = 1;
int highNum = 99;
int largerNum = lowNum < highNum ? highNum : lowNum;
```

This code is equivalent to the following:

```
int lowNum = 1;
int highNum = 99;
int largerNum;
if(lowNum < highNum) {
    largerNum = highNum;
} else {
    largerNum = lowNum;
}
```

Working with Inner Classes

You learned (we hope) about the object-oriented programming and class hierarchy in your basic Java instruction, but not all instructors or books talk about inner classes or, perhaps more importantly, anonymous inner classes.

An *inner class* is a class whose scope and definition are encompassed in another class. Most classes in Java are top-level classes. These classes, and the objects they define, are standalone. You can also create nested classes to encapsulate and define subordinate objects that make sense only in the context of the outer class. Nested classes are called inner classes. Inner classes can have all the features of a regular class, but their scope is limited. Inner classes have another benefit: they have full access to the class in which they are nested. This feature makes inner classes perfect for implementing adapter or builder functionality, as you frequently see them used in Android.

Inner classes exist only to help the developer organize code; the compiler treats inner classes just like any other class, except that the inner classes have a limited scope and are therefore tethered to the class they are defined with.

Here is an example of a top-level class with two inner classes:

```
public class Car {
    // Car fields, including variables of type Engine and Wheels
    // Misc car methods

    class Engine {
        // Car engine fields
        // Get/Set engine methods
        // Functional engine method (goForward, goReverse, etc.)
        // Can access Car fields/methods
    }
```

```
class Wheels {
    // Car wheel fields
    // Get/Set wheel methods (getTirePressure, etc.)
    // Functional wheel method (turnRight, turnLeft, etc.)
    // Can access Car fields/methods
}
}
```

The Car class has two inner classes: Engine and Wheels. Although all user-related data and functionality can be defined in the Car class, using the inner classes to compartmentalize functionality can make code easier to read and maintain. The inner classes Engine and Wheels also have access to the protected/private fields and methods available within the Car class, which they might not otherwise have due to security, if they were defined as standalone classes. Remember that you cannot use or instantiate the Engine or Wheels classes except with an instance of the Car class, but the inner classes can access any fields or methods available in the outer class Car, as needed.

Tip
One specific use for inner classes is as static inner classes. A *static inner class* defines behavior that is not tied to a specific object instance but applies across all instances.

Let's look at another way inner classes are used. Android developers often use anonymous inner classes to define specialized listeners, which register callbacks for specific behavior when an event occurs, on the fly. For example, to listen for clicks on a Button control, the developer uses the setOnClickListener() method, which takes a single parameter: a View.OnClickListener object. You can define an entirely new MyOnClickListener class, or you can simply define the class inline in code, without naming it at all (thus, the anonymous part). The following code uses the anonymous inner class technique to create, define, and assign a custom View.OnClickListener to a Button control:

```
Button aButton = (Button) findViewById(R.id.MyButton);
aButton.setOnClickListener(new View.OnClickListener() {
    public void onClick(View v) {
        // User clicked my button, do something here!
    }
});
```

You often see threading done in a similar fashion:

```
new Thread() {
    public void run() {
        doWorkHere();
    }
}.start();
```

This code defines a new Thread class, implements the run() method, and starts the thread, all in one "line" of code.

Summary

To program Android applications, a basic understanding of object-oriented programming and Java is essential, in addition to being able to utilize the ADT. Java is an evolving language. Some older reference books do not cover the latest the language has to offer, and different developers have different coding styles. We have tried to make our examples easy to read, even if that means they are a bit verbose.

Quiz Questions

1. True or false: Method stacking means interim method return values are not stored in their own named variables but are simply used "on the fly."
2. What is the syntax for creating an infinite `for` loop in Java?
3. What is the syntax for creating a `for-each` loop involving an array of strings in Java?
4. Provide an example line of code that uses the += unary operator.
5. Provide an example line of code that uses the ternary operator in a `Boolean` evaluation that returns a `Boolean` `true` or `false` value.

Exercises

1. Read the official Java documentation for learning the Java language found here: *http://docs.oracle.com/javase/tutorial/java/index.html*.
2. Read the official Java documentation for learning the essential Java classes found here: *http://docs.oracle.com/javase/tutorial/essential/index.html*.
3. Read the official Java documentation for learning Java collections found here: *http://docs.oracle.com/javase/tutorial/collections/index.html*.
4. Read the official Java documentation for learning Java generics found here: *http://docs.oracle.com/javase/tutorial/extra/generics/index.html*.

References and More Information

Oracle Java Tutorials: "Java Tutorials Learning Paths":
   http://docs.oracle.com/javase/tutorial/tutorialLearningPaths.html

D

Quick-Start Guide: Android Studio

Android Studio is an integrated development environment (IDE), similar to the ADT Bundle or Eclipse with the ADT Plugin, but is based on IntelliJ IDEA, which is a very popular tool for Java development. Many of the same features that you have become accustomed to in the ADT Bundle are available within Android Studio, although Android Studio has many new features that are not yet available in the ADT Bundle or Eclipse with the ADT Plugin, and there are some differences in the Android Studio project structure. This appendix introduces you to Android Studio and brings you up to speed on the features available for Android developers to leverage.

Warning

At the time of writing this book, Android Studio was available only as an early access preview. This means that there may be features in Android Studio that have not yet been implemented, features that are subject to change, in addition to bugs that may be present. Regardless, Android Studio is a powerful tool and worth a serious look. If you are not comfortable using an early access preview product, you may want to stick to using the ADT Bundle or Eclipse with the ADT Plugin.

Getting Up and Running with Android Studio

This appendix shows you how to get up and running with Android Studio on a Windows-based machine. Android Studio is also available for Mac OS X and Linux. Aside from installation and basic configuration, the available Android Studio tools behave the same regardless of the operating system you use for development.

You first need to install Android Studio, so if you have not already done so, please see *http://d.android.com/sdk/installing/index.html* and follow the appropriate instructions to install Android Studio for your platform.

Note

Version updates for Android Studio are released approximately every two weeks. Major bug fixes may be released more frequently, so be aware that the version number is constantly changing.

Figure D.1   The Welcome to Android Studio screen.

Tip

Make sure you have the Java JDK version 6 or higher installed on your development machine. If you have been following along with this book so far, we assume that you already have one installed. We have found that the 64-bit version of the Java JDK, version 7, is the easiest Java version to configure for working with Android Studio. Ideally, you would install the JDK before installing Android Studio because Android Studio searches for a compatible JDK during the installation process. Depending on your system setup, your experience may be different.

Launching Android Studio for the First Time

Now that you have Android Studio installed, the next step is to launch the IDE so that you can begin experimenting. Proceed to launch Android Studio. Once it is launched, a screen titled Welcome to Android Studio presents the available Quick Start actions you can take (Figure D.1).

Configuring Android Studio

Before creating your first application, you need to configure Android Studio by installing at least one Android SDK using the Android SDK Manager, so select the Configure action. You will be presented with a list of Configure actions (Figure D.2), and the one you want to select is SDK Manager. Selecting this action launches the SDK Manager on your system. If you have not already done so, go ahead and install at least one version of the Android SDK so that it is available to Android Studio. We recommend installing the most recent version of the Android SDK, Android KitKat 4.4 (API Level 19), in addition to installing the necessary Tools and Extras.

Figure D.2   The Welcome to Android Studio Configure actions.

Warning

Even if you have installed versions of the Android SDK using the ADT Bundle or the command-line tools, you will have to install them again for Android Studio. If you have not yet installed a version of the Android SDK for Android Studio, you will receive errors when creating new projects or when importing projects into Android Studio.

Creating an Android Studio Project

Now that you have installed at least one version of the Android SDK for Android Studio, close the SDK Manager, and from the Android Studio wizard, select the back button located to the left of the Configure title, and navigate back to the Quick Start action list. From this list, select the New Project. . . action to begin creating your first Android application with Android Studio.

To create your project, proceed through the New Project wizard, like so:

1. The first page (Figure D.3) asks you to enter an Application name. Name this project Hello Studio Project. For the Module name, enter HelloStudio in the text field. For the Package name, enter com.advancedandroid.hellostudio in the text field. Check Create custom launcher icon. Keep all other settings at their defaults and click the Next button.

2. The second page (Figure D.4) of the wizard allows you to edit the custom launcher icon information. For our purposes, keep everything at their defaults, and click Next.

3. The third page (Figure D.5) of the wizard lets you create a particular type of Activity. Keep the default selection of Blank Activity and click Next.

Figure D.3   The first page of the New Project creation wizard.

Figure D.4   The second page of the New Project creation wizard.

4. The final page (Figure D.6) of the wizard lets you name your `Activity`. Change the name of the `Activity` to `HelloStudioActivity` and click Finish.

The project you just created should now open in Android Studio, with the `Hello StudioActivity.java` file open and ready for editing. The Project structure is visible in the left-hand pane (see Figure D.7).

Figure D.5   The third page of the New Project creation wizard.

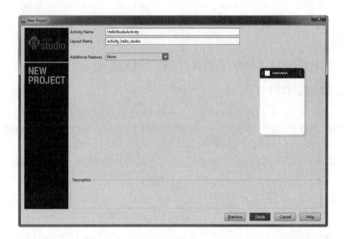

Figure D.6   The final page of the New Project creation wizard.

Figure D.7   The `HelloStudioActivity.java` (center) file
and the Project tool window (left).

Understanding the Android Studio Project Structure

Now that you know how to create a new Android application project in Android Studio, let's go over how a new project is structured. On first glance, the structure of an Android Studio project looks very different from a project created with the ADT Bundle or Eclipse with the ADT Plugin. The project files and folders can be grouped into two categories:

- The first category consists of files and folders associated with your Android application, found within the `/libs` and `/src` folders of the `HelloStudio` module.

- The second category consists of files and folders associated with Android Studio and the powerful Gradle build system, which includes virtually all other project files and folders not included in the `/libs` and `/src` folders.

Tip

This project structure may look intimidating at first glance. Most of the modifications you will need to perform occur within the `/src` folder. For managing your application's build process, you will need to modify the `build.gradle` file located within the `HelloStudio` module. We talk more about the Gradle build system in the following section.

Learning about the Gradle Build System

Gradle is an open-source tool used by Android Studio to simplify and automate the building of applications. Gradle combines many of the powerful features of the Ant and Maven build management tools into a single build automation tool, easily managed by a domain-specific language (DSL) built on top of the Groovy programming language (a Java Virtual Machine dynamic language).

In addition to using Gradle from within Android Studio, Gradle may also be invoked from the command line. The following list of features should help you better understand Gradle's purpose as a build system:

- Resources and code are made easy to reuse.
- It is easy to create different forms of your application for distributing multiple APK variations.
- It makes the build process totally configurable, extendable, and customizable.

Tip

Gradle is an extremely powerful tool for use with Android application development. There are entire books dedicated to using Gradle, so rather than writing another book, we recommend learning about Gradle from the Android documentation found at *http://d.android.com/sdk/installing/studio-build.html* and *http://tools.android.com/tech-docs/new-build-system/user-guide*. If you want to go even further, we recommend the official Gradle documentation, which can be found here: *http://www.gradle.org*.

Overview of the Android Studio User Interface

The Android Studio user interface is composed of many parts. When we first created the HelloStudioProject, Android Studio opened the HelloStudioActivity.java file in the code editor (Figure D.7), which takes up a majority of the UI. To the immediate left of the code editor is the project file and folder hierarchy, which has also been opened. Above the code editor and project file and folder hierarchy are menus, toolbars, and a project navigation bar. To the far left, far right, and immediate bottom relative to the code editor and project file and folder hierarchy, there are easily accessible tool windows that, when clicked, expand or contract to reveal functions related to specific tasks. At the very bottom of the UI resides a status bar showing information related to the status of the IDE and your project.

Introducing the Layout Editor

A Layout Editor has been included in Android Studio to make it easy to develop an application layout by dragging and dropping Android user interface components onto a canvas in a design view or by editing an XML file in a text view. The Layout Editor is accessible when editing layout files, which can be found within the /src/main/res/layout folder located in your project module. To toggle between

Figure D.8   The Android Studio Layout Editor design view.

the design view and text view, you simply click the Design or Text buttons found toward the bottom of the Layout Editor.

Working in Design View

When in design view (Figure D.8), the main UI shows an editable preview or canvas of how the layout most likely will be displayed on a sample device. Directly to the left of the editor is the Palette panel, which contains a list of drag-and-drop components, such as various layouts, widgets, text fields, containers, date and time, as well as expert and even custom components.

Tip
One advantage of using Android Studio when working in design view is the ability to show how an application will look on multiple screen configurations simultaneously. To see this, select the device drop-down, such as Nexus 4 (see Figure D.8), then choose the Preview All Screen Sizes option from the list.

Working in Text View

When in text view (Figure D.9), the main UI provides an XML editor for marking up the layout using code. To the right of the XML editor is the Preview window that displays a preview of how the layout most likely will be displayed on a sample device. This looks similar to the editable canvas of the design view.

Figure D.9   The Android Studio Layout Editor text view.

Using the Preview Controls

To the top of the Layout Editor in design (Figure D.8) and text (Figure D.9) view are preview controls for:

- Choosing the type of device you would like to visualize, such as a Nexus 5
- Changing the layout orientation
- Selecting the application theme
- Changing the Android API version
- Adding translations and previewing a right-to-left layout

Debugging Your Android Studio Applications

The Android Studio debugger makes it easy to track down errors present in your applications. The debugger can be used to debug applications running on real devices as well as applications running on emulator instances.

Setting Breakpoints

It is easy to get started debugging your applications. The first step you must take is to set one or more breakpoints within your application code. To set a breakpoint, simply click in the column directly to the left of the line of code where you would like to place the

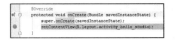

Figure D.10   Setting a breakpoint.

breakpoint (Figure D.10). Once the breakpoint is set, you should see a red dot, and the line of code where you set the breakpoint should be highlighted. Now you are ready to run your application in debug mode. To run your application in debug mode, click the Debug button (▮) located on the toolbar. You will then be prompted to select the device to launch your application.

Stepping through Code

Your application is then launched on the chosen device, and the debugger opens and halts the execution of your application at the first breakpoint you have set (Figure D.11). To resume execution of your application, there are a few action buttons for stepping through your code at the top and left-hand sides of the debugger tool window. These actions are Step Over (▮), Step Into (▮), Force Step Into (▮), and Step Out (▮).

Note
To learn more about debugging, see the online documentation titled "Debugging with Android Studio" found here: *http://d.android.com/sdk/installing/studio-debug.html.*

Figure D.11   The Android Studio debugger.

Table D.1 **Common Keyboard Shortcuts**

Key Combination	Action
ALT + ENTER	Quick fix
CTRL + P	Show method parameters
CTRL + SHIFT + A	Command lookup
CTRL + Y (Win), CMD + Backspace (Mac)	Delete line
SHIFT + F10 (Win), CTRL + R (Mac)	Build and run
ALT + left arrow or ALT + right arrow (Win), CTRL + left arrow or CTRL + right arrow (Mac)	Navigate open tabs
ALT + Insert (Win), CMD + N (Mac)	Generate method (Win), Generate. . . (Mac)

Useful Keyboard Shortcuts

One useful way to speed up programmer productivity is to use keyboard shortcuts. Android Studio is a keyboard–centric IDE. This means that a keyboard is all you need to perform the necessary actions for Android development, without the need for a mouse. The actions you need to perform are controlled with certain keys and key combinations. A few of the most common keyboard shortcuts and their respective keymappings are displayed in Table D.1.

Tip

There are many more keyboard shortcuts available. For a keymap quick reference card, select Help from the menu, then choose Default Keymap Reference. To view this quick reference card, an Internet connection is required along with a PDF viewer.

If you are coming from Eclipse development, there is even an option for selecting an Eclipse keymapping from the Keymaps drop-down from the Keymap settings. Selecting the Eclipse keymapping allows you to use the Eclipse keyboard shortcuts you are already familiar with, rather than having to learn an entirely new keymap.

Summary

There are many more features available within Android Studio than what we have covered in this appendix. The best way to go about learning what features you have at your disposal is to begin using Android Studio and experiment with all the available controls, menus, toolbars, options, and interfaces.

Quiz Questions

1. For what operating systems is Android Studio available?
2. True or false: Installing versions of the Android SDK with the ADT Bundle or Eclipse with the ADT Plugin will automatically make these SDKs available to Android Studio.

3. What programming language is the Gradle DSL built on top of?

4. True or false: The Layout Editor allows you to edit layout files using a design view or text view.

5. What is the keyboard shortcut for quick fix?

Exercises

1. Install the Android SDK for Android Studio using the SDK Manager.

2. Read through all of the Android documentation titled "Android Studio" found here: *http://d.android.com/sdk/installing/studio.html*.

3. What are the keyboard shortcuts for the Android Studio Debugger actions Step Over, Step Into, Force Step Into, and Step Out?

References and More Information

Android Tools: "Android Studio":
   http://d.android.com/sdk/installing/studio.html
Android Tools: "Using the Layout Editor":
   http://d.android.com/sdk/installing/studio-layout.html
Android Tools: "Building Your Project with Gradle":
   http://d.android.com/sdk/installing/studio-build.html
Android Tools: "Debugging with Android Studio":
   http://d.android.com/sdk/installing/studio-debug.html

Answers to Quiz Questions

Chapter 1

1. False
2. `onPreExecute()`
3. `executeOnExecutor(AsyncTask.SERIAL_EXECUTOR)`
4. The `Loader` class
5. False

Chapter 2

1. False
2. `bindService()`
3. A remote interface
4. False
5. `IntentService`

Chapter 3

1. False
2. `ContentValues`
3. `setTransactionSuccessful()`
4. True
5. Store the location as a file path or URI

Chapter 4

1. `onCreate()`, `delete()`, `getType()`, `insert()`, `query()`, `update()`
2. `content://`
3. False
4. False

Chapter 5

1. Normal and ordered
2. False
3. Register to receive broadcasts and implement a broadcast receiver class
4. `ACTION_MY_PACKAGE_REPLACED`
5. True

Chapter 6

1. `getSystemService(Context.NOTIFICATION_SERVICE);`
2. False
3. True
4. `setNumber()`
5. Causes notifications to be canceled when the user clicks them

Chapter 7

1. False
2. `always`, `ifRoom`, `never`, and `withText`
3. `setDisplayHomeAsUpEnabled(true)`
4. `hide()`
5. `setTheme(R.style.themeToSet)`

Chapter 8

1. True
2. `ViewTreeObserver`
3. `GestureDetector` and `ScaleGestureDetector`
4. `onScroll()`
5. False

Chapter 9

1. False
2. `android.speech.RecognizerIntent`
3. `LANGUAGE_MODEL_WEB_SEARCH`
4. False
5. `shutdown()`

Chapter 10

1. True
2. Use flexible layouts; use dimension values; provide alternative resources; use various resource types to your advantage; adjust the UI when hardware features aren't present on the device; use `Fragment`-based layouts
3. False
4. Chrome web apps and native Android apps
5. Stack them

Chapter 11

1. False
2. `java.net.HttpURLConnection`
3. True
4. `ConnectivityManager`
5. `android.permission.ACCESS_NETWORK_STATE`

Chapter 12

1. True
2. `android.permission.INTERNET`
3. `WebChromeClient`
4. `@JavascriptInterface`
5. True

Chapter 13

1. True
2. `SurfaceView`
3. `getSupportedFocusModes()`
4. True
5. `android.permission.RECORD_AUDIO`

Chapter 14

1. `android.permission.READ_PHONE_STATE`
2. `TelephonyManager telManager = (TelephonyManager) getSystemService(Context.TELEPHONY_SERVICE);`

3. False

4. You must add an `Activity`, an SMS `BroadcastReceiver`, an MMS `BroadcastReceiver`, and a `Service`, each with special options

5. False

Chapter 15

1. False

2. `getSystemService(Context.SENSOR_SERVICE)`

3. `sensorManagerObj.getDefeaultSensor(Sensor.TYPE_STEP_COUNTER)`

4. `onSensorChanged()`

5. False

Chapter 16

1. False

2. `android.permission.BLUETOOTH` and `android.permission.BLUETOOTH_ADMIN` respectively

3. `UsbManager`

4. NFC Data Exchange Format

5. `startScan()`

Chapter 17

1. False

2. `ACCESS_FINE_LOCATION`

3. `getLastLocation()`

4. False

5. `getMap()`

Chapter 18

1. False

2. 4096 bytes

3. False

4. A broadcast receiver

5. True

Chapter 19

1. Where apps are published free of charge but contain content for purchase
2. A role-playing game with a shop where users can purchase items; wallpaper, ringtone, music, or video download application, pay per download; photo filter app, pay per filter; for more see all the options as detailed earlier in the "What Is In-App Billing?" section
3. False
4. False

Chapter 20

1. False
2. UA
3. `google-play-services_lib`
4. `INTERNET, ACCESS_NETWORK_STATE`
5. False

Chapter 21

1. Google Play Developer Console
2. False
3. `CLIENT_PLUS`
4. If a particular achievement builds on another required achievement
5. Four-byte arrays each worth 256 kilobytes for a total of 1024 kilobytes
6. False

Chapter 22

1. True
2. `getHeight()` and `getWidth()`
3. Anti-aliasing makes a graphic look smoother, and use the `Paint.ANTI_ALIAS_FLAG`
4. True
5. Application, `Activity`, `Window`, `View`

Chapter 23

1. Frame-by-frame animation

2. Alpha, rotate, scale, translate

3. False

4. `AnticipateInterpolator`

5. `android.transition`

Chapter 24

1. `<uses-feature android:glEsVersion="0x00020000" />`

2. False

3. `SurfaceView` and `GLSurfaceView`

4. False

5. True

Chapter 25

1. False

2. C and C++

3. `ndk-gdb`

4. `ndk-build`

5. False

Chapter 26

1. Provide an XML App Widget configuration, determine whether the App Widget requires a configuration `Activity`, provide an `AppWidgetProvider` class implementation, provide a `Service` class implementation to handle App Widget content updates (as needed), and update the application Android manifest file to register the App Widget provider information and any information about the update service

2. `minWidth` and `minHeight`

3. False

4. $(70 \star n) - 30$, where n is the number of cells you want the App Widget to occupy

5. False

6. Provide an XML wallpaper configuration, provide a `WallpaperService` implementation, and update the application Android manifest file to register the wallpaper `Service` with the appropriate permissions

7. `android.permission.BIND_WALLPAPER`
8. `<uses-feature android:name="android.software.live_wallpaper" />`

Chapter 27

1. True
2. `searchSuggestThreshold`
3. `android:voiceSearchMode="showVoiceSearchButton|launchWebSearch"`
4. False
5. `android:includeInGlobalSearch="true"`

Chapter 28

1. True
2. `android:requiredAccountType`
3. `AbstractThreadedSyncAdapter`
4. `onBackup()` and `onRestore()`
5. False

Chapter 29

1. True
2. `/res/layout-fr`
3. `/res/drawable-fr-rCA`
4. False
5. Add `android:supportsRtl=true` to the `<application>` tag in the Android manifest file

Chapter 30

1. Use secure coding practices, obfuscate your binary code using ProGuard, and leverage the LVL
2. False
3. Add the line `proguard.config=proguard.cfg` to the file `project.properties`
4. False
5. `mapping.txt`

Chapter 31

1. True
2. **A**ndroid **R**untime
3. `<uses-feature android:glEsVersion="0x00030001" />`
4. False
5. `elevation`

Appendix A

1. `adb devices`
2. False
3. `-d`
4. False
5. `bmgr backup <package>`

Appendix B

1. `/data/data/<application package name>/databases/<databasename>`
2. False
3. `.schema <tablename>`
4. INTEGER, REAL, TEXT, BLOB
5. False

Appendix C

1. False
2. `for (;;) {/* Loop infinitely */}`
3. `for (String str : aStrs) {/* Loop over str */}`
4. `int value = 0; value += 1;`
5. `bool value = true ? true : false; // one possibility`

Appendix D

1. Windows, Mac OS X, and Linux
2. False
3. Groovy
4. True
5. ALT + ENTER

Index

E

T

U

offload processing of main, 12

starting OpenGL ES, 349–350

Thread class, 15–16

Unary operations, Java, 502

unbindService() method, remote interface, 27–28

Uninstallation, of applications using ADB, 473

uninstall command, 473

UNKNOWN, activity recognition APIs, 262

updateAppWidget() method, 398

update() method

building content provider, 59–60

records in SQLite database, 38–39

updatePeriodMillis attribute, App Widgets, 394

Updates

Android Studio versions, 507

antipiracy tips, 453

App Widgets, 394–399

content provider, 62

data in SQLite database tables, 495

global search, 425

UriMatcher class, 57, 58–59, 419

URIs

building content provider, 56

enabling search suggestions, 419

locating content, 63–64

URL object, 165–166, 171

URLUtil class, WebKit API, 182

USB, 239–241

UsbAccessory object, 240

UsbManager class, 240–241

Use case. *See* Extending Android application reach

User accounts

backup service. *See* **Backup service**

managing with Account Manager, 427–428

multiple users, restricted profiles and, 428–429

overview of, 427

synchronizing data, 429–430

User dictionaries, 118

User input methods

accessibility with alternative, 140

fine-tuned control over, 116

gestures. *See* **Gestures**

quiz Q & A, 137, 520

screen orientation changes, 134–136

speech recognition services, 141–145

textual, 115–119

user events, 119–123

User interface

action bars. *See* **Action bars**

Android guidelines, 97–98

Android Studio, 513–515

binding data to application, 48–53

challenges of games, 154

content provider and, 55–56

contextual action mode, 105–106

creating devices with flexible, 152

defining App Widgets, 396–397

device diversity and, 151–154

Google TV variations, 156–158

overview of, 97

quiz Q & A, 113

state animations with scenes/transitions, 342

style inheritance, 109–111

styles, 106–109

themes, 111–113

V